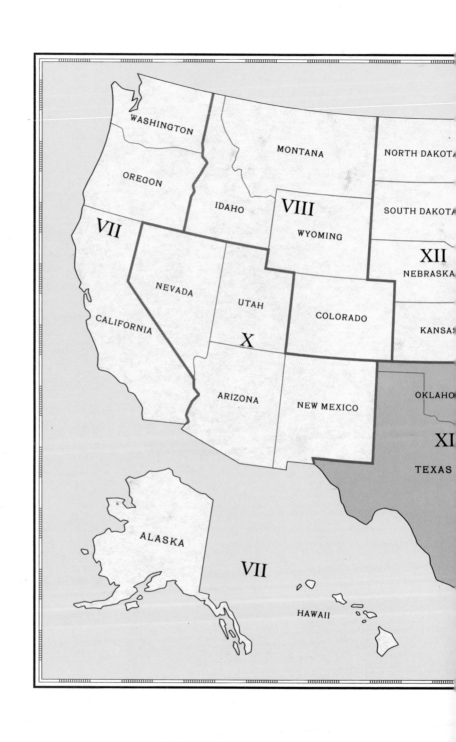

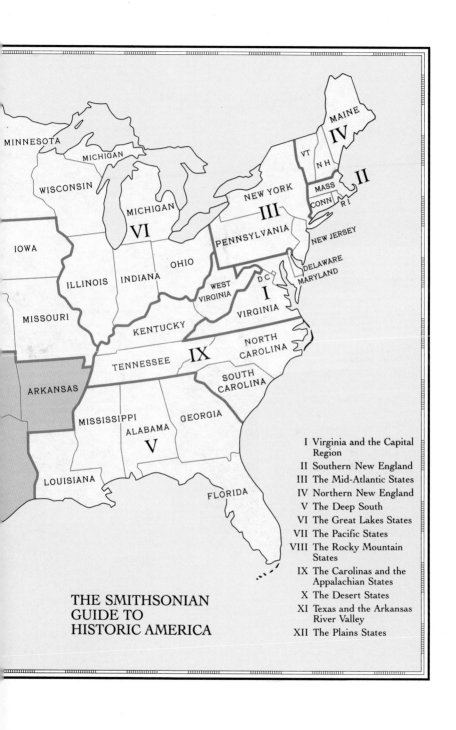

I Virginia and the Capital
   Region
II Southern New England
III The Mid-Atlantic States
IV Northern New England
V The Deep South
VI The Great Lakes States
VII The Pacific States
VIII The Rocky Mountain
   States
IX The Carolinas and the
   Appalachian States
X The Desert States
XI Texas and the Arkansas
   River Valley
XII The Plains States

THE SMITHSONIAN
GUIDE TO
HISTORIC AMERICA

THE
SMITHSONIAN
—— GUIDE TO ——
HISTORIC AMERICA

TEXAS & THE ARKANSAS
RIVER VALLEY

TEXT BY
ALICE GORDON
JERRY CAMARILLO DUNN, JR.
MEL WHITE

SPECIAL PHOTOGRAPHY BY
TIM THOMPSON

EDITORIAL DIRECTOR
ROGER G. KENNEDY
DIRECTOR OF THE NATIONAL MUSEUM
OF AMERICAN HISTORY
OF THE SMITHSONIAN INSTITUTION

Stewart, Tabori & Chang
NEW YORK

Text copyright © 1990 Stewart, Tabori & Chang, Inc.
Photographs copyright © 1990 Tim Thompson.

Due to limitations of space, additional photo credits appear on
page 496 and constitute an extension of this page.

All information is accurate as of publication. We suggest
contacting the sites prior to a visit to confirm hours of operation.

Published in 1990 by Stewart, Tabori & Chang, Inc., 740 Broadway,
New York, NY 10003.

FRONT COVER: Ysleta Mission, El Paso, TX.
HALF-TITLE PAGE: Lucas Gusher, Spindletop, TX, January 10, 1901.
FRONTISPIECE: Lewis-Wagner House, Winedale Historical Center, TX.
BACK COVER: Texas State Capitol, Austin, TX.

SERIES EDITOR: HENRY WIENCEK
EDITOR: MARY LUDERS
PHOTO EDITOR: MARY Z. JENKINS
ART DIRECTOR: DIANA M. JONES
ASSISTANT PHOTO EDITORS: BARBARA J. SEYDA, REBECCA WILLIAMS
EDITORIAL ASSISTANT: MONINA MEDY
DESIGN ASSISTANT: KATHI R. PORTER
CARTOGRAPHIC DESIGN AND PRODUCTION: GUENTER VOLLATH
CARTOGRAPHIC COMPILATION: GEORGE COLBERT
DATA ENTRY: SUSAN KIRBY

LIBRARY OF CONGRESS CATALOGING-IN-PUBLICATION DATA

Gordon, Alice.
    Texas and the Arkansas River valley/text by Alice Gordon and
Jerry Camarillo Dunn, Jr., Mel White: special photography by Tim
Thompson; editorial director, Roger G. Kennedy. — 1st ed.
        p. cm. — (The Smithsonian guide to historic America) Includes index.
    ISBN 1-55670-122-5: $24.95 — ISBN 1-55670-124-1 (pbk.): $18.95
    1. Arkansas River Valley—Description and travel—Guide-books.
2. Texas—Description and travel—Guide-books. 3. Arkansas—
Description and travel—1981—Guide-books. 4. Oklahoma—
Description and travel—1981—Guide-books. 5. Historic sites—
Arkansas River Valley—Guide-books. 6. Historic sites—Texas—
Guide-books. 7. Historic sites—Arkansas—Guide-books.
8. Historic sites—Oklahoma—Guide-books. I. Dunn, Jerry
Camarillo. II. White, Mel, 1950-   . III. Thompson, Tim, 1942-
IV. Kennedy, Roger G. V. Title. VI Series.
F417.A7G67 1990   917.67'30453—dc20

89-4605
CIP

Distributed by Workman Publishing, 708 Broadway, New York, NY 10003

Printed in Japan

10 9 8 7 6 5 4 3 2 1
First Edition

C O N T E N T S

INTRODUCTION   10

SOUTH TEXAS AND THE GULF COAST   18

CENTRAL TEXAS   126

NORTH AND EAST TEXAS   204

WEST TEXAS   270

EASTERN OKLAHOMA   332

WESTERN OKLAHOMA   376

ARKANSAS   426

NOTES ON ARCHITECTURE   484

INDEX   486

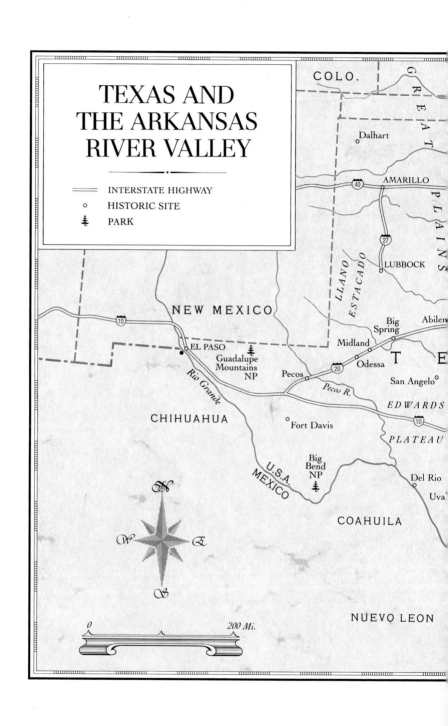

TEXAS AND THE ARKANSAS RIVER VALLEY

INTERSTATE HIGHWAY

o HISTORIC SITE

🌲 PARK

COLO.

GREAT PLAINS

Dalhart

AMARILLO

40

27

LUBBOCK

NEW MEXICO

LLANO ESTACADO

10

Big Spring

Abilene

Midland

San Angelo

EL PASO

Guadalupe Mountains NP

Pecos

20

Odessa

Rio Grande

Pecos R.

EDWARDS

CHIHUAHUA

Fort Davis

PLATEAU

10

Big Bend NP

Del Rio

Uva

U.S.A. MEXICO

COAHUILA

T E

NUEVO LEON

0   200 Mi.

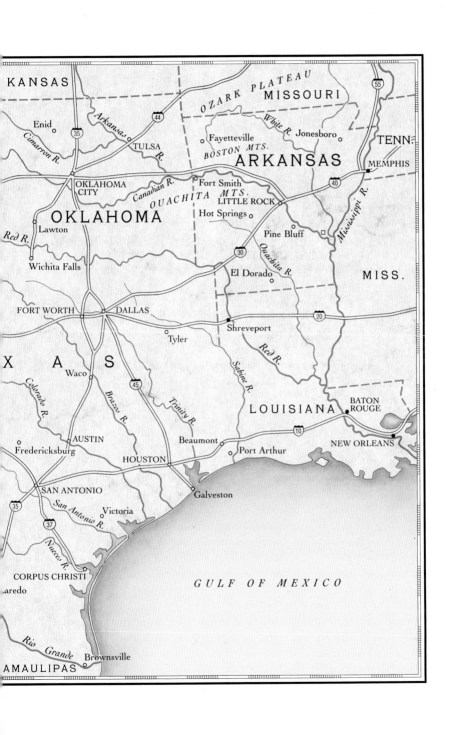

INTRODUCTION

ROGER G. KENNEDY

General Sam Houston's victory at San Jacinto gave Texas its independence in 1836. It also created a new power in a region that was beyond the effective control of any of the European empires or of their successors, the United States and Mexico. For more than half a century, the region between the Mississippi and the Rio Grande had been an open stage, offering adventurers an invitation to become sovereigns.

Colonel Aaron Burr died in 1836, having noted Houston's achievements and observing that he himself had been "thirty years too early." In 1805 and 1806, Burr had attempted to set up his own domain in Arkansas. No one knows how independent he intended it to be, but it was conventional at the time to assume that the U. S. government could not hold onto its western provinces. The seat of that government was weeks away, across a formidable mountain range still largely in the hands of independent Indian nations, beyond an immense, unbroken, hostile, and forested mystery—Kentucky and Tennessee. And between Texas, Louisiana, and Arkansas and the rest of the United States lay the Mississippi, a moat so broad and unpredictable in its moods as to seem beyond bridging to the Easterners who first beheld it. James Madison said that "no colony beyond the river could exist under the same government, but would infallibly give birth to a separate State having in its bosom germs of collision with the East."

As early as 1795, Burr discussed an expedition to found a colony beyond the river with anyone who would listen, while Alexander Hamilton consulted his friends about a competing colony for himself. John Jay, first chief justice of the United States, was not at all affronted by Burr's disclosure of his plan in 1796; it apparently seemed inevitable to him that energetic military heroes, disappointed in politics in tranquil terrain, would seek more exciting careers.

In the end, Houston achieved what Burr and Hamilton had intended. It is well to recall that until their final duel—fatal to Hamilton in the literal sense and to Burr politically—*both* those colonels were military heroes, and Burr the more heroic of the two. In the Revolutionary War, he may well have saved Hamilton's life

OPPOSITE: *Sandbars in the Rio Grande's Santa Elena Canyon.*

during the fighting on Manhattan. At Quebec Burr carried the corpse of his commander, General Richard Montgomery, through a snowstorm from the field of battle; engravings of this scene once offered inspiration to schoolboys.

Burr has not had a good press. Like Adlai Stevenson, he had the burden of wit. He could not resist cynical "one-liners." He was not admired by Thomas Jefferson—indeed, one can say with certainty that he was feared by Thomas Jefferson. And he killed a former secretary of the treasury. Those are not good ways to assure a chorus of praise from American historians. Furthermore, many Southern historians have, until very recently, seen him not only as an enemy to Jefferson, whose ambiguities they felt a need to simplify, but as an enemy to southern institutions. Burr actively opposed slavery, proposing its abolition in New York in the 1790s, where it had powerful defenders, especially among Dutch farmers who had as many slaves, per capita, as the people of North Carolina. Burr provoked Jefferson on the subject; in his final act as Jefferson's vice president, Burr broke a tie in the U. S. Senate to ensure that, despite the President's strenuous efforts to cut off all trade with the black republic of Toussaint-Louverture on Haiti, trade would continue. (This does not mean that Jefferson favored slavery. He was stuck with it—"a wolf by the ears," as he said.)

One of the chief reasons given by members of Jefferson's cabinet for opposing Burr's colony in the West was that Burr would forbid slavery and provide an asylum for runaways. This nearly came to pass as a result of the Mexican constitution of 1824, which barred slavery. However, Stephen Austin managed to persuade the Mexican government to allow his colonists to bring slaves with them. Slave owners were urged to settle in Texas by Andrew Jackson and James Polk, who looked to Texas as a slave-owning buffer territory against the contagion of emancipation sweeping up from Latin America.

The idea of creating one or more proto-Texases, American satellite states situated between the United States and Spanish possessions, was probably first proposed by General Francisco de Miranda. Miranda was a Venezuelan patriot who hatched such a scheme while commanding one wing of the French revolutionary armies in Flanders in 1792-1793. By doing so, he brought into this story that theme of French swashbuckling which is as important in the region as the grand adventures of American military colonizers.

Miranda and the French commander Charles-Francois Dumouriez shared a proto-Texas scheme with American soldiers of fortune in their army, while other French leaders took it up with George Rogers Clark and John Paul Jones. The highest-ranking Revolutionary War hero to pursue the thought was, however, not a Frenchman but a German, Baron Friedrich Wilhelm Ludolf Gerhard Augustin von Steuben, godchild of King Frederick William of Prussia and drillmaster of George Washington's army. After the Revolutionary War, Steuben came to believe himself rudely treated by a Congress that should have been more grateful and by fellow officers who should have been more respectful. He was conspiring with the Spaniards for independent status in the West at the time of his death. Soon thereafter, William Blount, governor and senator from Tennessee, turned to the British. Blount was caught so red-handed in the attempt to make himself satrap of a secessionist western state under British protection that he was drummed out of the U. S. Senate in 1798.

These were the plots of the 1790s, when it was very doubtful that the United States could extend itself to take control of the other side of the Appalachians, much less the other side of the Mississippi River. The exhausted Spanish empire was relinquishing its feeble control over the immense expanse of desert, rock, swamp, prairie, and savannah lying beyond the line of missions and forts guarding its truly valuable possessions, the silver mines about San Luis Potosí.

Treaty title to portions of this region was, on occasion, assigned to Spain, Britain, France, Mexico, the United States, and Texas, but claims manufactured in distant chancelleries and salons did not have much effect upon people in the bayous, the dry mountains, or the Staked Plains. It was never very important whether a king in Madrid or in Paris or in London or a president in Washington or Mexico City was currently the asserted suzerain of the sagebrush kingdom, the marshlands of Barataria or the fastness of the Davis Mountains, the Ozarks and Ouachitas. The absence of a real ruler was an immense invitation to adventure, especially after two events that occurred during Burr's lifetime.

The first was the invention of the cotton gin, a contraption that arrived just in time. The world's population was surging for reasons we still do not fully understand, and surging with it was the demand for cloth to cover these new human bodies. Southern uplands quite

suddenly became good for something beyond subsistence agriculture. Their only cash crop had been a little corn whiskey—now they
were to clothe the world. Aaron Burr was one of the first to recognize that the world's rapt and rapacious attention would fall upon
the upland South on both sides of the Mississippi River, with profitable consequences.

A second great event drew the attentive Burr to the trans-
Mississippi West. This was a coup not of invention but of finance,
which threw the spotlight of the world of finance upon Mexico's silver mines around the city of San Luis Potosí. Between 1804 and
1809, 70 million pesos of San Luis Potosí silver, shipped from
Veracruz to Europe, kept Emperor Napoleon solvent. The agents of
that transfer were largely American, working on commission; a number of Burr's friends were conspicuously enriched, and several of
them regaled him with tales of ingots tarnishing in warehouses in
Veracruz, or stored in the vaults of churches at San Luis. So it
became established in the minds of every ambitious scalawag in the
western world that he who controlled a source of silver might control much else. A vacuum on the edge of a bonanza will not go long
unoccupied. In 1804 Burr was in New York, competing for expedi-
tionary talent with Miranda. He put all his remaining capital into a
bloc of land lying along the Ouachita River. Upon his domain of
350,000 acres, Burr could be far enough into Arkansas to be safe
from any casual rake of claws by President Jefferson and also suffi-
ciently distant from the Mexican garrisons to train without interfer-
ence a disciplined army of invasion. When he was ready, that army
might make a cross-country expedition to San Luis Potosí or
progress downriver to New Orleans, and in alliance with the pirates
of Barataria, he could set sail for Veracruz.

Burr began assembling a general staff of experienced French
officers, headed by Colonel Julien de Pestre, to aid in recruiting
French trappers on the plains. Apparently he also opened negotia-
tions with the brothers Jean and Louis Lafitte, French pirates who
knew the shores of the Gulf of Mexico. The wisdom in his method
belied the apparent madness of his plan, a madness, like Hamlet's,
that was quite sane south by southwest. His compass was drawn not
by iron but by silver. This Franco-American group found in Arkansas
a well-watered and fertile plain, unoccupied by permanent settlers,
upon which he might grow cotton and plot about silver.

In 1805-1806, Burr made his move. He was, in fact, both too
early and too late. Jefferson was ready for him—and pounced. The

Sage of Monticello had weakened Burr by acquiring as his own agent Burr's duplicitous second-in-command, James Wilkinson. Jefferson and Wilkinson had led Burr along, over more than a year of open discussion. At first, they thought it possible that Burr could be a useful weapon against the Spaniards. But Burr was unmanageable. In a war with Spain he might prove heroic once more, restoring his political reputation. Alternatively, he might not bother with such mundane matters and might set himself up as an independent power, the true beneficiary of Jefferson's labors to acquire Louisiana. Furthermore, in such a role he would serve the British, French, and Spanish objective of preventing the further expansion of the United States into the Southwest.

So Burr's manifest, full-disclosed, and entirely public activity was suddenly described as a "conspiracy" and disavowed. (Like Miranda's, at the same time, and by the same people). In each of five trials and hearings, the allegation that Burr's intentions were treasonous failed of proof before judge or jury. But his career as a public figure was over. He was driven into exile.

In 1818-1820, a new group of Frenchmen, generals and colonels of Napoleon's staff, attempted a renewal of Burr's plan, with the base and the contemplated invasion route shifted a little to the south. Soon after Waterloo they had come to Philadelphia, gesturing westward with their muscles bulging, limping a bit, scarred somewhat, but still very energetic, terrifying the Quaker merchants, and demanding ships, recruits and money to depart in the general direction of Texas. They received some of their supplies and money from Stephen Girard, the French-American banker who by that time had become the owner of Burr's property in Arkansas. Probably more important to Girard, however, was a political objective he held in common with other Bonapartists—the establishment in Texas of a base to acquire financial resources (silver would do) to liberate Napoleon from his island-prison on Saint Helena. Burr had left maps and proposals with Napoleon that could be used for the Texas portion of such a Bonapartist expedition.

The heroes of the South's first Lost Cause, veterans of Waterloo, established themselves at a place they called "le Champ d'Asile," in the valley of the Trinity River above Galveston. After Texas—an assault upon the silver mines! But the brothers Lafitte, who might have aided Burr to reach those mines, were, as usual, playing two games; they were still in the pay of Spain, hiking their "rates" to match those paid by the Napoleonic heroes. Worse, from the point of view of Bonapartist historians, they failed to instruct those heroes in desert nutrition. Dysentery is always a threat to armies, but the consumption of "desert lettuce" can bring it on fearsomely. Though a passing Indian offered another plant as palliative, the heroes were so weakened that they had difficulty in building the three small forts constituting their threat to the Spanish empire. Though that empire could summon only a puny expedition to deal with them, rumor magnified that force. After an orderly but inglorious French retreat to Galveston, the final humiliation was provided by a hurricane, which flooded the island and destroyed their remaining stores and morale. They crept away into civilian life. Their leader, General Jean-Joseph-Amable Humbert, who once captained the famous invasion of Ireland in 1798, died a drunken tavern crawler in New Orleans. This was not the end of the French connection in Texas. In 1839, when the republic's frontier was threatened by the Comanche and Kiowa and the resurgent Mexicans, Sam Houston and General Albert Sidney Johnston, Secretary of War for Texas, proposed that Texas re-import French soldiers of fortune—a new set, the Bonapartists were getting old—to man a series of nine forts along the 98th meridian. The plan came to nothing, for Texas pride balked at the proposed pay for these mercenaries (3 million acres of land) and the implication that their country would become "the puny fraction of a French colony." (Visitors to the French Legation in Austin might wish to bear this in mind).

Even after Texas was folded into the Union in 1845, the hopes of adventurers for independent sovereignties were not extinguished. Governor John A. Quitman of Mississippi, a hero of the Mexican War, asserted publicly that his leader, General Winfield Scott, should make himself emperor of Mexico, distributing to his fellow officers titles, lands, and mines. Scott disappointed him, so Quitman thought next of Cuba. But that is another tale. There is a very handsome mansion in Natchez, called Monmouth, to which Quitman repaired when his Cuban ambitions were disappointed. It is said, locally, that he was poisoned by abolitionists while attending a banquet for President James Buchanan.

In this region the most magnificent of possibilities for lovers of architecture is a dream, not a historic site. This was an imperial capital to be designed by the great Benjamin Henry Latrobe. Latrobe was an adventurer too, and he was enthusiastic when he was invited to build a capital for Aaron Burr, among whose admirable qualities was a love of good architecture. The site for this magnificent creation was found for them by yet one more military adventurer, as tall as Houston and as crafty as Burr—"Baron" Felipe de Bastrop. Burr had acquired his Arkansas holdings from the Spanish Crown by way of Bastrop and two Kentucky speculators. The *soi–disant* baron was *very* tall, and had once been handsome enough to catch the eye of Frederick the Great of Prussia. According to Bastrop, Frederick bestowed the title of baron upon him when very young but not even then naive. After a scrape with Napoleon in France, the beautiful Bastrop found favor with a Spanish official from whom came the grant of land.

Thomas Jefferson told Latrobe that Burr's empire was an impregnable valley surrounded by ramparts of mountain (Jefferson's view of the Ozarks was a trifle emphatic), and Latrobe's imagination was so much engaged in assisting Burr's army to get there that he even designed riverboats to serve as Burr's troop ships. Then, despite encouragement from their mutual friend Colonel de Pestre, he lost his nerve—just in time. Soon thereafter, Burr was betrayed by Wilkinson, who had been persuaded to expect greater preferment from Jefferson.

If the notion of a Latrobian, Neoclassical capital city for Aaron Burr seems too fanciful, one can get a more concrete sense of what Burr might have had in mind by visiting the Old State House in Little Rock. It is a classical complex designed by Gideon Shryock, a mystical Kentuckian who learned the style from Latrobe's own student, William Strickland. Burr's capitol might have looked like that. And, with Latrobe about for encouragement, Arkansas might have had many Neoclassical villages over the ensuing decades. It does have one, Old Washington, where Sam Houston plotted the fulfillment, in Texas, of Burr's design for Arkansas. Although there was no Emperor Aaron the First, and Burr probably had no intention that there should be, we can imagine the white Latrobian domes of Burr's capital—like those built in our own time for the National Gallery and the Jefferson Memorial in Washington, DC—glimmering above the great trees of Arkansas, reflected in basins drawn from the meandering Ouachita River.

SOUTH TEXAS
AND THE
GULF COAST

OPPOSITE: *The staircase of the Bishop's Palace in Galveston, designed by Nicholas J. Clayton and completed in 1893. The stained-glass window of Saint Teresa was installed after the original jeweled glass window was blown out in a hurricane.*

The first Spanish exploration of the Gulf Coast and possibly the Rio Grande took place in 1519—we know that Alonso Alvarez de Pineda surveyed the coast. Although Alvarez left a journal before he was killed by Indians, Alvar Nuñez Cabeza de Vaca was the first Spaniard to land on Texas soil, in 1528, and live to tell about it. After a forced sojourn with the fierce coastal Karankawa, he escaped across Texas to the western coast of Mexico. In 1543 Luis de Moscoso Alvarado, continuing the expedition started in 1539 under Hernando de Soto, sailed from the mouth of the Mississippi to the mouth of the Sabine—the present-day boundary between Texas and Louisiana—where he stopped to caulk his expedition's brigantines with pitch from oil seepage, the first recorded use of Texas petroleum.

The Spanish claims on Texas were unsupported by a Spanish presence in the region for many years: The Indians along the Gulf Coast were hostile, the climate was unhealthy with fever, and no gold was found. But a counterclaim was entered in 1685, when René-Robert Cavelier, sieur de La Salle, established Fort Saint Louis on Garcitas Creek above Matagorda Bay, having missed the mouth of the Mississippi, where he had intended to establish a French empire "by seizures of provinces rich in silver, and defended only by a few indolent and enervated Spaniards." Building a log fort for the colonists he had brought with him, La Salle then left to search for the real Mississippi, first exploring south as far as the Rio Grande, then heading east to the Neches and Trinity rivers. This was his final journey: He was shot, possibly in an argument over food, by companions disgusted with the rigors of the expedition.

News of La Salle, Fort Saint Louis, and French designs on Texas alarmed the Spanish and led them to establish their first mission in eastern Texas, southwest of present-day Nacogdoches (Alonzo de León discovered in 1689 that Fort Saint Louis had been ransacked by the Karankawa and its settlers killed). Some years passed, and the French threat seemed to have subsided until Louis Juchereau de Saint-Denis established a fort at Natchitoches in Louisiana and traveled undetected across Texas to Mexico in 1714. His good relations with the east Texas Indians gave the French influence there that alarmed Spain even more. The Spanish built more missions, this time not only in the east but also in southern Texas. The most important was San Antonio de Valero—later the Alamo—in San Antonio, which was to be the center of the missionizing effort and

The red, white, and blue Lone Star flag of the Third Republic of Texas was based on the Stars and Stripes of the United States. It is said to have been designed in 1836 by Oliver Jones, an Austin Colony settler from Connecticut who headed the committee responsible for creating a new flag and seal for the republic.

the only real Spanish settlement north of the Rio Grande. The mission effort was sustained into the late eighteenth century. It was near San Antonio that the Spanish had their first battles with the Apache and, by the mid-eighteenth century, the more powerful Comanche, who made their way down from the Rockies to the Great Plains and as far south as the buffalo herds and raidable Spanish livestock could support them.

While the missions struggled along, a successful Spanish colonizing effort took place farther south. Don José de Escandón was commissioned to colonize the area between Tampico and Corpus Christi Bay in 1746. In 1748 Escandón led 755 soldiers and 2,513 Spanish-Mexican colonists up from Querétaro to the Rio Grande in the area just across the river from what is now known as the Lower Rio Grande Valley. He avoided the coast, which was still inhabited by the Karankawa and known to be rife with fevers (smallpox had cut down the French at Fort Saint Louis before the Indians came to finish them off). By 1755 Escandón had founded twenty towns, all but Laredo on the south side of the Rio Grande (Rio Bravo to the

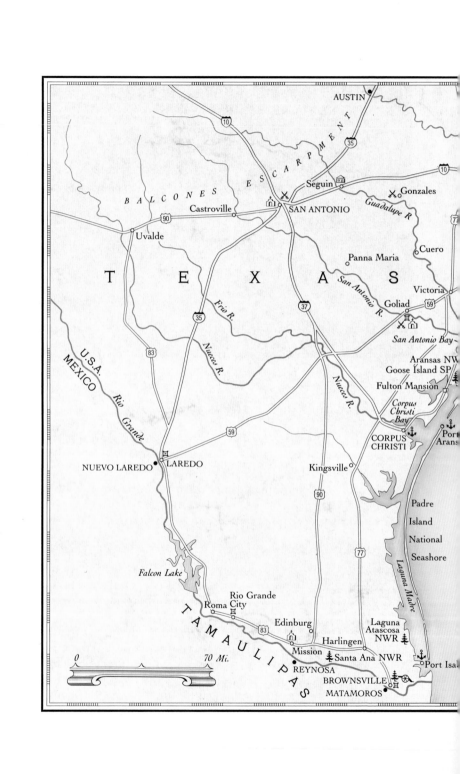

Neches R. Sabine R.
BEAUMONT
Orange
Buffalo   LOUISIANA
Bayou   PORT
Trinity R.   ARTHUR   Sabine Lake
HOUSTON
Brazos R.
Sugar Land   San Jacinto Battleground SHP
Colorado R.   Richmond   Johnson Space Center
Galveston
Bay
GALVESTON
Varner-Hogg
Plantation SHP
Freeport
Lavaca
Bay
Indianola

GULF   OF   MEXICO

SOUTH TEXAS
AND THE
GULF COAST

══════	INTERSTATE HIGHWAY
○	HISTORIC SITE
⚔	CIVIL WAR BATTLE
🏠	RECONSTRUCTED VILLAGE
✕	TEXAS REVOLUTION BATTLE
⊟	FORT
⚓	PORT

🏠	MISSION
🌲	PARK

Spanish), many of them still in existence today. The land was more suitable for ranching than agriculture. The cattle brought over by Cortés in 1521 had propagated into huge herds and, aided by Cortés's institution of branding (slaves were branded first, and from that practice came the idea of branding cattle), ranching developed in northern Mexico. Indian slaves rode out to work the cattle. The mestizo vaqueros were the first cowboys, developing a vocabulary to describe the elements of their life, from *rancho* to *corral* to *bronco,* and their masters were the first *rancheros,* the cattle kings. Escandón brought the rancheros to Texas. Although their settlements were on the south side of the river, their cattle roamed across it to graze on the lush grasses of the south Texas chaparral. By the turn of the eighteenth century Spanish rancheros had moved as far north into Texas as the Nueces River, whose mouth is at present-day Corpus Christi.

The Indian barrier to further Spanish colonization of Texas and Spain's inability to interest other European emigrants opened Texas to Anglo and American colonization under the *empresario* system established under the reinstated Spanish constitution of 1812. There was a further opening after Mexico gained independence from Spain in 1821. *Empresarios* were given land grants by Mexico as well as responsibility for the distribution of land to the colonists and the establishment of local governments according to Mexican law. By the time Stephen F. Austin brought his Old Three Hundred settlers to his colony, extending over parts of south, central, and east Texas in December 1821, Mexico was eager to fill up Texas, to let outsiders try to succeed where Spain's lack of funds, colonists, and cultural adaptability had failed. Colonists were given the large land grants and exempted from taxes and customs for the first seven years of their residency. Austin made sure that his colonists were upstanding people. Most of them were literate and were chosen carefully; no "drunkard, no gambler, no profane swearer, no idler" was allowed, and when such people were discovered in the colony they were removed or punished publicly for their misdeeds. The other successful colony besides Austin's was the Green DeWitt colony south of San Antonio. Its headquarters were at the old mission at Refugio; it also established the towns of Gonzales and Goliad, where the Mission La Bahia had been established a century earlier.

In the late 1820s and early 1830s turmoil in the Mexican government sowed the seeds of revolution in Texas. Several Mexican presidents were deposed amid a struggle over limiting or expanding the power of the central government. Texas, like the rest of Mexico, was placed under military rule. In 1830 Mexico suspended land grants in an attempt to hold back the wave of Anglo immigration, and new arrivals found themselves without land or work. In 1833 General Antonio López de Santa Anna was elected president. Regarded as a liberal, he was a popular figure, a war hero who had repelled Spanish invaders in 1829. Stephen Austin went to Mexico City to present grievances over taxes, the ban on immigration, military rule, and the Mexican legal system (which did not provide for trial by jury). Most of Austin's requests were met, but on his way home he was arrested by the order of Santa Anna, who was justifiably suspicious that some Texans intended to break away from Mexico. Austin spent a year and a half in prison. In 1835 the liberal constitution of 1824 was voided, and with it went the principle of decentralized government by which Texans had hoped for a degree of autonomy. Mexican dissidents took refuge in Texas, clandestine committees of correspondence were organized, and Austin, released from prison in July 1835, appealed to Americans to take up arms and settle in Texas. The Mexican government sent troops under General Martín Perfecto de Cós to arrest agitators and seize weapons. When his troops tried to confiscate a cannon at Gonzales, Texans unfurled a banner over it reading COME AND TAKE IT, fired a shot, and the Texas Revolution was on. After the skirmish at Gonzales, the Texans ousted Cós from his stronghold in San Antonio. Without orders, a few Texans decided to hold San Antonio, barricading themselves at the Alamo. Santa Anna himself directed the successful siege of the Alamo but took so long in reducing the fort that Texans were given time to rally at San Jacinto, where Sam Houston won a sudden, decisive victory.

The revolution was brief—lasting from the fall of 1835 to the spring of 1836—and not, in the eyes of the Mexican government, final. In 1842 a Mexican invasion force retook San Antonio but remained only a few days. Expeditions were sent out by the Texans, and fighting continued until 1844, when a truce was called. In the U.S. presidential election that year, James Polk campaigned on a platform of expansion, calling specifically for the annexation of Texas, which took place in early 1845. However, the Mexicans refused to sell New Mexico or California or to recognize the Rio Grande as the border; for them, Texas ended at the Nueces River. To bring the dispute to a head, President Polk ordered General

Zachary Taylor to lead U.S. forces into the contested area southwest of the Nueces. As anticipated, the Mexicans retaliated; war was declared in May 1846. The first battles in this short war were fought along the Rio Grande near Brownsville, the rest mostly in Mexico. By the Treaty of Guadalupe Hidalgo, ratified in July 1848, Mexico was forced to sell, for $15 million, not only the disputed area of Texas, but also California, New Mexico, Arizona, Utah, Nevada, and parts of Wyoming and Colorado.

The bloodiest wars in Texas were fought with the Comanche. Peace was very briefly thought to be possible in 1840, when the Comanche agreed to come to San Antonio and return white hostages and talk of a treaty, but they only brought one hostage, and the Texans trapped and killed the Comanche party. It was the last time the Comanche would consider peace with the Texans, and they fought against white encroachment to the bitter end, when the buffalo were gone and a reservation in Indian Territory became the only remaining option open to them.

As W. W. Newcomb, Jr., writes in *The Indians of Texas*: "The facts of history are plain: Most Texas Indians were exterminated or brought to the brink of oblivion by Spaniards, Mexicans, Texans, and Americans who often had no more regard for the life of an Indian than they had for that of a dog, sometimes less. What happened during this era is largely a tale of bloodshed and massacre, yet it is also part of a larger unfolding, that of the emergence of a powerful industrial nation."

Between the founding of the Texas republic and the outbreak of the Civil War, hordes of immigrants flooded into Texas. The economy continued to be agricultural. Those who settled along the coastal prairies and riverbottoms established new cotton and sugar plantations, worked, as in the Southern states, by slave labor. Farther north, small farms flourished. Texas held onto its public lands after annexation, was as eager as the Mexicans had been to fill the land with productive settlers, and continued a generous land-grant system. In the 1840s an influx of European merchants and traders began along the Rio Grande. The towns these new arrivals formed opposite older ones on the Mexican side were based on trade with Mexico, and although the Mexican-American population on the border continued to grow, the government of the area was con-

OPPOSITE: *Mexican guerrillas observe American troops fording a river in September 1846, after the capture of Monterrey, during the Mexican-American War.*

Paso el Diablo
Tres leguas d'Parras.

trolled by the European immigrants. So were vast lands—merchants who stayed in the area often became ranchers. Richard King and Mifflin Kenedy established their ranching domains in south Texas in the 1850s, and large ranches are still the rule in the area.

The major activity in Texas during the Civil War was the blockading of the growing ports of Galveston and Indianola. In the final days of the war, diehard Confederates (including Jefferson Davis) tried to reach Texas for a last stand, but few made it. The last land battle of the Civil War took place in Texas, near Brownsville, on May 12–13, 1865. The Battle of Palmito Ranch was, ironically, a Confederate victory. Nonetheless, on June 2, aboard a steamer in Galveston harbor, General Edmund Kirby Smith signed documents that formalized the surrender of the last Confederate army (which had in fact surrendered in New Orleans on May 26). General Stand Watie's Indian battalion remained in arms for a few more weeks, as did scattered irregulars. Some Confederates crossed into Mexico.

After the war Galveston became the largest and most sophisticated city in Texas, although Houston, which had built railroads before the war, had ambitions to catch up. Indianola, founded by the Germans, was a major port for immigration until the railroads came to central and northern Texas in the 1870s and 1880s and two hurricanes wiped out the port. After the Civil War, the great cattle drives began. The longhorns that had roamed freely during the conflict were rounded up and driven north to markets paying forty dollars a head for what before the war had gone for four. The culture of the rancher, the cowboy, and the open range spread from Texas all the way to Canada. The twentieth century came to the Gulf Coast with the oil strike at Spindletop in 1901, and the oil business was added to the thriving agriculture along the coastal plains, bringing more wealth to the region and turning Houston into the international port and business center it is today. Ranchers in south Texas had oil on their lands too, but for the most part it was taken out of the ground alongside ranching operations.

This chapter begins with San Antonio and nearby towns, proceeds southeast to the Gulf Coast at Indianola, follows the coast to the Rio Grande, then covers sites along the river to Laredo. The next section covers southeastern Texas, beginning at Houston.

OPPOSITE: *A seaweed-covered beach in the Padre Island National Seashore, one of the longest stretches of undeveloped ocean shoreline in the United States.*

S O U T H   T E X A S

SAN ANTONIO

San Antonio is the only major city in the state that existed before Texas won its independence from Mexico in 1836. Its many layers of history and purpose give it a unique character, as much European as American, seemingly less "Texan" to the casual observer, but on closer observation encompassing all that made Texas what it is. In 1718 Father Antonio Olivares was sent to start a Franciscan mission on the San Antonio River. Don Martín de Alarcón, military governor of Texas, was authorized to establish a fort and village. Seventy-two settlers, priests, and soldiers, and a considerable number of livestock made the 600-mile trek across Mexico. The mission was named San Antonio de Valero after the viceroy of Mexico, the marquis de Valero—100 years later it would be given the name Alamo. It was founded on May 1, 1718; four days later the Presidio San Antonio de Bexar and the Villa Bexar, where the soldiers would live with their families, were established. Both were named for Alarcón's brother, the duke of Bexar.

As did all thirty-six of the missions founded by Spain in Texas between 1680 and 1793, Mission San Antonio de Valero served both the church and the king. It had two purposes: conversion of the Indians to Catholicism and expansion of the kingdom of Spain. The native Payaya and Coahuiltecan were nomadic, subsisting on roots, pecans, insects, and mesquite beans. They were under constant threat by the Apache, whose lives had been greatly improved by their acquisition and mastery of the horses introduced to America by the Spanish but who were being pushed farther and farther south as the Comanche made their way down from the High Plains. In return for the protection and food the Franciscans provided, the Payaya and Coahuiltecan worked in the mission fields and built the mission churches. The Indians became the first Texas cowboys, learning to tend cattle from horseback as their neighbors farther south in Mexico did. Some used their horses to escape.

The Franciscans asked that settlers be sent to set a good example for the Christianized Indians, and finally Spain was able to find some

OPPOSITE: *A romantic vision of the defense of the Alamo, painted in 1901 by Robert Onderdonk, shows Davy Crockett wielding his rifle, Betsy, while defending the south wall gate. Eyewitness accounts placed him nearer the chapel at the end of the battle.*

Canary Islanders willing to move to the Texas frontier. In 1731, after a year's journey, fifteen exhausted families arrived. For their pains, the Canary Islanders had been given titles of gentility from the crown; they were angered upon arrival that there was neither a town nor townspeople to whom their new social position would be superior. The priests did not allow the Indians to work for the settlers, so for several years these titled folks chose not to work any harder than it took to subsist in their Villa de San Fernando (named in honor of the king's son and heir), more or less as the Indians had before the missions had been established. They did lay out a plaza, now Main Plaza, and eventually built a church, now San Fernando Cathedral. Other settlers joined them as new missions were built in a string along the San Antonio River. San Jose had already been established in 1720, then in 1731—after the failure and closing of the missions in east Texas—Concepción, Espada, and San Juan Capistrano were built. The church kept the missions open for seventy-five years, until 1793, when disease and the Comanche had so severely reduced the livestock and farming population that the lands were secularized and distributed among the remaining Indians. San Antonio by this time was well established as the most important frontier outpost and the capital of the province of Texas. By 1806 the city had a population—mostly Mexican—of 1,000.

In 1813 San Antonio was the scene of the short-lived First Republic of Texas, declared by a group of filibusters led first by Augustus Magee and after his death by Samuel Kemper. The group was called the American Volunteers and was associated with Mexican republicans rallying around Bernardo Gutiérrez de Lara in the Gutiérrez-Magee Expedition. On April 6 the Volunteers issued the Declaration of Independence of the State of Texas, based largely on the American Declaration. The first republic collapsed when Gutiérrez insisted that Texas remain part of Mexico and drew up a constitution based on Spanish models.

When the Texas Revolution broke out, Mexican General Martín Perfecto de Cós marched from Mexico, stopped briefly at Goliad, then proceeded to make his headquarters at San Antonio, which the Anglos often referred to as Bexar. In October 1835 Cós and his 800 men were besieged by a ragtag army of enthusiastic but ill-equipped and ill-trained Texans, augmented by American volunteers in search of adventure and a piece of whatever prizes this war might yield. For six inconclusive weeks, Cós was not inclined to risk a bloody break-out, and the Texans were equally disinclined to fight their way in—a standoff known as the Siege of Bexar. Just as the Texans and their allies were ready to quit, a Mexican deserter informed them that the defenders' supplies and morale were dwindling. On the spot a Texan named Ben Milam called for volunteers to join him in attacking. Milam's men fought house-to-house, sometimes room-to-room, undeterred by the occasional blasts from Mexican artillery, steadily pushing the defenders back, until Cós agreed to surrender. Some Texans decided to defend San Antonio by fortifying an old mission called the Alamo, but General Santa Anna resolved to take it, and finally did on March 6, 1836, in one of the most famous episodes in the history of American warfare. After the fall of the Alamo, San Antonio was under Mexican authority only until the Texans, led by Sam Houston, won the decisive Battle of San Jacinto on April 21. Bexar County was established by the Republic of Texas in 1836, and the period of heavy immigration to San Antonio began. The arrival of German and French immigrants in the 1840s had a profound effect on the city. In a town with only a few substantial buildings and commercial enterprises, the Germans established mills and breweries and constructed houses of great beauty, a concentration of which can be seen in the area of town known as King William.

Great changes were also brought about by the cattle drives that began forming in south Texas after the rounding up of all the animals that had been left to roam during the Civil War. San Antonio came to be called "the capital of south Texas" because it was a major trade and supply center for the ranchers, and it continued to supply the forts built in apprehension of the "Indian Problem" to the west. The first railroad arrived in San Antonio in 1877, and the railroads brought more immigrants. Businesses thrived; saloons flourished along with variety theaters and banks.

The agricultural development of the Rio Grande Valley brought Mexican nationals flooding into Texas, and many more made their way to San Antonio during and after the Mexican Revolution early in this century. Today, as in the days before Texas independence, Mexicans make up well over half the population and profoundly affect the social and political character of the town. Because of its rich and well-preserved history, modern San Antonio is a major tourist center. And, as at the beginning of its history, the city depends mightily on the military, with four air force bases and the army's Fort Sam Houston.

The Alamo (Mission San Antonio de Valero)

If there is one symbol Texans share with the outside world, it is the Alamo, where a heroic, hopelessly uneven battle between 188 Texans and 5,000 Mexican troops took place for thirteen days in February and March 1836. The four-acre Alamo compound includes the former mission church, now called the Shrine, a memorial to the Texans who defended it. Much of the fighting on the last, decisive day actually took place in the Long Barracks, the former *convento* (living quarters) of the mission priests, in the northwest corner of the grounds. The Mission San Antonio de Valero was moved from its original site to its present location in 1724. A stone church begun in 1744 was destroyed by hurricane and fire, and construction of a second church, the present Alamo, began in 1756.

The Alamo, originally the mission of San Antonio de Valero, was one of five missions established by the Spanish along the San Antonio River .

Stone quarried in the vicinity was used in a cruciform plan with barrel vaults, buttresses, and solid and low-lying forms. The delicately carved facade is typical of the other San Antonio missions. The upper part of the church was never finished. In 1793 the mission was secularized, and in 1801 a Spanish cavalry unit called El Alamo (cottonwood), after the town in Coahuila, Mexico, from which they hailed, was stationed here and remained with their families until 1825. The church was closed in 1812, and in 1814 the former *convento* was made a hospital, San Antonio's first.

After the surrender of General Cós at San Antonio in December 1835, General Antonio López de Santa Anna, ruler of Mexico, moved to put down the rebellion. By mid-February Santa Anna was in Texas, marching his army toward San Antonio. Colonel James Bowie—the frontiersman of bowie knife fame (it was actually patent-

A courtyard at the Alamo. The defenders of the Alamo could have escaped through the Mexican lines, but they chose to stay and fight, facing certain death.

ed by his brother) and the widower of the daughter of the Mexican vice-governor of Texas—arrived at the Alamo on January 19, 1836, under orders from General Sam Houston to destroy the fort and evacuate the town. Bowie found eighty Texans determined to defend the fort with the artillery Cós had left behind, which happened to be the best between Mexico City and New Orleans and too heavy to take anywhere without transport, which the Texans did not have. Bowie decided to fortify the Alamo. "The salvation of Texas depends in great measure on keeping [San Antonio] out of the hands of the enemy," he wrote to Governor Henry Smith. Colonel William B. Travis arrived on February 3 and assumed joint command. On February 8 the famous frontiersman David Crockett, at age 49 the oldest man at the Alamo, arrived to much fanfare with his fiddle and fifteen Tennessee volunteers. The Texans now had 150 men at the Alamo. Santa Anna arrived February 23, received intelligence from the townspeople of the tiny and ill-armed force inside the Alamo, and hoisted the red flag of no quarter from the San Fernando Cathedral. Travis fired the Mexican eighteen-pounder cannon in response.

On February 24 Bowie, who had been ill (possibly with tuberculosis), collapsed. He gave over his share of the command to Travis, a hotheaded young man in his mid-twenties who was eager for action and glory. Santa Anna's bombardment began, and Travis sent his famous appeal for help "To the People of Texas and All Americans in the World." His letter concluded, "If this call is neglected, I am determined to sustain myself as long as possible and die like a soldier who never forgets what is due to his own honor & that of his country, VICTORY OR DEATH."

Crockett had asked for the most dangerous position for himself and for his volunteers. Travis granted it. Bowie had been placed in a small room on a cot, which was carried out from time to time during the siege so that he could rally the men. The siege and bombardment continued steadily. Travis sent more pleas for help to the outside world. On March 1, thirty-two men from Gonzales arrived, and the men at the Alamo rallied, believing that James Walker Fannin, Jr., was coming too, with some 400 to 500 reinforcements. Fannin did not come. The Texans were able to hold off the Mexicans because of their extraordinary marksmanship and skill at loading and firing cannon rapidly and accurately. Mexican attacks were repeatedly beaten back with heavy losses, particularly among the officers, whom the Alamo's sharpshooters singled out. By March 5 no Texans had been killed, but Santa Anna's forces had moved closer while the Alamo's ammunition was depleted. It was clear that there was no hope for success. Travis gathered his men in the plaza and told them the three choices available to them: surrender, attempt to escape, or stay and fight. Then, according to legend, Travis drew a line in the dirt with his sword and asked all those who would choose the last option to cross it. All crossed but the Frenchman Moses Rose, who escaped over the wall. The Mexican siege was not a tight one—all the defenders probably could have escaped.

At dawn March 6, the Mexicans advanced on the Alamo. Twice they were repulsed by the Texans, but the third time they breached the north wall and swarmed into the plaza. The fighting now became pure slaughter. Enraged by the heavy losses they had suffered, the Mexican soldiers needed no encouragement to carry out their government's orders to annihilate the rebels. The victors mutilated the corpses of the defenders. The body of Jim Bowie, who was killed in his sickbed, was thrown into the air and impaled on bayonets. By 9:00 AM the killing was finished. The only people spared were a black slave, the wife of one of the defenders, and some Mexican families that had lived at the Alamo. The bodies of the defenders were burned in a huge pyre. The Mexicans had suffered some 600 casualties. At San Jacinto several weeks later Santa Anna would hear the vengeful cry, "Remember the Alamo!".

After the revolution and through annexation, the Alamo lay empty and abandoned, until 1849, when the U.S. Army restored it to use as a warehouse for supplying frontier forts, adding the parapet (probably copied from the one on a mission in California where they had also been stationed). By the turn of the twentieth century, the *convento* at the Alamo had been covered with a two-story wooden "castle," a mercantile concern, and local developers planned to buy it and turn it into a hotel (the church had been purchased in 1883 by the state). With the legislature not in session to help them, the Daughters of the Republic of Texas could raise only a fraction of the money needed to head off the developers. Then Clara Driscoll, member of a wealthy Corpus Christi ranching family, bought the property in 1903 for $65,000. She was eventually repaid by the state of Texas. Today the museum is still administered by the Daughters of the Republic of Texas. The sales museum was built in 1936 to celebrate the Texas centennial, marking 100 years of independence. The Daughters of the Republic of Texas Library, built in 1950, is a research library and archive. The Alamo Cenotaph, honoring the defenders, outside the museum grounds, is by Pompeo Coppini.

LOCATION: Alamo Plaza at Houston Street. HOURS: 9:30–5 Monday–Saturday, 10–5:30 Sunday. FEE: None. TELEPHONE: 512–225–1391.

Across the street from the Alamo, the **Menger Hotel** (204 Alamo Plaza, 512–223–4361) was built in 1859 as a hostelry of "eight rooms with adjoining baths" next to the Menger Brewery. The hotel's popularity was immediate. After the Civil War and during the great migration west and the cattle drives north, the Menger became the most famous hotel in the Southwest. William Sydney Porter (O. Henry) mentioned the hotel in several of his short stories; Sidney Lanier stayed here during the winter of 1872–1873 while he worked on a sketch called "San Antonio de Bexar." In 1898 Theodore Roosevelt used the Menger as a headquarters for recruiting ranchers for the Roughriders of the Spanish-American War. As a result the Menger Bar, which had been installed in 1887, roughly replicating the taproom in the House of Lords—complete with solid cherry bar, French mirrors, and gold-plated spittoons—came to be called the Roosevelt Bar. In 1909 the San Antonio architect Alfred Giles did a splendid Renaissance Revival refurbishment and addition to the Menger, which included a three-story rotunda with balconies supported by Corinthian columns and decorated with filigreed balustrades.

Saint Joseph's Catholic Church (623 East Commerce) was built by German Catholics who had worshiped at the San Fernando Cathedral with the Hispanic community since their arrival but wanted a church of their own after the Civil War. They first asked to use the Alamo, but the U.S. Army denied the request, preferring to retain the church as a warehouse. The limestone Gothic Revival Saint Joseph's was built between 1868 and 1876 by Theodore E. Giraud. In 1898 the spire was added by James Wahrenberger, a local architect. The interior has art-glass windows imported from Munich in 1902.

Between 1938 and 1941 the Works Progress Administration completed an ambitious landscaping of the banks of the San Antonio River as part of a flood-control project. (A flood in 1921

The Arneson River Theater, part of the Paseo del Rio, has its stage on one side of the San Antonio River and its seating on the other.

had killed fifty people and damaged $50 million worth of property.) **Paseo del Rio,** designed by the architect Robert H. H. Hugman, was intended to create a "quaint atmosphere" such as that of "old cities in Spain." Beautifully landscaped stone paths wind along both sides of the river, where cypress trees have been transplanted from the Guadalupe River. Thirty-one stairways lead down to the river from twenty-one bridges in the downtown area.

La Villita

La Villita ("Little Village"), a complex of twenty-seven restored buildings on the site of a Coahuiltecan village on the San Antonio River, is a material chronicle of 200 years of white settlement in the city. In the mid- and late eighteenth century, the village was temporary and ramshackle, a community of huts. A flood in 1819 destroyed the dwellings on the opposite side of the river but did not damage the higher La Villita, which thereafter gained larger houses.

La Villita was the scene of house-to-house fighting during the final days of the siege of San Antonio in December 1835. The Mexicans capitulated to the Texans here on December 10, 1835, at the **Cós House** (ca. 1800), which is the oldest in the village. After Texas statehood Germans and later Swiss and French immigrants interspersed graceful cut-stone structures, including the 1876 **Little Church,** among the earlier Spanish and Mexican stuccoed-adobe houses. La Villita had become derelict by the early twentieth century; under the guidance of Mayor Maury Maverick, the Villita Ordinance established La Villita as an arts and crafts center. The area was restored by the National Youth Administration under the supervision of O'Neill Ford, a noted San Antonio architect. Artists and craftspeople work in view of the public in almost all the buildings, which have been sensitively restored and house cafés and shops. In **Bolivar Hall** the **Old San Antonio Exhibit** (512–224–6163) traces the history of the village from its beginnings through its restoration. The village, located between Durango, Navarro, and Alamo streets and the San Antonio River, is now a park.

There are over 20,000 circus artifacts in the **Hertzberg Circus Collection** (210 Market Street, 512–299–7810), making it one of the largest circus collections in the country. Exhibits include a 1902 parade wagon for a dog-and-pony show; Tom Thumb's coach (thought to have been built in 1843 to the order of P. T. Barnum), along with various Tom Thumb accoutrements; a miniature circus; poster, broadside, and photograph collections; and circus prints. The extensive library includes rare sixteenth- and seventeenth-century books on gymnastics. The collection, donated by the San Antonio civic leader Harry Hertzberg to the city library, is housed in the **Old San Antonio Public Library** (also known as the Library Annex) designed in 1930 by Herbert M. Green. Flanking the main entrance are statues of Cervantes and Shakespeare and an inscription from Ralph Waldo Emerson: "Books are the homes of the American people."

The **Main Plaza de Las Islas,** laid out in 1731 to the specifications of Philip V of Spain, was the heart of the original Canary Islander settlement called Villa de San Fernando and of later San Antonio as well. In 1749 the Apache signed a peace treaty here (although it would not end hostilities between them and the whites); Moses Austin negotiated his land grant here. During the

Siege of Bexar late in 1835, General Cós placed breastworks and batteries on the plaza.

The anchor of Main Plaza is the Gothic Revival **San Fernando Cathedral** (115 Main Plaza). Designed by François Giraud and constructed between 1868 and 1873, it was added to the front of a Spanish Baroque church completed in 1749—now the oldest cathedral sanctuary in the United States. The Texans flew a flag of victory from the old church's tower after driving out General Cós; General Santa Anna flew the red flag of no quarter from one of the towers of the church on the first day of the siege of the Alamo. In an alcove just inside the simply appointed cathedral is a white marble crypt, decorated with small photographs of Travis, Bowie, and Crockett. Bones said to be theirs were rescued from the funeral pyres after the battle and buried at the church. Across the plaza from the cathedral is the 1895 **Bexar County Courthouse** (20 Dolorosa Street), a massive pink granite and Pecos sandstone building with a terra-cotta frieze by James Riely Gordon, whose beautiful Romanesque Revival courthouses adorn many Texas county seats.

Separated from Main Plaza by the cathedral, **Military Plaza (Plaza de Armas)** is the former drilling ground of the Spanish troops from the presidio, which was moved here in 1722 from its original site farther north. In the nineteenth century, chili stands lined the plaza, the city's business center. In 1876 Military Plaza was the scene of a landmark event in the history of the cattle business: John Warne "Bet-A-Million" Gates had met with sneers from some cattlemen who had come to San Antonio with their huge herds to buy supplies for the drive north when he hawked a new-fangled product from Illinois called barbed wire. Gates talked city officials into letting him build a corral in Military Plaza and invited the stockmen to send in their least disciplined cattle. The cattle charged ahead, but they balked again and again at the barbs. On the spot Gates received more orders for the fencing than his company could possibly fill. The days of the open cattle range were coming to an end. **San Antonio City Hall** was built on the plaza in Second Empire and Renaissance Revival style in 1891 by Otto Kramer, a Chicago architect (the building was altered in 1927).

OVERLEAF: *A painting by William G.M. Samuel, an amateur artist who was later a city marshal, shows the west side of San Antonio's lively main plaza in 1849. An American flag flies behind the San Fernando Cathedral.*

West Side Main Plaza, San Antonio

Texas 1849　　WGMSamuel

The Spanish Governor's Palace

Military Plaza's only remaining Spanish Colonial structure has a keystone dated 1749 and bears the Habsburg coat of arms in honor of King Philip V. It became the governor's residence after it had been the *comandancia*. In the early nineteenth century, the palace fell into private hands and went on to become a clothing shop, a saloon, a tailor's shop, a restaurant, and a schoolhouse. The city of San Antonio rescued it in derelict condition in 1929 and restored it as a museum. Spanish Colonial antique furnishings and artifacts include a fine seventeenth-century rosewood bed and, from the sixteenth century, fringed leather chairs, a spice cabinet with locks, and a conquistador's brass stirrups.

LOCATION: 105 Plaza de Armas. HOURS: 9–5 Monday–Saturday, 10–5 Sunday. FEE: Yes. TELEPHONE: 512–224–0601.

The courtyard of the Spanish Governor's Palace, used as the comandancia, or captain's residence, in the Presidio de San Antonio de Bexar.

José Antonio Navarro, born in San Antonio, was a rancher and lawyer who was present at the enactment of the Texas Declaration of Independence in Washington-on-the-Brazos while Santa Anna was besieging the Alamo. Navarro went on to help draft the constitution of the Republic of Texas and serve in its congress. The **José Navarro House** (228 South Laredo Street, 512–225–4801) is part of a complex of three adobe and limestone buildings—home, kitchen, and office in an expressive amalgam of Mexican, German, French, and pioneer styles. These were built a block from Military Plaza around 1850. Exhibits include historical displays and period furnishings.

The west side of **Milam Square** (bounded by West Commerce, West Houston, North San Saba, and North Santa Rosa) is the site of the grave of Ben Milam, who led 300 Texan volunteers against the Mexican garrison of 1,200 in the battle for San Antonio in December 1835—"Who will go with old Ben Milam into San

The dining room at the Governor's Palace is furnished with sixteenth-century Spanish chairs. The tall and narrow fireplace accommodated logs standing on end.

Antonio?" he is said to have asked—and became the Texans' first casualty. The east side of the square was the cemetery for the Canary Island settlers and for San Fernando Cathedral from 1808 to 1860. A bit north at 500 Santa Rosa is the limestone-rubble **Menger Soap Works** (1850), probably the oldest industrial building in Texas and possibly the first soap factory in the Southwest; it operated as such until the turn of the century.

The **Southwest Craft Center** (300 Augusta, 512–224–1848) is a complex of six structures built between 1851 and the early 1900s, which housed the **Old Ursuline Academy** until the middle of this century. The academy was established in 1851 by Bishop Jean-Marie Odin, who came with the Ursuline nuns from New Orleans, the order's U.S. headquarters, and bought ten acres on the river. The first building was constructed that year by François Giraud and Jules Ponsard, who used the *pise de terre* (rammed earth) process, very few examples of which are seen in the United States. In the 1860s dormitories and a chapel were built and in the 1880s a priest's house, all of limestone blocks in Gothic Revival style. They are at once rustic and very French, melding into a harmonious Gallo-Texan aesthetic. The complex was saved from development or razing by the San Antonio Conservation Society, which asked the Southwest Craft Center to make its headquarters here.

Noteworthy commercial buildings from the early twentieth century abound in the downtown area. Beginning on East Houston Street from Main Plaza are the **Rand Building** (number 100) by Sanguinet & Staats, early Texas skyscraper architects from Fort Worth; the small but big-bayed **Book Building** (number 130) of 1906; and the **Gunter Hotel** (number 205), completed in 1909. The queen of the block is the **Majestic Theater Building** (number 214) of 1929, an eighteen-story Spanish Colonial- and Mission-style office building by John Eberson, six stories of which are occupied by the theater. The interior of the 4,000-seat theater has two elaborately ornamented balconies beneath a sculptural ceiling full of clouds and thousands of twinkling stars. The triangular **G. Bedell Moore Building** (110 Broadway at East Houston Street) of 1904 is one of the finest commercial buildings of the San Antonio architect Atlee B. Ayres.

South on Alamo Plaza, the **Crockett Block** (numbers 317–323) of 1882–1883 was designed by architect Alfred Giles of San Antonio.

Only a portion of the 1926 terra-cotta Texas Theater, designed by the Bowler Brothers of Kansas City, survives today. The rest of the building was demolished to make way for a skyscraper constructed by a Texas bank.

These four three-story buildings with a common Italianate facade were discovered under less appealing false fronts when the **Paseo del Alamo** (connecting the Alamo and the Paseo del Rio) was being constructed. The **Reuter Building** (217 Alamo Plaza) was built in 1891 by James Wahrenberger, who designed its two projecting bays to allow unobstructed views of its neighbor, the Alamo. On Commerce Street heading west: The **Clifford Building** (numbers 423–431) with its huge rounded end alongside the river was designed by James Riely Gordon; the 1867 **Stockman Restaurant** (number 409) preserves a bit of Old West style in a cattle-era commercial building; the Renaissance Revival-style **Old Alamo National Bank Building** of 1902 (number 316) is by James Wahrenberger, Coughlin & Ayres; the **Stevens Building** (number 315) of 1891 and the **Staacke Brothers Building** (number 309) of 1894 were built with complementary details by James Riely Gordon.

The finest small commercial building in San Antonio is the **First National Bank,** also known as the Old San Antonio National Bank (number 213), built in 1886 by Cyrus L. W. Eidlitz for George Washington Brackenridge, a cotton merchant, banker, entrepreneur, Union colonel, and generous philanthropist. Brackenridge, who studied engineering at Harvard, apparently was inspired by Islamic architecture when he contributed to the design of this building. Attached to the bank, but apparently a separate edifice, is Brackenridge's less dramatic **San Antonio Loan & Trust** (number 235), also by Eidlitz, built in 1903.

Located in the former Texas Pavilion of the 1968 World's Fair, the **Institute of Texas Cultures** (801 South Bowie Street, 512–226–7651) is devoted to research and educational programs that preserve and re-create the lifestyles of the native peoples of Texas and the many immigrant groups who settled in the state. Interpreters and hands-on exhibits in the gigantic exhibition hall illustrate the history of twenty-seven different ethnic groups, including Indians, Mexicans, Hungarians, Germans, and Irish. An outdoor exhibit area depicts rural Texas life with reconstructions of a one-room schoolhouse, adobe house, barn, windmill, and fort. The **Mexican Cultural Center** (600 HemisFair Park, 512–227–0123) has four galleries with changing exhibits of Mexican art, contemporary as well as historic.

San Antonio's most famous residential area and first suburb (also Texas's first official historic district), **King William** was carved out of irrigated farmlands that once belonged to the Mission San Antonio de Valero. The greatest concentration of German-influenced buildings in the San Antonio area can be seen here and in New Braunfels. The first German in the area was Karl Wilhelm Guenther, who established a mill on the river in 1859. The area was begun as an actual neighborhood in 1866 when a lawyer, Ernst Altgelt, moved from nearby Comfort in the Hill Country. Altgelt had a grand plan: three parallel avenues intersected by five streets and bordered by a triangular park. He named the central avenue after Kaiser Wilhelm I of Prussia and the flanking avenues after Presidents Washington and Madison. Kaiser Wilhelm Street was

OPPOSITE: *The towers of J. Riely Gordon's Richardsonian Romanesque Bexar County Courthouse, constructed between 1892 and 1895, juxtaposed with the Neo-Gothic Tower Life Building, designed by Atlee B. Ayres and completed in 1929.*

later anglicized to King William, and during World War I it was nervously and temporarily renamed Pershing Street.

The houses in King William were built over a period of more than thirty years; this architectural unfolding—combined with a distinctive local architectural aesthetic—gives the neighborhood its tone. The **Wulff House** (107 King William Street, 512–224–6163) was built in 1870 by a merchant, Anton Wulff, in the Italianate style according to the precepts expressed a generation earlier in the books of Andrew Jackson Downing. The house serves as the offices of the San Antonio Conservation Society, which provides a walking tour of the area. The district includes many noteworthy private houses.

Steves Homestead

A rather homespun name identifies the museum showpiece of King William, built by Alfred Giles in 1875 for the retail lumber merchant Edward Steves. Sited on the river among old pecan, magnolia, cypress, and palm trees, the house is Second Empire with proud restraint, appointed with antiques collected to correspond as closely as possible to the original interiors as documented in family photographs. Among the furniture is a seven-piece Belter parlor set, a Chickering piano, and a canopy bed where (it is said) Robert E. Lee once slept. On the grounds are a carriage house and the River Haus, which was built to cover a swimming pool fed by an artesian well.

> LOCATION: 509 King William Street. HOURS: 1–5 Monday–Tuesday,
> 10–5 Wednesday–Sunday. FEE: Yes. TELEPHONE: 512–225–5924.

Once on the grounds of Mission Concepción, the **Yturri-Edmunds Home and Mill** (257 Yellowstone Street, 512–534–8237) is a rare example of the farmhouses on the San Antonio River in the 1840s. Built of adobe bricks and recently restored, the house spans a portion of the Spanish-built Pajalache acequia, or irrigation ditch.

San Antonio Missions National Historical Park

These four beautiful missions in a string along the San Antonio River are among the oldest and most important structures in the United States. Each has a compound of about four or five acres. Thick stone walls were built as defense against Apache and Comanche raids, and within them, the missions were laid out like

The elegant Second Empire Steves Homestead, in San Antonio's King William district, was built in 1875 by Edward Steves for $12,000. It was the first house in San Antonio to be lighted electrically.

small towns. Around a central court were houses for the Indians, a *convento* (quarters for the priests), cloisters, workshops, and a mission church. Water was obtained from an ingenious system of acequias, little channels dug from the nearby river. There were also *ranchos* and acequia-irrigated croplands outside the mission compounds, where the Indian workers carried weapons in case of Apache or Comanche attacks. The mission church was always the last structure to be completed, so that it could be given the most time, care, and elaboration in the Spanish tradition. Spanish artisans would travel among the missions and teach building techniques and supervise the craftsmanship. The friar contractors and their Indian construction workers used local materials; the river was rich in clay, and limestone was quarried nearby. Metal was brought raw from Mexico and wrought at the missions into hardware. Some important items, such as bells, were made in Mexico or Spain.

Churches were painted by Indians and Spaniards with exotic colors made from local pigment sources such as rocks and plants. All mission churches still serve active parishes.

The **Mission Concepción (Nuestra Señora de la Purísima Concepción de Acuña)** at 807 Mission Road, has an unrestored stone church completed in 1755. Originally established in east Texas, the mission (not the church building) was moved in 1730 to an area now occupied by Zilker Park in Austin, then to San Antonio in 1731. Concepción's interpretive theme is "The Mission as Religious Center." Traces of brightly colored frescoes remain on the twin towers of the church. Abandoned for many years after secularization, the mission became the campground for Stephen F. Austin's Texas volunteers, including Jim Bowie and James W. Fannin, Jr., after the nearby Battle of Concepción (leading up to the Siege of Bexar).

The **Mission San Juan Capistrano** (9101 Graf Road), ca. 1731–1756, was never fully completed, and most of the original square is preserved within the mission walls. The delicate bell tower at San Juan is unique among the Texas missions. In the church are rare cornstalk-pith figures of Christ and the Virgin Mary. The **Mission Espada (San Francisco de la Espada)** at 10040 Espada Road, built between 1731 and 1756, was created by an east Texas mission reestablished here in 1731. Although the mission was not secularized until 1794, the church was in ruins by 1778. The present chapel was built in 1886. The interpretive theme at Espada is "The Mission as a Vocational Education Center."

The **Espada Aqueduct and Dam** (9044 Espada Road), built between 1731 and 1740, are the only surviving parts of the extensive, sophisticated water system built by the Franciscans to serve the missions. The remaining five-mile section of the system begins here at the dam and still carries water over Piedras Creek via the limestone-rubble aqueduct.

The **Mission San José (San José y San Miguel de Aguayo)** at 6539 San Jose Drive was the second mission founded on the San Antonio River after Mission San Antonio de Valero. Built between 1768 and 1782, the church, with its exquisite carved-stone ornamentation, is one of the finest in Texas. Pedro Huizar, who moved

OPPOSITE: *Unlike most eighteenth-century stone churches in this country, the church at Mission Concepción, built in 1755, has never been restored. At one time it was used as a cattle and horse barn.*

ABOVE *and* OPPOSITE: *Mission San José is the most elaborate of the five San Antonio missions. Its baroque facade was carved by Pedro Huizar between 1768 and 1777. During the 1840s, soldiers used it for target practice.*

to Bexar from Aguascalientes, Mexico, is credited with sculpting the famous Rosa's Window. According to mission legend, he created the window as a tribute to Rosa, the woman he loved, who died at sea on her way to join him at the mission. San José was founded by one of the most ambitious missionaries, Antonio Margil de Jesús. Mission San José, The mission's interpretive theme is "The Mission as a Social Center and as a Center of Defense;" it is the most completely restored mission of the four.

In the residential areas known as **Laurel Heights, Monte Vista, Alamo Heights, Olmos Park,** and **Terrell Hills** are some of the most interesting and beautiful houses in the state, many of them built during the first thirty years of this century. A few examples (all privately owned) are the eclectic **Halff House** (601 Howard Street) of 1908 by Atlee B. Ayres; the exotic Bavarian Victorian **Koehler House**

(Belknap at French Place) of 1900, by Carl von Seutter; the baronial 1936 **Oak Court** (636 Ivy Lane), the finest residential work by Atlee B. and Robert M. Ayres; and one of the oldest houses in the area, the **Argyle** (734 Patterson Avenue), built in 1854 as the headquarters for a horse ranch, converted into a stylish hotel in 1893 and converted into a private dining club in the 1950s. **San Pedro Springs Park** (1500 San Pedro Avenue), a former Indian village, was declared public land in 1729 by the Spanish. It has been a city park since 1852 and still has an early bandstand.

San Antonio Museum of Art

Completed in 1981 by the architectural firm Cambridge Seven Associates, San Antonio's newest art museum (whose collections were once housed at the Witte Museum in Brackenridge Park) is an imaginative adaptive reuse of the old Lone Star Brewery built in 1903 for Adolphus Busch by the Saint Louis firm of Jugenfeld and Company, brewery-design specialists. Forced to shut down by Prohibition, the brewery was used variously for manufacturing and storage. The museum space was skillfully incorporated into the old building. Collections range from pre-Columbian pottery to contemporary American painting and sculpture.

LOCATION: 200 West Jones Avenue. HOURS: 10–5 Monday–Saturday, 10–9 Tuesday, 12–5 Sunday. FEE: Yes. TELEPHONE: 512–226–5544.

Fort Sam Houston

This active army post was established in San Antonio in 1845 and moved to its present location in 1876, when the Quadrangle was constructed. Originally a supply depot, the Quadrangle encloses a plaza of about nine acres and features a ninety-foot-tall tower in the center. The post went through successive building programs and represents a physical record of more than a century of military architectural styles; it is now a 550-acre National Historic District. The museum in Building 123 depicts the history of the installation from 1845 to the present. Numerous historic markers are located on the post.

LOCATION: Grayson Street and New Braunfels Avenue, off Route I-35. HOURS: *Quadrangle:* 8–6 Daily; *Museum:* 10–4 Wednesday–Sunday. FEE: None. TELEPHONE: 512–221–6117.

Brackenridge Park

Sections of this city park were part of an original Spanish land grant to the city. Much of the land was donated by Colonel George W. Brackenridge. At the edge of the park is the **Witte Museum** (3801 Broadway, 512–226–5544), which is devoted to Texas natural history, anthropology, and archaeology. Three historic San Antonio houses have been moved to the grounds of the museum. The Spanish Colonial–style **Ruiz House** was built in 1745 by José Francisco Ruiz, a native San Antonian who was the town's first official schoolmaster, served in the Mexican army, signed the Texas Declaration of Independence, and sat in the first Texas congress as a representative from Bexar. The limestone **Celso Navarro House,** built in downtown San Antonio in 1835 by a descendant of Angel Navarro, the *alcalde* (mayor) of San Antonio's Canary Islanders' settlement in 1790, was reconstructed behind the museum in 1948. The **John Twohig House** was the home of an Irishman who had a mercantile business in San Antonio and took part in the Siege of Bexar in 1836. In 1842, when a Mexican army, led by the French soldier of fortune Adrian Woll, invaded San Antonio, Twohig was captured and taken to Perote Prison in Veracruz. In response, Texans launched the punitive Mier Expedition, during which the Texans were captured after they had pillaged the Mexican border town of Mier; a number of them escaped but 176 were recaptured a week later. The Mexicans had received orders to kill every tenth escapee. The Texans were passed a jar of 176 beans, seventeen of which were black, the "beans of death." John Twohig and eight other men escaped from Perote Prison via a tunnel in 1843. Next door to the Witte is **Memorial Hall** (3805 Broadway, 512–822–9011), built in 1936 for the Texas centennial. It has three exhibits: the Trail Driver Exhibit Room, housing memorabilia from the cattle era; the Texas Ranger Exhibit Hall, which traces the history of this statewide police force; and the Pioneer Parlor, which exhibits furniture and clothes of early settlers. Outside the building is the bronze cast for the *Trail Drivers Memorial* by Gutzon Borglum, sculptor of Mount Rushmore. The full-scale piece was not completed.

The **McNay Art Museum** (5000 North New Braunfels Avenue, 512–824–5368) was built as a Spanish Colonial-style mansion for Marion Koogler McNay, an oil heiress from Kansas who settled in Texas when her first husband was stationed in the Army at Laredo.

Atlee B. Ayres and his son, Robert, eminent San Antonio architects, designed the building with the close participation of Mrs. McNay, who was trained as an artist. It was completed in 1928. Mrs. McNay began collecting art with a painting by Diego Rivera; in 1942 she decided to open the San Antonio Art Institute in the former aviary of her house and set about building an important collection for the museum, focusing on Mexican art as well as Impressionist and Postimpressionist paintings. In the years since Mrs. McNay's death in 1950, the museum has broadened the scope of the collections, which occupy the entire mansion and newer additions to the building.

The **Southern Pacific Passenger Station** (1174 East Commerce) is a Mission–style station of 1903 with a Beaux-Arts interior that includes art-glass windows. Across the street is the Mission Revival **Heimann Building,** built about 1906. West of downtown is the tiny **Chapel of Miracles** (113 Ruiz Street), built as a devotional chapel in the 1870s by Don Juan Ximenes and tended by his descendants, who live across the street. Inside the chapel is an eight-foot-high wooden Spanish Colonial crucifix, which is said to have hung in the church of the Mission San Antonio de Valero. Worshipers attribute miracles to the cross, and the chapel is filled with tiny tin *milagros* left by the faithful who have come for healing.

CASTROVILLE

Founded under a colonization contract by the French entrepreneur Henri Castro, this small town west of San Antonio on the Medina River was settled in 1844 by a group of immigrants. They were soon joined by more, from Alsace-Lorraine. It is sometimes referred to as "the Little Alsace of Texas," and indeed, its simple stone-cottage architecture—built and maintained through difficult early years of drought, Indian attacks, and cholera—is like other north French colonies in the Hudson Valley and along the Saint Lawrence. There are ninety-six historic structures in the village; those marked with Castroville Garden Club markers can be visited by appointment with the club (512–538–2298). The Gothic Revival **Saint Louis Catholic Church** (Angelo Street and Route I-90) was completed in 1870 and replaced the **First Church** (Angelo Street between Paris and Madrid streets), a tiny whitewashed stone chapel built in 1847 next to the first **Saint Louis School.** The French Provincial–style **Carle House** and Store (Angelo and Madrid streets, private) was built in 1855; the **Tarde Hotel** (Fiorella and Madrid streets) is an Alsatian-style building, now a private residence. At **Mount Gentilz Cemetery** (Route I-90 and Alsace Street) is buried Amelia Castro, wife of the founder. **Cross Hill,** above the cemetery, offers a stunning view of the Medina River valley.

Landmark Inn State Historic Site

The French immigrant Cesar Monod, who was the mayor of Castroville in 1852, built the first floor of what is today called the Landmark Inn in 1849 and used it as his home and as a general store. The complex included a detached stone kitchen, and the walls of both buildings are of plastered limestone twenty-two inches thick. In 1853 an Irish immigrant named John Vance bought the house and added a second floor as well as galleries to both floors. He started renting rooms to travelers on the well-used road from San Antonio to El Paso, and the place came to be known as the Vance Hotel. Robert E. Lee is said to have stayed here. A stone grist-mill and a wood-and-stone dam built later have also been preserved. The property is operated as an inn by the Texas Parks and Wildlife Department. Exhibits on the history of the inn and its restoration are at the site.

LOCATION: Florence and Fiorella streets. HOURS: 8–6 Daily. FEE: None. TELEPHONE: 512–538–2133.

UVALDE

A sheep- and goat-ranching and agricultural town founded in the 1850s, Uvalde was the home of John Nance "Cactus Jack" Garner, Speaker of the U.S. House of Representatives and vice president under Franklin D. Roosevelt (1933–1941). As a congressman, Garner promoted an income tax according to one's ability to pay and was among the first to conceive of insurance for bank deposits, the fore-runner of the FDIC. He donated his two-story brick house to the city of Uvalde to be made into the **Garner Memorial Museum** (333 North Park Street, 512–278–5018). Displays include Speaker Garner's gavels plus memorabilia from the early days of Uvalde. Downtown is the

Grand Opera House (100 Northwest Street, 512–278–4082), which was built in 1891 and is once again a performance hall.

SEGUIN

Founded in 1838 as Walnut Springs, this town on the Guadalupe River was renamed in 1839 for Colonel Juan Nepomucena Seguin, a native San Antonian who led a detachment of Mexican Texans at San Jacinto and was later a Texas state senator. At the corner of Camp and Gonzales downtown are the **Ranger Oaks,** under which the first settlers and signers of the town charter camped until the survey was completed and lots were drawn for homesites. According to local tradition, Texas Rangers Jack Hays and James Callahan made some captive Indians dig a trench under the oaks, ordered the prisoners to stand in it, and then shot them, thereby saving themselves the trouble of grave digging.

In the nineteenth-century downtown commercial district is the **Los Nogales Museum** (415 South River Street at East Live Oak Street), a tiny pioneer house of sun-baked bricks built in 1849. Next door is the white gingerbread **Doll House** built in 1908–1910. Just east is the **Campbell-Hoerman Cabin** of 1850, which employs a pioneer design element common from North Carolina to New Mexico—the dog run or dogtrot, a wide central breezeway separating two rooms or parts of a house to promote air circulation. In back of the cabin is a late-nineteenth-century **calaboose** from what was once the nearby Guadalupe County Poor Farm. Originally mounted on wheels, the 4,000-pound rolling wooden jail car with a metal lining, whose inside walls still show graffiti, was used to transport prisoners to the fields to pick cotton.

The unusual **Sebastopol House State Historic Site** (704 West Zorn Street, 512–379–4833), a one-story Greek Revival house with a partially raised basement, was built from 1854 to 1856 by Colonel Joshua Young from an early form of concrete. It was later the residence of Joseph Zorn, Jr., mayor of Seguin from 1890 to 1910. The house displays a few pieces of furniture from the Zorn family and the Seguin area, but the major installation is an exhibit on the history of concrete construction.

The first federal building to go up in Galveston was **Old Galveston Custom House** (20th Street and Avenue E) of 1858–1861 by Ammi B. Young. Made of local brick and iron imported from restored nineteenth-century structures, including an 1830s log cabin (one of the few remaining in the state), a cypress-sided church from the 1870s, and a two-story German-style house built in the 1890s. Costumed interpreters demonstrate pioneer crafts and household tasks.

GONZALES

The plat of this charming town on the Guadalupe River, with its seven public squares, is unchanged from 1825, when it was laid out as the capital of a colony of 400 families led by Kentucky-born Green DeWitt. Gonzales is where the first shot of the Texas Revolution was fired. A Mexican corporal was sent to Gonzales in late September 1835 to retrieve a small cannon that had been lent to the Texans a few years earlier for protection against the Tawakoni Indians. A group of 18 Texans told the corporal that the cannon

The Knowles-Townsend Log House, constructed in the late 1840s, has been moved to Gonzales Pioneer Village Living History Center from Gonzales County.

would have to be taken by force; the Mexicans responded by sending 150 dragoons to do so. On October 1 the Gonzalians met the soldiers at the Guadalupe River (the battleground is marked near the community of **Cost,** south on Route 97). In three days the 18 men had grown to a force of 180; they had unearthed the little cannon from its hiding place in a colonist's peach orchard and filled it with pieces of chain and scrap iron. The Texan battle flag, made quickly by two women out of a wedding dress, was white with a black star and stitched with the words COME AND TAKE IT. The Texans fired one shot out of what would come to be called the "Come and Take It Cannon," killing one Mexican. The Mexican commander, under orders not to fight over the cannon, retreated to San Antonio. (A WPA mural in the **Gonzales Municipal Building** on Saint Joseph Street commemorates the event.) A few weeks later, several hundred Texans marched from Gonzales to San Antonio to join in besieging General Cós at the presidio of Bexar. In February of the following year, when the call for help came from the Alamo, Gonzales gathered thirty-two reinforcements who fought their way into the Alamo and died there.

Historic sites are marked by green-and-white signs. Information about tours is available from the Gonzales Chamber of Commerce and Agriculture, housed, along with the **Old Jail Museum** (512–672–6532), in the Gonzales County Jail on Courthouse Square. The Italianate and Neoclassical brick jail by Eugene T. Heiner, a Houston architect, was built in 1887 in a style and at an expense some townspeople likened to "putting a fifty-dollar saddle on a twenty-five-dollar horse." The cells and jailers' rooms have been restored. The Victorian eclectic brick-and-limestone **Gonzales County Courthouse** was built in 1894–1895 by Otto P. Kroeger after plans by courthouse architect James Riely Gordon. Opposite the courthouse is the **Heroes of Texas Independence Monument,** by the sculptor Pompeo Coppini. East from the courthouse, the **Kennard-Bowden House** (621 Saint Louis Street, private) is a restored High Victorian house built in 1895. The **Gonzales Memorial Museum** (Smith and Saint Louis streets, 512–672–6350) is one of the museums built to commemorate the Texas centennial in 1936. The limestone structure

OPPOSITE: *The Gonzales County Courthouse, built in 1894-1895, replaced a pre-Civil War structure that was destroyed by fire in 1893.*

is small but grand in scale; a monument overlooking a reflecting pool is inscribed with the names of the "Old Eighteen" who rallied around the "Come and Take It Cannon" and the "Immortal Thirty-two" who lost their lives at the Alamo. The "Come and Take It Cannon" is displayed here periodically.

The **Eggleston House** (1300 block of Saint Louis Street) was one of the first to be built in Gonzales after the revolution; as the army retreated and citizens fled after the fall of the Alamo, Sam Houston had commanded that all buildings be burned. The log house was built by Austin colonist Horace Eggleston in 1840 of black walnut and put together with beautiful half-dovetail notches.

Southeast of Gonzales, twelve miles from a gravel road off Route I-90, is the privately owned Greek Revival **Braches House** (1848) and the **Sam Houston Oak,** under which Houston established his temporary headquarters after the fall of the Alamo. The 374-member volunteer army he gathered here became a fighting force as it retreated east to the final showdown with Santa Anna at San Jacinto a month later.

CUERO

Cuero means "rawhide" in Spanish, and this sleepy town is named for Cuero Creek, in whose muddy bottom many a cow got stuck and consequently was skinned for profit. The town was a starting point for a leg of the Chisholm Trail; from 1866 to 1895 approximately 10 million cattle traveled up the trails from Texas. The **DeWitt County Historical Museum** (312 East Broadway, 512–275–6322) has period furnishings and ranching artifacts housed in a two-story frame house. It is housed in the **Bates–Sheppard House,** built in 1886, partially with lumber from the Sheppard family home in Indianola, which had been wrecked earlier that year by a hurricane that caused the abandonment of the entire town. The **Reiffert–Mugge Inn** (304 West Prairie) actually survived the Indianola storm, and not pressing his luck, its owner had it dismantled and moved sixty miles northwest to Cuero. It is now a bed-and-breakfast inn. The 1894–1896 **DeWitt County Courthouse** (307 North Gonzales) is Richardsonian Romanesque in style, designed by A. O. Watson.

A few miles southwest of Cuero, the **Yorktown Historical Museum** (Eckhardt and Main streets, Yorktown, 512–564–2661) displays furniture, tools, and local memorabilia. The museum is housed in the stuccoed limestone **Eckhardt & Sons Store,** built in 1876.

PANNA MARIA

This town, the first permanent Polish settlement in the United States, was founded in 1854 by 800 settlers from Upper Silesia. Seeking a refuge from Prussian oppression and from a poor economy, the Poles came to this fertile land near the San Antonio River at the invitation of Father Leopold Moczygemba, a Franciscan missionary who had settled here two years earlier. The immigrants, including Father Leopold's brothers, endured a long voyage to Galveston (which was in the grip of a yellow fever epidemic when they arrived) and an arduous overland journey. Devout Catholics, they named their settlement after the Virgin Mary. **Immaculate Conception Church,** a Gothic Revival structure of stuccoed limestone with a hand-painted interior, was put up in 1877 to replace a church that had been struck by lightning. Also of interest are the **John Gawlik House** of 1858, whose owner was one of the builders of the church; the steep roof, practical in Poland to shed snow, has not often had that use in Texas. Other stone cottages of the settlement period include the house of Father Leopold's brother, just across F.M. 81 from the church. There is also a community cemetery. Some of the older townspeople still speak a Silesian dialect that modern Polish speakers have difficulty understanding.

Another Polish settlement, called **Cestohowa,** was established just north of Panna Maria in 1873. Its gray stone **Nativity of the Blessed Virgin Mary Church** was built in 1877.

GOLIAD

Goliad is one of the oldest municipalities in Texas. It was an Aranama Indian village when early Spanish explorers passed through and named it Santa Dorotea. It first saw European settlement in 1749 when the Mission Espíritu Santo and the attendant Presidio La Bahia were relocated for the second time. The town was renamed Goliad in 1829, its name chosen as an anagram of Hidalgo (without the *H*) after the leader of the first revolt against Spanish rule in 1810. Goliad has a long military history; the Gutiérrez-Magee Expedition occupied the town briefly during its American filibustering and Mexican revolutionary activities in 1812. Goliad played a prominent role in the Texas Revolution, and it was occupied by the Mexicans during the Mexican invasions of 1842.

The Second Empire **Goliad County Courthouse** (10 Courthouse Square) was built in 1894 by the San Antonio architect Alfred Giles, with additions in 1964. It dominates a group of turn-of-the-century commercial, public, and residential buildings that covers parts of nine blocks. On the courthouse lawn is a Goliad landmark, the oak **Hanging Tree,** under which court was held between 1846 and 1870, where guilty persons were hanged on the spot. During the "Cart War" in 1857, about seventy Mexican cart drivers were killed, some of them lynched here by Texans who were trying to break the Mexicans' hold on the freight-hauling route between Indianola and San Antonio. Before the episode was over, a few months after it had begun, Texans had started lynching fellow Texan competitors as well as Mexicans. The Texas Rangers ended the conflict. The **Old Market House Museum** (Franklin and Market streets, 512–645–3563) started out in the early 1870s as a city-owned market with stalls rented to meat and produce vendors. In 1886 it was converted to a firehouse and meeting hall. The museum's holdings include documents and artifacts depicting the lifestyles of farmers and ranchers in the Goliad area from the mid-nineteenth to the early twentieth century. The **Captain Barton Peck House** (1 Hill Avenue, private) is a stuccoed limestone residence completed in 1852 by an Easterner who arrived too late to fight for Texas independence and went home but, remembering the beauty of Goliad, returned in 1842. Peck's Greek Revival house, which took ten years to build, is one of the finest early examples of the style in the state.

Mission Espíritu Santo
(Nuestra Señora del Espíritu Santo de Zuñiga)

Mission Espíritu Santo was founded on the site of La Salle's Fort Saint Louis to Christianize the untamable Karankawa on Matagorda Bay. It was called Mission La Bahia (*bahia* means bay) even after it was moved inland. The mission was moved in 1726 to the Mission Valley area of Victoria and finally to this site in 1749. It did not thrive in its missionary purpose, but it did succeed in becoming the first large-scale ranching operation in Texas—at one time the herds numbered 40,000 and supplied all the Spanish settlements from here to Louisiana. Marauding Comanche, as well as Anglo rustlers, sharply reduced the number of cattle. The mission was secularized in 1831 and rebuilt in 1848 by the Goliad City Council. It was made into a college for Spanish-speaking Texans, Aranama College, rendered defunct in 1861 when its entire student body joined the Confederate Army. Left in ruins, many of its stones were hauled away and are now part of other structures in the area. The mission was meticulously rebuilt in the 1930s.

> LOCATION: Goliad State Historical Park, Route 183. HOURS: 8–12 and 1–5 Daily. FEE: Yes. TELEPHONE: 512–645–3405.

The ruins of Mission Nuestra Señora del Rosario, known as **Mission Rosario** (Route 59, 512–645–3405) lie four miles west of Goliad. This mission was established in 1754 by Franciscans from the College of Zacatecas in Mexico, who apparently thought they could succeed in converting the Karankawa if the tribe was separated from the Aranama at nearby Mission Espíritu Santo. The ruins are now part of Goliad State Historical Park.

Presidio de la Bahia

The only fully reconstructed Spanish Colonial presidio in the western hemisphere, this fort was established in 1721 on the site of Fort Saint Louis and moved to its current location in 1749. The objective of the presidio was to secure Spanish territories in Texas. During the American Revolution, from 1779–1782, Spanish soldiers from the presidio assisted the armies of the Spanish general Bernardo de Galvez, who defeated the British at Baton Rouge, Natchez, Mobile, and Pensacola in alliance with the American colonists.

The fort was the scene of several conflicts during the Mexican struggle for independence from Spain. In 1812 a rebel army of Mexican republicans, Americans, French, and Indians led by Bernardo Gutiérrez de Lara and Augustus Magee captured the fort and held it through the longest siege of a fortress in American history. The rebels pushed the Spaniards back to San Antonio and captured the city in April 1813. The Americans took this opportunity to declare the first Republic of Texas, in the hope that it would be joined to the United States. Gutiérrez, however, insisted that Texas remain part of Mexico, and the republic quickly collapsed.

In 1817 a group of American veterans of the War of 1812 made an unsuccessful bid to capture the presidio. Another impromptu army, this one raised in Mississippi and led by Dr. James Long, invaded Texas in 1819 and declared the second Republic of Texas. This time La Bahia was the scene of the revolution's final act: Long, leading an army of fifty-two men, occupied the fortress in October 1821 but was quickly surrounded by the Spanish and forced to surrender. That same year, Mexico won its independence from Spain, and the Mexican army took control of the fort.

In the early days of the Texas Revolution the presidio was the first military target secured by Mexican troops, in 1835, when General Martín Perfecto de Cós marched 600 soldiers from the coast on the way to San Antonio. On October 9, 1835, a group of Texans (composed mostly of Irish Catholics) captured the fort, the first offensive action of the revolution. At the presidio, on December 20, 1835, ninety-two colonists signed the first Declaration of Texas Independence from Mexico. (The official declaration was enacted on March 2 at Washington-on-the-Brazos.)

One of the most controversial episodes of the revolution took place at Presidio de la Bahia in 1836. As in almost every important event of the revolution, accounts differ as to what happened and why. Colonel James Walker Fannin, Jr., was encamped at La Bahia with a force of 400 to 500 American volunteers, including a handful of Texans. He had vague instructions from the provisional Texas government to raid the Mexican town of Matamoros. William B. Travis, commanding the Alamo, requested aid from Fannin, who refused. Another desperate request came from Travis as the siege was reaching its conclusion. Fannin marched, but damage to his ammunition wagon caused him and his officers to decide to turn back. Historians still debate whether Fannin thereby saved his men from certain death at the Alamo, or if Fannin's detachment could have prolonged the siege until Texas rallied to Travis's aid.

OPPOSITE: *Our Lady of Loreto, the military chapel at Presidio de la Bahia, was the site of the signing of a declaration of Texas independence from Mexico on December 20, 1835.*

On March 14 Fannin received an order from Sam Houston to retreat to Victoria—1,600 well-trained troops under General Don José Urrea were on their way to the presidio. Fannin sent a third of his men to Refugio to help Anglo settlers evacuate; most of this detachment was killed when Urrea's army suddenly appeared. Fannin's main force fled La Bahia, halted at Coleto Creek to rest the transport animals for the artillery, and was surrounded by a portion of Urrea's army. (The **Fannin Battleground** is nine miles east of Goliad on Route 59.) After fighting for a day and a half, Fannin was forced to surrender because Urrea's artillery had arrived. Fannin's men were marched back to the presidio, where Urrea informed Fannin that the Mexicans would not execute men who asked for clemency, in spite of the Mexican government's decree that foreigners who aided the rebellion were legally to be regarded as pirates and executed. Fannin's men were nearly all from the United States, and thus liable to the penalty specified by the decree. Santa Anna refused Urrea's request to spare the prisoners. On Palm Sunday, March 27, 1836, the Mexicans shot all but twenty-seven. The 390 who were massacred were left unburied for three months; they were given a full military burial by Texas general Thomas Rusk. (The **Fannin Grave Site** is marked by a monument built in 1939.) This infamous episode, known as the Goliad Massacre, was the event that solidified U. S. support for the Texans' cause. Santa Anna was to hear the shout "Remember Goliad!" as well as "Remember the Alamo!" at the Battle of San Jacinto.

The reconstructed compound appears as it did in 1836 and includes the officers' quarters, the barracks, the guardhouse, and bastions at each corner of the quadrangle. The beautiful **Our Lady of Loreto Chapel,** where masses are still held regularly, has a fresco mural painted in 1946 by Antonio García. Re-enactments and living history events are held throughout the year.

LOCATION: Route 183, 2 miles south of Goliad. HOURS: 9–5 Daily. FEE: Yes. TELEPHONE: 512–645–3752.

Around Presidio La Bahia there grew up a small colonial town, the civil, religious, and military center of the region. Archaeologists are investigating the area, but nothing remains to be seen of the old town. One structure from this period has been re-created: The

Ignacio Zaragoza Birthplace (Route 183 South, adjacent to La Bahia, 512–645–2282) is a reconstruction, erected in the early 1960s, of the house where General Zaragoza was born in 1829. The original house was built about 1755. On May 5, 1862 at the Battle of Puebla, Zaragoza defeated an elite French army twice the size of his own. The anniversary of the battle is a holiday (Cinqo de Mayo) in Mexico and in Goliad. Exhibits here examine the general's career and the shared history of Goliad and Mexico.

VICTORIA

Victoria was laid out in 1824 by Don Martín de León, a prominent Mexican citizen who had been given a large land grant on the lower Guadalupe River. The town was called Nuestra Señora de Guadalupe de Jesus Victoria for Guadalupe Victoria, the first president of Mexico; the name was shortened to Victoria after Texas gained its independence. De León brought ten of his friends and their families, forty-two settlers in all, to the new town and established them on Main Street, which was then called Calle de los Diez Amigos (Street of the Ten Friends). A cattle- and horse-ranching capital, Victoria was mostly Mexican by the time of the Texas Revolution but had a few Anglo settlers—one of whom, John or "Juan" Linn, served as mayor and later as a diplomatic communicator between clashing Mexican and Texan townspeople. After independence Mexican families who had been loyal to the Texan cause were nonetheless ill-treated amid an atmosphere of general hatred toward Mexico.

The 1840s saw a great influx of European immigrants to Victoria—many of them Germans on their way from the nearby port of Indianola to points farther west who decided to stay in the charming town. Many victims of the great cholera epidemic of 1846 were buried in a common burying ground, now **Memorial Square** (400 block of East Commercial street), also the site of the **Dutch Wind Grist Mill,** brought by settlers from Germany in 1860. After the Civil War, the cattle business surged again, and Victoria, the so-called cradle of the Texas cattle industry, was in the heart of the great roundups; well into the twentieth century, wealthy ranchers refused to lease lands to petroleum companies because they did not want their pastures fouled by oil.

The prosperity of the cattle business produced many fine houses in Victoria. Historical sites include **De Leon Plaza** (100 block of
North Main Street), with an 1885 bandstand; **Saint Mary's Catholic
Church** (101 West Church), a Gothic Revival building completed in
1904 to designs by Galveston's noted architect Nicholas J. Clayton;
the **Old Victoria County Courthouse** of 1892, another limestone castle by James Riely Gordon; and the **O'Connor-Proctor Building** (202
North Main Street), built in 1895 for local ranchers, beautifully
restored and maintained by the Victoria Junior League. The
McNamara House Museum (502 North Liberty, 512–575–8227) was
built in 1876 by a prominent cotton and hides merchant and civic
leader; the Southern Coastal vernacular house, with mid-Victorian
ornamentation, has been partially restored and contains period
rooms and changing exhibits on local history.

WESTERN GULF COAST

INDIANOLA

Texas Route 316 ends at Indianola, once a thriving port, now a
quiet, empty beach marked by a historical marker and a granite
statue of the explorer La Salle. It is thought by some that La Salle
landed at Indianola, a natural port, in 1685. In 1843 Prince Carl of
Solms-Braunfels brought the first group of German immigrants to
Texas via Indianola, and the same route was used by waves of
European immigrants. The town was chosen as a landing place in
1849 by Charles Morgan for his shipping concern, the Morgan
Lines. During the Civil War, Indianola was blockaded by the
Federal navy. The *Handbook of Texas* says, "Of the many ghost towns
of Texas, none lived longer, none throve better, none died as tragic a death as Indianola." The end was signaled in 1875, when a
hurricane destroyed three quarters of the town. Indianola was
rebuilt; but when another hurricane struck in 1886, the residents
abandoned the town, finally convinced that storms would come no
matter how well and how often they rebuilt. Some stones of the
courthouse foundation still can be seen under the waves, along
with the outlines of a few crumbling concrete cisterns.

ARANSAS NATIONAL WILDLIFE REFUGE

These 55,000 acres of grassland, live oak, blackjack, sweet bay, brush, and marshland, on a peninsula bounded by San Antonio and Saint Charles bays and Matagorda Island, are the last, best hope for the survival of the rare whooping crane. Whooping cranes, named for their bugle call, are the tallest birds in North America, standing five feet. Each October they fly 2,500 miles from their breeding grounds in Canada to the Aransas refuge and stay until early April. Earlier this century their numbers had dwindled drastically because of hunting and the practice of draining and filling almost all their wetland habitat. When the refuge was established by the executive order of President Franklin D. Roosevelt in 1937, only eighteen of the cranes were known to exist. In the years since, conservation efforts have brought up their numbers to nearly 130. Also thriving in the refuge are roseate spoonbills, ibis, egrets, herons, Canada geese, and most of the diving ducks, as well as white-tailed deer, American alligators, armadillos, and javelinas (the last two are indigenous to Texas). Facilities include a Wildlife Interpretive Center, which has displays and exhibits about the refuge; an observation tower; hiking and walking trails; and an automobile tour loop.

LOCATION: On F.M. 2040, off Route 35, 7 miles south of Austwell. HOURS: *Refuge:* Dawn–Dusk Daily. *Wildlife Interpretive Center:* 7:30–5 Daily. FEE: Yes. TELEPHONE: 512-286-3559.

On the edge of **Goose Island State Park** (Park Road 13, off Route 35, 512-729-2858) grows the largest and most venerable live oak in Texas, estimated to be 2,000 years old. **Big Tree,** as it is called, is thirty-five feet wide and forty-four feet tall and has a canopy spread of eighty-nine feet.

FULTON MANSION
STATE HISTORIC STRUCTURE

On a coastline otherwise populated by beach houses and tourist enterprises looms this house in the Second Empire style, built in 1876 by George W. Fulton, partner in the Coleman, Mathis, and Fulton Pasture Company. Fulton was a Philadelphian who arrived

in Texas to fight for independence in 1837, after independence had already been won. He worked in the General Land Office of the republic, went into business locating land claims, and married Harriet Smith. The Fultons moved to Baltimore so their children could receive a good education, and Fulton became a machinist and structural engineer, building railroads and bridges. He returned to Texas with his family after the Civil War to oversee his wife's inheritance and eventually entered the cattle-raising and shipping business when prospects were high.

Fulton's goal was a house that matched the grandeur of his friends' houses in Philadelphia and Baltimore. Sparing no expense, he had all the materials shipped from New Orleans or the East Coast. Oakhurst, as the Fultons called their new mansion, was a marvel of construction. The house was built to withstand hurricane-force winds—or to topple over in one piece that could be righted again. The unusually thick timber walls are made of one-by-five-inch planks stacked on top of each other and held together with railroad spikes. Fulton's engineering interests inspired him to fit the house with conveniences unheard of in Texas at the time. A cast-iron furnace in the basement heated the rooms through a series of ducts and flues connected to false decorative fireplaces in the major rooms. A tank in the tower fed water to bathrooms, allowing for flush toilets. Hot air was piped into the laundry room for drying clothes, and water ran through troughs in the larder to keep food cool. Although only a few of the original furnishings remain, the restoration team found all the family's original invoices for the house and were able to fill it with Renaissance Revival pieces similar to the Fultons' own.

LOCATION: Henderson Street and Fulton Beach Road, Fulton. HOURS: 9–11:30 and 1–3:30 Wednesday–Sunday. FEE: Yes. TELEPHONE: 512–729–0386.

PORT ARANSAS

In this once quaint fishing resort on Mustang Island, a few miles northeast of Corpus Christi, the **Tarpon Inn** was built in 1886 from an abandoned Civil War barracks. It was rebuilt after storm damage

OPPOSITE: *The formal parlor of the Fulton Mansion, furnished according to detailed inventories listing the house's original contents. The fireplace is a disguised hot air duct, a rarity in South Texas.*

in 1904, then again in 1919 and in 1924, retaining the character of
the original each time. On the inn's walls are some 7,500 tarpon
scales, signed and dated by the fishermen. The most famous scale is
from a tarpon caught by Franklin D. Roosevelt.

From Port Aransas can be seen the **Aransas Pass Light Station**
on Harbor Island. The third-oldest lighthouse on the Texas coast, it
is a privately restored, tapered octagonal brick tower built by the
U.S. government in 1854 and commissioned in 1856. Local tradition
holds that during the Civil War residents of the island buried the
lens in the marshes to keep it from the Union; they also tried to
blow up the tower but caused only minimal damage. A new
lens—still in use—was installed after the Civil War.

CORPUS CHRISTI

This port and resort town is set on fine white Gulf beaches just
southeast of the mouth of the Nueces River. Alonso Alvarez de
Piñeda named Corpus Christi Bay in 1519 and claimed the barrier
Mustang Island and "all land beyond" for Spain. Attempts by the

*A birds-eye view of Zachary Taylor's troops encamped near Corpus Christi in
October 1845, awaiting orders. In the spring of 1846, they invaded Mexico.*

Spanish to establish missions were thwarted by the hostility of the Karankawa and other bands. The pirates commanded by Jean Lafitte lurked in the Corpus Christi area between 1817 and 1821. The first permanent settlement here was begun in 1839 by Henry Lawrence Kinney, an adventurer from Pennsylvania who moved to Texas after a disappointing romance (it is said) and founded Kinney's Trading Post. At the time Corpus Christi was on the edge of territory between the Nueces River and the Rio Grande still claimed by Mexico and ruled by Mexican law, even though Texas had gained its independence three years earlier. The Mexican War settled this ambiguity, and it was during the war, when General Zachary Taylor's troops built a tent city on the beach at Kinney's Trading Post (the first U.S. military camp on Texas soil) and made it a supply base, that Corpus Christi began to take on the character of a town.

After the war ended in 1848, Kinney promoted the sun-drenched little town as "the Italy of America." Among the military men smitten enough to return and settle on the Gulf Coast was Captain Forbes Britton of Virginia, who retired from the army in 1850, moved to Corpus Christi with his wife, and entered the ranching business and eventually the state government. The Greek Revival **Britton-Evans (Centennial) House** (411 North Upper Broadway, 512-992-6003), on property Britton bought from Kinney, is the oldest existing structure in the city. Built in 1848–1850, the brick house has foundations of shellcrete, a cement made of oyster shells that is peculiar to the coast. During the Civil War, the house was used as a hospital, first by the Confederacy, then the Union.

Henry L. Kinney moved away from Corpus Christi in 1854 in an unsuccessful attempt to establish a colony in Nicaragua. Where and how he died is disputed. The city of Corpus Christi continued to grow as a ranching and farming center in the nineteenth century, then as a port and resort in the twentieth. A number of turn-of-the-century houses have been restored and moved to **Heritage Park** in "Old Irishtown" near downtown, including the **Charlotte Scott Sidbury House** (1609 North Chaparral Street, 512-883-9352), a two-story Queen Anne–Eastlake frame house built as a rental property by a prominent rancher and civic leader. At 1617 North Chaparral Street is the **S. Julius Lichtenstein House** of 1905, in a style transitional between Queen Anne and Colonial Revival. It now houses the Creative Arts Center. Information about the houses in

Corpus Christi's Simon Gugenheim House, built in 1905 by a man who arrived in the town with $40 and prospered in the petroleum industry. OPPOSITE: *The Charlotte Scott Sidbury House features decorative woodwork in the Eastlake style.*

the park are available at the 1908 **Galvan House** (1581 North Chaparral Street, 512–883–0639).

The **Corpus Christi Museum** (1900 North Chaparral Street, 512–883–2862) emphasizes natural history, anthropology, archaeology, and marine science. Holdings include dioramas, fossils, ancient artifacts, and a study collection on the natural history of south Texas. Permanent exhibits include a survey of naval aviation history and artifacts recovered from three Spanish ships wrecked off nearby Padre Island in 1554. The **Corpus Christi Seawall** (Shoreline Boulevard), a reinforced-concrete stair leading to the water, was built after a 1919 hurricane to designs by Gutzon Borglum, the sculptor of Mount Rushmore. **Padre Island National Seashore** (south via South Padre Island Drive and John F. Kennedy Causeway, 512–949–8173) preserves sixty-seven-and-a-half miles of the barrier island.

KINGSVILLE

The site of the headquarters for the King Ranch, one of the largest in the world, the town of Kingsville was established on land provided by Henrietta King, Captain Richard King's widow, in 1904. Henrietta King also established companies to sell land and provide building

materials to settlers; built a school for the city; and donated land for
the establishment of churches and parsonages of several denomina-
tions, as well as for Texas A & I University (formerly South Texas
State Teachers College).

The King Ranch

Bigger than the state of Rhode Island, the King Ranch is today the
largest ranch in the continental United States—826,000 acres
spreading over four counties. (The ranch holdings once included
38,400 acres in Cuba.) The King Ranch was originally named Santa
Gertrudis for the 75,000-acre former Spanish land grant Captain
Richard King purchased in 1853. He had been a steamboat operator
on the Rio Grande during the Mexican War and for some years
afterward. His first herd of cattle was made up of Texas Longhorns,
bought largely from a northern Mexican village whose citizens
accepted the invitation to move with their cattle to work at King's
new ranch. Besides introducing to Texas such strains as Hereford,
Shorthorn, and Brahman, the King Ranch in 1915 crossed

*The main house at King Ranch, located on its Santa Gertrudis Division, with quarter horse
and cattle pastures in the distance. This section of the ranch is named after the original Spanish
land grant settled by Captain Richard King in the 1850s.*

Shorthorns and Brahmans to develop the now-famous Santa
Gertrudis breed. In the 1930s the King Ranch was more than $3 mil-
lion in debt and in danger of being broken up. It was saved by
Humble Oil, which paid the debt in exchange for leases that eventually brought in 650 wells, enriching both Humble and the King
Ranch. In addition to oil and cattle, the King Ranch's operations
include quarter-horse raising. A self-guided tour travels a twelve-mile
loop through the ranch, which is still family-owned.

> LOCATION: Off Route 141, just west of Kingsville. HOURS: *Loop Road:*
> 9–5 Daily. FEE: None. TELEPHONE: 512–592–8516.

The **Henrietta Memorial Museum** (405 North 6th Street,
512–595–1881), occupying an old icehouse by the railroad tracks,
houses King family memorabilia including a mounted Santa
Gertrudis bull's head, saddles from the different areas of the ranch,
and King son-in-law Robert Kleberg's specially manufactured
General Motors hunting car with running boards and a seat that can
be attached to the top of the fender. In the **John E. Conner Museum**
(821 West Santa Gertrudis Avenue, 512–595–2819), on the campus
of Texas A & I University, 900 branding irons are on exhibit, as well
as farm and ranch equipment, Indian and Mexican artifacts, and displays of natural history and the history of south Texas, much of
which is also the story of the King family.

LOWER RIO GRANDE VALLEY

One of only three semitropical regions of the United States, the
Lower Rio Grande Valley, or the Valley, as it is called, is not so much
a valley as a fertile delta and an approximately 100-mile strip of the
upriver plain. Starting in the late nineteenth century, its natural
cover of palm trees and dense, thorny brush was cleared and the
land covered instead with neat rows of citrus trees and crops of
every variety. The Valley today has a growing season of 340 days a
year—at least one crop is harvested each month. The first large
immigration of Anglos to the area occured after irrigation was introduced in 1898, but the region retains a strongly Hispanic character.
Permanent Spanish settlements were established in this part of the
province of Nuevo Santander by Don José de Escandón in the 1750s
on the south side of the river at Reynosa, Mier, Camargo, and
Revilla. The settlers followed their cows into Texas to ranch, a north-

ward expansion that had an enormous impact on the American West. The Mexican cattle kingdom and its customs—the *charro*, or cowboy, culture—were extended to the Rio Grande and far beyond.

The **Port Isabel Lighthouse** ((Route 100, Port Isabel, 512–943–1172) was begun in 1851 and completed in 1853. For a while during the Civil War Confederate forces held the tower, but they gave it up when Union troops strengthened their blockade in 1863. The lighthouse guided commercial vessels to this busy port for twenty years after the war. The tower now shines with a mercury-vapor light and aids recreational navigation.

BROWNSVILLE

Today the Valley's largest city, Brownsville grew up around **Fort Brown** (International Boulevard at the river), an earthen fortification established by General Zachary Taylor in 1846 (a year after Texas became a state), to confirm the Rio Grande as the boundary between Mexico and the United States. The fort was originally called Fort Taylor until the commander, Jacob Brown, was killed by cannon fire from Matamoros across the river and the soldiers renamed the fort in his honor. Fort Brown was briefly taken over in 1859 by Juan Cortina, who is described by some as a bandit, by others as the rescuer of Mexican citizens he believed to be mistreated by Americans. Confederates occupied the fort during the Civil War; it was retaken by the Union, then burned and evacuated by the Confederates. The oldest building on the grounds, the **post hospital** (now the Texas Southmost College administration building), dates from the reconstruction of the fort in the 1860s and was the place where Dr. William Gorgas did some of the pioneer work in treating yellow fever that resulted in his being knighted by King George V of England in 1920. Decommissioned in 1945, its grounds are now the campus of Texas Southmost College.

The **Brownsville Art League Museum** (512–542–0941), within old Fort Brown, is housed in the William Neale house, built in 1834 and believed to be the oldest frame house in Brownsville. The permanent collection includes paintings by N. C. Wyeth, who once taught at the league. The **Historic Brownsville Museum** (641 East Madison, 512–548–1313) is housed in an attractive Spanish Colonial–style depot, one of several built in the Valley in the 1920s by the Southern Pacific Railroad. The museum offers changing exhibits

The ca. 1894 Field-Pacheco complex in downtown Brownsville, conveniently located one block away from the Rio Grande Railroad Station. Henry M. Field and later Andreas Pacheco, hardware and hide merchants, ran their businesses from the ground floor while living on the second floor.

of photography and historical documents on the city of Brownsville and the Valley.

Charles Stillman, a merchant across the river in Matamoros since 1828, saw that a town could grow around Fort Brown during peacetime and purchased the land near the fort shortly after the Mexican War. The **Stillman House Museum** (1305 East Washington Street, 512-542-3929), the founder's 1850 Greek Revival house (which shows Mexican influences also), contains memorabilia of the Stillman family, period furnishings, and exhibits on Brownsville history. The town's architecture has a French as well as a Mexican flavor, because of the influx of French who settled in Matamoros. A typical example of Creole architecture, **La Nueva Libertad** (1301 East Madison Street at 13th) originally housed Andrés Cueto's store on the first floor, a residence on the second.

The Gothic Revival **Immaculate Conception Cathedral** (1218 East Jefferson) was built between 1856 and 1859 by Father Pierre Yves Keralum, a priest who had studied architecture in France before arriving in Texas to join the Oblate Fathers. (The order was known as "the Cavalry of Christ" because they ministered to rancheros scattered over a 100-square-mile area, necessitating almost continuous travel on horseback.) A later house of architectural interest is the **Augustine Celaya House** (504 East Francis Street, private), a showplace when it was built in 1904 by a prominent lawyer. The unusual brick house has a front facade formed by three two-story polygonal towers joined together. The 1912 Classic Revival **Cameron County Courthouse** (1150 Madison Street), by the San Antonio architect Atlee B. Ayres, has a stunning plaster-and-art-glass rotunda.

There are three important battlefields in the Brownsville area. **Palo Alto Battlefield** (near the junction of F.M. 1847 and F.M. 511) was the site of the opening battle of the Mexican War on May 8, 1846. The engagement continued the next day at **Resaca de la Palma Battlefield** (Parades Line Road), where the Americans under General Zachary Taylor forced the Mexicans under General Mariano Arista to withdraw. The rest of the war was fought only on Mexican soil. **Palmito Hill Battlefield** (Route 4, about twelve miles east of Brownsville) is the site of the last land engagement of the Civil War, the Battle of Palmito Ranch (May 12–13, 1865), in which Confederates defeated Federal soldiers marching to take possession of Brownsville.

The **National Audubon Society Sabal Palm Grove Wildlife Sanctuary** (ten miles southeast of Brownsville off F.M. 1419, 512–541–8034), on land that was a part of the old Rabb Plantation, preserves the last portion of the virgin native-palm forest that inspired Alonso Alvarez de Piñeda in 1519 to name the Rio Grande "Rio de las Palmas." The huge **Old Rabb Plantation Headquarters** can be seen on the way to the sanctuary.

The 45,187-acre **Laguna Atascosa National Wildlife Refuge** (F.M. 106, twenty-seven miles east of Harlingen, 512–748–3607), established in 1946, is the largest protected tract of wild land remaining in the Lower Rio Grande Valley. It includes several life zones, among them aspects of the desert Southwest, the temperate North, and the tropical South. A crucial point on the central and Mississippi flyways, the refuge sees several species of endangered birds and animals, including peregrine falcons and bald eagles. Two threatened species of wildcats, the jaguarundi and the ocelot, depend solely on Laguna Atascosa and the nearby Santa Ana Refuge for their survival in the Valley.

HARLINGEN

Founded in 1904 by Lon C. Hill, a major Valley real estate developer, this agricultural and food-processing center was named after Harlingen, Holland, because the area's irrigation system reminded Hill of Dutch canals. For part of its early life, Harlingen was referred to as Six-Shooter Junction by railroad conductors, who more than once pulled into the station to see it populated by Texas Rangers and immigration officers. The **Rio Grande Valley Museum** (Industrial Air Park, Boxwood Street, 512–423–3979) is located in the old jail of the former army air force base. Its displays tell the story of the Valley from the days of the Karankawa and the Coahuiltecan through the early part of this century; also on exhibit is a stone tablet incised with the name Alonso Alvarez de Piñeda and dated 1519. The museum complex includes the **Lon C. Hill Home,** the first house built in Harlingen (relocated from its original site), which is filled with turn-of-the-century furniture and Hill family possessions, and the **Paso Real Stagecoach Inn,** an 1850s way station on the stage line from Brownsville to San Antonio.

The **Confederate Air Force Museum** (1 Heritage Way, adjacent to Valley International Airport, 512–425–1057) preserves a collection of World War II combat aircraft in flying condition. An air show featuring the 150-plane fleet in re-creations of major battles of World War II is held annually.

The **Chapel of Our Lady of the Visitation** (Route 281, one-half mile east of Santa Maria) was built in 1880–1882 to the designs by Father Yves Keralum. The steeple was lost in a hurricane in 1933. The 2,000-acre **Santa Ana National Wildlife Refuge** (Route 281, south of Alamo, 512–787–3079), the largest remaining stretch of virgin chaparral in the Valley, is a tangled jungle of thorny brush and ebony trees teeming with life. The nearly tame hordes of chachalacas are the biggest attraction, but over 325 other species of birds have been spotted here—more than at any other refuge in the country—many of them considered peripheral, threatened, or endangered. More than fifty other species that are endangered or threatened live here as well. Near one of the oldest ebony trees in the refuge is a nineteenth-century cemetery where the remains of the Leal family are buried; they were the owners of the Spanish land grant on which Santa Ana lies.

LAREDO

Laredo was one of the few major Spanish settlements in Texas to be established without a mission or presidio. The town was founded at a ford in the river in 1755 by Tomás Sánchez de la Barrera y Gallardo and three ranching families, with the approval of Don José de Escandón. Almost immediately Villa San Agustín de Laredo, as it was named by Spanish authorities some time later, became an important point of exchange between the interior provinces of Mexico and Texas, although attacks by the Comanche and Lipan Apache were a problem for settlers until well after the Mexican War. Santa Anna marched his troops through Laredo on his way to the Alamo and was honored with a ball; Mexican forces retreated through Laredo with less fanfare following the Battle of San Jacinto. In 1839–1840 Laredo was the capital of the Republic of the Rio Grande when separatists in northern Mexico seceded in protest against Santa Anna's government. The republic lasted for 283 days, until Santa Anna's Mexican troops overran the town. Just outside Laredo they captured and killed the republic's military leader, Antonio Zapata, cut off his head, and displayed it on a pole, which discouraged further dissent or secession. Mexican jurisdiction over the city was not seriously challenged until the Mexican War. During the Civil War, Confederate troops held Laredo and it became the center of cotton shipping to Mexico, since Brownsville and Corpus Christi had been taken by the Union. Expanded railways in Texas brought many settlers from the north in the 1880s and 1890s, and the Mexican Revolution of 1910 brought immigrants from the south.

Nuevo Santander Museum Complex

Three restored buildings of **Fort McIntosh,** established on the banks of the river by the U.S. Army in 1849 as Camp Crawford, now house museums devoted to local history, pioneers, military history, and science and technology. The **Chapel Museum** is a repository for historical archives, traveling exhibits, and a photographic collection about Laredo; the **Guardhouse Museum** has a permanent collection of World War I memorabilia as a well as photographic exhibits about Camp Crawford and Fort McIntosh. The **Science and Technology**

OPPOSITE: *Laredo's San Agustín Church, built between 1872 and 1877 to replace two earlier churches, the first of which had been erected in 1767.*

An early hand-cranked washing machine, made in San Antonio, is on display at the Museum of the Republic of the Rio Grande.

Museum encompasses a ranch house, carriages, and a kitchen, all showing the technological changes that have occurred in Laredo from about 1850. The remains of the original star-shaped Fort McIntosh can still be seen.

> LOCATION: Laredo Junior College Campus, Washington Street at the river. HOURS: 9–4 Monday–Thursday, 9–12 Friday, 1–4 Sunday. FEE: None. TELEPHONE: 512–722–0521, ext. 321.

The **San Agustín Plaza** was the heart of the old Sánchez settlement. It was named for Laredo's patron saint, San Agustín, and laid out as a city in 1767 around the first **San Agustín Church** (214 San Bernardo Avenue), which was erected in 1764. The present Gothic Revival church was built between 1872 and 1877 by Father Pierre Yves Keralum. Across the plaza is the **Museum of the Republic of the Rio Grande** (1005 Zaragoza Street, 512–727–3480), a plaster-covered stone-and-adobe house built in 1834 that served as the capitol of the Republic of the Rio Grande in 1840. The museum's displays include three rooms furnished in the period of the republic as well as Indian artifacts and memorabilia from families of old Laredo. The eclectic three-story brick **Webb County Courthouse** (1000 Houston Street) was built by San Antonio architect Alfred Giles in 1909.

SOUTHEASTERN TEXAS

HOUSTON

In 1836, on the heels of the decisive Texan victory at the Battle of San Jacinto, the brothers Augustus C. and John K. Allen, two shrewd land speculators from New York, began looking for a town site that might win the competition for the permanent capital of the Republic of Texas. Unable to acquire the village of Harrisburg (now on the Houston Ship Channel, eight miles from downtown), Augustus Allen hopped into a pirogue and started paddling up the Buffalo Bayou. Described by a contemporary observer as "an enchanting little stream . . . overhung with lofty and graceful magnolias," the bayou, though relatively deep, was also narrow and full of roots and stumps and sandbars. Nonetheless, Allen sounded the depth of the stream all the way and came to a stop at Buffalo Bayou's junction with White Oak Bayou. This, he proclaimed, with a speculator's flair for exaggeration, was "the head of navigation"—the bayou was not deep and wide enough for decent navigation until it met the San Jacinto River at Harrisburg. But, legend has it, Augustus Allen climbed up the steep bank at "Houston," propped a piece of paper on his hat, and sketched himself a city. Shortly thereafter, and with much legal maneuvering, the Allen brothers bought their city from descendants of the original grantee—6,642 acres south of Buffalo Bayou, for $9,428.

John Allen was a member of the Texas congress, then meeting in the temporary capital at Columbia, and he displayed a map of a sixty-two-block grid, named after Sam Houston, hero of San Jacinto and first president of the republic. To seal the bargain the Allens promised to build a capitol, which was clearly drawn on the map. The Allen brothers' heavy advertising in national newspapers implied the existence of a real urban locale, but when prospective investors traveled on the *Laura* in January 1837 to the town, the steamboat captain went three miles too far upstream before discovering he had missed Allen's Landing. When the government arrived

in May 1837, their temporary capitol building was finished and "painted peach blossom," according to an observer, although chairs for the members of congress were not ordered until the session was already under way. The Allens priced the first lots in the new town exceedingly high, but by summer their promotion showed returns: 1,000 people from all over the country had moved to Houston, drawn by the prospect of a brand-new start in a brand-new capital.

In the early years, drunkenness and gunfighting were common, even among the legislators. The forty-inch yearly rainfall made the unpaved streets thoroughfares of pure mud. The sultry heat and its attendant mosquitoes annually threatened outbreaks of yellow fever. All these factors, along with his distaste for Sam Houston, helped Mirabeau B. Lamar, Houston's successor, convince the congress to move the capital to Austin in 1839. But the city of Houston was already established as a commercial center, and as early as 1839 improvement of Buffalo Bayou was begun. In 1841 the shallow-water Port of Houston was created by city ordinance for steamships coming up the bayou from the deep-water port of Galveston to pick up cotton and other crops grown on the fertile prairie. A railroad was planned in 1840, though not built until 1853. Houston later became the railroad hub of the state, "where eleven railroads meet the sea." When the Houston Ship Channel opened in 1915, the city became one of the country's and the world's most important ports.

Oil was struck at Spindletop in 1901, then at Humble in 1903, then seemingly everywhere. Oil millionaires and those who profited from supporting the oil business joined real estate, cotton, and timber magnates such as William Marsh Rice, George Hermann, Jesse Jones, Will C. Hogg, and Hugh Roy Cullen and made indelible and often controversial marks on the city's financial, social, and cultural character. The oil business protected Houston from the worst ravages of the depression—not a single bank in town failed. During World War II defense and chemical industries flourished. The postwar years saw the rise of the natural gas business, a building boom, and between 1950 and 1970 a doubling of the population. NASA came to town in the 1960s, and another building boom started that did not end until the crash in oil prices in the early 1980s.

OPPOSITE: *Sam Houston, hero of the battle of San Jacinto, in a daguerreotype taken ca. 1850, when he was president of the Republic of Texas. He also served as governor and as U.S. Senator.*

Sam Houston Historical Park

On the western edge of downtown, the nineteenth-century buildings at Sam Houston Historical Park—the city's first public park—are an oddity viewed against the overscaled modern skyline, which starts across the street. The Harris County Heritage Society administers the park and gives tours of each of the buildings. The original **Long Row** (the present one is reconstructed) was Houston's first commercial building, constructed in 1837 by the Allen brothers to house a row of stores and shops and lost to fire in 1860. The Creole-style **Kellum-Noble House,** the park's only restoration on its original site, is the oldest surviving brick house in the city, built in 1847 by a Virginian, Nathaniel Kellum, Houston's first contractor. Mrs. Zerviah M. Noble, the second owner, ran a school for girls. After Mrs. Noble's death in 1894, the house served briefly as a park

The parlor of the San Felipe Cottage, furnished as a workingman's house ca. 1870, features a Texas German-style walnut corner cupboard of the period and an Eastlake-style organ made in Boston in 1880.

office and the yard as Houston's first zoo. The Greek Revival **Nichols-Rice-Cherry House,** built in 1850 by Ebenezar B. Nichols of Cooperstown, New York, is furnished with fine early- to mid-nineteenth-century American antiques. The house was owned between 1856 and 1873 by the merchant and financier William Marsh Rice, one of Houston's most famous early citizens and the benefactor of the William Marsh Rice Institute (today's Rice University). Rice was murdered in New York City in 1896 by his valet and a lawyer who had designs on his deceased second wife's estate.

Other buildings moved to the park include the simple **Saint John Evangelical Lutheran Church,** a frame structure built northwest of Houston in 1891 by German immigrant farmers, still furnished with its original pews; **San Felipe Cottage,** a six-room cottage from the 1870s; **The Old Place,** a cedar log cabin built about 1824 on Clear Creek by John R. Williams; the **Pillot House,** of 1868, a Carpenter–Queen Anne cottage with later Eastlake additions and what is said to be the first attached kitchen in Houston; and a copy of the **Houston City Park Bandstand.** The newest addition to the park is the **Staiti House,** an Arts and Crafts residence built in 1905 for the oilfield pioneer Henry Staiti. The **Gallery of Texas History** has permanent exhibits on the history of Texas since Spanish exploration. Among several works in the sculpture area of the park is a winged figure called *Spirit of the Confederacy* (1908) by Louis Amateis.

LOCATION: 1100 Bagby Street at Lamar Street. HOURS: 10–4 Monday–Saturday, 1–5 Sunday. FEE: None. TELEPHONE: 713–655–1912.

In the original city of Houston, Main Street ended at **Allen's Landing** (Main and Commerce streets), now a city park on the bayou marking the spot where Augustus Allen disembarked from his pirogue. Almost overhead, to the east of the park, is the **Main Street Viaduct,** built in 1910 across Buffalo and White Oak bayous. One block away from Allen's Landing is **Market Square** (bounded by Congress, Travis, Preston, and Milam streets), called Congress Square when the Allens designated it as the site of the permanent capitol. Market Square, the heart of the early city, preserves a cluster

OVERLEAF: *The Pillot House parlor is furnished with American furniture in the French taste dating from the 1850s and 1860s. The Aubusson carpet was made in France in 1860.*

of fine old commercial buildings. The oldest is **Kennedy Bakery (La Carafe)** (813 Congress Street), built ca. 1860 by the Irish immigrant John Kennedy, an Indian trader, miller, merchant, planter, and baker who supplied the Confederacy with hardtack during the Civil War. The small two-story Creole-style building with wrought-iron grille decoration remained in the family unitl 1970 and is still virtually unaltered. The High Victorian brick-and-iron **Old Cotton Exchange Building** (202 Travis Street), built in 1884 by a Houston architect, Eugene T. Heiner, is where the Board of Trade and Cotton Exchange regulated the operation of the industry. Heiner also redesigned the **William L. Foley Building** (214–218 Travis Street) in 1889 (the original went up in 1860) for John Kennedy's son-in-law, who founded a dry-goods store that evolved into one of the state's largest department store chains, Foley's. The eclectic brick **Sweeney, Coombs and Fredericks Building** (301 Main Street), with its three-story corner turret and Eastlake detailing, was built in 1889 by George E. Dickey for a Houston jewelry firm; it now houses the Harris County Engineering Department. At San Jacinto and

Houston's Classic Revival U.S. Post Office and Customs House, designed by James Knox Taylor.

Rusk streets is the imposing Classic Revival **U.S. Post Office and Customs House,** built from 1907 to 1911 by James Knox Taylor. It was the first example of the French Classical style in Houston.

In the 1910s and 1920s, commercial monuments to oil prosperity went up in Houston. Built on the site of the house of Augustus Allen the thirty-six-story **Gulf Building** (712 Main Street) was completed in 1929 by the Houston architect Alfred C. Finn. It was built for Jesse H. Jones, the lumber, real estate, banking, and publishing magnate whose Texas Commerce Bank shared the building with the oil company and the Sakowitz department store. Art Deco in style with Gothic-inspired crenelation, the building was the tallest in town until 1963. In its lobby are fresco murals depicting Texas history. Jesse Jones was the most powerful man in Houston for many years and a formidable national presence. He put up $200,000 of his own money to the Democratic National Committee to make Houston the site of the 1928 Democratic National Convention. Franklin D. Roosevelt made Jones chairman of the Reconstruction Finance Corporation, through which he pioneered federal deposit insurance to rescue the nation's depositors. He went on to serve as secretary of commerce and is said to have been called "Jesus H. Jones" by Roosevelt for his autonomous bent. The Gulf Building was the biggest of thirty substantial pre–World War II structures that Jones's construction companies put up in Houston. After a trip to Paris, Jones expressed regret that he had not kept Houston to a height of ten stories.

Other oil-business buildings include the 1921 **Humble Building** (1224 Main Street), designed by Clinton & Russell of New York for the Humble Oil and Refining Company. Humble was a company created by the merger of several Houston oil concerns and was responsible for more than a few Houston fortunes. The thirty-two-story **Neils Esperson Building** (802 Travis Street) was built in 1927 by Mellie Esperson, carrying out the dream of her late husband, oil man Neils Esperson, who had meant to pay homage to the industry that had made him a rich man. It was designed by a Chicago architect, John Eberson, who also designed the adjacent nineteen-story **Mellie Esperson Building.** The **Texas Company Building** (717–720 San Jacinto Street), built as the headquarters for the oil company founded in 1903 by Joseph S. Cullinan (now called Texaco), is a modern Renaissance structure of thirteen stories erected in 1915 by Warren & Wetmore of New York, the architects of Grand Central

Terminal and Houston's own Classic Revival **Union Station** (501 Crawford Street).

Three nineteenth-century churches of note still stand downtown. The first Episcopal congregation in town built **Christ Church Cathedral** (1117 Texas Avenue) in 1892. The Gothic Revival structure has intricately carved woodwork and fine stained-glass windows, including one from Tiffany and Company in New York. Only about ten years after it was completed in 1869 for the city's oldest existing Catholic parish in the city of Houston, **Annunciation Church** (1618 Texas Avenue) was found to have dangerous cracks in the walls, the church towers leaning away from the main building. The Galveston architect Nicholas J. Clayton was brought in to remedy the situation. Clayton remodeled the limestone building in the Romanesque Revival style, adding buttresses, a new roof, and a 175-foot tower and spire between the old towers. The church was then stuccoed and trimmed in brown marble and completed in 1884. The interior includes a frescoed dome over the sanctuary, marble altars, and impressive stained glass. The Gothic Revival **Antioch Missionary Baptist Church** (500 Clay Street) was built in 1879 for one of the oldest black congregations in Houston. Its first pastor, John Henry Yates, is credited with designing sections of the buildings; its builder, Richard Allen, was a member of the congregation, a Reconstruction legislator, and a city official. Until the Gulf Freeway was built between them, Antioch was part of the black neighborhood within what is still called the Fourth Ward.

Glenwood Cemetery (2525 Washington Avenue, 713–864–7886) is the final resting place of many prestigious Texans, including Samuel and Henry Allen, the brothers of Augustus and John Allen; the last president of the Republic of Texas, Dr. Anson Jones, who committed suicide in 1858; Texas governors James Wilson Henderson, William P. Hobby, and Ross Sterling; Benjamin F. Terry, commander of the Civil War's famous Terry's Texas Rangers; George Hermann, eccentric lumber and real estate magnate and philanthropist (Hermann Park and Hermann Hospital are two of his namesakes); and the industrialist and aviator Howard Hughes, whose father, Howard Hughes, Sr., invented the famous rock drill bit that changed the oil industry. Next to Glenwood lies the smaller **Washington Cemetery,** located on land bought in 1887 by local German businessmen. Its most famous occupant is Emma (Edmondson) Seelye, a veteran of the Civil War who, using the name Frank Thompson, served two years as a soldier, scout, brigade postmaster, and orderly on the staff of General O. M. Poe.

Bayou Bend

On fourteen acres a few miles west of downtown, the twenty-eight-room Bayou Bend was built in 1927 as a residence for the philanthropic siblings William C., Michael, and Ima Hogg, whose father, James Stephen Hogg, was the first native-born governor of Texas. Designed by the Houston architect John C. Staub, the house was an amalgam of New Orleans and Spanish influences dubbed "Latin Colonial" by Staub and Miss Ima, as Ima Hogg was known throughout her life. Staub's highly original and graceful interpretations of European and American Colonial mansions on a scale appropriate to Houston set the tone for several Houston residential areas. Miss Ima's love for "old things with a history" came from a childhood spent in the governor's mansion in Austin, where she slept in Sam Houston's mahogany four-poster bed. She began collecting seventeenth- to nineteenth-century American furniture and decorative arts in 1920, when she bought a Queen Anne chair. (She would say many years later, "I cannot imagine why I was so excited over that simple chair.")

Miss Ima carefully supervised the ten-year conversion of the house into a museum, and it was opened as the Bayou Bend Collection of the Museum of Fine Arts in 1966. The collection includes substantial American holdings by such furniture makers as Duncan Phyfe, John Townsend, and John Henry Belter; paintings by John Singleton Copley, Charles Willson Peale, Gilbert Stuart, Edward Hicks, and Thomas Cole; drawings by Benjamin West; and significant Federal silver by Paul Revere and others. The grounds comprise formal and woodland gardens and are at their best when the azaleas and dogwood bloom in the spring.

> LOCATION: 1 Westcott Street, off Memorial Drive. HOURS: *House:* September through July: By appointment. *Gardens:* 10–5 Wednesday–Saturday, 1–5 Sunday. FEE: Yes. TELEPHONE: 713–529–8773.

Bayou Bend is in Houston's largest and grandest residential area, **River Oaks,** laid out in the 1920s under the sponsorship of Will C. Hogg, perhaps Houston's most civic-minded philanthropist. The

area is known today for its mansions on River Oaks Boulevard —modified Tudor, Colonial, and Mediterranean residences set back on deep, shady lawns—built by John Staub, William Ward Watkin, and Birdsall Briscoe. Even Ralph Adams Cram, architect of Princeton and Rice universities, took a rare residential commission here, the 1925 Spanish Colonial Revival **Cleveland Harding Sewall House** (3452 Inwood). River Oaks is across the bayou from **Memorial Park,** named in honor of Houston's veterans of World War I. It is a rare spot of unspoiled—if well-used—bayou ecology.

Museum of Fine Arts

Texas's first museum exclusively devoted to art grew out of the Houston Art League, founded in 1900 to provide works of art to the public schools. The museum is built on a triangular plot, donated by George Hermann, across Main Street from Rice University. The original section was built in 1924 in the Classical spirit of the American City Beautiful movement by William Ward Watkin with Ralph Adams Cram as consulting architect. The museum's collections range from Renaissance paintings to contemporary paintings, sculpture, and photography; Impressionist and post-impressionist paintings; and works by Frederic Remington.

LOCATION: 1001 Bissonet Street at Main Street. HOURS: 10–5 Tuesday–Saturday, 10–9 Thursday, 12:15–6 Sunday. FEE: Yes. TELEPHONE: 713–639–7300.

Rice University

Rice Institute was created by William Marsh Rice in 1896 with an endowment of $200,000. The campus was not built until 1912 because of Rice's murder and litigation over his estate. Rice's estate subsequently increased the endowment to $10 million—seventh in collegiate endowments in the nation at the time. In 1909 the Rice estate trustees appointed Edgar Odell Lovett, then a professor of astronomy at Princeton, as the institute's first president. With the means and the mandate to build a university of excellence, Lovett gave the commission for design of the campus to Boston's Cram,

OPPOSITE: *A statue of Clio, the muse of history, stands in the fourteen acres of formal and woodland gardens surrounding Bayou Bend, the house turned into a museum by Ima Hogg, the noted collector of Americana.*

Goodhue, and Ferguson, who built the "Collegiate Gothic" campuses of Princeton and West Point. Faced with a flat and treeless prairie site, and influenced by the heat and humidity of the climate, the firm decided that the Gothic style in Houston would be "manifestly out of place . . . the only thing to do was to invent something approaching a new style"' something with a "Southern" character. Best effected in the Administration Building (now **Lovett Hall**), the new style for Rice was a colorful yet dignified amalgam, combining the warm-climate architectural traditions of southern France, Italy, Dalmatia, the Peloponnese, Byzantium, Anatolia, Syria, Sicily, Spain, and northern Africa. Lovett Hall's double-height sally port leads to **Academic Court** with its cloistered passages and richly sculptured ornament by the Austrian-born stonecutter Oswald J. Lassig.

LOCATION: 6100 South Main Street. TELEPHONE: 713–527–8101.

Residential enclaves grew up with Rice University as the city's growth spread south from downtown. **Montrose** is today Houston's most fashionable bohemian neighborhood. Montrose Boulevard was laid out in 1911 as the major thoroughfare of the Montrose Addition, but most of its grand old mansions are gone. An exception is the **Link-Lee Mansion** (3812 Montrose Boulevard, 713–522–7911), now part of the **University of Saint Thomas.** Near the Saint Thomas campus is the **Rothko Chapel** (3900 Yupon Street, 713–524–9839), built between 1970 and 1971 by the architects Philip Johnson, Howard Barnstone, and Eugene Aubry. The abstract artist Mark Rothko was commissioned to create a space for meditation and prayer—the chapel is the result of his efforts, which include fourteen of his paintings.

A real estate man in the late 1800s, George H. Hermann became a millionaire after oil was struck at Humble in 1903. In 1914 he donated 285 acres of the present-day 410-acre **Hermann Park** (6000 Fannin Street), south of the Montrose area. Within the park is the **Houston Museum of Natural Science** (1 Hermann Circle Drive, 713–639–4600), one of the largest natural science museums in the Southwest, with a fine gem and mineral collection, a planetarium,

OPPOSITE: *Houston's Rice University was designed by Cram, Goodhue, and Ferguson in a mix of many Mediterranean styles.*

and exhibits on such diverse subjects as health, petroleum science, butterflies, and seashells.

Houston's violent beginnings in the 1830s and 1840s evoked descriptions of it as "the most uncivilised place in Texas" and "the greatest sink of disipation [sic] and vice that modern times have known." The **Houston Police Department Museum** (17000 Aldine-Westfield Road, 713–230–2300), in the north part of town, has artifacts and equipment from the city's early days to the present as well as exhibits on homicide detectives and other special divisions.

SAN JACINTO BATTLEGROUND STATE HISTORICAL PARK

On a small delta in the midst of the Houston Ship Channel lies probably the most hallowed ground in the state of Texas apart from the Alamo: San Jacinto, the site of the battle that won Texas its independence from Mexico. After Santa Anna captured the Alamo, Sam Houston withdrew from Gonzales to the east with 374 men who had gathered at Gonzales, too late to rescue Travis at the Alamo. For a month he retreated, despite political injunctions to stand and fight Santa Anna's vastly superior army. "The enemy are laughing you to scorn," wrote President David G. Burnet. Houston also had to contend with the impatience of his own untrained, inexperienced, but fiercely independent men determined on revenge. But Houston wrote, "We cannot fight the enemy ten to one in their own country." By retreating he was buying time to gather more volunteers and train them to fight, and he was waiting for the right moment. Meanwhile Santa Anna and his four generals marched in pursuit and burned every settlement they came upon. Many Texans fled ahead of Santa Anna, in what came to be called the "Runaway Scrape," and joined Houston.

After burning Harrisburg, where he had arrived only a few minutes too late to capture the interim government, Santa Anna burned New Washington as well. Then he moved toward the San Jacinto River and its juncture with Buffalo Bayou, where Sam Houston was waiting. When Santa Anna arrived, just before noon on April 20, the Mexican commander realized that the Texan force had grown to be almost equal in number to his own. He fell back and started setting up camp to await reinforcements.

Both sides were tense that evening, but Houston did not attack at dawn as Santa Anna expected. General Cós arrived to reinforce Santa Anna at 9:00 AM. At 3:30 on the afternoon of April 21, 1836, while Santa Anna was sleeping in his tent, the Texans attacked. Taken by surprise, the Mexicans had no time to form a battle line. The Texans charged into the confused mass with shouts of "Remember the Alamo!" and "Remember Goliad!" The battle itself lasted just eighteen minutes, but carnage went on into the evening, as the Texans killed without mercy. By sunset 630 Mexicans were dead. About 600 more were put under guard, 200 of them wounded. Two Texans were killed in action, seven were fatally wounded, and twenty-three wounded survived.

Santa Anna, who had disappeared, was found the next day disguised in a private's uniform—his identity confirmed by Mexican prisoners shouting "El presidente! El presidente!" Santa Anna was taken to Houston, who was lying under a tree with a badly wounded ankle, and there the president of Mexico agreed to cease all hostilities and order withdrawal of all remaining troops from Texas.

The **San Jacinto Monument,** built between 1936 and 1939 to honor those who gave their lives for Texas's independence, is 570 feet high, made of reinforced concrete faced with Texas fossilized buff limestone. An elevator takes visitors to an observation tower at the top of the monument, which is surmounted by a 35-foot-high, 220-ton Star of Texas. The 125-square-foot base of the obelisk is covered with eight massive panels depicting the history of the Texas Revolution, and above them a frieze shows significant phases in Anglo-American colonization of Texas. Inside the base, beyond bronze doors with reliefs of the six flags that have flown over Texas, the **San Jacinto Museum of History** traces the history of Texas from Spanish exploration and includes rare maps, manuscripts, and memorabilia from the families of the men who fought at the battle. The **Battleship *Texas*** has been moored at San Jacinto Park since 1948. Commissioned in 1914, it is the only surviving naval vessel to have served in both world wars. In World War II the *Texas* took part in the Normandy invasion and the landings at Iwo Jima and Okinawa.

LOCATION: 3800 Park Road 1836, La Porte. HOURS: *Park:* 8–7 Daily. *Museum:* 9–6 Daily. *Battleship:* 10–5 Daily. FEE: For monument elevator and battleship. TELEPHONE: 713–479–2431.

NASA LYNDON B. JOHNSON SPACE CENTER

The Manned Spacecraft Center, opened in September 1963, is a complex of 100 buildings, each with a separate function, designed and built to develop spacecraft, train astronauts, and control space missions, among other purposes. The Mission Control Center, a three-story building at the complex, has been controlling space flights since the launch of *Gemini 4* on June 3, 1965. Since then, more than fifty manned missions have been controlled from this center. During missions a team of engineers, technicians, and medical attendants use sophisticated communication and data display equipment to monitor prelaunch and ascent phases of flights, electricity distribution systems, cabin pressure control systems, vehicle lighting systems, and the crew's health status. The Manned Spacecraft Center, renamed in honor of President Johnson in 1973, usually has five buildings open for tours, beginning at the visitor center, where moon rocks, space suits, and Mercury and Apollo spacecraft are on display. The Mission Simulation and Training Building exhibits simulators currently used by astronauts to train for Space Shuttle missions. The Space Shuttle Orbiter Training Building holds the Space Shuttle dubbed "Space Truck," used in astronaut training. At the Lunar Sample Building scientists work on material brought back from the moon. Lectures on the history and future plans of NASA are held in the Mission Control Center hourly by appointment.

LOCATION: Route I-45 South to NASA/Alvin exit, 3 miles east on NASA Road. HOURS: 9–4 Daily. FEE: None. TELEPHONE: 713–483–4321.

THE FORT BEND MUSEUM

Approximately thirty miles southwest of downtown Houston, the old town of Richmond is in the area settled in 1822 by members of Stephen F. Austin's "Old Three Hundred" families. This multiresource museum has artifacts from the Austin colony, including furniture, clothing, and manuscripts, as well as exhibits on Mirabeau B. Lamar, second president of the republic, and Carry Nation, the hotelier, mystic, and temperance crusader. Also administered by the museum are the ca. 1850 **McNabb House,** where Carry Nation's daughter lived, in **Decker Historical Park**; the exuberant 1896 **Fort**

Bend County Jail; the 1901 **Southern Pacific Railroad Depot**; and a reconstructed log cabin.

LOCATION: 500 Houston Street, Richmond. HOURS: 10–4 Tuesday–Friday, 1–5 Saturday–Sunday. FEE: None. TELEPHONE: 713-342-6478.

Southeast of Richmond, the **George Ranch Headquarters** (F.M. 762, 713-545-9212) re-creates life on a 20,000-acre Coastal Plain cattle ranch through five generations of the George family. It offers living-history exhibits, tours of the 1890s J. H. P. Davis mansion and the 1930s George Ranch House, and demonstrations of cowboy life, blacksmithing, crafts, and domestic tasks. Located on three acres of the "Old South Plantation"' the **Confederate Museum** (2740 F.M. 359, 713-342-8787) features a large collection of mid-nineteenth-century Texas memorabilia and exhibits on the Civil War, including uniforms and guns.

The **Imperial Sugar Company** (Route 59/I-90A, Sugar Land, 713-491-9181), opened in 1843 to process the sugar cane grown in this area of Stephen F. Austin's original colony, is the oldest continuously operating business on its original site in the state and the first known sugar plantation in Texas. In 1853 the plantation was sold to William Jefferson Kyle and Benjamin Franklin Terry (of the famous Terry's Texas Rangers of the Civil War), who named it "Sugar Land."

VARNER-HOGG PLANTATION STATE HISTORICAL PARK

Before he died in 1906, Governor James Stephen Hogg begged his four children: "Don't sell the plantation!" For about five years Hogg had unsuccessfully drilled on his plantation for oil, but apparently he had just chosen the wrong spots. Eventually farmhands' reports of cattle pastures catching fire led the Hoggs to drill again. In 1918 they hit what was called the West Columbia Field, and the siblings Will, Mike, Tom, and Ima Hogg were transformed from genteel poor into one of the richest families in the state. Ima Hogg gave the plantation house to the state of Texas in 1956 after she had appointed it with fine early American and antebellum Texas furniture, antiques, paintings, objects, and Hogg family memorabilia. The rooms are arranged according to specific historic themes. Collections include Staffordshire "Texian Campaigne" china commemorating the Texas Revolution.

LOCATION: 1702 North 17th Street, F.M. 2852, West Columbia.
HOURS: 9–11:30 and 1–4:30 Wednesday–Saturday, 1–4:30 Sunday.
FEE: Yes. TELEPHONE: 409–345–4656.

NORTH GULF COAST

GALVESTON

The Bay of Gálvez (now Galveston Bay) was christened by Spanish surveyors charting the Texas coast in the 1770s for Bernardo de Galvez, acting governor of Louisiana from 1777 to 1783 and later the successor to his father as viceroy of Mexico. Alvar Núñez Cabeza de Vaca was the first Spaniard to set foot on Galveston Island, after being shipwrecked with some of his followers in 1528. In 1817 Jean Lafitte, the pirate, and his brother Pierre established the first European settlement on the island, which came to be called "Galveztown." Lafitte and his plunderers of the Gulf of Mexico departed in 1820 in a negotiated arrangement with the government of the United States.

By 1836, as Texas was fighting for her independence, about 300 mostly Anglo settlers lived in Galveston. The provisional government under David G. Burnet took refuge here in April 1836, and the city was briefly the capital of the republic. Galveston formally became a city in 1838 when Michael Branamour Menard, a French-Canadian Indian trader and one of the signers of the Texas Declaration of Independence, purchased a large tract of land from the republic and organized the Galveston City Company to sell lots. Almost immediately the town became a thriving port, and for the rest of the century it was the most sophisticated city in Texas as well as the point of entry for most goods shipped to the state's interior and to the western and northern frontiers of the United States. Galveston claims a number of firsts in the history of Texas, including the first chamber of commerce, in 1845; the first convent, in 1847; the first private bank, in 1854; the first national bank, in 1865; the first telegraph, in 1854; the first electric lights, in 1883; and even the first golf course, in 1898.

Cotton was the biggest export in the glory days, and the wealth the crop generated brought in goods from all over the world. The port was the arrival point of European immigrants headed for the interior, many of whom remained in the city. During the Civil War, Galveston was under constant blockade. Shortly after the war's end, the Union army returned to take over Galveston, and on June 19, 1865, U.S. general Gordon Granger read the proclamation freeing the slaves in Texas, a day celebrated in Texas as "Juneteenth."

Postwar Galveston became a city of progress, wealth, and civic splendor. The architect Nicholas J. Clayton, an Irishman who grew up in Ohio and came to the city in 1872, had a pronounced influence on the city's appearance, building over 200 commercial, government, and residential buildings before his death in 1917. Because Galveston was a world-class port, luxurious and exotic building materials were easily procured. In the latter half of the nineteenth century, the city came to be known as the "Queen of the Gulf."

Although Galveston was familiar with hurricanes, having suffered and survived several, none had prepared its citizens for September 8, 1900, when the most destructive storm in the recorded history of Texas crashed over the island, killing over 6,000 people and washing away a huge amount of land. Much rebuilding took place; the ground level was raised an average of five feet, and a seventeen-foot-high, four-mile-long **Seawall** (since extended) was completed in 1910 to protect the city from future devastations. But Houston had long argued that Galveston's vulnerability to the weather (not to mention its increasingly exorbitant docking fees) made it an unsuitable port, and while Galveston attempted to recover, the Port of Houston, with the backing of the federal government, began building the Houston Ship Channel, which dealt a major blow to Galveston. Because the declining economy allowed for little rebuilding or demolition, Galveston's splendid architectural legacy remained largely unaffected by twentieth-century progress.

The first successful bridge to span Galveston Bay was the reinforced-concrete-and-steel **Galveston Causeway,** with a 100-foot Scherzer rolling-lift drawbridge, which can be seen just to the north of the present causeway. Built from 1909 to 1912, the old causeway was reconstructed in 1917 after a devastating hurricane in 1915 and is still in use for railroad traffic. After the bridge, Route I-45 from Houston turns into the main thoroughfare of Broadway, the 5000 and 4000 blocks of which are lined with the **Cotton Concentration Company warehouses,** dating from 1910 to the 1940s. A long line of low concrete buildings overgrown by semitropical vines and towered over by palm trees, the warehouses are a powerful evocation of the last phase of the cotton era.

Samuel May Williams Home

Samuel May Williams was an early citizen of Galveston with an illustrious background as private secretary to Stephen F. Austin, who
induced him to go to Texas and eventually made him a partner in
one of his colonization contracts. Williams became one of the
largest landowners in the territory. During the Texas Revolution, he
bought fighting ships with his own money and thus came to be
called "the Father of the Texas Navy." (The navy was stationed at
Galveston.) In 1837 he was appointed commissioner under
President Sam Houston to contract the building of six new ships for
the new republic. Also in 1837 Williams moved to Galveston, where
he became the city's first banker. The Williams Home was begun in
1838, completed in 1839, and extensively renovated in 1854. It is
one of the oldest in Galveston, in a Creole–Greek Revival style, with
cupola and widow's walk. Though it has such characteristics of
Louisiana and Deep South architecture as wide galleries and Tuscan
or Roman Doric columns, it was in fact partially framed in Maine
and shipped to Galveston.

LOCATION: 3601 Avenue P. HOURS: September through May: 10–4
Monday–Saturday, 12–4 Sunday; June through August: 10–5
Monday–Saturday, 12–5 Sunday. FEE: Yes. TELEPHONE:
409–765–1839.

A few blocks from the Williams Home is **Sydnor's 1846–47 Powhatan
House** (3427 Avenue O, 409–763–0077), a Greek Revival mansion
now used by the Galveston Garden Club. John S. Sydnor, a Virginia
merchant who moved to Texas in the early 1840s, was mayor of
Galveston and the founder and promoter of schools, the First
Baptist Church, and general public improvement, as well as being
the city's major slave dealer. Powhatan House was named after a tribal sachem in Virginia. The house was divided and moved from its
original location and extended on the west side about 1895.

Grace Episcopal Church (1115 36th Street), a late Gothic
Revival white-limestone structure, was built in 1894–1895 by
Nicholas J. Clayton. The most historically important house in
Galveston, the two-story early Greek Revival **Michel B. Menard**

OPPOSITE: *Galveston's Trueheart-Adriance Building, which is richly decorated with
different varieties of bricks, was designed by Nicholas J. Clayton, one of the first professional architects in Texas.*

House (1605 33d Street) is boarded up, its future unknown. Built in 1838–1839, it was the residence of the founder of Galveston.

Ashton Villa

James Moreau Brown's expansive three-story mansion, built in 1859, was among the first in the Italianate style in Texas. Brown moved to Galveston in the early 1840s from New York and quickly became active in its civic and business affairs. A mason by trade, he designed and built the house himself, and its bricks were made on the site. Saved from demolition by the Galveston Historical Foundation in the late 1960s (for a while the house served as El Mina Shrine Temple), Ashton Villa is now a museum furnished with appropriate nineteenth-century antiques and possessions of the Brown family. Ashton Villa served as a hospital during the city's yellow fever epidemics, and it is said that U.S. major general Gordon Granger accepted the surrender of Galveston here in 1865. The museum offers an audio-visual program on the 1900 hurricane. An open excavation viewed through an arched breezeway shows the grade of the city before the storm.

LOCATION: 2328 Broadway. HOURS: Memorial Day through Labor Day: 10–5 Daily; Labor Day through Memorial Day: 10–4 Monday–Friday, 10–5 Saturday–Sunday. FEE: Yes. TELEPHONE: 409–762–3933.

Open Gates (2424 Broadway, private) was the first Renaissance Revival house in Texas, designed by Stanford White and built from 1889 to 1891 for George Sealy, president of the Gulf, Colorado & Santa Fe Railroad. The house was given to the University of Texas Medical Branch when the last Sealy heir died; some of its furnishings are at Ashton Villa.

The Bishop's Palace

Perhaps the finest private house designed by the Galveston architect Nicholas J. Clayton, the sumptuous Bishop's Palace was begun in 1886 and completed in 1893 for Colonel Walter Gresham, a native of Virginia who fought in various regiments in the Civil War and surrendered with Lee at Appomattox. Shortly after the war, Gresham moved to Galveston, where he would become a prominent local attorney, a founder of the Gulf, Colorado & Santa Fe Railroad, and a representative in both the Texas state legislature and the U. S. Congress.

Clayton's High Victorian building is made of native Texas lime-stone, pink and gray granite quarried near Marble Falls, and red sandstone, all of it cut in a special workshop on the building site. Clayton had trained as a stonecutter in Cincinnati before becoming an architect, and he hired a notable group of craftsmen to sculpt the exterior elements, which range in style from French Renaissance to Richardsonian Romanesque to Moorish to Tudor. The architect also had a strong hand in the interiors. Rosewood, satinwood, mahogany and other exotic woods, as well as American oak and maple, were intricately hand-carved into paneling—each downstairs room is sheathed in a different wood. Decorative fabrics, furniture, and *objets d'arts* from Europe fill the house. Two of its fireplaces were purchased at world's fairs—the first-prize winner at Philadelphia in 1876 graces the front parlor, and a Mexican onyx piece from New Orleans, valued at $10,000 in 1886, is in the music room. Mrs. Gresham, an accomplished artist, painted murals throughout the house; on the ceiling of the dining room, she portrayed some of her children as angels.

The palace was bought in 1923 by the Catholic Diocese of Galveston-Houston for Bishop Christopher Byrne, whose thirty-year tenure in the house gave it its current name. The house is still owned by the church and serves as the current bishop's residence when he visits Galveston.

LOCATION: 1402 Broadway. HOURS: June through August: 10–5 Monday–Saturday, 12–5 Sunday; September through May: 12–4 Daily. FEE: Yes. TELEPHONE: 409–762–2475.

Across 14th Street from the Bishop's Palace is the Moorish-style **Sacred Heart Catholic Church,** erected in 1903 to designs by one of the parish priests; the original 1890s structure by Nicholas J. Clayton was destroyed by the great 1900 hurricane, although Clayton is thought to have designed the present dome in 1915 after another major storm. Both the Bishop's Palace and Sacred Heart are at the edge of the **East End Historic District,** which covers about forty blocks south of Broadway near downtown. Virtually all of the raised houses in this area (mostly private), even the most neglected or over-grown, have a graceful, romantic character, including an exuberant evocation of a German castle, the **John Clement Trube House** (1627 Sealy, private), by Alfred Muller, once described as "the strangest house in a city of strange houses"; the 1876 **Burr-Alvey House** (1228 Sealy, private), by Nicholas J. Clayton, a Classic Revival and Gothic

Galveston's East End Historic District preserves some forty blocks, with many gingerbread-covered houses. Shown here are three examples located along Sealy Avenue and Winnie Street. OPPOSITE PAGE: *The John Clement Trube residence, popularly known as Trube's Castle, built in 1890 by a Danish immigrant who sought to reproduce the ambience of a European castle.* ABOVE: *The 1890 Liberty S. McKinney House, more commonly known as the McDonald House after the family that purchased it in 1909.* OPPOSITE: *The Jacob Sonnenthiel House, which may have been designed by the noted local architect Nicholas J. Clayton.*

Victorian blend and one of the most elaborate frame structures in the city, built for a cotton broker; the graceful Carpenter Gothic **Jacob Sonnenthiel House** (1826 Sealy, private); and the **Landes-McDonough House** (1602 Postoffice, private), an 1886 Richardsonian Romanesque brick residence built for a merchant.

The Strand was Galveston's major commercial street in the city's heyday, the so-called Wall Street of the Southwest. The **Strand Historic District** includes about ten blocks of landmark buildings. Before the Civil War, The Strand itself had been lined with wooden buildings on pilings extending into the bay; ships were able to transfer cargo directly to and from the warehouses, and employees would sometimes fish from upper floors during their lunch breaks. New construction from the 1870s until the hurricane of 1900 caught up aesthetically with Galveston's commercial success, and The Strand turned into one of the most colorful and beautifully made commercial districts in the country.

Nicholas J. Clayton was responsible for many of the important buildings in the business district. Among the most notable is the **Trueheart-Adriance Building** (210 22d Street), built for H. M. Trueheart & Co., the first chartered real estate firm in Texas. The three-story building, the first in The Strand to be restored, is a celebration in masonry, with pressed bricks of different molds and patterns framed and ornamented by carved-stone capitals and bases. On either side is the **First National Bank,** with its red brick and white ornamentation, built in 1878, and the **Kauffman and Runge Building** (now the Stewart Title Building), designed by Eugene T. Heiner in 1882, which lost an elaborate cornice in the 1900 hurricane. The bank has been restored and adopted by the Galveston Arts Center. Other Clayton buildings of interest include the 1883–1884 **Galveston News Building** (2108–2116 Mechanic Street), built with pressed red-and-yellow brick and iron with ornament in white and pink marble (the facade has been covered over); the **Hutchings, Sealy, and Company Building** (2326 Strand), a Classic Revival structure built in 1895–1897 for a prominent banking firm; and the nearby **Greenleve, Block, and Company Building** (2120–2128 Strand) of 1881–1882, at four stories tall the height of a typical present-day seven-story structure.

The *Elissa* (Pier 21, 409–763–1877) is a restored iron three-masted bark docked at the north end of 22d Street, just beyond The Strand. Built in 1877 in Scotland, the ship carried cargo in and out of the Port of Galveston in the 1880s. Restored to sailing condition, the ship is also a maritime museum. On board are interpretive displays of the era when tall ships reigned over the seas and the ports of the world. The captain's and seamen's quarters have been restored.

The first federal building to go up in Galveston was **Old Galveston Customs House** (20th Street and Avenue E) of 1858–1861 by Ammi B. Young. Made of local brick and iron imported from New York, it is one of the finest Greek Revival structures on the Gulf Coast. Inside, the cast-iron stairway's designs include the Star of Texas. The Customs House is still owned by the federal government and is used as a courthouse and post office substation. The Romanesque Revival **Grand 1894 Opera House** (2020 Postoffice Street) was built in 1894–1895 and heralded by the *Galveston Daily News* as "the greatest temple of Thespis to be found in the broad confines of Texas or the Southwest." Oscar Wilde, Sarah Bernhardt, John Philip Sousa, and Edwin Booth are among the well-known figures who appeared at the opera house. At one time made into a movie theater, it has been restored as a performance hall.

The brick Gothic Revival **Saint Mary's Cathedral** (2011 Church Street) is the oldest religious structure in the city, built with a gift of 500,000 bricks from Belgium in 1847–1848 and altered in the 1870s and 1880s by Nicholas J. Clayton. Bishop Claude-Marie Dubuis brought three nuns of the order of the Sisters of Charity of the Incarnate Word here in 1866; they founded the first Catholic hospital in Texas, Charity Hospital (today **Saint Mary's Hospital**) in 1867, only weeks before the outbreak of the yellow fever epidemic. **Trinity Episcopal Church** (2216 Ball Street) is a Gothic Revival complex whose first building of worship was built in 1855–1857 by John DeYoung. The smaller **Eaton Memorial Chapel** is by Nicholas J. Clayton, built in 1878 as a memorial to Reverend Benjamin Eaton, Trinity's first rector. Extensive rebuilding of the complex took place after the 1900 storm, including the installation in 1904 of a Tiffany window. **First Presbyterian Church** (1903 Church Street), constructed between 1872 and 1889, was the building that brought Nicholas J. Clayton to Texas. He came to Galveston as supervising architect for the Memphis firm of Jones & Baldwin, which designed the Romanesque Revival–style building. Clayton remained in Galveston, where he became one of the city's most prolific architects.

German immigrants in particular made a mark on the city's appearance, contributing such representative present-day landmarks as **Saint Joseph's Church** (2202 Avenue K), a simple frame building with Gothic and Greek Revival elements and a superb painted wood interior, designed by Joseph Bleicke and dedicated in 1860. In the **Silk Stocking Historic District** (roughly bounded by 23d and 26th streets and avenues L and Q), the **Garten Verein,** an octagonal frame dancing pavilion designed by Clayton and built about 1876, has been restored and is the centerpiece of Kempner Park.

Rosenberg Library

Henry Rosenberg came to Texas in 1843 from Switzerland and established what became the largest dry-goods business in Galveston; he went on to become a banker, civic leader, and philan-thropist. His numerous bequests included a trust for establishing a free public library for Galveston. The Rosenberg Library Association was incorporated in 1900, and its Renaissance Revival building, by the Saint Louis firm of Eames and Young, was completed in 1904. A year later it absorbed the collections of the Galveston Public Library. Along with impressive rare-book collections and research materials, the library houses a huge and historically invaluable Texana collec-tion in the Galveston and Texas History Center, which includes the archives of the Galveston Historical Society from 1871 onward. The Rosenberg Library also owns a number of important art collections and mounts regular exhibitions.

> LOCATION: 2310 Sealy. HOURS: Varied, phone for specific informa-tion. FEE: None. TELEPHONE: 409–763–8854.

The **Galveston County Historical Museum** (2219 Market, 409–766–2340) is housed in the Classic Revival City National Bank building of 1919, which has one of the finest unbroken barrel vault ceilings extant in Texas. Interpretive exhibits cover farming and ranching, the Texas navy, the work of architect Nicholas J. Clayton, fossils found in the area, a shipping company's office and opera-tions, a typical 1905 general store, and photography in Galveston County. The museum also displays a handsome brass beacon light from the South Jetty lighthouse, which was automated in 1972.

The **Center for Transportation and Commerce** (25th Street at the Strand, 409–765–5700) has the largest collection of restored rail cars and locomotives in the Southwest. Housed in the 1932 Santa Fe Railroad Depot at the foot of the Strand, this railroad museum has forty-three cars on five tracks. In the waiting room are thirty life-size

The Ashbel Smith Building, affectionately known as "Old Red," was one of some 200 buildings in Galveston designed by Nicholas J. Clayton. Fire, hurricanes, and progress have demolished all but about 50 of them.

sculptures of 1930s-era travelers. There are also sound-and-light shows on Galveston history and a working model in HO gauge showing the railroad's role in the commerce of the Port of Galveston. In 1881 Galveston was selected as the site of the Medical Branch of the University of Texas (now the University of Texas Medical Branch), home of a world-renowned burn center and Galveston's largest employer. The first building on the campus, intended to house classrooms, offices, laboratories, and physiology and anatomy amphitheaters, was commissioned from Nicholas J. Clayton at the height of his powers. Originally called the Medical College Building, the **Ashbel Smith Building** was nicknamed "Old Red" because it was built with red pressed brick from Cedar Bayou, Texas granite, and sandstone.

BEAUMONT

The Lucas gusher at Spindletop Hill in 1901 put Beaumont on the map, but the city had been around for three-quarters of a century before that. The first permanent settlers were a farmer named Noah Tevis and his wife, Nancy, who moved to the area from Louisiana in 1824. Other early settlers were Acadians from nearby Louisiana. In

1835 Tevis sold fifty acres of his land on the Neches River as a town site to Henry Millard, who commanded the right flank at the Battle of San Jacinto. Millard named the town for his wife, Mary Warren Beaumont. By the mid-nineteenth century the town's prime position between the great east Texas forests and the Gulf of Mexico had made it both a lumber center and a shipping center for coastal farmers' cotton, sugar cane, and cattle. Antebellum Beaumont life is re-created at the **John J. French Museum** (2995 French Road, 409–898–0348), built in 1845 by a tanner from Connecticut and filled with furniture made in Texas before the Civil War.

Considered by some to be as important in Texas history as the Battle of San Jacinto was, Spindletop opened a new chapter in the history of not only Texas but also the world—that of the modern petroleum industry. In the weeks after the famous Lucas gusher erupted on January 10, 1901, Beaumont's population rose from 9,000 to 30,000. Over 600 oil companies—including Gulf, Texaco, and Mobil—had their beginnings at Spindletop. By 1902 there were 285 active wells on the hill. Although Spindletop was played out from overproduction, better management of wells (and the discovery of more deposits on the flanks of the hill in 1925) ensured the industry's and the city's success. Beaumont became a major port when the Neches River was dredged for shipping in 1908, with subsequent widening and deepening in 1911, 1927, and 1930. With Port Arthur and Orange as the other two points, Beaumont is part of "the Golden Triangle" of the petroleum industry in Texas.

Oil wealth provided the funds for such monuments as **Saint Anthony Cathedral** (Jefferson and Wall streets), built in 1904 to designs by J. B. Brechlin, and the stone Romanesque Revival–style **Tyrrell Historical Library** (Pearl and Fannin streets, 409–833–2759), originally the **First Baptist Church.** Built in 1903 to designs by A. N. Dawson, it was bought by Captain W. C. Tyrrell in 1923 and donated to the city. The church's interior was altered very little during its adaptation into a library housing an impressive collection of Texana.

Gladys City Boomtown

A reconstruction of the boomtown originally platted in 1898, Gladys City was named after a 7-year-old girl in the Sunday school class of Pattillo Higgins, the real estate developer who was the first

OPPOSITE: *Oil wells, accessible only by boat or catwalk, in the bayous of the Neches River, within the Golden Triangle formed by Beaumont, Port Arthur, and Orange.*

to suspect that the gaseous vapors on Spindletop Hill indicated oil below. This museum, sited three-quarters of a mile from the actual Gladys City because of soil subsidence, reproduces the clapboard shacks, saloon, post office, general store, surveyors' and lawyers' offices, and pharmacy of the town where land was bought and sold for $200,000 an acre and men were told by the police chief to walk in the middle of the street after nightfall and "tote guns in your hands." All the buildings are fitted with period furnishings. The **Lucas Gusher Monument,** a fifty-eight-foot granite obelisk dedicated in 1951, is also on the site.

LOCATION: Off Route 287 at Highland Avenue–Sulphur Drive exit. HOURS: 1–5 Sunday, Tuesday–Friday, 9–5 Saturday. FEE: Yes. TELEPHONE: 409–835–0823.

W. P. H. ("Perry") McFaddin, the son of a Texas revolutionary, became a major force in the development of the Beaumont cattle and rice business and a part owner of Spindletop Hill when Anthony F. Lucas brought in his gusher. The dramatic Colonial

The McFaddin-Ward House, designed by Henry Conrad Mauer, who was the first formally trained architect in Beaumont. The family slept on the second floor porch during the influenza scare at the time of World War I. OPPOSITE: *A view of the Pink Parlor from the entry hall, lit with a crystal chandelier.*

Revival **McFaddin-Ward House** (1906 McFadden Avenue, 409–832–2134), with its gigantic Ionic columns, was sold to McFaddin by his sister in the midst of construction. It was designed by Henry Conrad Mauer and completed in 1906. All furniture, rugs, and decorative objects on display in the house belonged to the family, who occupied the house until 1982.

ORANGE

The second point on the so-called Golden Triangle, Orange was founded in 1836 and is said to have been named after the mayor's favorite color. Timber, cattle, rice, and shipbuilding (most intensely during both world wars) have been its major industries. The history of Orange County is explored at the **Heritage House Museum** (409–886–5385), the former Jimmy Ochiltree Sims house of 1902.

The beautifully crafted Queen Anne–Eastlake **W. H. Stark House** (610 Main Street, 409–883–0871) was built of longleaf yellow pine and cypress in 1894 for the lumber baron and prominent Orange businessman and his philanthropist wife, Mildred Lutcher Stark. Much of the interior is furnished with the original belongings of the Stark family. The **Stark Museum of Art** (712 Green Avenue, 409–883–6661) houses a significant collection of Western art including work by Remington, Russell, Bierstadt, and Moran as well as Indian art and artifacts and nonhistorical collections. The Stark family also funded the building of the **Lutcher Memorial Church Building** (902 West Green) of 1911, designed in the Beaux-Arts style by James Oliver Hogg. Between Orange and Port Arthur on Route 87 is the graceful, high-arching **Rainbow Bridge,** built in 1938.

PORT ARTHUR

This town was founded in 1895 by Arthur E. Stillwell, a railroad magnate who bought the site for the terminus of his Kansas City, Pittsburg, & Gulf Railroad. Stillwell claimed that the site for Port Arthur came to him in a dream and later wrote that no other city had ever been "located and built under directions from the spirit world." Stillwell also dreamed, incorrectly, that Port Arthur would be a resort community. Once oil was found in the area, the town quickly grew into a center for production and shipping.

The Pompeiian Villa

Virtually the only evidence of Stillwell's resort community is this peculiar pink stucco, U-shaped Classic Revival residence built in 1900 for Isaac Ellwood, the co-inventor of barbed wire, and sold within two years to James Hopkins of the Diamond Match Company, who in turn traded the house to George Craig for 10 percent of the Texas Company. Craig once was asked why he surrendered so much stock for a house. "Oil companies were a dime a dozen then," he replied. "How did I know the Texas Company would survive?" Today the Texas Company is Texaco. The Port Arthur Historical Society has restored and fitted the house with appropriately splendid furnishings.

LOCATION: 1935 Lakeshore Drive. HOURS: 9–4 Monday–Friday. FEE: Yes. TELEPHONE: 409–983–5977.

On the campus of Lamar University–Port Arthur is the Classic Revival **Gates Memorial Library** (316 Stillwell Boulevard, 409–983–4921), built in 1916 by the wife of John Warne "Bet-a-Million" Gates in honor of her husband and son. Gates, who introduced barbed wire to Texas, went into the oil business, becoming a strong promoter of Port Arthur. Housed in the building, which was designed by the noted New York firm of Warren & Wetmore, is the **Port Arthur Historical Museum,** which displays documents and memorabilia telling the story of Port Arthur.

Fifteen miles south of Port Arthur is the site of the most spectacular military engagement of the Civil War in Texas, **Sabine Pass Battleground State Historical Park** (F.M. 3322, off Route 87). On September 8, 1863, a Union fleet of twenty vessels and 5,000 men tried to invade Texas at Sabine Pass, the point of entry from the Gulf of Mexico to Sabine Lake. Although the Confederates under Lieutenants Dick Dowling and N. H. Smith numbered merely 42, with only six cannon, they sank three Union gunboats in forty-five minutes, killed 65 Federals, and took 315 prisoners while suffering no casualties themselves. The Union forces retreated to New Orleans.

CENTRAL
TEXAS

OPPOSITE: *Pompeo Coppini's statue of a Terry's Texas Ranger, a member of a Civil War unit, guards the steps to the Texas State Capitol in Austin, while the* Goddess of Liberty *stands atop the dome.*

Central Texas—"central" being a slippery concept in a state so vast that many inhabitants still argue about where is where—comprises several geographic areas: rich river bottoms in the southern portion, prairies to the northeast, plateaus and hills and rivers cutting through limestone to the west. Indian trails, Spanish roads, and stage routes crisscrossed the center. In 1534 central Texas was the homeland of Indians including the Wichita, Huaco, Tonkawa, and Lipan Apache when Alvar Núñez Cabeza de Vaca escaped from the Charucco tribe near the Gulf Coast and crossed northwest through the Hill Country to the area of El Paso. The next European to cross central Texas was Louis Juchereau de Saint-Denis, a French trader along the Red River in northern Louisiana, who traveled a southwesterly route in 1714 looking to establish a trade route between Louisiana and Mexico. In the years to follow, between Nuestra Señora de Guadalupe de los Nacogdoches in the east and the missions in San Antonio and farther south, the Spaniards trekked through much of central Texas in response to the French threat but actually established few and always temporary outposts in the central part of the interior. One such failure was the San Francisco Xavier Mission; established in 1755 at present-day San Marcos northeast of San Antonio, it lasted only fifteen months. In 1757 the mission of San Saba de la Santa Cruz was founded in what is now Menard County. Two years later, the Spaniards had their first encounter with the Comanche—who destroyed the mission. The Apache, whom the Comanche had forced southward, had already caused trouble for the Spaniards in San Antonio and farther south. The expansion of missions was over. Spain's retreat from central Texas was accelerated by its diminishing coffers and strife in Europe.

Although there were unauthorized Anglo-American incursions into and explorations of Texas before 1821, not until that year was Texas significantly opened for colonization by non-Spaniards. The first Anglo colonist was Moses Austin, whose fortunes had suffered in the Panic of 1819; he went west to recoup. With the help of a soldier of fortune, "Baron" de Bastrop, Austin was made an *empresario* and given permission to bring 300 families into Texas. He died

OPPOSITE: *A portrait of the Texas colonizer Stephen F. Austin by an unknown painter. It hangs in the Senate Chamber of the Capitol.* PAGES 132-133: *A dog-trot cabin, at right, and a smaller smokehouse, at left, surrounded by the Texas State flower, the Bluebonnet, on the homestead of Casper Danz. The site is now part of the LBJ State Historic Park.*

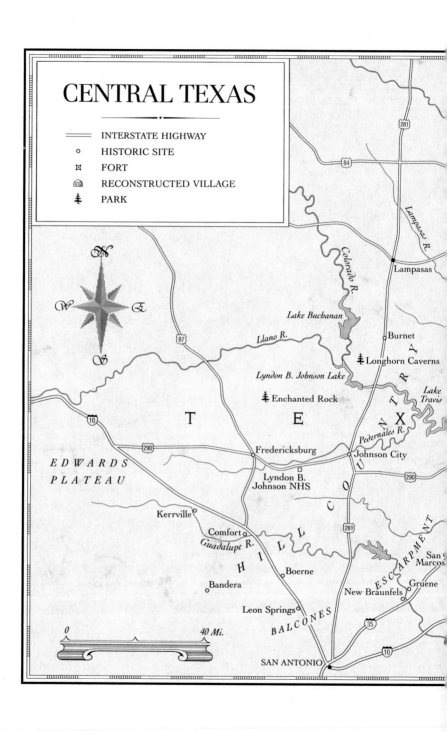

CENTRAL TEXAS

=== INTERSTATE HIGHWAY
○ HISTORIC SITE
⊞ FORT
🏛 RECONSTRUCTED VILLAGE
🌲 PARK

Lampasas R.

281

84

Colorado R.

Lampasas

Lake Buchanan

Burnet

87

Llano R.

🌲 Longhorn Caverns

Lyndon B. Johnson Lake

Lake Travis

🌲 Enchanted Rock

T   E   X

Pedernales R.

10

290

Fredericksburg

Johnson City

Lyndon B.
Johnson NHS

290

EDWARDS
PLATEAU

C

281

Kerrville

Comfort

San
Marcos

Guadalupe R.

Boerne

ESCARPMENT

Bandera

New Braunfels

Gruene

Leon Springs

BALCONES

35

0   40 Mi.

SAN ANTONIO

10

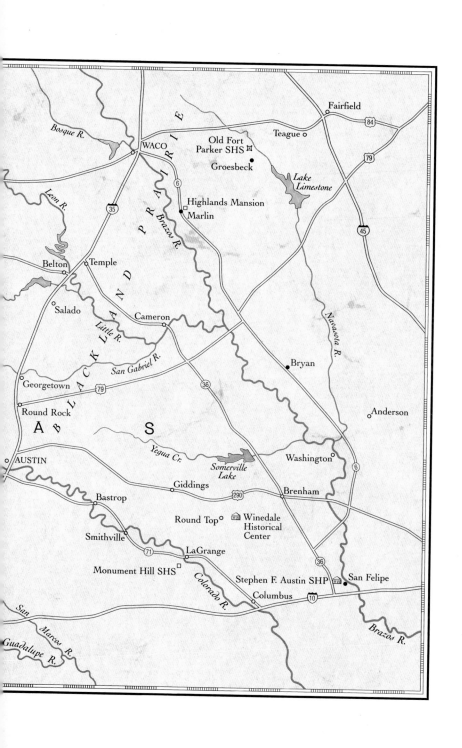

before he could take up his empire. From his deathbed in 1821 the elder Austin requested of his wife that she and their son Stephen take over. Within a few months Stephen F. Austin was choosing his colony in the rich Brazos and Colorado River valleys. But newly independent Mexico was cautious in approving the Spanish grant, and it was not ratified until 1823.

Thus began the era of log cabins and cotton farms and independent Anglo settlements. Each of Austin's first families of colonists—the Old Three Hundred—were given more than 4,500 acres of land in a district bordered by El Camino Real to the north, the Colorado River to the west, and the Neches to the east. A number of other grants were given to Anglo *empresarios* in central Texas, but the Austin colony was the only one in the region to succeed during the years before the republic was founded in 1836. By then, 8,000 Americans had been drawn to Texas by the free lands and had

King Cotton being lifted into place on a festive archway constructed of bales of cotton at the entrance to the Waco Cotton Festival, in a photograph from the 1920s.

settled in an area roughly bounded by the San Jacinto River to the east, the Old San Antonio Road (El Camino Real) to the north and west, and the Lavaca River to the southwest.

Texas's independence from Mexico was fragile, based as it was upon the secret Treaty of Velasco, which Santa Anna had been forced to sign while held in captivity by the Texans after the Battle of San Jacinto in 1836. Sam Houston, as the first nonprovisional president of the republic, knew that a new nation with no money was wise to keep the peace. Houston respected the Indians, and he believed they should have the right of title to land. But he was succeeded in 1838 by Mirabeau B. Lamar, who reversed Houston's policies and brought to an end the period of peaceful coexistence with the Indians and with Mexico. Lamar thought the Indians should be removed from Texas or eradicated. He repudiated the treaties Houston had made; thereafter, many lives were lost in battles between Texans and Indians, and the coffers of the republic were emptied. However, Lamar's harsh approach opened up more land to white settlement. By the time Houston returned to office in 1841 and began slowly trying to rebuild relations with the Indians, Anglos had already begun to move into previously unsettled parts of Texas.

The new Republic of Texas continued the Mexican policy of granting a league of land, or 4,605 acres, to families and smaller parcels, 1,476 acres, to unmarried men to encourage settlement. Central Texas in the mid-nineteenth century experienced a surge of Anglo-American settlement as well as a rush of immigration from Europe. European settlement was concentrated in the Hill Country. Although a few Germans had come to Texas before the revolution, many more came after a general colonization act, offering generous land grants to colonizers, was passed by the congress of the Texas republic in 1842. The first wave of German immigrants to the Colorado and Brazos River valleys had sent back reports of the opportunities and good land available in Texas.

Most of the other Indian groups remaining in Texas at mid-century were "removed" in 1854 to reservations in north-central Texas. Later, they were excluded from Texas altogether. After Texas entered the Union in 1845, the U.S. Army was given the responsibility of dealing with the Indians. The army began building forts along the Indian frontier in west-central Texas, and this in turn encouraged more incursions by settlers in a great American migration. Farming and ranching took hold; more sophisticated wooden or rock houses replaced log cabins and "soddies." Between 1845 and 1860, central Texas was composed of slave-driven cotton plantations to the south and east, yeoman farming in the north, and subsistence farming and livestock raising to the west. Towns grew up along all the trade and travel routes through the heart of Texas and to serve the farming communities. In the 1840s and 1850s, Czechs and Poles, Norwegians and Swedes followed the Germans to Texas. Theirs were tightly knit communities, and many of them remain so today. There are still German-, Czech-, Polish-, and Wendish-speaking communities in Texas.

After the Civil War, the great days of cattle drives began, first along the Shawnee Trail through Lockhart and Austin, then, after 1867, along the great Chisholm Trail to Kansas; and after 1876 along the Western Trail to the west of the Chisholm. A few railroads came through the center of the state before the Civil War, and afterward a spidery network was laid down to serve existing towns and create new ones. Even after the growth of cities and a more service-oriented economy, central Texas remains the agricultural heartland it was in the beginning of American settlement here.

This chapter begins with the capital city of Austin. It then radiates to the east, along the Colorado and Brazos River valleys; to the north, to Waco and its surroundings; and finally west, to the Hill Country.

AUSTIN

Although Sam Houston is a more appealing figure, it is Mirabeau B. Lamar whom Texas has to thank for its capital city of Austin. In 1838 only a handful of people lived here in crude circumstances among verdant, gentle hills on the banks of the Colorado River, in what is now the heart of Austin. The community, called Waterloo, had been started in 1832 and consisted of five families, including the first settler, Reuben Hornsby, an Indian-fighting ranger in the Texas army, and Jacob M. Harrell, a pioneer who was living near the present-day capitol. In the fall Lamar came to Waterloo to hunt buffalo with Harrell. Lamar was enamored of the site for, among other things, its "well-watered" climate. A few months later, in 1839, after he was elected president of the republic, Lamar sent five commissioners to see Waterloo, and the commission approved, even though the settlement was on the edge of Comanche country. Waterloo was renamed

Austin, in honor of Stephen F. Austin, the father of Texas, and construction was begun on the capital's streets and government buildings in May 1839.

The streets were laid out by Edwin Waller (who would become the city's first mayor in 1840) in a grid surrounding Capitol Square. North–south streets named after Texas rivers intersected those named for Texas trees (the tree streets now are numbered). Armed guards protected the early construction workers from the Comanche, who watched the building from the nearby hilltops. By the mid-1840s the audaciously located city boasted almost a thousand citizens, but it was still essentially a pioneer village.

In 1842 the modestly built town was virtually abandoned when Mexican forces led by Adrian Woll invaded and captured San Antonio. Sam Houston, president once again, feared that the Mexicans would continue on to Austin. He called an emergency session of the congress, and it was decided that the government would retreat to Houston. The president sent men to gather some of the archives for the temporary exile. The remaining Austinites thought removal of the archives portended their losing the capital forever, and thus began the "Archives War." A local vigilance committee formed, packing up the archives and posting an armed guard to protect the boxes. When Houston sent a company of rangers some months later to try again to collect the papers and take them to Washington-on-the-Brazos, the rangers surprised the now-relaxed vigilance committee and made away with a wagonload of boxes. A day or two later, the vigilance committee caught up with the wagons. Under orders from President Houston to avoid bloodshed, the rangers gave up the archives, which remained in Austin until the government returned in 1844. In the state election of 1850, Austin was made the permanent capital.

By 1860 Austin had nearly 3,500 citizens. Greek Revival houses of beauty were built, and commercial and government buildings also flourished. When the Confederacy was being formed, Austin voted against secession from the Union, but the state voted for it. Austin did not see any fighting, but Confederates did maintain military establishments in the city. Much of Austin's most impressive building took place after the railroads came in 1871. Turn-of-the-century houses can still be seen in Austin, particularly in **Hyde Park** and the central city just west of downtown. Austin's grandest old neighborhood backs onto Shoal Creek and is known as **Pemberton**

Heights. This is where Governor Elisha Pease's former house, **Woodlawn** (6 Niles Road, private) was built in the Greek Revival style in 1853 by the master builder Abner Cook.

Texas State Capitol

This Renaissance Revival statehouse is several feet taller than Washington's Capitol and comparatively grand in many other ways. It is the fourth capitol constructed in Austin but only the second one to occupy the site that was designated in Edwin Waller's city plan as Capitol Square. (The first capitol, a wooden structure, was situated at the corner of Colorado and 8th streets.) In 1876 a new state constitution had authorized the sale of some 3 million acres of state-owned land to finance the building of a new capitol, the fourth to be constructed. From eleven proposals the Capitol Commission chose that of Elijah E. Myers, a 48-year-old Detroit architect who also designed courthouses and city halls in the Midwest and capitols in Idaho, Michigan, and Colorado. Myers proposed a limestone building in an extended Greek cross with a Second Empire dome, which would resemble that of the U.S. Capitol. The third capitol, built in 1854, burned in November 1881. Soon after, construction on the new capitol began. It was discovered, however, that the local limestone was embedded with pyrite, which disintegrated when exposed to air and made yellowish brown streaks on the creamy white stone. More costly Texas red granite was substituted. To save money the state provided convict labor to operate the quarry, which aroused the ire of the International Association of Granite Cutters. The contractor hired sixty-two Scottish stone cutters, quietly brought into Texas from Virginia via train.

Completed in 1888, the structure has a dome of metal painted to match the red granite, and its lantern is topped by a Goddess of Liberty statue (the original zinc version was replaced in 1987 with a sturdier aluminum replica, painted the original white). The interior structure was done using the original limestone, surfaced with plaster and painted white. Wainscoting and door and window frames are made of white oak, yellow pine, mahogany, cherry, cedar, and walnut. Some metalwork was imported from Belgium, although the

OPPOSITE: *The Senate Chamber in the Texas State Capitol.*

grand iron columns were cast by convicts in the East Texas Penitentiary at Rusk.

Flanking the south entrance are twin cannons used in the Texas Revolution and the Civil War. In the south entrance hall are two murals by William H. Huddle, *The Surrender of Santa Anna* and *David Crockett,* as well as marble statues of Sam Houston and Stephen F. Austin by Elisabet Ney. Off the rotunda hang paintings of the governors of Texas, including Miriam A. Ferguson, Texas's first woman governor, and the presidents of the republic. Monuments by Pompeo Coppini on the grounds commemorate the Alamo, volunteer firemen, the Confederacy, and the Texas cowboy. Coppini also sculpted the east lawn's *Monument to Hood's Texas Brigade,* honoring a famous Confederate unit.

LOCATION: 100 East 11th Street. HOURS: 8:30–4:30 Daily, tours every 15 minutes. FEE: None. TELEPHONE: 512–463–0063.

Just east of the capitol, the **Texas State Library** (Brazos between 12th and 13th streets, 512–463–5480), housed in the Lorenzo de Zavala State Archives and Library Building (named for the first vice president of the republic), has cases displaying facsimiles of the Texas Declaration of Independence, William B. Travis's impassioned letter from the Alamo "To the People of Texas & all Americans in the World," and other documents pertaining to the republic and the state. A forty-five-foot mural painted in 1964 by the English artist Peter Rogers depicts the history of Texas from Indian domination through the Spanish conquest to industrial society. Looming in the mural's foreground are the likenesses of Stephen F. Austin; Alamo heroes William B. Travis, David Crockett, and James Bowie; and presidents Sam Houston, Mirabeau B. Lamar, and Anson Jones.

On a hill on the southeastern portion of the capitol grounds, the **Old Land Office** (112 East 11th Street) was designed by the German immigrant architect C. Conrad Stremme, a former professor of architecture in Russia under Czar Nicholas I, who awarded Stremme the Russian title of hereditary nobleman for his distinguished work. The General Land Office was established in 1836 to administer public lands. With statehood Texas retained ownership of its public lands—the only state in the Union ever to do so—and the comptroller was charged with commissioning a building to house the land office and its records. Stremme's design, built in

1856–1857, was a fireproof stuccoed limestone structure in the Romanesque Revival style, unusual at a time when the Greek Revival was all the rage in the state, with such good-humored Texas elements as horseshoe-shaped chamfered arches at the entrance and five-point Texas stars in the masonry and in the leaded glass above the south doorway. In the early days, offices included one for Spanish land grants, the administering of which became complicated after independence from Mexico. The writer William Sydney Porter (O. Henry) worked in the drafting room on the second floor from 1887 to 1891.

Near the capitol are the offices of the Texas Historical Commission, which occupy the limestone Federal-style **Carrington-Covert House** (1511 Colorado Street, 512–463–6100), built by a merchant in 1856 and saved by the commission from demolition.

The Gothic Revival **Gethsemane Church** (1510 Congress Avenue) was constructed by Texas's first Swedish Lutheran congregation from handmade bricks and stone salvaged from the burned 1854 capitol. The **Daniel H. Caswell House** and the **William T. Caswell House** (1404 and 1502 West Avenue, private) were built by father and son of rusticated limestone in 1899 and 1906. They are among the most comfortably elegant of the Victorian structures on this street.

The Governor's Mansion

The master builder Abner Cook was responsible for the final design of the Governor's Mansion, built from 1854 to 1856 across 11th Street from the capitol. Cook, a native North Carolinian, had come to Austin in 1839 after working in Tennessee and Georgia. Before he took on this important building, Cook had constructed several fine Greek Revival houses in Austin. Opposition to financing such a fine edifice for the head of state was strong in the early days of Austin, but Governor Pease prevailed. The mansion is made of Austin bricks, which were originally unpainted, its fine Ionic columns built of cypress and pine from the Bastrop area. Historical paintings in the house include San Antonio artist Robert Onderdonk's *The Fall of the Alamo*. Sam Houston's bed, Stephen F. Austin's desk, and Governor Pease's sofa are among the furnishings.

LOCATION: 1010 Colorado Street. HOURS: 10–11:40 Monday–Friday. FEE: None. TELEPHONE: 512–463–5516.

The Greek Revival-style Texas Governor's mansion has remained nearly unchanged since 1854, due to limited appropriations from generations of Texas legislators who considered the house an extravagance. OPPOSITE: *The library contains American Federal-style furniture, including a settee that belonged to Elisha M. Pease, the first Governor to live in the mansion.*

Scrubbed and rehabilitated nineteenth- and early-twentieth-century commercial buildings line broad Congress Avenue, which slopes down from 11th Street to the river and affords the city's longest view of the capitol. On the southwest corner of 11th and Congress are the **Old Capitol Ruins,** where a temporary capitol stood after the 1854 building burned and before the present one had been completed. The **Old Lundberg Bakery** (1006 Congress Avenue, 512–477–5961), built in 1876, is a brick-and-limestone building with a pressed-metal cornice topped by a carved stone eagle. It is now a visitor center. **Saint Mary's Cathedral** (201–207 East 10th Street) is a High Victorian Gothic church of 1874, designed by the noted Galveston architect Nicholas J. Clayton. Its stained-glass windows were imported from Munich. The **Millet Opera House** (112 East 9th Street), by architects Jacob Larmour and Charles Wheelock, was built in 1878 for Charles F. Millet and at the time was the second-biggest opera house in Texas, after Galveston. Leading ladies from Sarah Bernhardt to Helen Hayes have played the **Paramount**

Theater for the Performing Arts (713 Congress Avenue), an intimate Beaux-Arts performing house built as the Majestic Theater in 1915. The sophisticated Venetian Gothic **Walter Tips Building** (712 Congress Avenue) was designed in 1876 by J. N. Preston, who also created the Driskill Hotel. Next door is the earlier (1865) and simpler **Edward Tips Building**; Walter's older brother ran a hardware business here. The 1859 **Sampson Building** (620–622 Congress Avenue) is the oldest building still standing on Congress Avenue, three stories in limestone designed by Abner Cook for a dry-goods merchant. The Classic Revival **Claudia Taylor Johnson Hall** (220 West 6th Street) is an office of the University of Texas system named for Mrs. Lyndon B. Johnson. It was designed as a post office and federal building from 1912–1914 by James Knox Taylor to complement the earlier (1878–1881) Renaissance Revival post office and federal building at 601 Colorado Street. That structure, now a university building named **O. Henry Hall,** was where the writer William Sydney Porter was tried and found guilty of embezzlement.

The curvaceous Beaux-Arts **Littlefield Building** (106 East 6th Street) was designed in 1910 by C. H. Page, Jr., for Major George W. Littlefield, a colorful cattleman-turned-banker and powerful civic force. The **Scarborough Building** (522 Congress Avenue) was built in 1910 and was later given an appealing Art Deco facade. The **Koppel Building** (318–320 Congress Avenue) was built by Burt McDonald and his brother John (later mayor of Austin) in 1888. The architects James Riely Gordon and Burt McDonald designed the Romanesque Revival **McKean-Eilers Building** (317 Congress Avenue) for a dry-goods concern. It was built in 1897.

The most concentrated area of Victorian residential elegance in town, the **Bremond Block** was originally an enclave of houses built by two families connected by intermarriage, the Bremonds and the Robinsons. The historic district comprises ten buildings (all private) on parts of three blocks. Particularly striking are the **John Bremond, Jr., House** (700 Guadalupe Street), designed by George Fiegel in 1886, with an elaborate wraparound double gallery and decorated mansard roof; the late Victorian (1898) **Pierre Bremond House** (402 West 7th Street); the **Eugene Bremond House** (404 West 7th Street), built in 1877, the only frame house on the block, with a semicircular colonnaded gallery; the 1872 **Catherine Robinson-**

OPPOSITE: *The John Bremond, Jr., House in Austin is distinguished by lacy ironwork on its double gallery.*

McBee House (705 San Antonio Street), originally one story, with a second story and Classic Revival detailing added in 1885; the New Orleans–style **Walter Bremond House** (711 San Antonio Street), built in 1882 (George Fiegel's addition of a second story in 1887 was a wedding present to Mr. Bremond); and the **North-Evans Chateau (Bellevue)** (708 San Antonio Street), which was a modest chateau nicknamed "North's Folly" when it was built in 1874 for Harvey North, but was turned into a Romanesque Revival castle with additions by Major Ira H. Evans in 1894.

The most exuberant building on 6th Street, once the main easterly road between Austin and the earlier Anglo settlements in Texas, is the **Driskill Hotel** (6th and Brazos, 512–474–5911), a Richardsonian Romanesque corner-turning hotel built by J. N. Preston in 1886 for Jesse Driskill, one of the early cattle kings to drive herds north after the Civil War and later a business tycoon. The hotel is brick with limestone trim and is ornamented with distinctive carved stone accents: busts of Driskill and his sons, a longhorn, and the Texas Lone Star. J. N. Preston also designed the Renaissance Revival **Hannig Building** (206 East 6th Street), which belonged to a cabinetmaker who married Suzanna Dickinson; she and her baby were at the Battle of the Alamo and, according to legend, afterward were escorted by the Mexicans to Gonzales, where she delivered the news of the Alamo's fall. The Gothic Revival **Saint David's Episcopal Church** (304 East 7th Street), built in 1854 for the second-oldest Episcopal congregation in the state, has undergone several subsequent additions and alterations. Some of the stained-glass windows are by Tiffany and Company.

Back on 6th Street, number 422–424 is the **Risher-Nicholas Building** (1873), rented by its owner to J. J. Jennings, a black druggist. The black doctor J. H. Stevens made his home and office in the building, and a black newspaper called the *Austin Watchman* was published here at the turn of the century.

O. Henry Home and Museum

William Sydney Porter moved to Austin in 1885, seeking good health and better fortune. He worked as a bookkeeper, a draftsman, and a bank teller, marrying Athol Estes along the way. In 1894 he started publishing a weekly newspaper of humor, usually four to ten pages, called *Rolling Stone*. It carried short stories, cartoons, jokes, news, politics, and advertising, but apparently not enough advertising to make

Porter a living; publication stopped the next year. Of Porter's embezzlement of funds from the First National Bank, *The Handbook of Texas* says, "It is possible that, had he obeyed the summons, he would have been acquitted." But the accused Porter fled to New Orleans, then Honduras, returning when his wife became seriously ill in 1897. This time he voluntarily faced trial, was convicted, and was sent to jail in Columbus, Ohio, until 1901. It was in prison that he wrote many of the works published under the pseudonym O. Henry. This little Victorian cottage, which was moved from its original site a block away, was where Porter, his wife, and his daughter lived from 1893 to 1895. It has period furniture and family memorabilia.

> LOCATION: 409 East 5th Street. HOURS: 12–5 Wednesday–Sunday.
> FEE: None. TELEPHONE: 512–472–1903.

French Legation

The oldest surviving house in Austin, and one of few houses surviving from the Republic of Texas era, the French Legation was completed in 1841 for Jean Pierre Isidore Alphonse Dubois de Saligny, France's representative to the republic. Dubois sold the house before it was completed, and although he retained the right to use the house until 1842, he probably lived here for only a few weeks. Originally located on a twenty-one-acre site, the Legation was the most elegant house in a rough frontier town. Dubois may have received architectural advice from Thomas William Ward, an Irishman who had worked as a builder in New Orleans. The house combines Anglo elements (such as the central hall) and Louisiana elements (French doors and a hipped roof). In 1839, during Dubois' tenure as chargé d'affaires, France and the Republic of Texas recognized each other. A contentious man who paid little attention to his duties, Dubois became embroiled in a petty squabble called the "Pig War," which arose when an innkeeper's pigs repeatedly raided his rented house (not the Legation) and grounds. Dubois and one of his servants scuffled with the innkeeper several times, and Dubois brought charges against him. Dubois left Austin, in April 1841, before the case was settled. He did not return.

Operated by the Daughters of the Republic of Texas, the museum has Republic of Texas-era furnishings, including an English piano and two pieces original to the house, an armchair and daven-

Maze-like hedges, designed by the Austin landscape architect C. Coatsworth Pinkney, were planted on the grounds of the restored French Legation in the 1950s.

port, both of rosewood and probably made in New Orleans. On display are copies of some of Dubois' dispatches to the king, supplied to the museum by the French government.

> LOCATION: 802 San Marcos Street. HOURS: 1–5 Tuesday–Sunday. FEE: Yes. TELEPHONE: 512–472–8180.

The grave of Stephen F. Austin is marked by a Pompeo Coppini bronze statue on the highest point in the **Texas State Cemetery** (East 7th and Canal streets). Other notable Texans buried here include Albert Sidney Johnston, commander in the Texas army, secretary of war in the Republic of Texas, and later a general in the Confederate army, beneath an Elisabet Ney statue of him reclining; eight governors of Texas; and 2,047 Confederate veterans. A few blocks north is **Oakwood Cemetery** (East 16th Street and Navasota), whose first occupant was a black man killed by Indians.

The **George Washington Carver Museum** (1165 Angelina Street, 512–472–4809), a black-history museum, opened in 1980. It has changing exhibits and hosts cultural events. The **Henry G. Madison**

Log Cabin (2300 Rosewood Avenue) was originally on East 11th Street, built by the black homesteaders Henry and Louise Madison. Henry Madison became a police officer and in 1886 built a frame house around the cabin, which was uncovered during a recent demolition and moved to Rosewood park.

The University of Texas

Although the high ideals of the republic created the University of Texas in 1839, the high costs of building a republic and a state on the frontier during two wars delayed the actual establishment of the university for more than forty years. The university officially opened in 1883 on College Hill, forty acres of land north of the capital that the republic had set aside. The **University of Texas Visitor Center** (512–471–1420) is housed in the complex known since 1925 as the **Little Campus** (Red River Street at Martin Luther King Boulevard). The square two-story building, now known as the **Arno Nowotny Building,** was the original Asylum for the Blind, the first such state school, built in 1857 by Abner Cook in the Italianate style. Other buildings for the institution were built in the late 1800s and early 1900s. From 1865 to 1866, the complex was made a barracks and was briefly home to Lieutenant Colonel George Armstrong Custer and his family. **Santa Rita Number 1** (Martin Luther King Boulevard at San Jacinto Street) was the first drilling rig to strike oil on University of Texas land in the Permian Basin, thus allowing for the creation of a very large permanent university building fund.

Battle Hall, an inspired building by New York architect Cass Gilbert (built after his U.S. Customs House but before his celebrated Woolworth Building in New York), was the first of the distinctive Beaux-Arts/Southwestern buildings that grace the older parts of the campus. Built in 1911, it is a cream-colored limestone edifice with generous round-arch windows, terra-cotta ornamentation, and painted wooden cornice; its style was described as "Spanish Renaissance" by Gilbert himself. Gilbert was made university architect in charge of creating a master plan for future building, which he worked on for twelve years; but only one other building in his plan, the 1918 **Sutton Hall** (southeast of Battle Hall), was actually constructed. A subsequent university architect, Paul Phillipe Cret of Philadelphia, was the author of a master plan adopted by the university in 1930 that developed the Renaissance Revival mode instituted by Gilbert. Cret's lega-

cy is more apparent; he designed nineteen major buildings for the university, including the **Texas Union** and **Hogg Auditorium,** both designed in association with Robert Leon White, and the **Architecture Building,** designed in association with Greene, LaRoche and Dahl. Credit for the **Main Building,** completed in 1936 and today the university's symbol, goes to all of these architects.

One of the museums chartered to celebrate the Texas centennial in 1936, the **Texas Memorial Museum** (2400 Trinity Street, 512–471–1604) was completed in 1939 by the Houston architect John Staub in consultation with Paul Cret. Through brass doors visitors enter Memorial Hall, a thirty-five-foot-tall room lined with rouge marble from the Pyrénées and occupied by the original "Goddess of Liberty" statue from atop the State Capitol. The museum is devoted to natural history and anthropology, with an emphasis on Texas, and includes exhibits ranging from gemstones and mineral specimens to fossils, life-size dioramas of Texas wildlife, and Native American artifacts. A small adjacent building houses dinosaur tracks in pieces of a 105-million-year-old limestone bed removed from the Paluxy River in the Glen Rose area to the north.

Lyndon Baines Johnson Library and Museum

One of eight presidential libraries in the country administered by the National Archives and Records Administration, the Johnson Library and Museum traces the career and influence of Johnson in the House of Representatives, the Senate, and the White House. He was elected to the Senate in 1948 under dubious circumstances—three days after his opponent had been named the winner, the infamous Ballot Box 13 in Duval County yielded 203 "overlooked" votes for Johnson, all written in the same hand, and Johnson went to Washington. He rose to be the Senate Majority Leader, served as vice president under John F. Kennedy, and assumed the presidency upon Kennedy's assassination. His administration's "Great Society" programs sought to broaden civil rights and ameliorate the lot of the poor. Johnson also heightened American involvement in the Vietnam War and declined to seek re-election in the face of intense opposition to his war policy. The LBJ Library has 35 million documents for use by scholars and researchers, some of which are still

OPPOSITE: *The Littlefield Memorial Fountain at the University of Texas at Austin, sculpted by Pompeo Coppini, with the 307-foot tower of the Main Building behind it.*

classified. Exhibits for the general public cover significant periods in LBJ's life and career as well as the reconstructed Johnson Oval Office; cases of American political memorabilia; gifts to the president; and the presidential limousine.

LOCATION: 2313 Red River Street. HOURS: 9–5 Daily. FEE: None. TELEPHONE: 512–482–5137.

Eugene C. Barker Texas History Center

Just behind the LBJ Library is one of the state's most important historical repositories, named after Eugene C. Barker, history professor, author, editor, and director of the Texas State Historical Association for over twenty years. Among Barker's major accomplishments were the establishment of a strong University of Texas history department, and the explosion of the widely accepted myths that the Texas Revolution and the Mexican War had been all the Mexicans' fault. Changing exhibitions display selections from the center's holdings, which include 142,000 volumes of printed material, 3,000 broadsides, and 35,000 clippings files; the personal libraries of philanthropist Ima Hogg and Dr. Ashbel Smith (president of the university's first board of regents); the Natchez Trace Collection, a large archive of documents from 1780 to 1900 relating to the Lower Mississippi Valley; rare imprints such as Cabeza de Vaca's *La Relación* (1555); and the papers of Stephen F. Austin. Major photographic holdings include work by Russell Lee, and oral history holdings include field recordings by the folklorists John A. Lomax and John Henry Faulk.

LOCATION: Sid Richardson Hall, South Mall. HOURS: 8–5 Monday–Saturday. FEE: None. TELEPHONE: 512–471–5961.

Cattle king, Confederate veteran, and major University of Texas philanthropist Major George W. Littlefield built the **Littlefield Home** (24th Street and Whitis, 512–471–5424) in 1893–1894. By then the most ornate Victorian styles were giving way to the simpler Classic Revival in much of the United States, but were the height of fashion in Texas. The Littlefield Home, designed by the San Antonio architect James Wahrenberger, features a turreted bay, wraparound double gallery with wrought-iron work, and many ornate details. The red bricks of the house, which cost ten cents apiece, were shipped from Saint Louis, and the pointed joints consist not of mere cement but of an extremely fine compound of white marble dust. Red sandstone, limestone, blue granite, tile, and slate are also worked into the exterior. The interior features fifteen different kinds of wood. The first floor, the only one open to the public, has been furnished to reflect typical High Victorian taste, although the family's original interior decoration, created by the Chicago department store Marshall Field, was quite different. The Littlefield Home is now occupied by the University of Texas Development Office.

The architect Charles O'Connell designed the exuberant Classic Revival **Goodall Wooten House** (700 Martin Luther King Boulevard, 512–472–1343), which was built in 1898 for an Austin physician and civic leader and altered in 1910. The brick house now serves as a medical facility.

Neill–Cochran House

Another Abner Cook gem, this antebellum mansion a few blocks west of the university was built for the Washington Hill family in 1855 and is named for the last two owners, Colonel Andrew Neill and Judge T. B. Cochran. Originally the house was on forty acres of land and was reached via a tree-lined path, now West 23d Street. In 1856 it became the first Blind Institute in the United States. Built of hand-cut limestone rubble slabs, the house also has striking Doric columns marching across the front, using native materials for a Texas version of the Greek Revival style. The house had an unstable existence until after the Civil War. The Hills never lived in it, apparently because Mrs. Hill thought it too far from town, and sold it to Union sympathizers; during the war it was seized by the Union army as a hospital (apparently George Armstrong Custer made this arrangement); and after the war it was considered to be haunted by the ghosts of Union soldiers interred in the yard. The house was renovated in 1876, when Colonel Neill bought it, and in 1895 it was sold to Judge Cochran. Now a museum, it is furnished with antiques spanning three centuries.

LOCATION: 2310 San Gabriel Street. HOURS: 2–5 Wednesday–Sunday. FEE: Yes. TELEPHONE: 512–478–2335.

After the Civil War, Governor Elisha M. Pease set aside some of his estate lands for freedmen to settle upon. In 1871 one freedman, Charles Griffin Clark, bought two acres and invited other blacks to settle around him. The **Clarksville Historic District** (West Lynn, Waterston, Mopac Expressway, and West 10th Street) comprises about ninety small frame houses built from Clark's time into the early twentieth century. Of particular interest are the **Tucker-Haskell House** (1702 Waterston, private), built in 1875 by a former slave, Peter Tucker, and sold in 1885 to a former buffalo soldier and Union trooper, Hezekiah Haskell; and the **Sweet Home Baptist Church** (1727 West 11th Street), a frame structure built in 1882 with a basilica plan and clerestory, whose congregation has been active since that time. The 500-year-old **Treaty Oak** at 503 Baylor was, according to legend, a meeting place for Indians and whites.

Laguna Gloria Art Museum

A contemporary art museum whose permanent attraction is its setting and architecture, Laguna Gloria is a Mediterranean-style stuccoed villa built in 1916. Stephen F. Austin once owned this land and meant to build his last home here on the Colorado River at the foot of Mount Bonnell. The villa was built by Clara Driscoll Sevier, who at the age of 22 led the fight and provided the money to save the Alamo from exploitation or destruction by commercial interests. A carved fireplace mantel, made from a beam from the Alamo, depicts the famous battle. Mrs. Sevier's husband, Henry, whom she met during her campaign to save the Alamo, was a journalist who went on to become a legislator and U.S. ambassador to Chile. Mrs. Sevier gave Laguna Gloria to the Texas Fine Arts Association in 1943. She landscaped the grounds in a natural style with native plants. The gates to the museum, which bear Texas stars, once protected entrances to the state capitol. The rose window at the east entrance is a copy of the original at Mission San José in San Antonio.

LOCATION: 3809 West 35th Street. HOURS: 10–5 Tuesday–Saturday, 1–5 Sunday, 5–9 Thursday. FEE: Yes. TELEPHONE: 512–458–8191.

Elisabet Ney Museum

This museum preserves the last sculpture studio of Elisabet Ney, who was born in Münster in 1833. During the late 1850s and early 1860s, Ney modeled the likenesses of some of the most influential European figures of the day, among them King Ludwig II of Bavaria, Alexander von Humboldt, Arthur Schopenhauer, Otto von Bismarck, and Giuseppe Garibaldi. During the Franco-Prussian War, Ney and her husband moved to Georgia and two years later to a plantation near Hempstead, just west of Houston, where they began farming and raising their two boys. By the late 1880s, Ney was ready to resume

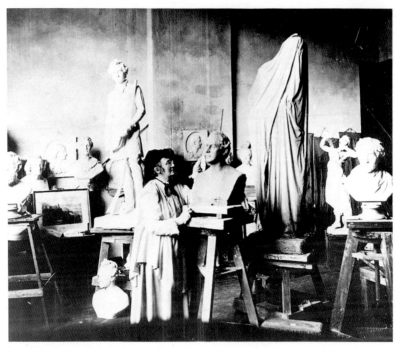

Elisabet Ney putting finishing touches on a bust of William Jennings Bryan in her Austin studio in 1900.

her career. She was commissioned to do statues of Sam Houston and Stephen F. Austin for the World's Columbian Exposition in Chicago in 1893. By 1892 she had built the first part of her studio in what was then the countryside north of Austin. The studio began as a tall plastered-limestone building with a wooden platform in a corner on which there were a sleeping hammock and a small bathtub. Ney reached the platform by ladder, and from the platform she could go onto the roof through a little door she called the "skytrap."

As Ney's reputation grew, her studio became a gathering place for art lovers. During her years in Austin, Ney sculpted such important figures as Sul Ross, Albert Sidney Johnston, and Swante Palm. The studio—a romantic amalgam of Texan and German architecture—now displays a large collection of plaster models and finished marbles of many of Ney's most famous works.

LOCATION: 304 East 44th Street. HOURS: 10–5 Wednesday–Saturday, 12–5 Sunday. FEE: None. TELEPHONE: 512–458–2255.

One of the oldest houses in town, the Greek Revival **Michael Paggi House** (200 Lee Barton Drive, private) was built in 1860 by a prominent early Austin businessman, an Italian immigrant, at what had been a Colorado River crossing on the frontier. Farther south is **Saint Edward's University** (3001 South Congress Avenue), chartered in 1885 by the founder of Notre Dame, Edward Sorin. The campus is located on 180 acres on a hill overlooking downtown Austin. The **Main Building** was first constructed in 1887 by Galveston architect Nicholas J. Clayton and is of the Gothic Revival style. Its towering red steeples can be seen for many miles in any direction. Although totally destroyed by fire in 1903, it was reconstructed the same year. The third floor houses the Maloney Room, once the school chapel, resplendent with its rose-patterned stained-glass window. Another historic campus building is **Sorin Hall,** built in 1913 to house the French Sisters of Saint Mary of the Presentation. The Sorin Oak, a large umbrella oak thought to be more than 100 years old, was said to have caught Father Sorin's eye and caused him to choose this site for the "Notre Dame of the Southwest." **Our Lady Queen of Peace Chapel** was built in 1897 as an auditorium. Over the years it has served as an engineering shop, a storage facility, and as a classroom, and it was used during World War II as an armory and rifle range. When converted into a chapel in 1948 it was named Our Lady Queen of Victory. The name was changed in 1973 to honor Saint Edward's students who lost their lives in war.

A score of old street lights called **Moonlight Towers** still operate in Austin. Each is a 150-foot-high triangle-shaped wrought-iron and cast-iron tower, the only remaining such municipal fixtures in the country. Built in 1894 and 1895, they were once common.

Northeast of Austin, off Braker Lane on Route I-35, is the **Jourdan Bachman Pioneer Farm** (11418 Sprinkle Cut-off Road, 512–837–1215). This 1880s living-history museum re-creates the daily lives of three Texas "families": the Homesteaders, typical Appalachian and Southern immigrants to Texas who independently worked the frontier; the Commercial Cotton Farmers, wealthier farmers who raised cotton for the world market and lived somewhat higher on the hog; and the Tenant Farmers, featuring the stark injustices of the sharecropping life.

OPPOSITE: *In the Texas Room of the Elisabet Ney Museum, formerly the artist's studio, are the plaster models of her statues of several noted Texans, and Lady Macbeth.*

COLORADO RIVER VALLEY

BASTROP

Established in 1832 in the northwestern corner of the Austin colony, Bastrop was named in honor of "Baron" Felipe Enrique Neri de Bastrop, a swindler and poseur who was able to pass as a nobleman. He became the first Texan representative elected to the Mexican legislature. He enjoyed the favor of the Mexican governor, sold real estate to Aaron Burr, and later negotiated the establishment of the Austin colony. As land commissioner he issued the original land grant titles to Austin's Old Three Hundred. It is said that Bastrop had fled Holland because he was accused of embezzlement; a reward of 1,000 ducats was posted in Holland for his return.

Housed in the **Old Haynie Building** (1010 College Street, 512–321–2419), the chamber of commerce provides information and a walking and driving tour of historic sites. Many early structures employed the much-prized wood from the nearby forest of "Lost Pines," now **Bastrop State Park** (off Route 71). Among the more important buildings are three Greek Revival houses: the 1857 **Henry Crocheran-McDowell House** (1502 Wilson Street), built for a prominent merchant; the **Allen-Bell House** (1408 Church Street), with unusual board-and-batten sheathing, built in 1855; and the **Josiah Wilbarger House** (1403 Main Street), built in 1842 for one of Bastrop's earliest settlers, who is said to have survived a scalping. The **Governor Joseph D. Sayers House** (1703 Wilson Street) was built in 1868 as a "bachelor's cottage" for a Confederate soldier turned politician who was elected governor in 1899. The stuccoed brick **Bastrop County Courthouse** (805 Pine Street) was built in 1883 and shares Public Square with the **Bastrop County Jail** (1892).

LA GRANGE

La Grange is the seat of Fayette County (named for the Marquis de Lafayette), one of the most picturesque in the state, with a landscape of gently rolling Colorado River bottomlands and blackland prairie, dotted with evidence of mid- and late-nineteenth-century Anglo-American and German-Czech settlement. La Grange, part of the original Austin colony, was founded in 1831 by Colonel John

Henry Moore from Tennessee. In 1835 Moore raised volunteers to go to Gonzales, where he commanded the force that fired the first shot of the Texas Revolution. The **Fayette Heritage Museum and Archives/Fayette Public Library** (855 South Jefferson Street, 409–968–6418) has exhibitions of documents, photographs, and artifacts reflecting the history of the area, as well as a Texana Collection of 600 titles and extensive genealogical records. The **N. W. Faison Home and Museum** (822 South Jefferson Street, 409–968–5532) started out as a simple frame house in 1841. Three rooms were added to the front in 1855, and the facade was embellished with jigsaw detailing including an unusual balustrade. Faison bought the house in 1866 and lived here until his death in 1870. The house has the furnishings and paintings of Faison's brother's family, who moved into the house in 1870. Faison himself was a survivor of the Dawson Massacre during the Mexican Invasion in 1842, when Texans fighting under Nicholas Dawson were killed by Mexicans after they had already dropped their arms.

On Courthouse Square stands the **Fayette County Courthouse** (1890–1891), an exuberant Richardsonian Romanesque structure of limestone and blue sandstone with granite and red Pecos sandstone details, designed by James Riely Gordon. Also on the square is the Gothic Revival **Fayette County Jail,** built in 1881 by Andrewarthe and Wahrenberger, with a crenelated tower and angled wings. In the mid-1930s two members of the Bonnie and Clyde gang were jailed here for robbing a bank in nearby Carmine. The Shingle-style **Saint James Episcopal Church** (Monroe and Colorado streets, 409–968–3810) was built in 1885 by Richard Mitchell Upjohn, the son of the prominent church architect Richard Upjohn. The wooden-framed church with a steeply pitched roof and geometrically decorated tower was also built to respond well to the climate; the pews are flanked with louvered and screened openings. Reverend W. G. W. Smith designed the altar, lectern, bishop's chair, and communion rail, which are still in use, as well as the memorial window.

MONUMENT HILL AND
KREISCHE BREWERY STATE HISTORIC SITE

In September 1848, with Sam Houston among the attending dignitaries, the remains of Texans who had died in the Dawson Massacre

and on the Mier Expedition were entombed on a high bluff overlooking the Colorado River, which then came to be called
Monument Hill. Within a few months, the land on which the tomb
lay was purchased by Heinrich Ludwig Kreische, an immigrant
stonemason from Saxony who built a homestead and a brewery.
After his death in 1882 the brewery fell into ruin, as did the tomb.
A new tomb encasing the old one was completed in 1933. During
the Texas centennial in 1936 the state erected the present forty-
eight-foot monument. The Kreische family continued to occupy
their house until 1952, when the last family member died. The
charming three-story house, which has German *Fachwerk* elements,
is built into the side of a slope and made of coursed rubble sandstone quarried on the site.

> LOCATION: Spur 92 off Route 77 just south of La Grange. HOURS:
> 8–5 Daily. FEE: Yes. TELEPHONE: 409–968–5658.

COLUMBUS

On the Colorado River, Columbus, with a population of about
4,000, is the oldest surveyed and platted Anglo-American town in
the state. A former Karankawa campsite, it was settled in 1821 by the
Kentucky brothers Robert and Joseph Kuykendall and Red River settler Daniel Gilleland, who were among the Old Three Hundred
land grantees. In 1823 Stephen F. Austin and "Baron" de Bastrop
surveyed the village as a potential capital of the colony; that capital
ended up being San Felipe, but this village remained. During Sam
Houston's retreat to San Jacinto, and the "Runaway Scrape" of men,
women, and children fleeing the Mexican army, the Texas army
burned Columbus's buildings to keep them from the Mexicans;
after the victory at San Jacinto, the town was rebuilt. The **Abram and
Nancy Alley Log Cabin** (1226 Bowie Street, 409–732–5135), one of
the first houses to be rebuilt, was moved from its original site about
eight miles southeast and is furnished in the style of the Texas colonial period. The area around Columbus is rich farmland, and after
the revolution, plantations and a wealthy planter class grew up. The

OPPOSITE: *Raumonda, built in 1887 by Henry Ilse, is one of many turn-of-the-century houses in Columbus, a town founded in the 1820s by members of Stephen F.
Austin's colony.*

town was a cotton shipping point as well, as the Colorado was navigable by steamships to this point.

The Columbus Chamber of Commerce, which offers tours of some of the fifty-five historic houses and sites in town, has offices in the **Stafford Opera House** (Spring Street, across from Courthouse Square, 409–732–5881). Built in 1886 by Galveston architect Nicholas J. Clayton, the High Victorian Italianate opera house with intricate brick detailing was funded by millionaire rancher Bob Stafford, who, it is said, situated his own house next door in such a way that he could lie in bed and see the opera house stage.The **Colorado County Courthouse** (Courthouse Square) was built by the Houston architect Eugene T. Heiner in 1890–1891 on the site of several previous courthouses. Recent restoration uncovered a stained-glass dome above the district courtroom. Also on Courthouse Square is the unusual **Confederate Memorial Hall Museum,** housed in an 1883 water tower made of 400,000 handmade bricks. Collections include memorabilia and documents relating to early Anglo Texas.

The **Senftenberg-Brandon House** (616 Walnut Street, 409–732–5135) was built in the 1860s by the Phoecian Tate family (he was later the mayor of Dallas) as a four-room Greek Revival cottage. The Senftenberg family bought the house in the 1880s and added the second floor, verandahs, and elaborate Victorian detailing. The house is now a museum depicting small-town life. Some nineteenth-century houses have been turned into bed-and-breakfast inns, including the 1887 **Raumonda** (1100 Bowie Street), the 1870 **Gant House** (936 Bowie Street), and the ca. 1865 **Montgomery House** (1419 Milam Street). The restored Greek Revival **Dilue Rose Harris House** (602 Washington Street, 409–732–5881) was built with tabby construction, a West Indian technique mixing gravel, sand, and lime with water and pouring it into molds; while drying, the mixture was scored to resemble blocks of stone. This is the only tabby house remaining of at least ten in town. Built in 1860 by Ira and Dilue Rose Harris, it has been furnished with Texas furniture provided by local citizens or acquired by a previous occupant, a historian. Dilue Harris wrote memoirs about her early family life and her father's acquaintance with the leaders of the Texas Revolution. The memoirs, which incorporate her father's diary, are among the most important primary sources of Texas colonial history.

BRAZOS RIVER VALLEY

STEPHEN F. AUSTIN STATE HISTORICAL PARK

This historical park on the muddy Brazos River occupies part of the original town site of San Felipe de Austin. (Residents of the town pronounce it "San Phillip"—Austin himself spelled it "Fillip" in an early letter to his sister.) Founded in 1823 on a high prairie at the old Atascosita crossing, the village was the seat of the Stephen F. Austin colony. During the march of Mexican president Antonio López de Santa Anna in pursuit of Sam Houston and the revolution's "Runaway Scrape," San Felipe, like so many other settlements on the armies' path, was burned to the ground by Texans before they fled. After the Battle of San Jacinto, the village of San Felipe was rebuilt, but Houston became the capital of the new republic. When the county seat was moved from San Felipe to Bellville in 1848, the former lost its prominence. About 1880 the town was moved a mile and a half from its original site (but still within the original plat) to be close to the railroad. The historical park features a replica of the log cabin in which Stephen F. Austin ran the affairs of his colony, and the original J. J. Josey General Store Museum, built in 1847, which displays local pioneer artifacts as well as Stephen F. Austin's desk, flag, and a dish of splinters from his coffin. The old ferry crossing, monuments, and statues are also on the grounds.

> LOCATION: Park Road 38, just north of San Felipe. HOURS: *Park Headquarters:* 8–5 Daily; extended hours in summer months. *J. J. Josey General Store Museum:* 1–5 Saturday–Sunday. FEE: Yes. TELEPHONE: 409–885–3613, –2181.

On country roads in the vicinity of San Felipe are the Romanesque Revival **Austin County Jail** (417 North Chesley), built in 1896, in **Bellville;** the old **Industry Post Office** in **Industry** (Main Street and F.M. 109), the only post office west of Galveston when it opened in 1838 (Industry is one of the oldest German settlements in Texas); and the octagonal frame **Cat Spring Agricultural Society Hall** in **Cat Spring.** Several of the bottomland counties have German and Czech churches with fine painted interiors. The wooden frame **Wesley Brethren Church** was built in 1866 in **Welcome,** with trompe l'oeil architectural patterns. The Gothic Revival stone **Church of the Guardian Angel** (5614 Demel Street) in **Wallis** has a polychromed, stenciled, and marbled interior. Built in **Praha** in 1895, **Saint Mary's Church of the Assumption** (F.M. 1295) is another Gothic Revival rusticated stone church with an interior marked by freehand religious symbols and floral patterns. In **Ammansville** is **Saint John the Baptist Catholic Church** (F.M. 1383), a frame Gothic Revival structure built in 1907 with freehand and stenciled floral patterns inside. **Nativity of Mary, Blessed Virgin Catholic Church** (F.M. 2672) in **High Hill,** is brick with stone trim and freehand symbols and floral patterns decorating the interior.

ANDERSON

The tiny town of Anderson grew up in the Austin colony as Fanthorp in 1834 with the establishment of the Fanthorp Inn on La Bahia Road, an east–west trail between southwestern Louisiana and southeastern Texas used by Indians for hundreds of years and later by Spanish explorers. The **Anderson Historic District** runs along Main Street, the location of the **Grimes County Courthouse,** an Italianate brick-and-stone building built in 1891 with an outside stair; and the Greek Revival **Anderson Baptist Church** of 1853–1855.

Fanthorp Inn State Historic Site

Visitors at Henry Fanthorp's frontier hotel and tavern included Texas presidents Sam Houston and Anson Jones, Jefferson Davis (before he became president of the Confederacy), Generals Robert E. Lee and Stonewall Jackson, and two future U.S. presidents, Zachary Taylor and Ulysses S. Grant. The first part of the structure was a cedar dogtrot house built in 1834; Fanthorp, an Englishman, added a second story in late 1850. For years Fanthorp's was on all the stage lines through the area. Although there were other inns in the town, Fanthorp's was preferred for its food and entertainment. One guest wrote of a ball for 150 commemorating the Battle of San Jacinto in 1851: "Mr. & Mrs. Fanthorp took all pains in their power to get the supper up in good order & style & succeeded beyond my expectations if they had had nice furniture & crockery it would have been hard to beat." The hotel operated until Fanthorp and his wife died from yellow fever in 1867; their descendants lived in the house until the 1970s. The restored inn has been furnished by the state in mid-nineteenth-century style, as travelers would have found it, without the luxury of chamber pots, stoves for heat, or wash basins in the rooms. The grounds include the family cemetery and a barn for stagecoaches and horses. A replica of the nine-passenger Concord stagecoach, the type used throughout the West, is on view and is used for special events.

LOCATION: Main Street, south of the courthouse. HOURS: 8–5 Wednesday–Sunday. FEE: Yes. TELEPHONE: 409–873–2633.

WASHINGTON-ON-THE-BRAZOS STATE HISTORICAL PARK

The village of Washington arose after Andrew Robinson began operating a ferry across the Brazos River here in 1822. It was the first and last capital of the Republic of Texas and was the scene of the enactment of the Texas Declaration of Independence on March 2, 1836, while the Alamo was under siege. The declaration was based on the Jeffersonian model, opening with: "When a government has ceased to protect the lives, liberty and property of the people, from whom its legitimate powers are derived . . . ." A constitution was written by March 16, and an interim government was elected—David G. Burnet as president, Lorenzo de Zavala as vice president, and Thomas Rusk as secretary of war. Sam Houston was appointed commander in chief with full powers over the Texas army, which he had to create before he could command. Washington was a town of about 100 when the convention took place; the meetings were held in what came to be called **Independence Hall,** an unfinished frame building of which a replica now stands in the historical park. The park headquarters features an orientation exhibit and film about the convention of 1836. The home of the last president of the republic, Anson Jones, was moved to the park from nearby. Called **Barrington** after his birthplace in Massachusetts, it is a one-and-one-half-story white frame house built in 1844 with two chimneys at each end. It is appointed with republic-era furnishings. The **Star of the Republic Museum,** a star-shaped edifice, is devoted to the history of the Republic of Texas and includes a research library.

LOCATION: F.M. 1155, Washington. HOURS: *Park:* 8 AM–Dusk Daily. *Museums:* March through August: 10–5 Daily; September through February: 10–5 Wednesday–Sunday. FEE: Yes, for Barrington. TELEPHONE: 409–878–2214.

BRENHAM

The seat of Washington County, Brenham was founded by Jabez Deming Giddings in 1844 and was named for Richard Fox Brenham, who was killed during a rebellion of the Mier Expedition prisoners. After the Civil War, Brenham was made a military post; friction arose between the citizens and the black troops garrisoned there and resulted in the troops partially burning down the town. A heavy influx of German immigrants moved into Brenham during Reconstruction. Among the historic buildings in town are the frame Greek Revival **Giddings-Wilkin House** (805 Crockett Street, private), the first house (1843) of the town founder, lawyer and civic leader Giddings. In 1870, after a yellow fever epidemic, Giddings built the **Giddings-Stone Mansion** (204 East Stone Street, private) on the highest hill in Brenham. He had noticed that people living at higher elevations were less likely to contract the fever (his widow remodeled the house in the 1890s, adding bay windows and columned galleries). The Carpenter Gothic **Pampell-Day House** (409 West Alamo) started out as a Greek Revival cottage in 1840 and was remodeled in 1875.

Just north of Brenham in the little village of **Independence,** the **Texas Baptist Historical Center-Museum** (F.M. 50 and F.M. 390, 409–836–5117) has historical and genealogical records pertaining to the congregation of the **Independence Baptist Church,** the third-oldest Baptist church in Texas and the one to which Sam Houston's very devout third wife, Margaret Moffette Lea Houston, belonged. Mrs. Houston successfully urged Houston himself to join the church; he was baptized in 1854. The present church building was built in 1872. Mrs. Houston and her mother are buried in the cemetery across the street. Independence was first known as Coles Settlement, for Judge John P. Coles' land grant in 1823; the name was changed in 1836 after the signing of the Texas Declaration of Independence. The **Judge Cole House** (F.M. 390, private) was built in 1824. The **Toalson House,** built in 1835 of two-foot-thick adobe, is the only Spanish-style house in the area; at one time it was a jail. The ruins of **Old Baylor University,** which was founded in Independence (it moved to Waco in 1886), can be seen off F.M. 390 a quarter-mile west of town in Old Baylor Park.

OPPOSITE: *A frame house of about 1855, built by the Schuhmann family and preserved at Round Top, is decorated with elaborate stencils.*

ROUND TOP

As part of Fayette County, where many of the earliest German immigrants to Texas settled, Round Top is among the country towns in
the area where some German is still spoken. On the way into town
from Brenham, one encounters the **Festival-Institute** on Festival Hill
(Route 237, 409–249–3129), a music institute, part of whose facilities occupy two Victorian buildings, the 1884 **William Lockhart
Clayton House** and the 1902 **Menke House Conference Center.**

Henkel Square

The Texas Pioneer Arts Foundation has brought together six Anglo
and German buildings from early Texas, two of which were originally on the site and have been furnished by Mrs. Charles L. Bybee of
Houston with an excellent collection of Texas pioneer furniture.
Buildings include the **Edward Henkel House** (ca. 1852), a two-story
white clapboard frame house with an outside stair, built for Round
Top's hardware store owner and first justice of the peace and mayor;
the storybook white frame **Haw Creek Schoolhouse-Church** (1872),
complete with bell tower; the **Muckelroy House,** a log cabin built
around 1840 whose walls are brightly painted with wash-bluing and
Paris green (arsenic); two houses belonging to the Schuhmann family, one dating from 1838, with a lean-to and a mud-and-daub chimney, and a more ornate frame house of about 1855 with a stenciled
interior; and the one-story frame-and-clapboard **Zapp–Von
Rosenberg House,** built in 1875.

LOCATION: Live Oak and Main streets. HOURS: 12–5 Daily. FEE: Yes.
TELEPHONE: 409–249–3308.

The stuccoed sandstone ashlar **Bethlehem Lutheran Church** (Route
237, just south of town) was built in 1866–1867 by Carl Siegismund
Bauer for a German congregation. Its most arresting features are
the stone buttresses on the south side, added in 1881 and 1882.
Inside the church is a cedar organ handmade locally in 1867 by
John Traugott Wantke. Also on Route 237 South are the tiny 1915
Saint Martin's Church, thought to be the world's smallest active
Catholic church—it has only twelve pews and one service a year but
is open at all times—and **Moore's Fort,** a very early (1828) struc-

ture built by an Indian fighter, Colonel John Henry Moore, and moved from La Grange. Two miles northwest of Round Top is the iron **Cummins Creek Bridge,** built in 1890.

WINEDALE HISTORICAL CENTER

Out in the country just four miles east of Round Top, Winedale Historical Center is an outdoor museum for the preservation and study of Texas's German and Anglo-American heritage. It was the last restoration project by Houston's famous philanthropist and decorative-arts expert, Ima Hogg. The Winedale acreage features more than ten historic buildings, but the center was started with only the **Lewis-Wagner House,** which Hogg bought in 1963 because she was drawn to its painted walls and ceilings. The house had been locally known as the Winedale Stagecoach Inn, but research showed that even though coaches on the La Bahia Road stopped for refreshments at the Lewis place, it had never been an inn.

The original portion of the Lewis-Wagner House was a log cabin built around 1828 by an Austin colonist, Will Townsend, for himself and his bride, Mary Burnham Townsend. Townsend sold the house in 1840 to a dashing frontier soldier, Captain John York, who owned it for five years before selling it to Samuel K. Lewis, a surveyor who had served in the ninth (and last) congress of the Republic of Texas. Lewis brought the house to its present size and appearance, enclosing the cabin in wood framing, turning the sleeping loft into a full second story, duplicating the whole structure to the north, and connecting the two halves with a breezeway, or double dogtrot. He also built a broad gallery across the front of the house, which gave it almost as much space outdoors as in—a boon in the hot Texas summer. Then he heard that the area had gained a most talented decorative artist, the immigrant Rudolph Melchior, and Lewis hired him to paint the interior. In contrast to the simple stenciled leaves, berries, and flowers common in many German homes of the time and area (and present in one room of this house), Melchior painted beautiful, intricate freehand designs—garlands of roses, bowls laden with fruit, parrots on the wing. The house was sold in 1882 to a successful immigrant shoemaker and farmer, Joseph George Wagner, Sr., whose family lived in the house until 1961. The interior of the house is a textbook of early Texas furniture. Hogg also furnished one room with examples of German-immigrant furniture from other parts of the country, such as Pennsylvania and Missouri, to compare regional differences in German-American design. The original Lewis farmstead included an animal barn and horse lot that still stand on the property. In 1894 the Wagners built a splendid barn from the cedar beams of an abandoned cotton gin of the 1850s. It has been adapted to serve as a meeting place and theater.

Between the Lewis-Wagner House and the original Lewis barn, Hazel's **Lone Oak Cottage,** built in 1865 by another German immigrant, Franz Jäntschke, and moved to Winedale from about two miles away, is a simple frame house with breezeway and decorated stair leading to a loft. The other major house on the property, moved here from its original site in Washington County, is the Greek Revival **McGregor-Grimm House.** It was built in 1861 by Dr. Gregor McGregor, a planter and land speculator who started a colony of Scottish North Carolinians in Texas and soon became one of the richest men of his time. In contrast to the rich materials imported by wealthy families building houses in Galveston, those used in the McGregor house were all local, but the artist Rudolph Melchior ingeniously imparted grandeur by using the full range of decorative painting techniques. For example, he plastered over the brick chimney and then painted it with a finer trompe l'oeil red-brick pattern. In contrast to the middle-class character of the Lewis-Wagner House, the McGregor-Grimm House is furnished with pieces made by known Anglo-American and German immigrant furniture makers working in Texas whose clients were equal to McGregor in wealth and position. Both houses also display textiles of the period, including a number of particularly fine quilts.

LOCATION: F.M. 1457, off F.M. 2714, 4 miles east of Round Top. HOURS: 10–5 Saturday, 12–5 Sunday, Monday–Friday by appointment. FEE: Yes. TELEPHONE: 409–278–3530.

GIDDINGS

This town, named for early Texas settler Jabez Deming Giddings, was settled by Wendish immigrants who moved from nearby

OPPOSITE: The walls and ceiling of the Melchior Room in the Lewis-Wagner House were painted by Rudolph Melchior, whose sense of order caused him to center an overmantle mural despite the actual location of the fireplace.

Serbin—the first Wendish colony in Texas—to be near the
Houston & Texas Central Railroad laid from Brenham to Austin in
1871. *The Handbook of Texas* says that "Wend is a general term used
by the Germans to designate the few remnants of the old Slavic
elements in their country." Texas and Australia have the two
largest Wendish colonies in the world. The history of this mostly
Lutheran people, who were persecuted for their religious beliefs
and emigrated to Texas from Lusatia, Germany, is explored at the
Texas Wendish Heritage Museum (Route 2, 409–366–2441).
Exhibits include an interpretive center where literature is translat-
ed from the old Wendish language and replicas of kitchens,
schoolrooms, and two log buildings. The **Lee County Museum**
(190 East Industry, 409–542–3455), housed in the late-nineteenth-
century house of a prominent Giddings physician, has local artifacts, photographs, and memorabilia. The octagonal
Richardsonian Romanesque **Lee County Courthouse** was built on
the public square in 1899 by James Riely Gordon.

NORTH-CENTRAL TEXAS

ROUND ROCK

This is the oldest town in Williamson County. The area was first settled by Anglos in the 1830s, and the little village that grew up was
called Brushy Creek. But the postmaster did not like that name when
it was formally submitted to the post office in 1854, and so a familiar
round rock in the bed of Brushy Creek gave its name to the town
instead. The rock can be seen from Chisholm Trail Road. The limestone creekbed still shows wheel ruts made by the many wagons that
crossed the creek at this spot following herds of cattle on their way
north.

The comfortable Greek Revival **Captain Nelson Merrell House**
(1514 Palm Valley Boulevard, 512–255–7852) was built in 1870.
Merrell was a frontiersman, Indian fighter, and buffalo hunter who
turned to farming. The house has a deep double gallery and a
square balustraded cupola, which some say is an Indian lookout,
although the Indians had left central Texas by this time. **Old Round
Rock and Old Slave Cemetery** (Sam Bass Road) is the final resting
place of the legendary bandit Sam Bass. In July 1878 Bass and two
members of his gang, casing Round Rock for a bank robbery, were

recognized by a deputy as they stepped into a store. As one deputy waited outside, another went into the store and asked one of the bandits if the bulge under his shirt was a gun. They shot him dead and then tried to shoot their way out of town. Although seriously wounded, Bass managed to ride out of town, but Texas Rangers soon found him, sitting in the shade of a tree, near death. The rangers carried him back into Round Rock, where he died on his twenty-seventh birthday. In years to come, he began to be regarded as a heroic figure, a Texas Robin Hood—it was said that Bass had waved his gun far more than he had shot it (the Round Rock deputy was the first and only person he killed), and Round Rock's annual Frontier Days celebration features a re-enactment of the Sam Bass shootout. Round Rock Cemetery, with graves dating back to the 1850s, is divided into an Anglo section, a Mexican section, and a slave and freedmen's section, the last of which has the most poignant markers and atmosphere.

The old **Palm House** (212 East Main Street, 512–255–5805) houses both the Chamber of Commerce, which provides information on historic sites in Round Rock, and the Palm House Museum, with period furnishings and exhibits including a Swedish kitchen. The oldest structures are found in what is now known as **Old Town,** just west of Route I-35. **Harris Stagecoach Inn** (Chisholm Trail at F.M. 620) was built around 1850 of locally quarried limestone. The **Old Post Office** (8 Chisholm Trail) dates from 1853; the **Saint Charles Hotel,** next to it, was originally the home of a local physician, Dr. William Owen. Descendants of Williamson County pioneer settlers still gather in Round Rock each July at week-long reunions sponsored by The Old Settlers Association, chartered in 1900.

GEORGETOWN

The seat of Williamson County, named for "Three-Legged Willie" Williamson, a crippled hero of San Jacinto, Georgetown was founded in 1848 on a site donated by land developer George Washington Glassock, Jr., whose gift depended on the town being named for him. Georgetown is now best known for **Southwestern University** (University Avenue, 512–863–6511), a Methodist school founded in 1840 by merging several older colleges. (Southwestern and Baylor both claim to be the oldest college in the state.) In the early days of the university, students tended toward gun toting and had to check their arms with the authorities; nonetheless, the school managed to produce ten ministers in the first nine years of its operation. The Richardsonian Romanesque **Cullen Building (Old Main)** was built in 1898 by Robert S. Hyer, the second president of the university, employing the same Scottish craftsmen who had built the granite state capitol ten years earlier; the simpler **Mood-Bridwell Hall,** by C. H. Page, went up in 1900. Originally a men's dormitory, the building now houses offices and the **Mood-Heritage Museum** (512–836–1997) with exhibits on local and area history, natural history, science, and religion.

The remarkably intact pre-World War I **Williamson County Courthouse Historic District** (city center) comprises thirty-eight buildings on parts of nine blocks, including the Beaux-Arts brick **Williamson County Courthouse** (1911); the limestone **Williamson County Jail** (1889); the 1896 **M. B. Lockett Building** (119 West 7th Street), limestone with a red-brick facade, pressed-metal cornice, and domed turret; and the **Fire Station** (Main and 9th streets), an L-shaped limestone structure built in 1893 around a 150-foot-tall, 15-foot-diameter standpipe for the city's water supply.

SALADO

The railroad's bypassing of this town meant that its character was better preserved than many another town experiencing "progress." Salado (Spanish for "salty") was founded on Salado Creek (not a salty body of water) in 1859. Elijah Sterling Clack Robertson donated land near his plantation for the establishment of Salado College, and the town grew up with it. The stabilized ruins of the college, which was possibly the first nondenominational coeducational college west of the Mississippi, are on Main Street. The restored frame **Stagecoach Inn** (Main and Front streets) is the oldest structure in Salado (now housing a restaurant), built in 1853 to serve coach passengers on the old Military Highway. Its guests included Sam Houston, Robert E. Lee, George Armstrong Custer, and others. Houston made one of his antisecession speeches from the second-floor verandah. Across the street is the **Central Texas Area Museum** (1 Main Street, 817–947–5232), a good local museum. The **Colonel Elijah Sterling Clack Robertson Plantation** (Route I-35, west of town, private), home of the founder of Salado, is a two-story Greek Revival frame residence (1852–1857), unusual in Texas for the galleries balancing the central portico. President Lyndon B. Johnson's great-grandfather lived in the 1866 saltbox **George Washington Baines House** (Royal Street, private). A Baptist minister, Baines was one of the presidents of Baylor Female College. The Greek Revival **Twelve Oaks** (Center Circle, private) was completed in 1869 for Dr. D. B. McKie; during the Civil War, a distillery had been run on the property to make alcohol for medical use in the Confederate army. **Salado Methodist Church** (Thomas Arnold and Episcopal Church roads) is a simple white frame Gothic-style structure built in 1890.

BELTON

Belton was established in 1850 as a center for nearby farms and ranches. In the early days, one entrepreneur sold dry goods from a wagon, another opened a "saloon," consisting of a barrel and a tin cup, under a tree. The Renaissance Revival **Bell County Courthouse** (Public Square) was built by J. N. Preston and Son in 1884–1885, and in spite of the removal of a 125-foot tower and much pressed-metal detailing, the building is still handsome. The one-story Gothic Revival **Old Saint Luke's Church** (438 North Wall Street) was built in 1874 of hand-quarried stone for an Episcopal congregation. The **Miller-Curtis House** (1004 North Main Street) is a two-story brick mansion with Queen Anne elements, eclectic millwork, and art-glass windows, built for a cotton broker in 1902. In a 1905 Carnegie Library building, the **Bell County Museum** (North Main Street and First Avenue, 817–939–2169) has exhibits on local and pioneer history. The **Beamer-Jones House** (1202 South Beal Street, private) was built in 1897 by William Frank Beamer, who owned Belton Brick, which produced the white brick used throughout central Texas.

TEMPLE

Established in 1880, Temple was served by two railroads, the Gulf, Colorado, & Santa Fe, and the Missouri, Kansas & Texas (Katy). Pioneer history and the development of the railroad in Texas is explored at the **Railroad and Pioneer Museum** (710 Jack Baskin Street, 817–778–6873), housed in the restored 1907 Santa Fe depot that once stood in Moody, Texas. (The rail line through these parts followed the old Chisholm Trail.) The **SPJST Museum** (520 North Main Street, 817–773–1575) of the Slovanská Podporující Jednota

The Grove's W.J. Dube General Store Building of 1917, with a general store, the post office, and Planters State Bank under one roof, was purchased outright to become The Grove Country Life Museum in 1972.

Státu Texas, or Slavonic Benevolent Order of the State of Texas, is an institution devoted to the preservation of the state's Czech heritage. The library and archives have a genealogical section, over 18,000 books in Czech, and hundreds of photographs. The museum has artifacts from early Czech immigrant life including costumes, costumed puppets, pioneer artifacts, and memorabilia.

West of Temple, the tiny town of The Grove is the site of **The Grove Country Life Museum** (512-282-1215). The town's general store, post office, and bank have become the repository of a collection of thousands of objects from rural Texas, amassed by a single collector. The museum also includes a saloon, a blacksmith shop, and a late-nineteenth-century doctor's office.

CAMERON

This farming town, established in 1845, was named for Ewen Cameron, a Scottish early Texas pioneer and Texas Ranger who was one of the members of the Mier Expedition to be executed. On the public square is the Renaissance Revival limestone **Milam County**

Courthouse, built in 1893 by Larmour and Watson. Also on the square is the **Milam County Historical Museum** (817-697-4770) in the old Milam County Jail, a Romanesque Revival structure of crenelated brick and limestone topped by a tower. Its collections cover the history and natural history of the area and include authentic jailhouse equipment. In **City Park** is the concert and meeting pavilion where James S. Hogg and George Clark held a gubernatorial debate in 1892.

WACO

In the heart of the fertile Blackland Prairie where the Bosque River meets the Brazos, Waco was settled in the eighteenth century by the Huaco Indians, who built their village at a spring that is now a mere trickle. A battalion of Texas Rangers established a temporary outpost here, Fort Fisher, in 1837. A bit more than a decade later a town site was laid out. Waco served cotton plantations in the Brazos Valley, a commerce that suffered during the Civil War. After the war Waco was on the route of the Chisholm Trail, the earliest and most famous cattle trail north from south Texas and San Antonio to the markets in Fort Worth and Abilene, Kansas. Waco became a rowdy cow town like many another in the cattle-kingdom era. In 1870 the first bridge over the Brazos was built, ensuring that cattle and people alike would continue to come through Waco on their way north. Baptists established Baylor University here in 1887, moving Baylor College from Independence and incorporating Waco College. It has made Waco a religious headquarters in the so-called Bible Belt of the state.

The **Waco Suspension Bridge** (Bridge Street at the river), completed in 1870, was the first bridge across Texas's longest river and the most handsome in the state at the time. The original steel cables were manufactured in Trenton, New Jersey, by the firm owned by John A. Roebling, who later designed the Brooklyn Bridge and consulted on the design of Waco's much smaller span (475 feet). In 1914 the towers were stuccoed and stripped of crenelations, and toll buildings were removed. Cars have been banned from the bridge since 1971, but it is accessible to pedestrians.

The Historic Waco Foundation (817-753-5166) administers four historic houses. The Greek Revival **Earle-Napier-Kinnard House** (814 South 4th Street) began in 1858 as a two-room brick house that was considerably expanded by a well-to-do couple who had moved here from Alabama; their descendants lived in the house until the

The Waco Suspension Bridge, built in 1869 to be wide enough for two stagecoaches to pass in opposite directions, carried wheeled traffic across the Brazos River for a century. In 1971, it was turned over to pedestrians.

1950s. Interior details include grain-painted woodwork and marbled mantelpieces. Some of the Napiers' original furniture is still in the house, most important, a Sheraton-style rosewood and ormolu pianoforte of 1818. **East Terrace,** also known as the **John Wesley Mann House** (100 Mill Street), is a brick Italianate villa, inspired by the work of Andrew Jackson Downing, built in 1872 on the east bank of the Brazos. John Wesley Mann owned the kiln that supplied bricks for the Waco Suspension Bridge as well as his own house and many others. The house was set upon a sand-and-clay terrace reinforced with brick walls. The grounds had sunken gardens, peacocks, rose gardens, and an orchard. Over the years floods have deposited layers of silt on the gardens and terraces on all but the east side of the house. The pink-brick Greek Revival **Fort House** (503 South 4th Street) was built in 1868 by Colonel W. A. Fort, a planter who started what became the First National Bank of Waco. The Fort House was bought and restored in 1956 by the Junior League of Waco. The Greek Revival **Champe Carter McCulloch House** (407 Columbus Avenue) started out as a one-story structure, now the east wing, built by Josiah and Maria Caldwell in 1866. The Caldwells sold the house to a Confederate veteran (and future Waco mayor), Champe Carter McCulloch, and his wife, Emma, in 1871 for $6,000 in gold. The floor has wide random-width boards. Damaged by a tornado and years of vandalism, the restored house has period furniture and McCulloch memorabilia, including the family Bible, the couple's marriage certificate, and a daughter's silver tea service.

Texas Ranger Hall of Fame and Museum

In the nineteenth and early twentieth centuries, the Texas Rangers were a loosely-organized law enforcement group that patrolled the frontier, fighting Indians, thieves, rustlers, and, later, Mexican bandits. The first ranger units were formed in the 1820s under the auspices of the Austin Colony. Later, the rangers were occasionally funded and controlled by the state, but in their organization, tactics, and equipage they were always irregulars. Celebrated for their skills, stamina, and bravery as trackers, horsemen, and gunmen, they were implacable pursuers of Indians and criminals, quick with a gun when their quarry had been brought to bay. They were

Every bit as tough as the desperadoes they pursued, Texas Rangers were the bulwark of law and order on the Texas frontier for most of the nineteenth century.

among the first Westerners to use the Colt six-shooter, and suggested important improvements to Samuel Colt. Their exploits in the brutal fighting with the Comanche and Apache, particularly the deeds of Captain Jack Hays, were legendary. In the violent years after the Civil War they were a major force in taming the Texas frontier. As times changed, their methods came into question. In the first decades of this century, when murder and banditry were rife along the Mexican border, rangers summarily executed hundreds, perhaps thousands of Mexicans they suspected of being bandits. Public opinion turned against the rangers, who were regarded as an anachronism. In 1919 a state review of their activities resulted in the virtual abolition of the force. Today's Texas Rangers, numbering fewer than one hundred, operate as an investigative and enforcement group within the Department of Public Safety. The museum displays a large collection of antique firearms, badges, saddles, paintings, and wax figures of rangers, depicting their dress and equipment from frontier days to modern times.

LOCATION: Route I-35 and University Parks Boulevard. HOURS: September through May: 9–5 Daily; June through August: 9–6 Daily. FEE: Yes. TELEPHONE: 817–754–1433.

Masonic Grand Lodge Library and Museum of Texas

This massive edifice was built between 1948 and 1953 as the Grand Lodge Temple, the Masonic headquarters in Texas. The front steps pass through freestanding obelisks, the "Pillars of the Porch," to the entrance, which is flanked at the base by friezes depicting the building of King Solomon's temple. Inside are the temple, an auditorium, a Memorial Room to honor Masons who have lost their lives in war, and the library and museum. The lodge's collection includes original letters of Stephen F. Austin; some of Sam Houston's papers, as well as the gavel he used while presiding over the first Grand Lodge meeting in the Republic of Texas; jewels and aprons dating to the American Revolution; and a 4,000-year-old "terracotta cone" from Egypt. There is also a gallery of U.S. presidents who were Masons.

LOCATION: 715 Columbus Avenue. HOURS: 9–4 Monday–Friday. FEE: None. TELEPHONE: 817–753–7395.

Armstrong-Browning Library

In 1918 Dr. A. Joseph Armstrong presented Baylor University with his private collection of documents and artifacts associated with Robert Browning and Elizabeth Barrett Browning. From that gift grew the largest Browning collection in the world, including first editions, numerous original manuscripts, most of the scholarly articles and books written on the two English poets, and hundreds of drawings, paintings, and sculptures of the couple, including a bronze cast of their clasped hands made by the American artist Harriet Hosmer. The collection is housed in an Italian Renaissance-style building finished in 1951. The grandest room is the McLean Foyer of Meditation, a forty-foot cube with three cathedral windows, a twenty-three-karat-gold dome ceiling and eight Levanto columns from Italy. The library also owns furniture and other personal items of the Brownings.

> LOCATION: 700 Speight Street, Baylor University campus. HOURS: 9–12, 2–4 Monday–Friday, 9–12 Saturday. FEE: None. TELEPHONE: 817–755–3566.

Commercial buildings of historic interest in Waco include the architect James Riely Gordon's 1901 **McLennan County Courthouse** (Public Square) in the Beaux-Arts style; the 1915 **Praetorian Building** (601 Franklin Street) with a brick and terra-cotta facade, built for a life insurance company; and the **Home of Dr. Pepper (Artesian Manufacturing and Bottling Company Building)** (300 South 5th Street), a Richardsonian Romanesque brick structure with huge rusticated stone arches built for the bottling company that produced the Texas soda pop invented in 1885 by a local pharmacist, Charles C. Alderton. The **Hippodrome (Waco Theater)** (724 Austin Avenue) was built in 1913 with a Sullivanesque facade and remodeled in 1929 with Spanish Colonial Revival elements.

Torrey's Trading House Number 2 (east of Waco off Route 6) comprises the remnants—six or seven log houses and warehouses constructed about 1844—of the second in a line of trading posts set up along the Indian frontier by the brothers John, David, and Thomas Torrey. Torrey's, located on a tributary of Tehuacana Creek, was officially recognized as an Indian trading station by Republic of Texas law in 1843. Sam Houston was a partner in the post and

friend to the brothers, encouraging them to adopt his own peaceful approach to the Indians. During his terms as president of the republic, Houston tried to moderate the antipathy of Anglos toward the Indians and usurpation of their lands. From 1844 to 1846, it appeared that he might succeed. A series of great Indian councils—bringing together the Delaware, Caddo, Huaco, Shawnee, Hainai, Andarko, Tawakoni, Wichita, Kichai, Chickasaw, Biloxi, Cherokee, and ultimately the Comanche—and meetings with Texas officials, including Houston himself, took place in the vicinity of Torrey's Trading House. On November 16, 1845, the final treaty between the Texans and the Indians was signed at Torrey's. The result of these meetings and understandings was a brief period of dramatically improved relations. But slightly more than a month after the final treaty, Texas was admitted to the Union and surrendered "control" of the Indians to the United States. The ensuing decades saw the decimation or removal of most tribes from Texas.

HIGHLANDS MANSION

This chateauesque white-painted brick mansion was built in 1900 by Basil C. Clark as a wedding present to his wife. Clark, a Confederate veteran, moved to Marlin after the Civil War, founded the First National Bank of Marlin, and became a cotton broker and cattleman. Little expense was spared on the Clarks' latter-day plantation house: Twin parlors have cove ceilings richly ornamented with garlands and ribbons and gold-leaf borders; a two-and-a-half-story stained-glass dome curves over the great hall; the dining room has a silver-plated chandelier and a built-in china cabinet with doors of beveled and cut glass. The house was restored in the 1960s, with the addition of Victorian and French furniture complementary to five pieces original to the house. The grounds include a rose garden, and over the years the number of live oak trees planted by the several owners has grown to fifty-two.

LOCATION: 147 East Groesbeck Highway, Marlin. HOURS: 10–4 Monday–Saturday, 1–4 Sunday. FEE: Yes. TELEPHONE: 817–883–5234.

OPPOSITE: *The John Leddy-Jones Research Hall in the Armstrong-Browning Library has ten stained glass windows illustrating Robert Browning's poems.*

OLD FORT PARKER STATE HISTORIC SITE

One of the most famous stories of pioneer Texas began here. Fort Parker was a private stockade built in 1834 around a few pioneer cabins on the prairie fringed by the Post Oak Belt, then the western edge of the east Texas frontier. On the morning of May 19, 1836, a band of 50 to 200 Comanche and Kiowa Indians killed several people at the fort (perhaps in revenge for being cheated in a horse deal) and rode off with five captives—two women and three children. The two women were eventually returned to the whites. Two of the children were found and ransomed some years after the capture, but one of them, John Parker, refused to stay in white society. He returned to the Comanche and ultimately married a Mexican girl who had also been taken by the Indians. The last kidnapped child was John's older sister Cynthia Ann Parker, 9 years old at her capture. Cynthia Ann grew up to marry and bear the children of Peta Nocone, a Comanche chief. Twice when white men came across her in their meetings with the Indians she indicated that she had no desire to return to white society. Almost twenty-five years after her capture, in 1860, she and her eighteen-month-old daughter, Prairie Flower, were recaptured at a Comanche camp on the Pease River when they were surprised by Texas Ranger captain Sul Ross and a band of men. Mother and child were taken to Camp Cooper for positive identification. Cynthia Ann did not speak English, but she recognized her English name. Her family, who had become prominent in Texas in the years since they had lost her, took her back and tried their best to influence her to adopt their ways, but she refused to do so. She continually tried to escape and was kept under guard. Prairie Flower caught diphtheria and died at the age of 4. In mourning, Cynthia Ann Parker scarified her breast and starved herself to death in the same year. Peta Nocone, it is said, mourned profoundly at losing his wife, searched for her in vain, and died a few years later from a wound. Their older son, Quanah, grew up to be the last chief of the Kwahadi Comanche, leading them at the battles of Adobe Walls and the Palo Duro Canyon. In 1875 Quanah (who later took his mother's Anglo surname) led the few remaining members of his tribe to the reservation at Fort Sill,

Oklahoma. Quanah Parker went on to become a rancher, a judge, part-owner of a railroad, and a spokesman for Indian peoples. He also founded the Native American Church.

Old Fort Parker has been reconstructed as the place it was in 1836 at the time of Cynthia Ann and John Parker's capture, with cabins and blockhouses.

> LOCATION: Route 14, 4 miles north of Groesbeck. HOURS: 8–5 Wednesday–Sunday. FEE: Yes. TELEPHONE: 817–729–5253.

Northeast of the fort is the railroad town of **Teague,** where the **Burlington–Rock Island Railroad Museum** (208 South Third Avenue, 817–739–2645) occupies the 1906 Spanish Colonial Revival depot. Displays include railroad memorabilia, a two-room log cabin filled with period furniture, an old locomotive, local-history rooms, and a Boy Scouts Room. In **Fairfield,** the **Freestone County Historical Museum** (302 East Main Street, 214–389–3738) is housed in the old county jail, built of handmade bricks in 1857. Collections include documents, military uniforms from seven wars, and county memorabilia and photographs. On the grounds are two restored buildings, the 1845 Carter Log House and the 1851 Potter-Watson Log Cabin, both with period furnishings.

THE HILL COUNTRY

The Hill Country is formed by the Balcones Escarpment, the wide, crumbling edge of the Edwards Plateau, marked by limestone ledges (*balcones* means balconies) overlooking clear green rivers lined with cypress trees. Most of the Hill Country was held by the Apache and very sparsely settled until after statehood. The eastern edge of the Hill Country was settled in the 1840s by the earliest German immigrants to Texas; the German character is still very much in evidence in the architecture and cultural activities. The Western Trail (or Dodge City Trail) through the heart of the Hill Country was an important route north after 1876. Goat and sheep ranching has been prevalent, profitable, and environmentally destructive in the Hill Country since the 1850s.

BURNET

One of the earliest U.S. Army forts built to protect settlers moving into Indian country was Fort Croghan at present-day Burnet. Built in 1849, the fort was abandoned by the army in 1853 because the frontier had moved farther west. New settlers used the buildings for temporary housing. Several other historic stone and log buildings from the Burnet area have been moved to the grounds of the fort and now make up a part of the **Fort Croghan Museum** (703 Buchanan Drive, 512–756–8281), which also has exhibits of local pioneer artifacts. The two-story limestone **Badger Building** (South Pierce and Jackson) was built in 1883 by W. H. Westfall and Brandt Badger. Westfall was one of the owners of nearby Granite Mountain, from which came the donated stone to build the state capitol in Austin. The **Burnet County Jail** (Washington and Pierce) was built in 1884 by an Austin architect, Frederick Ruffini, and used until 1981. The oldest commercial edifice in Burnet is the **Old Masonic Lodge** (309 South Main Street), built in 1854 by Logan Vandeveer, the first postmaster of the village and a storekeeper who let the Masons meet upstairs. Private houses of historic interest in Burnet include the 1870 limestone **George Whitaker House** (802 South Main Street), which had an indoor cistern that would have enabled the family to hold out against Indian attacks (although the Indian threat had passed); the **J. G. Cook House** of 1873 (200 North Main Street), whose iron fittings were brought by ox wagons from New Orleans; and the limestone-and-log **Rocky Rest** (404 South Water), a two-story Greek Revival residence on Hamilton Creek built in 1860 by Adam Johnson. It served as a school after Johnson and his family moved to **Airy Mount** (Route 29, three-quarters of a mile east of town), another limestone house, which has been completely restored and is now a private residence.

About a million years old, **Longhorn Caverns** (Park Road 4, off Route 281, 512–755–5975) has remarkable stalactites, stalagmites, and stones worked into unusual shapes by water. During the Civil War, Confederates gathered bat guano here to make gunpowder. The outlaw Sam Bass may have used the cave as a hideout in the 1870s. The cave was briefly made into a nightclub in the 1930s, with a wooden dance floor in one of the naturally "air-conditioned" rooms.

LYNDON B. JOHNSON
NATIONAL HISTORICAL SITE

Founded in 1969 after President and Mrs. Johnson gave 200 acres of the LBJ Ranch to the National Park Service and the State Parks and Wildlife Department, the LBJ National Historical Park was designed to give visitors a feeling for the countryside to which the Johnsons retreated for relaxation. There are five parts to the site. The **LBJ State Historical Park** has a visitor center with presidential gifts and mementoes, exhibits on the history of the Hill Country and the Johnson family, and an auditorium featuring films on Johnson's life. Attached to the center is a two-room dogtrot cabin built in 1870 by a German immigrant named Johannes Behrens, fitted with pioneer furnishings. On the center's other side is the restored Danz log cabin, among the oldest structures in the area. Just east of the visitor center, the park also has an operating historical farm, the **Sauer-Beckmann Farmstead,** where interpreters in historical costume re-create the farm life of the early-twentieth-century Hill Country and conduct tours through three buildings: a one-room log cabin, a limestone house where the midwife who delivered LBJ grew up, and a frame house built in the early twentieth century. The limestone-and-frame **LBJ Ranch House,** which Johnson admired as a child when he would visit his uncle and aunt there, can be viewed from a distance but is closed to the public, as Mrs. Johnson still resides there. The **Johnson Birthplace** at the LBJ Ranch is actually a replica of the farmhouse where Sam Johnson, Jr., fresh from his term as a Texas state legislator, brought his wife, Rebekah Baines, to a hard new life in 1907, and where their first son, Lyndon, was born in 1908. The original house was built by Sam Johnson, Sr., in 1889, and some of its contents fill the replica. The house is comfortably furnished, as Rebekah Johnson attempted to keep it—she used real tablecloths where other farm wives used oilcloth, in spite of the extra washing and ironing with boiled wash water, caustic lye soap, and wooden washboards. East of the birthplace is the **Junction School,** an embossed-metal box which was practically new when LBJ started there at the age of 4. The **Johnson Family Cemetery,** where the president is buried along with his grandparents, parents, and siblings, is shaded by oak trees and overlooks the Pedernales River.

The **Johnson Boyhood Home** (a block south of Route 290, Johnson City) is the white frame house where the Johnsons moved

A painting of a Texas farm family dressed in their Sunday best for an outing in an ox-drawn car, shows the mid-nineteenth-century prosperity of Texas agriculture.

in 1913, imaginatively restored and furnished with toys scattered in the bedroom. The nearby **Johnson Settlement,** where early farm life is re-created, is a collection of structures belonging to Johnson's great-uncle Tom and grandfather Sam Johnson, who started in the cattle-driving business here after the Civil War.

> LOCATION: Johnson City sites, 1 block south of LBJ Ranch, 14 miles on Route 290 West, near Stonewall. National Park Service buses travel to sites outside of state park. HOURS: *Johnson City sites:* 9–5 Daily. *LBJ Ranch:* 10–4 Daily. FEE: None. TELEPHONE: 512–868–7128.

FREDERICKSBURG

A group of Germans settled Fredericksburg, in the Pedernales River valley, in 1846. The contingent of 120 farmers, doctors, lawyers, and merchants had been led from New Braunfels by John O.

Painted in the early 1850s by Richard Petri, a farmer and artist who lived near Fredericksburg, it now hangs in the Texas State Capitol in Austin.

Meusebach. The settlers were able to succeed partly because they were better than the Mexicans and Anglos at dealing with the Comanche. Shortly after Fredericksburg was founded, Meusebach signed a treaty with the Penateka Comanche in which the latter agreed to share their hunting grounds. It was never broken, making it unique among treaties made between whites and Indians in the history of the state. Fredericksburg, named in honor of a patron of the Adelsverein, Prince Frederick of Prussia, grew rapidly for a frontier settlement; by the middle of 1847 the town had eighteen stores and the Nimitz Hotel. Fredericksburg is one of the best-preserved and most well known historic communities in the state. Besides good examples of *Fachwerk*, the old timber-with-infill building technique the Germans sustained in the rocky landscape of their new frontier colony, the town also has a unique building type, the Sunday House. Most farmers would come into town with their fami-

lies to stock up with supplies, visit with friends and relatives, and spend the night and go to church the next morning before heading back to the farm, and for this purpose they built little dollhouselike structures. A number of these charming symmetrical wood or stone structures still stand, one of the best examples being on the grounds of the Pioneer Memorial Museum.

Pioneer Memorial Museum

There are five buildings in this museum complex, the largest of which, the **Kammlah House,** was built on the site by Henry Kammlah in 1849 as a home and store. Expanded several times over the years, the house has eight rooms illustrating pioneer life, including two displaying the store's old inventory, three pioneer kitchens with stone hearths, exhibits on the Meusebach and Nimitz families, and a wine cellar. The **Fassel House,** built for the town's wheelwright, has original Fredericksburg-made furniture. The **Weber Sunday House,** built in 1904 (most Sunday houses were constructed between 1890 and 1920, after which the automobile rendered them anachronistic), is a tiny (sixteen-by-twenty-foot) gray house with white trim and the typical lean-to kitchen and one-and-a-half stories: The boys of the family would ascend a ladder propped up against the porch roof and climb into a white-shuttered window to their sleeping loft. Other buildings on the grounds are the old **First Methodist Church,** built in 1855; the **Fredericksburg Volunteer Fire Department Museum,** with turn-of-the century firefighting equipment; and a reconstructed log cabin.

LOCATION: 309 West Main Street. HOURS: April through Labor Day: 10–5 Wednesday–Saturday and Monday, 1–5 Sunday; Labor Day through March: 10–5 Saturday, 1–5 Sunday. FEE: Yes. TELEPHONE: 512–997–2835.

Nimitz Hotel/Admiral Nimitz State Historical Park

Charles Nimitz's Nimitz Hotel is now a museum honoring his grandson, Fleet Admiral Chester William Nimitz, commander of all U.S. naval forces in the Pacific during World War II. The elder Nimitz had been a member of the German merchant marine before he came to Texas with the Adelsverein in 1846 and started his success-

OPPOSITE: A Fachwerk *Sunday House in the German settlement of Fredericksburg, constructed of timber, locally quarried stone, and stucco.*

Fredericksburg's distinctive Nimitz Hotel, now the Nimitz Museum, a part of the Admiral Nimitz State Historic Site.

ful hotel business. In 1852 Captain Nimitz built the first four rooms of the later much-enlarged hotel that is today the most distinctive building in town, a wood-frame "steamboat" with its "bridge" looking over Main Street. In its day the Nimitz Hotel (also known as the Steamboat Hotel) was the most comfortable stop on the military road between San Antonio and San Diego—indeed, the last civilized hotel before California. It had the frontier's first bathhouse, as well as a brewery, saloon, general store, and ballroom. Guests included Robert E. Lee, Ulysses S. Grant, Rutherford B. Hayes, and Elisabet Ney. Several rooms of the hotel are furnished as they were in the nineteenth century, but most are given over to the **Museum of the Pacific War,** which tells the story of Admiral Nimitz, who possessed, in the assessment of the naval historian Samuel Eliot Morison, "an almost impeccable judgement of men, and a genius for making prompt, firm decisions." Nimitz took charge of the Pacific fleet eighteen days after the disaster at Pearl Harbor, reorganized the shattered forces, and was one of the architects of the strategy that brought victory over Japan.

Behind the hotel is the **Garden of Peace,** a Japanese-style garden created with money raised by the Japanese people. After the war Nimitz behaved kindly toward the defeated Japanese, returning samurai swords to ancestral homes and starting a fund to restore the *Mikasa,* the flagship of the brilliant commander of the Japanese fleet during the Russo-Japanese War whom Nimitz greatly admired, Admiral Heihachir Tog. The garden includes a replica of Admiral Tog's study, built by the Japanese and reassembled in Fredericksburg. The **Pacific History Walk** a block from the Nimitz Hotel takes visitors through relics of World War II: a Japanese Chi-Ha tank; an Aichi D3A "Val" dive bomber, the kind of plane that dropped bombs on Pearl Harbor; and the conning tower of the USS *Pintado,* the submarine that sank Japan's largest merchant ship.

LOCATION: 340 East Main Street. HOURS: 8–5 Daily. FEE: Yes. TELE-PHONE: 512–997–4379.

Built in the geographic center of town in 1847, the **Vereins Kirche** (Market Square, 512–997–7832) was Fredericksburg's first "people's church" and community center. An octagonal frame structure topped by a cupola, the building was also called Die Kaffee-Mühle Kirch (Coffee Mill Church). Now a museum featuring a local-history collection and ancient artifacts found in the area, the Vereins Kirche was reconstructed in 1936. The original building was demolished at the close of the last century.

The masterful British-born architect Alfred Giles designed the graceful small Italianate **Pioneer Memorial Library** (Courthouse Square, 512–997–6513), which was built of rusticated limestone in 1882 and served as the courthouse until 1939. Giles had an affinity for European historical touches, as is apparent in the little tower topping his 1897–1898 **Bank of Fredericksburg** (120 East Main Street), a limestone building trimmed in pink granite. One of the most wonderful old buildings in town, by an unknown architect, shows German decorative fancy and skill. It is the **White Elephant Saloon** (242 East Main Street) of 1888. This former "place of resort for gentlemen" has beautifully cut masonry and three sets of French doors, over the center of which is a bas-relief of a white elephant framed above and on either side with a lacy wrought-iron rail.

Other notable buildings downtown include the **Felix Reinbach Building** (227 East Main Street) of 1904, with thin columns supporting the second-story verandah—there was a store below and living quarters above, as was the case in many German business buildings in Texas. At South Orange and West San Antonio are two churches built by one parish. The simple Gothic Revival **Marien Kirche** was built 1861–1863 by members of the congregation under the supervision of Father Peter Baunach, a Benedictine priest, with soapstone floors in the aisles but sand beneath the pews. The "new" Gothic-style **Saint Mary's Church** is where the congregation has met since 1906. **Saint Barnabas Episcopal Church** (Bowie and Creek streets) occupies a house built in 1848, one of the oldest examples of *Fachwerk* in town. Much *Fachwerk* in Texas is stuccoed on the exterior, with the result that the vertical and diagonal bracing timbers are not visible. Since this was not the case here, one can see the structure of this house. The restored **Kiehne Home** (now the Country Cottage Inn at 405 East Main Street), built in 1850 was the first substantial stone building to go up in Fredericksburg.

ENCHANTED ROCK STATE PARK

This giant dome of pink granite is the second-largest rock mountain in the country (after Georgia's Stone Mountain). Enchanted Rock is a seventy-acre dome of volcanic rock rising 325 feet above the bed of Sandy Creek, which flows beside it. Prehistoric hunters and gatherers left evidence of their habitation on and around Enchanted Rock; metates, or grinding concavities, have been found in the bedrock along with arrow points and stone tool-making sites. Comanche assembled here to worship their gods; there was power in the mountain—it gave off creaking sounds at night, believed to be made by the cooling of the rock after a day in the sun. A historical marker at the top of the rock tells of the most famous of all Texas Rangers, Jack Hays, in battle with the Comanche on the summit of Enchanted Rock in 1841. The rock was too coarse in texture to be exploited as a building material. A favorite recreational spot, Enchanted Rock was first opened to the public by its then-owner, Tate Moss, in 1927. The rock was designated a National Natural

OPPOSITE: *Miniature ferns among pink granite blocks at Enchanted Rock State Park.*

Landmark in 1971; and in 1978 the state of Texas, with the aid of the Nature Conservancy, purchased it and made it into a state park.

LOCATION: Ranch Road 965, 18 miles north of Fredericksburg. HOURS: 8 AM–10 PM Daily. FEE: Yes. TELEPHONE: 915–247–3903.

KERRVILLE

Kerrville, the unofficial capital of the Hill Country, started out in the late 1840s when Joshua Brown moved to the site to make cypress shingles at a mill beside the Guadalupe River. The settlement endured Indian attacks and the depredations of outlaws and rustlers during the Civil War and afterward. Kerrville owed much of its growth to Captain Charles Schreiner, who moved from France to Texas as a teenager, became a Texas Ranger, and by 1857 had staked a claim near Kerrville on Turtle Creek. Schreiner, founder of the famous Y. O. Ranch (now a native and exotic game ranch), went on to introduce large-scale sheep and goat raising in the area.

Hill Country Museum

Built by German masons to the design of Alfred Giles, Captain Schreiner's Romanesque Revival mansion was begun in 1879 and extended by Giles in 1897. Eight kinds of wood went into the parquet floors, and brass lighting fixtures and a copper fountain for the garden—where the post office now stands—were imported from France. The addition's round turret rooms upstairs and downstairs reflected Schreiner's French heritage. Upstairs, triple-hung floor-to-ceiling windows rather than doors open onto the balcony—Schreiner's way of avoiding a local door tax. After Schreiner's death in 1927, the mansion served as a Masonic temple until 1973. The Masons tore out some of the fireplaces in the house, but otherwise the interior is historically accurate; Victorian furniture, some original to the house, includes pieces by Edward Belter. Exhibits tell the history of the Schreiner family and of a hundred years of life in the Hill Country.

LOCATION: 226 Earl Garrett Street. HOURS: 10–12, 2–4:30 Monday–Saturday. FEE: Yes. TELEPHONE: 512–896–8633.

Alfred Giles also designed Kerrville's **Masonic Building** (211 Earl Garrett Street) in 1890, an Italianate rusticated-limestone structure financed by Captain Schreiner. In 1920, Louis Albert Schreiner, Charles Schreiner's son, built another mansion on a hilltop just outside of town and called it **Tulahteka** for "edge of town." The house was designed by a San Antonio architect, Atlee B. Ayres, and constructed of brick and cast concrete. It is now the headquarters of the L. D. Brinkman Corporation, which offers tours by appointment (512–257–2000). The **Cowboy Artists of America Museum** (1550 Bandera Highway, 512–896–2553) exhibits contemporary paintings and sculptures of western scenes by the formal association called Cowboy Artists of America, plus special theme exhibitions. The museum building was the last nonresidential building by the San Antonio architect O'Neil Ford. It has a remarkable entrance covered by a network of twenty-three *bóvedas,* beautiful brick arches made without a supporting structure according to a technique now plied by a few skilled artisans in Mexico.

To the south of Kerrville is the site of **Camp Verde** (Route 173), although little of it remains. In 1856 Jefferson Davis, as U.S. secretary of war, began his camel experiment here, importing the animals to see how they would do in the mountainous desert of western Texas, where horses had a very difficult time.

BOERNE

Boerne, the seat of Kendall County, grew up in the 1850s around the remains of Tusculum, one of the Latin settlements founded by radical intellectual German immigrants. The town soon became a haven for German settlers and a renowned early tourist resort. **Ye Kendall Inn** (128 West Blanco Street, 512–249–2138) occupies a building whose original limestone portion, which has twenty-inch-thick walls, dates to 1859. In 1878 the building was enlarged to accommodate the health seekers who came to Boerne for relief from respiratory ailments. Alfred Giles designed what is now the **Boerne City Utilities Building** (402 East Blanco Street) as well as an Italianate addition of 1909 to the **Kendall County Courthouse** (Main and East San Antonio), built in 1870. The limestone-and-cypress **Kuhlmann-King Historical House** (402 East Blanco Street,

512–249–2030), built in the 1880s for a local pharmacist, has period furnishings, including quilts and toys.

BANDERA

Bandera is a center of Texas dude ranching, a recreational industry
that began about 1920. The town started as a cypress-shingle-mak-
ing enterprise in 1852 and later became a staging area for south
Texas cattle being moved up the Western Trail. Mormons moved
into the area in 1854 but remained only a year. Sixteen Polish families came to Bandera by way of Panna Maria in South Texas in 1855.
One of the original settlers built the **Jureczki House** (607 Cypress,
private) in 1876, a limestone-block structure originally housing a
store on the first floor. In 1876 the Polish-Catholic congregation,
one of the oldest in the United States, built **Saint Stanislaus
Catholic Church** (300 South Seventh). The simple **Old Bandera
Courthouse** (12th and Maple) was built by Henry White as a store
in 1868, of local stone. The county bought it in 1877. Alfred Giles
designed the picturesque **Bandera County Jail** (202 12th Street) in
1881 with a castellated roofline. A cut-stone courthouse in modified
Italianate style was built in 1890 during the golden age of Texas
public buildings.

The fascinating ***Frontier Times* Museum** (506–795–3864) was
founded in 1933 by J. Marvin Hunter, publisher of the *Frontier
Times*. Among the some 30,000 items on display are paintings by
western artists, and such oddities as a shrunken head from South
America, a map of Texas made of rattlesnake rattles, and a Brahma
fetus mummy. In the middle of the room is a fireplace made of fossil snails and a millstone used by the Mormons at Bandera Mill.
Also on display are prehistoric Indian relics and pioneer artifacts.

NEW BRAUNFELS

New Braunfels was founded in the spring of 1845 by German immigrants. Their leader, Prince Carl von Solms-Braunfels, was a representative of the Adelsverein, the Society for the Protection of
German Immigrants in Texas, which had been formed in 1842 by
German noblemen wishing to establish a colony overseas. Texas
had a good reputation in Germany, no doubt because of reports
from earlier immigrants to the rich farmlands of the Brazos and
Colorado valleys. When the intended site turned out to be unavail-

The Museum of Texas Handmade Furniture, in the Andreas Breustedt House in New Braunfels, contains hand-crafted furniture made in Texas from the 1830s to the 1860s.

able, Prince Carl selected a site on the three-and-a-quarter-mile-long Comal River where it flowed into the Guadalupe, established a town site, which he named New Braunfels for his birthplace, and brought in the first 200 settlers. Meanwhile, thousands of Germans had begun arriving at Galveston and from there were taken to Indianola. The Mexican War had erupted, and there was an extreme shortage of transport. The new arrivals were left to camp for months in the unfamiliar hot, wet climate of the Gulf Coast. Typhus broke out, and many of the Germans died. Prince Carl resigned his commission to return to Germany, leaving the work of getting the rest of the settlers to their new home to his deputy commissioner, Baron John O. Meusebach. Meusebach led what was left of his countrymen on the trek to New Braunfels, arriving in 1845. In what was healthful and pretty country, the Germans established their enclave, although disease traveled with them; in the beginning many new Texans died in New Braunfels. But once the worst hardships were over, the Germans' industriousness paid off; many of the settlers were skilled artisans and craftspeople, and their town became a manufacturing center and the stepping-off point for thousands of other German immigrants who headed farther west to make new settlements. The New Braunfels **Chamber of Commerce** (390 South Seguin Avenue, 512–625–2385) offers information about the town sites.

Sophienburg Museum and Archives

Sophienburg was the name Prince Carl gave to the hill overlooking the new village, on which he intended to build a house for himself and his fiancée, Lady Sophia, princess of Salm-Salm. However, Sophia refused to come, and the prince returned to Europe to marry her. He had built a log cottage on the hill when he first came to New Braunfels, and, it is said, he greeted visitors in full military regalia. The cottage was destroyed by the hurricane of 1886. Exhibits in the contemporary museum building include a scale model of the prince's castle in Braunfels, Germany; pioneer artifacts; handmade furniture; needlework and textiles made by the female settlers of New Braunfels; and historical displays covering the history of the town. The archives comprise photographs, written and oral history, and German books and newspapers of the day.

LOCATION: 401 West Coll Street. HOURS: 10–5 Monday–Saturday, 1–5 Sunday. FEE: Yes. TELEPHONE: 512–629–1572.

Lindheimer Home

A great botanist and adventurer, Ferdinand Lindheimer came to Texas from Frankfurt-am-Main in 1834, estranged from his family for his revolutionary views on representative government and the unification of the separate German states. When the Adelsverein began to bring German immigrants to Texas, Lindheimer was hired by Prince Carl to guide him and the first colonists to the frontier. From a cabin on the Comal River, Lindheimer made excursions into the wilderness to collect botanical specimens. He put aside his interest in botany when asked to edit a German-language newspaper in 1852, the year he built this *Fachwerk* house of cedar and limestone. Lindheimer and his descendants occupied the house before it came into the hands of the New Braunfels Conservation Society, in 1964, and most of the furnishings belonged to the family. These include some of the botanist's specimens, his desk, his china coffeepot, and several pieces of locally made furniture.

LOCATION: 489 Comal Avenue. HOURS: May through August: 2–5 Thursday–Tuesday; September through April: 2–5 Saturday–Sunday. FEE: Yes. TELEPHONE: 512–625–8766.

Administered by the New Braunfels Conservation Society, **Conservation Plaza** (Church Hill Drive, 512–625–8766) has ten buildings either restored or in the process of restoration. The **Carl Friedrich Baetge House** (1852) is a two-story, authentically furnished *Fachwerk* house built by a civil engineer. The second story of the house is unfurnished to display the fine construction of the house. The German cabinetmakers who came to Texas in the 1840s and 1850s brought a new level of craftsmanship to pioneer furnishings.

The Fachwerk *house of Ferdinand Lindheimer, who guided Prince Carl of Solms-Braunfels' colonists to New Braunfels in 1844. An early Texas botanist, Lindheimer's name is associated with more than thirty species of plants native to Texas.*

The **Museum of Texas Handmade Furniture** (1370 Church Hill Drive, 512–629–6504), which occupies the 1858 Breustedt Haus, displays over seventy-five original pieces of furniture, including children's furniture hewn from mesquite. A log cabin display features furniture and tools made by even earlier settlers. Also on exhibit are English ironstone, pewter, beer steins, and a Munich clock. The Victorian Gothic **Comal County Courthouse** (Seguin and San Antonio streets), an exuberant limestone structure, was designed by James Riely Gordon and built in 1898. The **First Protestant Church** (172 West Coll Street) was built 1875–1879 (and added onto in 1955) for a New Braunfels Protestant congregation founded in 1845 upon the settlers' arrival on Good Friday of that year.

GRUENE

This small town just northwest of downtown New Braunfels is now a national historic district. Originally known as Goodwin, Gruene (pronounced Green) was renamed for the entrepreneurs Ernst Gruene and his son H. D. Gruene, who started the area's first cotton crops with tenant farmers and opened the first mercantile establishment, a white frame building, now the **Gruene Mercantile Store** (Gruene Road). Gruene boasts a number of preserved historic buildings. Across the road from the store are the **Gruene Antique Company;** the **Gruene Haus,** built around 1870 for the foreman of Gruene's farms; **Gruene Hall,** a dance hall and community center of the 1870s, which still has Saturday night dances attended from miles around; and the **Gruene Mansion Inn,** H. D. Gruene's original *Fachwerk* house built in 1872 and extended in 1886. Other sites include a *Fachwerk* cottage across Gruene Road from the inn, started in the 1850s and extended in 1898.

SAN MARCOS

In 1755 the Spanish established the short-lived San Francisco Xavier mission and presidio at the San Marcos Springs (today replicated on the property of a park called Aquarena Springs). Another settlement was attempted on the San Marcos River at the Camino Real by the Spanish in 1808 but lasted only until 1812 because of the impending revolt of Mexico from Spain. The first Anglo settlers moved to the area in 1846, encouraged by Edward Burleson, a Texas Revolutionary veteran and vice president of the Republic of

Texas, who had received a San Jacinto land grant in the area. The actual town site was laid out in 1851 along the river on land owned by Burleson, William Lindsay, and Dr. Eli T. Merriman. With immigration from southern states, it became a cotton-producing center. Most of the historic buildings in the town reflect the prosperity of the turn of the last century. The **Heritage Association of San Marcos** has printed a Historic Tour of Old San Marcos available from the chamber of commerce (202 C. M. Allen Parkway, 512–396–2495) or from the association itself (308 East Hopkins Street, 512–392–9997). Included are the **Burleson-Knispel Home** (Lime Kiln Road), a limestone rock house at the top of a rise, built by slave labor in 1854 for General Burleson's son and in the Knispel family for most of this century; the **Claiborne Kyle Log House** (Old Austin Stagecoach Road), an unusually large cedar-log house built in the 1850s by Kyle, a Mississippi senator, Texas farmer, legislator, and state senator; and the **Charles L. McGehee Cabin** on the San Marcos River at the Old Camino Real Crossing. The **Charles S. Cock House** (402 East Hopkins Street), near the river in Juan Martin de Veramendi Plaza, is a one-story limestone house built in 1867 by a Mississippi planter who was later mayor of San Marcos. Restored by the city of San Marcos and furnished to the period by the Heritage Association, it is the only remaining early stone house in town. The wooden Gothic-style **First United Methodist Church** (129 West Hutchison Drive) was built in 1894 for a congregation that originated with the founding of the town. The Renaissance Revival **Hays County Courthouse** (Public Square) was built of rusticated limestone by C. H. Page and Bros. in 1908. In the immediate vicinity of the courthouse is the beautifully restored 1908 Beaux-Arts **Courthouse Annex.**

The **Belvin Street Historic District,** a street lined with ancient live oak trees, has San Marcos's finest collection of Victorian houses (all privately owned). The oldest house on Belvin Street (no. 709) was begun in 1859 and extended later in the Victorian era. At 727 Belvin is the original G. T. McGehee–Lindstrom House, built in 1895 with gables, a turret, and steeply pitched shingled roof. An exuberant Eastlake porch highlights the 1889 **John F. McGehee House** (no. 832). The Classic Revival house called **Crookwood** at 227 North Mitchell Street is a departure from its Victorian neighbors and has handsome Corinthian columns and a hanging gallery.

NORTH
AND
EAST TEXAS

OPPOSITE: *The Art Deco Hall of State on the State Fair Grounds in Dallas.*

The east Texas Piney Woods are unique in Texas, massive forests extending down from the Red River to meet the Big Thicket just above Houston and Beaumont. The Piney Woods are where civilization took hold earliest in Texas. The Caddo confederacies had relatively sophisticated political and religious communities in the forest a millennium before the Spanish arrived; the Spanish established their first Texas mission here in 1690, and by 1779 the Spanish town of Nacogdoches had been established; the French conducted friendly commerce with the Indians in the seventeenth and early eighteenth centuries. Anglos started coming in before Stephen F. Austin's legitimate colonization was allowed—after the Louisiana Purchase, the United States laid claim to Spanish territory in Texas that Spain believed should not have been included in the purchase. To avoid armed conflict, the United States and Spain established the Neutral Ground, a vaguely bounded buffer zone in east Texas from which settlers were barred. But both Spaniards and Americans moved into the area—by way of "filibusters," which the Anglos had created—to supersede the agreement and take Texas either for the United States or Spain. The Adams-Oñis Treaty of 1819 formally gave the land to the Spanish.

After independence from Mexico, the Republic of Texas did everything in its power to lure settlers, and after annexation in 1845, the state continued the same policy. The first homestead legislation in America was passed in the republic in 1838, providing several hundred acres to settlers and ensuring that an original homestead could never be seized for debt—a law that still holds. The Spanish system of *empresario* grants was continued by both the republic and the state, and settlers mostly from the Southern states arrived in droves. Until the Civil War, east Texas had a cotton economy made profitable by the importation of black slaves and the fertility of cleared river bottomlands. East Texas was more Southern in character—both in its topography and its inhabitants—than any other part of the state, and the plantation was the major economic and social institution until slavery was abolished.

Logging started in east Texas in the nineteenth century and expanded in the first decades of the twentieth. A conservation ethic struggles against destruction of the forest; today east Texas tree farms take up much of the land that has not been cultivated, and national forests have been established. No virgin timber remains, and lumber companies operate there still.

Cowboys move a herd of Longhorns along the Chisholm Trail near Iredell. Clara Williamson, who had watched cattle drives as a child in Iredell, painted this scene from memory in 1952 when she was 77.

Cotton farming took hold in the north after the war, when more Southerners moved away from their ruined homelands. The soils of the Grand Prairie and the Blackland Prairie west of the forests were far richer than the lands they had left in Alabama, Mississippi, Georgia, and Tennessee. With the coming of the railroads, Dallas became the major agricultural shipping and marketing center—the overland answer to Galveston's port economy—attracting merchants who purveyed fine goods manufactured in the eastern and northern United States. Cattle raising flourished to the west and north of Fort Worth, which supported and thrived upon the great trail drives in the 1860s and 1870s.

Secure settlement of north and east Texas, as everywhere in the state, was not possible until the Indians were removed. This was accomplished over a number of years, but Mirabeau B. Lamar, second president of the republic, did much to dismantle Sam Houston's fairer policies toward the Indians—Houston believed Indians should be given title to their lands; Lamar proposed they be removed or exterminated. Houston's way was never tested; in any

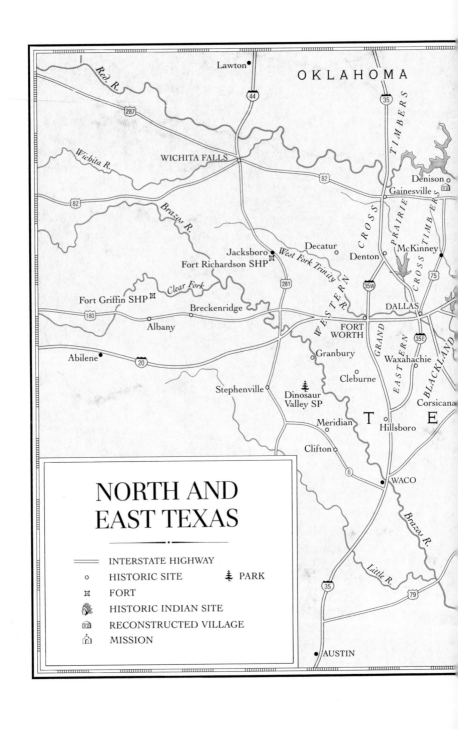

OKLAHOMA

Red R.

Lawton

44

WICHITA FALLS

Wichita R.

82

82

287

35

TIMBERS

Denison

Gainesville

CROSS

Brazos R.

Decatur

Jacksboro
Fort Richardson SHP

West Fork Trinity

Denton

281

PRAIRIE

CROSS

McKinney

TIMBERS

75

Clear Fork

Fort Griffin SHP

Breckenridge

DALLAS

180

Albany

WESTERN

FORT
WORTH

35W

35E

Abilene

20

Granbury

GRAND

Waxahachie

EAST

BLACKLAND

Cleburne

Stephenville

Dinosaur
Valley SP

T

Meridian

Hillsboro

E

Corsicana

Clifton

6

WACO

Brazos R.

NORTH AND
EAST TEXAS

Little R.

INTERSTATE HIGHWAY

o   HISTORIC SITE   🌲 PARK

Ħ   FORT

   HISTORIC INDIAN SITE

   RECONSTRUCTED VILLAGE

   MISSION

35

79

AUSTIN

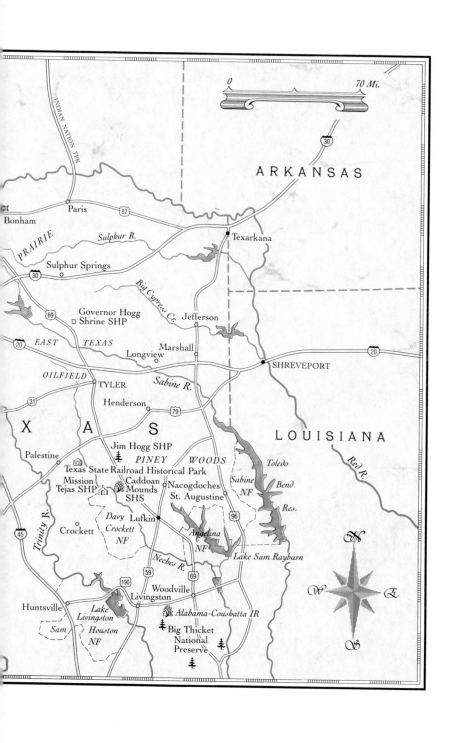

event, land-hungry white hordes made their way to Texas. Today much of north and east Texas is still farm- and timberland; oil came into the picture in northeast Texas with the discovery of the East Texas Oilfield in 1930. But there are places in east Texas where subsistence farming still goes on, as people hunt and trap in the woods and clear small areas for truck farming.

This chapter features three principal areas. The first begins with the sister cities of Dallas and Fort Worth, and fans out along Routes 45, I-35, and I-20 to include such towns as Corsicana, the site of Texas's first oil strike, and Fort Griffin State Historical Park in Albany. The next section starts with the northern city of Wichita Falls, which boomed in 1911 with its first oil strike. The third hub begins in Jefferson, known for its well-preserved historic homes, and moves south to Big Thicket National Preserve.

DALLAS

The popular image of Dallas is that of a city built on oil—but Dallas was founded on trade. The French were the first whites to regularly visit this area where the three forks of the Trinity River met, in the 1700s, and they came to trade with the Anadarko Indians, who lived by the river in cone-shaped huts. Almost 150 years later, in 1841, Tennessee-born John Neely Bryan traveled from Van Buren, Arkansas, to open a trading post (near what is now Courthouse Square) to serve a military highway planned by the Republic of Texas. Bryan actively sought neighbors. The town was marked, rather prematurely, on maps of the Peters colony, an *empresario* grant to W. S. Peters by the Republic of Texas in 1842. The Peters colony promoted the region both in America and abroad, attracting some 3,000 settlers by 1850. One Missourian who made his way to Dallas wrote in his journal, "We soon reached the place we had heard of so often; but the *town*, where was it? Two small cabins—this was the town of Dallas, and two families of ten or twelve souls was its population."

In the 1850s a French contingent came to the area and established the cooperative community of La Réunion west of Dallas. The first arrivals were twelve men in long robes, led by Victor-Prosper Considérant, a disciple of the Socialist François-Marie-Charles

Fourier. Within the year they were joined by about 300 more Socialists. La Réunion included artists, writers, musicians, and other highly educated settlers who knew nothing about farming. Within a few years, the thin and rocky soil, drought, grasshoppers, dissension, and mismanagement of funds caused La Réunion to go bankrupt; by early 1857 the community was officially dissolved. Some of the colonists moved back to France, some to New Orleans, and some to Dallas, where their skills went a long way toward giving Dallas a cosmopolitan feeling otherwise unknown in this region of the state.

During the Civil War, the population of Dallas increased with the influx of Confederate officials and troops who used the town as an administrative center. After the war Southerners came to the area; the rich soil of the Blackland Prairie turned out to be excellent for growing cotton, and soon cotton farms surrounded the town, along with smaller fields of wheat and corn. The coming of the railroad meant prosperity to many Texas towns, but to none so much as Dallas. Before the Civil War, only Houston was a rail center, and the railroads did not extend very far; in 1872 the Houston & Texas Central worked its way up to Dallas and then on to Denison to connect with the Missouri, Kansas & Texas (Katy) Railroad from Saint Louis. This was a significant juncture: For the first time Texas had a direct overland connection with major points east and northeast. Meanwhile, the Texas & Pacific started building west from Arkansas to California, passing through Saint Louis. Savvy leaders in Dallas sealed the future of their city through their legislator in Austin, who tacked on a seemingly insignificant amendment to the railroad-enabling act stipulating that the north–south tracks cross the east–west tracks at Browder Springs; few in the Texas House of Representatives had heard of this place, which happened to be the location of Dallas's water supply, one mile south from John Neely Bryan's original cabin. The first train to arrive in Dallas in 1872 was greeted with fanfare and ceremony, which John Neely Bryan attended, and the celebrants dined on barbecued buffalo.

Overnight Dallas became a major market. Cotton growers could ship their products far and wide. Manufactured goods that had taken weeks to reach the ports of Galveston and Indianola from New York and Boston now arrived from Saint Louis or Chicago in a matter of days, and merchants from those cities descended on the town with new wares and new deals. In 1873 alone $1,377,000 was spent on the construction of 725 new buildings in Dallas. The population grew from 1,200 to 7,000 in a matter of months. By 1890 Dallas was the largest city in Texas, and among the members of its board of aldermen were men from England and Ireland as well as Indiana and Pennsylvania.

Cotton and commerce continued to keep the city prosperous, economic slumps notwithstanding, and for years Dallas was the world's largest inland cotton market. The oil business never centered in Dallas; the oil fields were to the west, east, and south. But Dallas was a banking center, and it was in the realm of banking that it had a deep and lasting effect on the oil business by pioneering the creative financing of new drilling by using oil reserves as collateral. The city's closest tie to the oil business proper came when the tremendous East Texas Oilfield, a hundred miles east, was discovered in 1930 by Columbus M. "Dad" Joiner. Joiner, to his everlasting regret, sold his leases in the field to a man whose heirs are still very, very rich—H. L. (Haroldson Lafayette) Hunt.

Among the early-twentieth-century commercial structures that stand out in downtown Dallas is the 1903–1904 **Wilson Building** (1621 Main Street), an amalgam of the banded "Ruskinian Gothic" style with Beaux-Arts detailing by Fort Worth's Sanguinet & Staats. It sits directly across the street from the 1928 **Neiman-Marcus Department Store**. The 1921 Beaux-Arts **Magnolia Petroleum Building** (Commerce and Akard streets) was designed by New York's Alfred C. Bossom for that important early Texas oil company, which was eventually absorbed by Standard Oil and then merged with Mobil; this was Dallas's tallest building for twenty years and remains a landmark not only for its architecture but also for the trademark big red flying horse, "Pegasus," which Mobil placed atop it in 1934. The 1913 Gothic-style **Busch Building** (now called the **Kirby Building**), at 1509 Main Street, was designed by the Saint Louis firm of Barnett, Haynes & Barnett for the brewery king Adolphus Busch, who also commissioned the lavishly ornamented **Adolphus Hotel** (1912) at 1321 Commerce Street.

Old City Park Museum

Located in the city's first park, this "Museum of Architectural and Cultural History" began in 1966 when the Dallas County Heritage Society was formed to save Dallas's largest remaining antebellum house, **Millermore,** built from 1855 to 1862 by the early Dallas settler

William Brown Miller. The society dismantled and moved the house here from Oak Cliff, along with the **Miller Log House** (1847). Today a total of thirty-eight structures are on the park grounds, all authentically furnished. Tours begin at the 1886 **Railroad Depot,** which commemorates the early railroad era of Dallas and is sited alongside the **Section House** (1880s) and the **Drummers' Hotel** (1904). The Victorian era in Dallas is reflected in the late Queen Anne-style **George House** (ca. 1900), with typical detailing and stained-glass windows, and the **Doctor's Office and Apothecary** (1890). The **Shotgun House** (1906) is an example of African-American-influenced worker housing at the turn of the century. Rural housing is typified by the **Gano House** (1845–1846), a dogtrot log cabin, and the **Brent Place** (1876), a three-gabled farmhouse probably constructed according to the pattern books of the day (and now the park's restaurant). Outbuildings and support structures include an 1880s **Granary,** a **Curing Shed** (1860), a **Storm Cellar, Smoke House, Privy,** and **Log Kitchen.** There are several commercial buildings on the grounds as well, including the **Citizens Bank** (1905) from Justin, Texas, a **General Store** (1907), and the **D. B. McCall's General Store** (1904). Some of the buildings have living-history exhibits, with volunteer potters making stoneware, blacksmiths forging farm tools, and a printer setting type. Before this land became a park, it provided the city's water, which came from **Browder Springs,** the site of which is marked for visitors.

LOCATION: 1717 Gano Street. HOURS: *Grounds:* Dawn–Dusk Daily. *Houses* : 10–3 Tuesday–Saturday, 1:30–3:30 Sunday. *Depot Visitor Center:* 10–4 Tuesday–Saturday, 1:30–4:30 Sunday. FEE: Yes. TELEPHONE: 214–421–5141.

The Sixth Floor

On November 22, 1963, President John F. Kennedy was assassinated as his motorcade passed this spot. The sixth floor of the former Texas School Book Depository, where Lee Harvey Oswald allegedly fired the shot that killed the president, has been turned into an exhibition that examines the life, death, and legacy of President Kennedy. Operated by the Dallas County Historical Foundation, the

OPPOSITE: *In the midst of modern Dallas the Old City Park Museum preserves a number of historic buildings, including these early twentieth-century general stores.*

9,000-square-foot display includes nearly 400 photographs, six films, artifacts, and interpretive displays. The exhibition documents the social and political times of the early 1960s, the events of November 22, 1963, and the findings of the investigations that followed. The facts about the assassination are still debated, despite the conclusion of the Warren Commission that Oswald was the killer and that he acted alone. Some investigators claim that Oswald could not have fired as accurately and rapidly as the commission believed, and that the president was shot by others, perhaps from a nearby knoll. Visitors can see where Oswald stood and look out at the "grassy knoll," the triple underpass, and the presidential motorcade route.

LOCATION: Northwest corner of Houston and Elm streets. HOURS: 9:30–5 Monday–Thursday, 9:30–6 Friday–Sunday. FEE: Yes. TELE-PHONE: 214-653-6666.

Dealey Plaza (Houston and Elm streets) has a plaque describing the assassination of Kennedy as well as a monument to Dallas civic leader George Bannerman Dealey (1859–1946), who was an early executive of the *Dallas Morning News*. The **John F. Kennedy Memorial,** a cenotaph designed in 1970 by the architect Philip Johnson, a Kennedy family friend, is in **Memorial Plaza** behind the 1892 **Old Red Courthouse** (Main and Houston streets), a Richardsonian Romanesque blue granite and red sandstone structure designed by the Little Rock architects Orlopp and Kusener and one of the few nineteenth-century Dallas landmarks still standing. Just across the street, at Main and Record, the **Dallas County Historical Plaza** features a reconstructed cabin similar to that of John Neely Bryan, the first settler in Dallas in 1841.

    Old Oak Cliff Viaduct (also known as the Houston Street Viaduct, west on Houston Street from Union Station) was commissioned after a Trinity River flood in 1908 damaged much property. Fifty-one reinforced-concrete arches support the mile-long causeway, completed in 1912. The Beaux-Arts **Dallas Union Terminal** (400 South Houston Street), glazed in white brick, was designed by Jarvis Hunt of Chicago and built in 1916 to consolidate the five passenger terminals being used by the city's nine railroads. At its peak during World War II Union Station saw traffic from a hundred trains a day.

    The **Alfred Horatio Belo House** (2115 Ross Avenue, private) is the only remaining mansion on an avenue that was once lined with grand houses. The Classic Revival structure designed by Herbert M. Green was built in 1900 for the founder of the *Dallas Morning News*. The Gothic-style **Catedral Santuario de Guadalupe (Cathedral of the Sacred Heart)** (2215 Ross Avenue) has been the seat of Dallas's Roman Catholic bishop since its completion in 1902. The **Dallas Theater Center** (3636 Turtle Creek Boulevard) is housed in one of the last (1959) great projects of Frank Lloyd Wright, the only theater he designed in his long career. The **Kalita Humphreys Theater,** as it is known, shares the sculptural qualities of the Guggenheim Museum, in New York, which Wright designed about the same time.

Dallas Museum of Art

Housed in a building by Edward Larrabee Barnes, the museum has a varied permanent collection including Abstract Expressionist and modern paintings and sculpture, Impressionist works, important holdings of pre-Columbian and African art, and significant American

The Dallas Theater Center, the only theater designed by Frank Lloyd Wright.

works such as Frederic E. Church's 1861 *The Icebergs,* which was "lost" at an English boys' school for many years and bought for $2.5 million at an auction in 1979 by an anonymous bidder and donated to the museum. The decorative arts are represented here in two fine collections, the **Wendy and Emory Reves Collection** of mostly eighteenth- and nineteenth-century French furniture, donated to the museum on the condition that the pieces be housed in replicas of rooms from the Reveses' villa on the Mediterranean; and the **Bybee Collection of Colonial American Furniture,** donated to the museum by the Houstonian Mrs. Charles L. Bybee, who competed with Ima Hogg of Bayou Bend for primacy in this field.

LOCATION: Ross Avenue and North Harwood Street. HOURS: 10–5 Tuesday–Saturday (until 9 Thursdays), 12–5 Sunday. FEE: Yes. TELE-PHONE: 214–922–1200.

A private institution on 164 acres in residential University Park, **Southern Methodist University (SMU)** (Hillcrest Avenue and Mockingbird Lane, 214–692–2000) was established in 1911 and opened in 1915. **Dallas Hall,** the university's first building, was built in 1912 by the architects Shepley, Rutan & Coolidge and features an impressive rotunda; the four-story **Clements Hall** (1915) is by the same group of architects, who worked here in a three-part Palladian form; the **Perkins Hall of Administration,** built in 1926 by DeWitt & Washburn, has wrought-iron detailing and Corinthian pilasters.

Once situated alongside the crossroads of the Houston & Texas Central and Texas & Pacific railroads, **Deep Ellum** was the commercial core serving the adjacent black neighborhoods settled after the Civil War. Now officially spelled the way Deep Elm was originally pronounced, Deep Ellum has been called a miniature Harlem. Well into the 1930s it was a lively place, often hosting the blues master Leadbelly in its various nightclubs. It has had a resurgence of interest and renovation. The Renaissance Revival **Pythian Temple** (2551 Elm Street), built in 1916 as the state headquarters for the Black Knights of Pythius, was the community center of Deep Ellum. It was designed by the black architect William Sidney Pittman, son-in-law of Booker T. Washington.

Robert S. Munger built his **Continental Gin Company** (3311 Elm Street) in Deep Ellum in about 1888. The system he patented to move cotton to and from the ginning machines via air-suction tubes soon made Munger the largest gin supplier west of the Mississippi. The lower part of Swiss Avenue is actually a historic district within itself, the **Wilson Block** (2900 block). Frederick P. Wilson was a cattleman who bought this whole block in the 1890s, built a Queen Anne-style house for himself and his bride (number 2922), and then constructed five smaller but nicely adorned cottages to house his friends. The houses, which date from 1898 to 1902, make the most concentrated turn-of-the-century architectural grouping in Dallas, possible because the block remained in the hands of the Wilson family until 1977. The upper part of Swiss Avenue is lined with slightly younger buildings—generous Prairie-, bungalow-, and Classic Revival-style houses set well back from the street.

De Golyer Estate

Forty-four acres on White Rock Lake northeast of Swiss Avenue have as their focal point the Spanish Colonial Revival house of the petroleum geologist and oil man Everette Lee De Golyer, who has been dubbed "the grandfather of American geophysics." Designed

The De Golyer house, built for the famed petroleum geologist and energy consultant, Everette De Golyer. He decided to have it built in the Spanish style to remind him of Mexico, where he had his first, spectacular success locating oil deposits.

by Burton Schutt, the Los Angeles architect who built that city's renowned Bel-Air Hotel, the house is surrounded by and part of the Dallas Arboretum and Botanical Center. When restoration is complete, it will tell the story of both a beautifully made house and a Midas-touch geologist: In 1910, at the age of 24, De Golyer succeeded where others had failed in finding oil in Mexico—his discovery near Tampico was to be one of the most productive wells in history. In later years De Golyer was instrumental in developing oil in the Arab countries.

LOCATION: 8525 Garland Road. HOURS: 10–4 Tuesday–Sunday. FEE: None. TELEPHONE: 214–327–8263.

Hall of State/Fair Park National Historic Landmark

Dallas won the bid to hold the 1936 Texas Centennial Exposition, a world's fair celebrating the republic's 100th birthday. The Hall of State is the centerpiece of the 1,500-foot-long Esplanade of State, which itself is marked by a 700-foot-long reflecting pool lined with six pavilions. The T-shaped Hall of State, in its entirety, is like an architectural textbook on the history of Texas, emphasizing the heroic. A curved foyer called the Hall of Heroes has statues of the Texas revolutionary figures Stephen F. Austin, Sam Houston, Mirabeau B. Lamar, Thomas Rusk, and James Walker Fannin, above whose heads runs a frieze listing significant battles and events important in Texas history. Straight ahead is the most staggering space in this grand edifice: the Great Hall of Texas, with marble floors, squared-off fluted columns, and the twenty-five-foot great medallion. The four-story room speaks to the six flags over Texas: The seal has six parts, and there are six ceremonial side chairs built especially for the building, representing Texas, Mexico, Spain, France, the Confederacy, and the United States. Running clockwise around the room are giant murals depicting the history of Texas from 1528 to the 1930s, painted by Eugene Savage. The four other rooms in the building are devoted to the regions of Texas, each with murals depicting the life and business of those parts of the state. The Dallas Historical Society has its offices in the Hall of State and installs changing exhibits in the regional rooms.

LOCATION: Fair Park. HOURS: 9–5 Monday–Saturday, 1–5 Sunday. FEE: None. TELEPHONE: 214–421–5136.

The **Age of Steam Museum** (Washington and Parry, Fair Park, 214–421–8754) offers an outstanding display of American railroad history. The museum houses the Union Pacific Number 6913, "Big Boy," the largest diesel-electric locomotive in the world, as well as the world's largest steam-powered and electric engines. There is also a fine collection of passenger trains, including the Santa Fe Railroad's Pecos Valley Chief, which ran between Clovis and Carlsbad, New Mexico, and featured a Doodlebug engine that is still fully operational. A 1930s passenger train with seven cars, including Pullman and dining cars, is also on exhibit. Fifty dioramas focusing on the Southwest are in the **Dallas Museum of Natural History** (First and Grand avenues, Fair Park, 214–670–8457), showing wildlife in natural habitats. A 75-million-year-old Mosasaur skeleton towers in the museum along with a fifteen-foot mammoth skeleton, both uncovered in the Dallas vicinity.

FORT WORTH

The cattle drives stopped moving through the city streets by the 1880s and the meat-packing business is now just one livelihood among many, but Fort Worth will always be nicknamed "Cowtown." More than 10 million head of cattle rumbled through Fort Worth between 1866 and 1884, making their way north on the Chisholm Trail up through Oklahoma and on to the Kansas railheads. But the settlement of the town actually began in 1849, when Major Ripley Arnold led forty-one U.S. dragoons to the forks of the Trinity River to set up a military post at what was then the western border of the frontier. The post, on a bluff overlooking the Trinity, was one of the first established by the U.S. Army in the Indian Frontier Line, which ran south almost to Austin. That same year, settlers moved to the camp and opened stores. The fort put a stop to Indian attacks in the area; but in any case the Indians were already being pushed farther west by Tarrant County settlement, begun in the early 1840s under the auspices of the W. S. Peters colony. By 1853 the military had abandoned Fort Worth and removed its soldiers to Fort Belknap. Citizens used the post buildings to house commercial enterprises.

The first Texas & Pacific Railway engine pulled into Fort Worth in 1873, and almost immediately enterprising men built stockyards to handle those cows that drovers chose to sell at Fort Worth for lower prices—but less trouble—than they would get for going all the

The Texas photographer Erwin Smith (1886-1947) took some 1800 photos of cowboys, including this nighttime shot of cheerful cowpokes around a camp fire.

way to Kansas. Stockyards began to cover acres of land, cows grew fatter, and eventually enough lines connected northern markets to Fort Worth that trekking to Kansas was unnecessary. By 1890 the great trail drives were over; railroads had spread out in a web to transport herds, and barbed wire crossing the plains had made long, straight drives impossible. But in Fort Worth the cattle business remained the major industry through the 1920s, boosted significantly in 1902 when Armour and Swift added their major packing houses to the smaller ones already in operation around the stockyards, an area that is now restored. When oil was discovered in 1912 at Burkburnett, 125 miles north, and then in the Ranger Field, 100 miles west, Fort Worth was the logical center of operations, and oil companies and the usual contingent of schemers and dreamers converged on the town as the cattle ranchers had only decades before. Much of the commercial architecture of the city, particularly downtown, dates from the days when oil was king to cattle's queen.

The **Tarrant County Courthouse** (Belknap, Weatherford, Houston, and Commerce) is a Renaissance Revival structure built in 1893–1895 of the same red granite used for the state capitol in Austin. Tarrant County's massive structure has elaborate carved-stone detailing; on the front gable is a giant shield of Texas, the Lone Star nestled in a wreath of oak and laurel. The $408,840 price tag of this built-to-last hall of justice so infuriated the voters of Tarrant County that all the county commissioners responsible for the extravagance were ousted in the next election. A few blocks south of the courthouse, where Main and 2d streets intersect, is **Sundance Square.** The square was named for the Sundance Kid (a.k.a. Harry Longbaugh) who with his pal Butch Cassidy (a.k.a. Robert Leroy Parker) hid out in a part of downtown once known as Hell's Half Acre for its outlaw characters. Among the historic buildings restored in the Sundance Square area is the High Victorian Eclectic **Knights of Pythias Castle Hall** (3d and Main streets), built in 1901 by the prolific Fort Worth firm of Sanguinet & Staats. The ersatz medieval structure's front entrance is guarded by a seven-foot knight. Housed in a pleasant reconstruction of a turn-of-the-century brick building, the intimate **Sid Richardson Collection of Western Art** (309 Main Street, 817–332–6554) comprises about fifty paintings by western masters Frederic Remington and Charles M. Russell.

At 2d and Commerce streets stands the 1907 **Fire Station Number 1,** a yellow brick building occupied by the volunteer fire department and at one time the city hall. In it now is the **Fort Worth Interpretive Center,** a branch of the Fort Worth Museum of Science and History (817–732–1631), whose exhibits tell the story of the city through photographs, artifacts, and memorabilia relating to Camp Worth, ranching, the railroads, and the oil business.

Other buildings of interest include the Classic Revival **Neil P. Anderson Building** (411 West 7th Street), designed by Sanguinet & Staats in 1921 as a center for the cotton and grain trade—skylights over the grading room let buyers examine the cotton in good light. Sanguinet & Staats also designed the Classic Revival **Burk Burnett Building** (500–502 Main Street), built in 1914 as a bank and bought in 1915 by Samuel Burk Burnett, a famous early trail rider turned cattle king, the owner of the Four Sixes Ranch. The **Land Title Office Building** (4th and Commerce streets), built in 1889 of brick, sandstone, and cast iron to designs by Haggart and Sanguinet, features the stone carvings of an owl and a mockingbird and the initials

The Tarrant County Courthouse, a bold granite structure of the 1890s, stands next to Fort Worth's new City Hall.

of the lawyers who occupied the second floor. The twenty-story **W. T. Waggoner Building** (810 Houston Street) of 1920 was designed for the cattle baron and oil man by Sanguinet & Staats in a Chicago School mode. Its unique U shape aids ventilation; and it is the tallest building in Fort Worth. The **Flatiron Building** (1000 Houston Street) is a seven-story Sullivanesque building designed in 1907 by Sanguinet & Staats after the building of the same name and shape in New York, for Dr. Bacon Saunders, who performed the first successful appendectomy in Texas. The **Federal Courthouse** (10th and Lamar streets), completed in 1933 to designs by Wiley Clarkson and Paul Cret, is adorned inside with WPA murals by Frank Mechau depicting *The Taking of Sam Bass* and *Texas Rangers in Camp*.

Among the historic churches downtown is the Renaissance Revival **First Christian Church** (612 Throckmorton Street), designed in 1914 by Van Slyke & Woodruff for the oldest Christian congregation in the city, organized in 1855 (an annex dates from 1928). The

Gothic Revival **Saint Patrick Catholic Church** (1206 Throckmorton Street), dedicated in 1892, is next door to the oldest Catholic school in the county, the Second Empire **Saint Ignatius Academy** (1889). The Tudor-Gothic Revival **Allen Chapel African Methodist Episcopal Church** (1912–1914) at 116 Elm Street was built for a congregation organized in about 1870 by pioneer circuit rider Reverend Moody and five black settlers and named in honor of former slave Richard Allen, who became the first bishop of the African Methodist Episcopal Church. It was designed by W. S. Pittman.

Vestiges of the railroad days are found in the Renaissance Revival **Gulf, Colorado & Santa Fe Depot** (1601 Jones Street), built in 1899. The **Texas & Pacific Terminal Building** (1600 Throckmorton Street) is one of the outstanding Art Deco structures in Fort Worth, designed by Wyatt C. Hedrick and completed in 1931. The ornamentation on the exterior touches on Egyptian, Neo-baroque, American Indian, and Gothic themes. The interior is adorned by marble floors, gold- and silver-leafed ceilings with ornamental plaster, chandeliers, and grand mirrors. Nearby is the **Texas & Pacific Warehouse,** also an Art Deco beauty with stone and tile panels inlaid into the exterior brick as well as polychromed brick Zigzag ornamentation on the front façade.

As the railroads multiplied and the great trail drives came to an end, the Fort Worth stockyards were built to handle the cattle brought to be bought, sold, and slaughtered or shipped to northern points. This area, now the **Fort Worth Stockyards Historical District,** was developed in the 1880s when a group of investors joined together on the city's north side and built a complex of holding pens and railroad sidings. The stockyards saw increased activity in the 1890s when the Fort Worth Dressed Meat and Packing Plant established itself in the district. With the arrival of the huge Armour and Swift meat-packing companies in 1902, the district's ascendancy was ensured—Fort Worth grew to be the second-largest livestock market in the country. Exchange Avenue is the main thoroughfare in the district, lined with restored nineteenth-century buildings housing what is left of the cattle business. The **Livestock Exchange Building** (131 East Exchange Avenue, 817–625–5082) was the hub of activity in the old days and still has cattle auctions. This Mission-style structure was built in 1902 for commission companies, livestock brokers for the ranchers who brought their cows—and eventually hogs and sheep—to town. Headquartered here is the **North Fort Worth**

The Fort Worth stockyards. OPPOSITE: *The Booger Saloon, located in the Stockyards Historic District.*

Historical Society, which offers tours and administers a stockyards museum. West of the exchange is the Mission-style **Cowtown Coliseum,** designed in 1908 by the Chicago architect Berkley Brandt. The **Thannisch Building** (101–109 East Exchange Avenue) by Fort Worth's Field & Clarkson, built in 1907 as a hotel and added to in 1913, is very well preserved, with its original hotel and shopping functions re-created. To the east are the remnants of the enormous Swift and Armour plants and the Fort Worth Belt Railway, built as a switching yard for the cattle brought on the main railway.

West of downtown the cattle industry is explored in detail at the **Cattleman's Museum** (1301 West 7th Street, 817–332–7064), in the Texas and Southwestern Cattle Raisers Foundation Building. In addition to historic photographs of ranching in the Southwest and artifacts ranging from branding irons to a silver-mounted saddle, the museum shows films on the histories of the King Ranch, Burnett Estates, and the Waggoner Ranch. There is also a memorial hall honoring pioneers of the cattle industry such as Samuel Burk

Burnett, Charles Goodnight, Captain Richard King, Captain John Armstrong, and Cornelia Adair.

Amon Carter Museum

One of Texas's great civic leaders and philanthropists, Amon Carter was the editor and publisher of the *Fort Worth Star–Telegram* and an oil man par excellence, who numbered among his friends Franklin D. Roosevelt and Will Rogers. His ideals, through the Amon Carter Foundation, still exert force in promoting the arts and culture of the state. The collector was introduced to western art by Will Rogers, and his will established this museum to hold his superb holdings of drawings, paintings, and sculpture by Charles M. Russell and Frederic Remington. The institution opened in 1961, in a building designed by Philip Johnson. Today the museum has Albert Bierstadt's *Sunrise, Yosemite Valley* and the work of other Hudson River School painters; paintings by the nineteenth-century American painters William Merrit Chase, Jasper F. Cropsey, and William Michael Harnett; and works by twentieth-century artists including Georgia O'Keeffe, Arthur Dove, John Marin, Stuart Davis, and Grant Wood. The impressive photography holdings include works by Eadweard Muybridge, Carleton Watkins, Paul Strand, and Ansel Adams as well as the photographic estate of the Santa Fe photographer Laura Gilpin.

> LOCATION: 3501 Camp Bowie Boulevard (Amon Carter Square). HOURS: 10–5 Tuesday–Saturday, 1–5:30 Sunday. FEE: None. TELEPHONE: 817–738–1933.

From its beginnings as a children's exhibit housed in the De Zavala Elementary School, the **Fort Worth Museum of Science and History** (1501 Montgomery Street, 817–732–1631) has grown into 120,000 square feet filled with 100,000 scientific specimens, artifacts, and exhibits ranging chronologically from two Jurassic dinosaur skeletons to a spacesuit. Seven galleries focus on geological history, pre-Columbian artifacts, pioneer furnishings, the history of medicine, and computer science.

The **Kimbell Art Museum** (3333 Camp Bowie Boulevard, 817–332–8451) opened in 1972 to display the art collection of the Fort Worth industrialist Kay Kimbell. The exhibits consist mostly of British paintings from the eighteenth and nineteenth centuries, as well as masterpieces by European painters from the medieval period to the modern era, which have been added to the collection. The building is among the finest designs of Louis Kahn—rows of rectangles are roofed by barrel vaults and interrupted by open courts.

Log Cabin Historical Village

This living-history museum has seven log cabins of various sizes moved here from within a hundred-mile radius of Fort Worth. Dating from 1848 to 1866, the houses range from simple one-room cabins to one-and-a-half-story dogtrots to a two-story cabin with double gallery. Guides costumed as pioneers tell the stories of the families who occupied each house and demonstrate candle making, spinning, and the grinding of corn at a working gristmill (the cornmeal is sold at the museum). The oldest house in the village is the **Isaac Parker House** (1848), built by the Texas revolutionary and legislator for whom Parker County was named; Parker was the uncle of Cynthia Ann Parker, who was captured by the Comanche as a child, went on to marry and bear the children of chief Peta Nocone (including Quanah Parker, the last chief of the Comanche), was recaptured by Texas Rangers, and returned against her will to the house of her uncle, where she lived unhappily and died several years later.

LOCATION: 10 North University Drive. HOURS: 8–4:30 Monday–Friday, 11–4:30 Saturday, 1–4:30 Sunday. FEE :Yes. TELEPHONE: 817–926–5881.

Thistle Hill

The cattle baron W. T. Waggoner commissioned Sanguinet & Staats to build this Georgian Revival mansion in 1903 as a wedding present for his daughter Electra, who sold the house to an equally prominent rancher and oil man, Winfield Scott, in 1911. She and her husband, Philadelphian A. B. Wharton, decided to move to the ranch in northwest Texas—called Zacaweista—which had been given to them as a Christmas present by her generous father. Winfield Scott died before his family could move into the house, but his wife occupied it until 1938. On top of what was then known as Quality Hill, the house is still in the process of restoration; the pergola and tea-

OVERLEAF: *A barrel-vaulted gallery in the Kimbell Art Museum, illuminated by skylights. The architect, Louis Kahn, said that the natural lighting would change the mood of the museum day by day, "depending on the character of the light."*

house on the grounds have been refurbished, and among the turn-of-the-century furnishings are a few original pieces, including a Tiffany-style lamp and two Baronial-style chairs.

LOCATION: 1509 Pennsylvania Avenue. HOURS: 10–3 Monday–Friday, 1–4 Sunday. FEE: Yes. TELEPHONE: 817–336–1212.

Built in 1899 on a high bluff overlooking the Trinity River, the **Eddleman–McFarland House** (1110 Penn Street, 817–332–5875) is one of three remaining examples of Fort Worth's "Cattle baron" homes. Designed by English architect Howard Messer, the home was occupied by Carrie Eddleman McFarland for seventy-five years, was purchased by the Junior League of Fort Worth, Inc., in 1979, and now belongs to Historic Fort Worth, Inc. Built in the late Victorian style with turrets, gables, copper finials, red sandstone porches, and a slate tile roof, the elaborate exterior is amply matched by its interior, with its ornate mahogany and oak mantles, cornices, coffered ceilings, paneling, and parquet floors. The house has undergone several stages of restoration. Next door is the **Pollock-Capps House** (1120 Penn Street, private), a limestone-trimmed brick house also thought to have been built by Messer in 1898.

WAXAHACHIE

Waxahachie Creek was named by the Tonkawa Indians who inhabited the area for the cows they found by the stream. The first white settler, Emory W. Rogers, moved into this rich black prairie in 1846 and gave sixty acres for the town site. In 1850 Waxahachie became the seat of Ellis County. The Shawnee Trail and the Chisholm Trail brought cattle through Waxahachie before and after the Civil War, respectively. In the last two decades of the nineteenth century, the Ellis County Courthouse went up along with fine Victorian houses and commercial structures, the material expression of a town that considered itself the "Queen Cotton County of the World."

Built from 1894 to 1896, the **Ellis County Courthouse** was James Riely Gordon's definitive public structure, one of the courthouses he built in the state during his career and perhaps the finest courthouse in the state. Gordon was 31 when he got the Ellis County

OPPOSITE: *The tower of the Ellis County Courthouse in Waxahachie, one of the finest works by James Riely Gordon. The architect was only in his early thirties when he began designing the building.*

commission as the result of the acclaim of his first courthouse, for Bexar County (San Antonio). Although residents of the "Queen Cotton County" were suffering through a drop in cotton prices when construction on the courthouse began, they kept on with the original plans. The courthouse is often called Richardsonian Romanesque, but it is no mere imitation of the great Henry Hobson Richardson's style; the joyful building is constructed of three-foot-thick walls of gray granite, Texas pink granite, and Pecos sandstone, with stringcourses checkerboarded in color and texture; arches and turrets and columns and a cupola, also employing both smooth and rusticated surfaces, make the composition fanciful and rich. The elaborate stone carving was done by three Italian stone workers, one of whom reputedly fell in love with one Mabel Frame, a railroad telegraph operator whose family owned the boardinghouse where the Italian sculptors lived—her face appears in cornices and elsewhere in the building. Various legends are also attached to the uglier faces carved in the stone, some of them said to be Waxahachians the sculptors disliked.

Devoted to the history of Ellis County, the **Ellis County Museum** (201 South College Street, 214–937–0681) is housed in the Italianate red brick Waxahachie Masonic Lodge of 1889, whose first floor originally housed retail concerns; the second, offices; and the third, the Masons' meeting hall. The collections include Indian artifacts, toys and dolls, china, silver, and crystal, photographs, clothing, furniture, and memorabilia. The museum also administers the 1904 Classic Revival **Mahoney-Thompson House** (604 West Main Street), built in 1904 and furnished with period furniture and objects.

The imposing **Nicholas P. Sims Library** (515 West Main Street, 214–937–2671) was built with an endowment left by a Waxahachie farmer and later expanded with funds provided by J. Harry Phillips, inventor of the Phillips screwdriver. The Classic Revival structure has a double staircase of Carrara marble leading to its second floor, where a 270-seat lyceum, which serves as a local meeting hall and theater, has a proscenium arch decorated in gold leaf.

The **Chautauqua Auditorium** in Getzendaner Park (South Grand off West Main Street) may be the only such structure remaining west of the Mississippi from the famous literary and religious circuit of the late nineteenth and early twentieth centuries, when culture cravers from miles around would come to hear lectures, sermons, concerts, and other entertainments by Will Rogers, John Philip Sousa, and

William Jennings Bryan, among others. The 1,500-seat octagonal frame auditorium (1902) with its rectangular stage wing turns into an open-air pavilion when large wooden windows slide into the upper walls. Today the restored (1975) hall still hosts theater and symphony performances and local events.

CORSICANA

Although the gusher at Spindletop received all the publicity, the first oil strike in Texas had occurred seven years earlier, in 1894, in what is now downtown Corsicana. Oil drillers from Kansas came down to drill a water well for the city, and they struck oil in the 400 block of South 12th Street (commemorated with a historical marker). In 1895 the first producing well of the Corsicana Oilfield came in, and it can be seen at **Petroleum Park,** which has been developed around the site (it pulled up two-and-a-half barrels a day, considered quite a rich supply at the time). The Eastern oil man J. S. Cullinan established one of the state's first oil refineries in Corsicana in 1897, marketing crude oil for sprinkling over city streets to keep the dust down and as fuel for locomotives. Many major oil companies originated in Corsicana, including the Magnolia Oil Company (later Mobil) and the Texas Oil Company (which was to become Texaco).

The **Navarro County Courthouse** (300 block of West Third Avenue), built in 1905, was one of Texas's first Classic Revival halls of justice. The pre-oil-era **Roger Q. Mills Home** (1200 West Second Avenue, private) was built in 1855 for a U.S. senator around the 1847 house of the first owner, Hampton McKinney. **Temple Beth-El** (208 South 15th Street), a wooden frame synagogue built in 1898 for a prosperous Reformed Jewish congregation, is one of the few examples of the Moorish Revival style in Texas; its symmetrical onion-dome towers were an unusual architectural touch in this part of the country. The temple is now owned by the Navarro County Historical Society. The Gothic Revival **First Methodist Church** (320 North 15th Street) was built in 1896.

Pioneer Village

Thirteen structures built or restored and furnished by the Navarro County Historical Society make up this "village" reflecting life in Texas in the mid-nineteenth century. Among the structures is a general store thought to have been built from the logs of the so-called

Independence Hall, Noah Turner Byers's house in Washington-on-
the-Brazos, where the Texas Declaration of Independence was
signed. Byers, the blacksmith for the Texas army under Sam
Houston, was given a league (4,428 acres) and a labor (177 acres) of
land in the Corsicana area for his service. A blacksmith shop is
included in the village, as are a dogtrot house from the mid-1800s, a
freestanding kitchen, slave quarters, and an Indian trading post,
commissioned by General Sam Houston and filled with artifacts.

LOCATION: 912 West Park Avenue. HOURS: 9–5 Monday–Saturday,
1–5 Sunday. FEE: Yes. TELEPHONE: 214–872–1468.

HILLSBORO

In this small agricultural city founded in 1853 is the **Hill County
Courthouse** (Courthouse Square). Built in the Second Empire style
from 1889–1891 by the Waco architect W. C. Dodson, the three-story
limestone edifice was the subject of architectural debate in New York
upon its completion, likened to "an outstanding cathedral" by
Harper's and deemed "a monstrosity" by the *Saturday Evening Post*, but
it has always pleased its Texas constituents. It is at the very least
unusual, with all four facades having major entrances, each two
opposites identical in detailing; the portico on two sides is the height
of the building—elongated bases are the height of the first story,
with the columns themselves two stories tall. W. C. Dodson also
designed the two-story crenelated-brick **Hill County Jail** (125 North
Waco Street), built in 1893.

Other buildings of interest in Hillsboro include the **Hillsboro
City Library** (118 West Waco Street), built in 1913 as a post office;
the **Old Rock Saloon** (58 West Elm Street), constructed in 1876; and
the Classic Revival **Sturgis National Bank** (50 West Elm Street), built
in 1893 with a portico added in 1905. On the campus of **Hill Junior
College** (Lamar Drive, 817–582–2555) are two collections of interest: the **Confederate Research Center and Museum** and the **Audie
L. Murphy Gun Museum and Weaponry Library.** The first contains
Civil War documents, reference books, periodicals, photographs,
battlefield artifacts, and military art. The gun museum has rare
examples of Civil War and Texas guns and displays about Murphy, a
native Texan who was the most decorated American soldier in the
Second World War.

MERIDIAN

This town is the seat of Bosque County (pronounced "bosky" in Texas and meaning "woods" in Spanish), which itself is the seat of the densest concentration of Norwegian-immigrant architecture in the state. Meridian is the site of the Romanesque Revival **Bosque County Courthouse** on the public square, built of local limestone by J. J. Kane in 1886–1887. The **Bosque County Jail** (203 East Morgan Street) is a simple, two-story cube built in 1885 with a sympathetic addition of 1895 whose limestone blocks were creatively arranged—they start large at the bottom and gradually decrease in size as they head toward the top. The 1889 Romanesque Revival **First National Bank Building** (Main and Morgan streets) now houses Bosque County offices.

CLIFTON

In the **Bosque Memorial Museum** (301 South Avenue Q, 817–675–3845), visitors can see household and farming artifacts from the early Norwegian immigration to Texas in the 1850s—including the forerunner of the disc plow, which was invented here by a Norwegian. In the surrounding countryside is a significant architectural heritage that has seen little alteration since 1900. (Along paved, dirt, and gravel roads such as F.M. 219, F.M. 182, and Route 22, there are numerous examples of early rock and log construction done by the immigrants.) In the 1850s Cleng Peerson, the "Father of Norse Immigration to America," came to Texas from the Fox River settlement in Illinois, where he had found homes for immigrants for thirty years, to establish the first Norwegian settlements in Texas. Recognized as a gifted and tireless colonizer, he was granted 320 acres in Bosque County, half of which he exchanged for a home. His house no longer stands, but his grave is in the churchyard of **Our Savior's Lutheran Church** in what was once the thriving community of **Norse** (north on F.M. 182 off F.M. 219 west of Clifton). About eight miles south of this church are the **Reeder-Omenson Farm,** a substantial stone house with double gallery, and the **Norway Mill,** a massive two-story structure built about 1870 that once housed a steam-powered mill. Six miles west from Our Savior's Lutheran Church on F.M. 182 is **Old Saint Olaf's Lutheran Church,** a Gothic Revival stone structure dating from about 1890.

CLEBURNE

First known as Camp Henderson when it was settled in 1854, Cleburne was renamed after the Civil War for Confederate general Patrick Cleburne, killed in battle in Tennessee—this area of Texas was staunchly Confederate. The **Johnson County Courthouse,** on the public square, was built in 1913 by Lang & Witchell of Dallas to replace an architecturally significant courthouse by W. C. Dodson, which burned. The new courthouse was equally fine, and quite progressive for a small town in Texas. Although appearing to be Beaux-Arts, it also has Sullivanesque pendants and stylized capitals on the exterior; the spectacular interior has a six-story atrium topped by an art-glass dome. The **Layland Museum** (201 North Caddo Street, 817–641–3321), housed in the Classic Revival Carnegie Library built here in 1904, began with the collections of W. J. Layland, who enjoyed telling stories, mostly about cowboys and Indians, to rapt audiences. To Layland's Indian, Civil War, and frontier artifacts—including saddles that belonged to Kit Carson and Buffalo Bill—the museum has added genealogical materials and exhibits covering local history. The elaborate second-floor stage has been restored for community use.

DINOSAUR VALLEY STATE PARK

Dinosaur Valley State Park preserves dinosaur tracks and features two fiberglass dinosaur models, a seventy-foot brontosaurus (more correctly called by its genus name, *Apatosaurus*) and a forty-five-foot *Tyrannosaurus rex.* Since 1909 three kinds of tracks have been found in the bed of the Paluxy River in this area, called the Glen Rose Formation: giant, three-toed, birdlike imprints most probably made by the twenty- to thirty-foot-long *Acrocanthosaurus;* saucerlike depressions made by the thirty-to fifty-foot-long sauropod *Pleurocoelus;* and the mysterious three-toed tracks of an as-yet undetermined ornithopod. The first tracks found in the park are now in the American Museum of Natural History in New York—a dramatic double set made when a carnivorous dinosaur stalked an herbivorous one. Other tracks in the park allow scientists to discern how fast predators and prey were moving when one pursued the other.

LOCATION: F.M. 205, west of Glen Rose. HOURS: *Park:* 8–10 Daily. *Visitor Center:* 8–5 Daily. FEE: Yes. TELEPHONE: 817–897–4588.

Built on the Brazos River in 1871, **Granbury,** the seat of Hood County, saw new life when the river was dammed in the 1960s and Lake Granbury appeared at the town's doorstep; the dam was closed in 1969. The blocky **Hood County Jail** (1885) now houses the **Granbury Visitor Center** (208 North Crockett, 817–573–5548). Nine blocks of commercial structures make up the **Hood County Courthouse Historic District,** the highlights of which are on the public square: the **Hood County Courthouse,** by W. C. Dodson, built in 1890 of rusticated and detailed limestone in the Second Empire style; the Italianate **Granbury Opera House** (817–573–3779), built in 1886; and **Nutt House,** a simple two-story limestone store built in 1883 by two blind brothers, now restored and operated as an inn.

STEPHENVILLE

Named for John Stephen, who settled here in 1854 and donated the town site, this town on the Bosque River is the seat of Erath County, an agricultural and livestock center, site of one of the largest tree nurseries in the state, and a producer of coastal Bermuda grass. The Romanesque Revival **Erath County Courthouse** on the public square was built by James Riely Gordon between 1891 and 1892, with white limestone trimmed in Pecos red sandstone.

The **Stephenville Historical House Museum** (525 East Washington Street, 817–965–5880) started with the restoration and furnishing of a Gothic Revival cottage, built in 1869 of native limestone for the Confederate veteran Colonel J. D. Berry and his wife, Mary Elizabeth Wilkes Berry. The five-acre complex grew to include a carriage house, which displays local Indian and pioneer artifacts; the Carmack Log Cabin, reconstructed with logs from an original house (1854); the Center Grove two-room schoolhouse from 1890; and the Chapel on the Bosque, a Carpenter Gothic frame church (1899) built for a Presbyterian congregation, restored and fitted with its original pews. A nineteenth-century privy is also on the grounds.

Fort Griffin State Historical Park (Route 1, fifteen miles north of Albany, 915–762–3592) preserves the remnants of a post established in buffalo country in 1867. It was one of a line of forts protecting the frontier from the Comanche, Kiowa, and Kiowa Apache, whose hunting grounds these were. Although the fort was an important link in the frontier chain of defense—it would serve as a supply source for the Red River campaign, which ultimately removed the Comanche from the state—it was never an imposing complex. In 1874 the commander declared it "unfit for human habitation." All that remains today are the ghostly stabilized ruins of a few stone buildings. The fort was abandoned in 1881. The town of **Fort Griffin** that sprang up around the post was a supply point for famous cattle outfits—Loving, Goodnight, Slaughter—pushing north along the Western Trail (sometimes called the Fort Griffin Trail).

ALBANY

After the Western Trail had been blazed past Fort Griffin, cattle ranchers began using this town as a supply base on their drives. When the Texas Central Railroad came through Albany in 1881, the town also became a cattle-shipping center. An example of early frontier settlement, the **Ledbetter Picket House** (Bank Park) is a restored dogtrot cabin of a type built only in this area—slender upright boards, or pickets as in a picket fence, are supported on a sill, and the spaces between them are chinked as in a log cabin. The house is appointed with frontier furnishings and relics from the Ledbetter Salt Works, founded in 1860. The **Albany Chamber of Commerce** (Central and Main streets, 915–762–2525) is housed in the old Missouri, Kansas & Texas depot next to the museum house.

The **Shackelford County Courthouse Historic District** includes the mansard-roofed courthouse of 1883 on the public square, built by J. E. Flanders of Dallas, who was lauded for plans that combined "safety, durability, and grandeur"; the Gothic Revival **Matthews Memorial Presbyterian Church** (211 South Jacobs Street); and the stone **Jacobs House** (South Jacobs between Central and South 1st streets), built in 1877. One block east, the **Old Jail Art Center** (915–762–2269) is housed in the old Albany Jail, designed in 1878 by John S. Thomas. The collection includes works by modern artists; a Chinese collection with examples from the Han, Wei, Sui, T'ang, and Ming dynasties; and an extensive collection of pre-Columbian art dating back to as early as 1000 B.C.

OPPOSITE: *Wagons haul supplies and equipment to the oil field near Burkburnett in 1918, when a huge oil strike was made.*

WICHITA FALLS

Farming, ranching, railroads, and small industry were mainstays of this town's economy until the big oil discovery in Burkburnett, ten miles north, in 1918. One of the scams of those days was perpetrated by J. D. McMahon, who built the **Littlest Skyscraper.** McMahon advertised a four-story office building in which he sold stock. Construction, on a lot he did not own, proceeded according to plan, but in inches instead of feet. The structure, a part of the **Depot Square Historic District,** is located at La Salle and 7th streets.

The **Wichita Falls Museum and Art Center** (2 Eureka Circle, 817–692–0923) offers changing exhibits on science and art, as well as historical exhibits focusing mainly on northern Texas. Frank Kell commissioned Jones & Orlopp to build the Colonial Revival **Kell House** (900 Bluff Street, 817–723–0623) in 1909 for his wife, the former Lula Kemp, and their seven children. Kell, with his brother-in-law Joseph A. Kemp, helped establish Wichita Falls as a rail and milling center in its early years. The interior of the home features stippled walls with hand-stenciled borders, seven fireplaces, and original furnishings.

FORT RICHARDSON
STATE HISTORICAL PARK

The most northerly of the string of frontier forts established by the army in Texas after the Civil War, Fort Richardson was to come under command of the most successful army officer in the Indian wars, Colonel Ranald S. Mackenzie. In the 1870s Mackenzie led campaigns from Fort Richardson against the Comanche, Kiowa, and Kiowa Apache, who continually left their reservation at Fort Sill in Oklahoma in a desperate attempt to push back white settlement. Near Fort Richardson in May 1871, Kiowa and Comanche led by Satank, Big Tree, Satanta, and Eagle Heart killed seven teamsters traveling from Fort Griffin to Fort Richardson. The Indians were captured and put on trial in nearby Jacksboro. They were sentenced to death by hanging, but under pressure from President Ulysses S. Grant, Governor E. J. Davis commuted their sentences to life imprisonment, which, to a Plains Indian, was surely worse than being hanged. In prison Satanta, the oldest Kiowa warrior, tried to cut his wrists but was prevented by a doctor; he later jumped out of a hospital window to his death. By 1874, the campaign against the Plains

Indians was over in Texas. Fort Richardson (named for Israel B. Richardson, fatally wounded at Antietam in 1862) was abandoned in 1878. The fort consisted of picket huts before stone buildings were erected, and several buildings here have been restored and reconstructed, including enlisted men's barracks, a quartermaster's shop, a powder magazine, a bakery, and the original wooden picket-style officers' quarters. A museum in the impressive post hospital has displays relating the fort's history.

LOCATION: Route 281, just south of Jacksboro. HOURS: June through August: 9–5 Daily; September through May: 9–5 Friday–Sunday. FEE: Yes. TELEPHONE: 817–567–5687.

DECATUR

First named Bishop's Hill for Colonel Absalom Bishop, who laid out the town in 1857, a year after the settlement had been made the seat of Wise County, this town was also called Taylorsville for General Zachary Taylor before it finally settled on a name honoring one of the naval heroes of the Barbary Wars and War of 1812, Stephen Decatur. The Richardsonian Romanesque **Wise County Courthouse** (1895–1897), on the public square, was designed by James Riely Gordon. Exterior walls are of pitch-faced granite, and terra-cotta was used for the frieze, turrets, and dormers. The **Wise County Heritage Museum** (1602 South Trinity, 817–627–5586) is housed in the Richardsonian Romanesque Decatur Baptist College Administration Building (1892). Its collections feature Indian artifacts and local- and pioneer-history displays as well as the wall and windows from the old post office at nearby Chico.

In about 1850 Tennessee-born Dan Waggoner brought his first small herd of longhorns from Hopkins County to grassland about eighteen miles west of the present town of Decatur; twenty years later he and his son, W. T. Waggoner, drove their herd to Kansas and made the start of one of Texas's great ranching fortunes. In 1883 the elder Waggoner built his grand and finely detailed Italianate mansion known as **El Castile** (1003 East Main Street, private). The Waggoner fortune was boosted enormously when oil was struck on their ranchlands in 1911, and W. T. Waggoner's daughter, Electra, adopted shopping and entertaining habits that introduced to the rest of the country the extravagances of the Texas oil-rich.

DENTON

This site, set amid rich farmlands, was chosen for the seat of Denton County in 1857. The **Denton County Courthouse** (Courthouse Square, 110 West Hickory Street), built of granite and sandstone in 1895–1896 and combining the mansarded and Richardsonian Romanesque styles, is another monumental edifice by the Waco architect W. C. Dodson. The first floor of the courthouse—now called Courthouse on the Square to differentiate it from the newer building where most of the county business takes place—has been given to the **Denton County Historical Museum** (817–383–8073). Displays relating to the history of the county include a Victorian parlor, kitchen, and bedroom. The **Evers House** (1035 West Oak Street, private) and the **Lomax House** (723 West Oak Street, private) are two fine houses in what is called Silk Stocking Row, comprising a number of Victorian cottages on West Oak Street. On the campus of Texas Woman's University, the **Texas First Ladies Historic Costume Collection** (1117 Bell Avenue, 817–898–2683) contains inaugural ball gowns of governors' wives from the era of the Republic of Texas to the present. Housed in the university's Mary Ellen Bragg-Huey Library is the **Texas Women's Collection,** an extensive archival collection of items related to Texas women's history.

GAINESVILLE

Gainesville's California Street marks a route of the forty-niners on their way to California in the mid-nineteenth century. Gainesville was also on the Butterfield Stage Line and became a cattle supply point on the Western (or Dodge City) Trail. Cotton farming began in the area in the 1890s and produced the wealth that is evident in the town's interesting Victorian houses, particularly on Denton, Church, and Lindsay streets. The **Cloud-Stark House** (327 South Dixon Street, 817–665–4333) is a fine example of the Italianate style, built by a rancher, Isaac Cloud, in 1885. The Queen Anne-style **William and Anna Davis House** (505 South Denton, private) was built in 1891 for a future Gainesville mayor. The **Morton Museum of Cooke County** (210 South Dixon, 817–668–8900), housed in the Gainesville fire station (1884), displays pioneer artifacts. The **Santa Fe Passenger Depot** (505 East Broadway), a typical Mission Revival railroad station built in 1901, is undergoing restoration. Information about the town's sites can be obtained from the **Gainesville Chamber of Commerce** (101 South Culberson at California Street, 817–665–2831).

DENISON

Denison was established in 1872 as the railhead for the Missouri, Kansas & Texas Railroad. Among the workers for the railroad was Dwight D. Eisenhower's father, David, whose wife, Ida, gave birth here to the future president. The downtown **Denison Commercial Historic District** comprises 135 business and community buildings on parts of eighteen blocks dating from 1875 to the 1930s. Among the most notable structures are the Renaissance Revival brick **Waples-Platter Building** (104 East Main Street) of 1885; the Beaux-Arts **Missouri, Kansas & Texas ("Katy") Depot** (101 East Main Street), of 1909; and the **Ernst Martin Kohl Building (Hotel Traveler's Home)** (300 East Main Street), a store and saloon started in 1893 by a German immigrant sea captain turned railroad land agent and merchant.

Eisenhower Birthplace State Historic Site

President Dwight D. Eisenhower did not know he had been born in this white frame house until the 1940s when one Jenny Jackson, principal of Denison's Lamar Elementary School, suspected that the headline-making general might be the little baby she rocked in Denison nearly fifty years earlier. When Miss Jackson contacted General Eisenhower, he sent her the address of his mother, who confirmed that she and her husband had lived in Denison for three years while he worked as an engine wiper for the railroad. Jenny Jackson rallied community and state interest in preserving the Eisenhower birthplace. The restored house is not as it was at the time of Eisenhower's birth: For the purposes of the historic site, other houses in the neighborhood were cleared away, giving the Eisenhower place a somewhat peculiar, lonely feeling—a modest neighborhood house in a plantation setting. Only a quilt in the house actually belonged to the Eisenhowers; the rest of the 1890s furnishings were procured for the museum.

LOCATION: 208 East Day Street. HOURS: June through August: 8–5 Daily; September through May: 10–5 Daily. FEE: Yes. TELEPHONE: 214–465–8908.

The **Grayson County Frontier Museum** (Route 75, two miles southwest of Denison, 214–463–2487), a museum of rustic structures, includes a log schoolhouse with a teacher's sleeping loft; the **Davis-Ansley Log Cabin** dating from 1836, probably the first pioneer house in the area; the **Langford House,** built by slaves in 1847 from the first milled lumber in the area; and the **Dr. Ralph Bulloch–Nettie Bass House,** the oldest house in nearby Sherman (ca. 1855) before it was moved here. Newer cabins from the 1860s and 1870s also dot the grounds; all are furnished according to the period.

Just outside the town of **McKinney** is the **Heard Natural Science Museum and Wildlife Sanctuary** (F.M. 1378, four miles south of McKinney via Route 5, 214–542–5566), a small piece of preserved timberland surrounded by cleared farmland and development. In the museum are nature prints by John J. Audubon and others, collected by Bessie Heard, the philanthropist who created the private sanctuary, as well as natural-history exhibits.

BONHAM

Named for James Butler Bonham, the Alamo hero who was dispatched by William B. Travis to seek aid from James Walker Fannin and sneaked back into the Alamo through enemy lines, Bonham is the seat of Fannin County. This piece of the fertile Blackland Prairie was settled in 1837 and first named Bois d'Arc when Bailey Inglish brought a few families and built a blockhouse for his home and for protection against Indians on what was then the frontier. Today Bonham has several distinguished Victorian houses built during the days of wealthy planters and merchants, including the **David Rhine House** (318 East 8th Street, private), constructed in 1871. The house has been described as a Victorian hybrid—gable dormers combined with pilaster cornerboards and Italianate detailing. The Queen Anne-style **J. B. Shortridge House** (220 West Sam Rayburn Drive, private) is noted for its hipped roof, two-story bay, and Tuscan columns. Unusual window features on this 1873 house include portholes in the gables and semicircular dormers with sunburst designs. Across the street is the massive **A. B. Scarborough Home** (219 West Sam Rayburn Drive, private), also in the Queen Anne style. The **Fannin County Museum of History** (1 Main Street, 214–583–8042) features a collection of Indian artifacts found in the area, as well as vintage clothing, antique dolls, and a 1916 American LaFrance fire truck.

Fort Inglish Museum

This museum is a reconstruction of the log blockhouse Bailey Inglish built in 1837. On its grounds are three restored original log cabins representing the community that surrounded, and took refuge in, Fort Inglish. The sixteen-foot-square blockhouse has a projecting second floor with gun ports for defense against Indians—although it is said that Inglish himself was liked by the Indians. In those early days, the community posted two guards in hidden positions at the end of each field while it was being worked. In 1838 and 1839, Fort Inglish served as a rendezvous point for the local militia in their campaigns against Indians in the area. The museum is furnished with frontier artifacts and furniture.

LOCATION: Route 82 West. HOURS: April through September: 10–4 Tuesday–Friday, 1–5 Saturday–Sunday; October through May: By appointment. FEE: None. TELEPHONE: 214–583–4881, –3441.

Sam Rayburn House Museum

The legendary "Mr. Sam," born in Tennessee in 1882 and brought by his family to Texas in 1887, served twenty-five consecutive terms as a U.S. congressman (beginning in 1913) and was Speaker of the House for longer than anyone—from 1940 to 1946, 1949 to 1953, and 1955 until his death at age 79 in 1961 (during the 80th and 83d congresses, he served as House minority leader). Rayburn built his Colonial Revival white frame "home place" in Bonham in 1916. It was remodeled in 1934 and has been preserved as it was at the time of his death. All the furnishings and personal effects in the house are original; Rayburn's boots and saddle are still in his study, and his pickup truck is still parked in the driveway.

LOCATION: Route 82, 1 mile west of Bonham. HOURS: 10–5 Tuesday–Friday, 1–5 Saturday, 2–5 Sunday. FEE: None. TELEPHONE: 214–583–5558.

Sam Rayburn Library

In 1949 Sam Rayburn received the $10,000 Collier's Award for Distinguished Congressional Service, and this became the basis of an endowment to set up and maintain the Sam Rayburn Library. Rayburn's public and private papers, the most significant part of the library, illustrate his role in passing most of the important legislation of the first half of this century. Under President Woodrow Wilson, Rayburn introduced legislation to increase the power of the Interstate Commerce Commission and sponsored the War Risk Insurance Act; in the New Deal era he was the author of the Truth in Securities Act and of the acts creating the Federal Communications Commission and rural electrification. Besides his own papers, the library has the published congressional proceedings from the First Continental Congress of 1774 to the present, writings of U.S. presidents and other political leaders, a replica of Rayburn's Washington office, displays of the gifts he received during his many years on Capitol Hill (including a 2,500-year-old Grecian urn presented to Rayburn by the Athens Palace Guard), the white marble rostrum that was in the House from 1857 to 1955, and the Speaker's gavel.

LOCATION: 800 West Sam Rayburn Drive. HOURS: 10–5 Monday–Friday, 1–5 Saturday, 2–5 Sunday. FEE: None. TELEPHONE: 214–583–2455.

PARIS

This town, which was founded as Pinhook in 1839, became a railroad center in the 1870s and was called home by some colorful figures—Frank James, the outlaw Jesse James's brother and partner, who retired here to clerk in a dry-goods store; John Chisum, an early Paris citizen and pioneer antebellum cattleman; and Belle Starr, who lived on a farm near town before she began her career as "the outlaw queen of Indian Territory." The Renaissance Revival **First Methodist Church** (322 Lamar Avenue) was built in 1919–1924 and decorated inside with freehand and stenciled floral patterns and religious symbols. The **Scott-Roden Mansion** (425 South Church Street, private) is a two-and-a-half-story brick house with an Art Nouveau flavor, Dutch gable parapets, and cast-stone detailing, built from 1908–1910. Information on the town's many historic sites may be obtained from the **Paris Visitor Center** (1651 Clarksville Street, 214–784–2501).

Sam Bell Maxey House State Historic Site

This Italianate house was built in 1868 by Sam Bell Maxey, a West Point graduate, Mexican War veteran, Confederate brigadier general, and U.S. senator. The inspiration for the house apparently came from a similar one in Louisville, Kentucky (Maxey's native state), which Maxey directed his builder to copy as closely as possible. Decorative detailing on the exterior is most elaborate on the two-story portico and shouldered hood and carved brackets on the first-floor windows. The main house was remodeled in 1911 by Maxey's great-nephew Sam Bell Maxey Long. The furnishings represent typical high-style Victorian upper-middle-class decor. The state has restored the house to show how the generations of Maxeys lived here until 1967.

LOCATION: 812 South Church Street. HOURS: 10–5 Wednesday–Sunday. FEE: Yes. TELEPHONE: 214–785–5716.

In **Sulphur Springs** is another Romanesque Revival hall of justice by James Riely Gordon. The **Hopkins County Courthouse** (1895) is located on the northeast corner of the public square of this former resort town, whose mineral springs were advertised to cure-seeking travelers in the 1870s and 1880s. The **Hopkins County Museum and Heritage Park** (416 North Jackson Street, 214–885–4501) is a historical museum on eleven acres, to which have been moved old shops, mills, and houses, including the town's oldest brick home, the 1870 **Atkins House.** The **Wilson House,** built on the grounds in 1910, has historical exhibits on the county.

GOVERNOR HOGG SHRINE STATE HISTORICAL PARK

James Stephen Hogg was the much-admired and very effective first native-born governor of Texas, serving from 1891 to 1895. His children became rich when oil was discovered on family property. In an era when railroads and insurance companies, among others, exploited the public thoroughly, Hogg was known for his promotion of fair business, and legislation to ensure it. The "Hogg Laws" passed during his administration included the establishment of the still-powerful Railroad Commission, which regulates utilities, the oil industry, and transportation in the state of Texas. On the grounds are the **Honeymoon Cottage,** a 1952 replica of the first home of the governor and his wife, Sarah Ann Stinson Hogg. It is authentically furnished by Hogg's daughter, the decorative arts expert and philanthropist Ima Hogg, and includes family photographs and personal effects. The **Miss Ima Hogg Museum,** in a modern building, has exhibits ranging from Indian artifacts to the decorative arts. Moved thirteen miles to its present site, the **Stinson Home,** which was built in 1869 by Sarah Stinson Hogg's father, James A. Stinson, was where the future governor and his wife were married in 1874 and has been meticulously furnished by Miss Hogg.

LOCATION: Route 37 South, Quitman. HOURS: 8–12, 1–5 Wednesday–Sunday. FEE: Yes. TELEPHONE: 214–763–2701.

JEFFERSON

Although Jefferson's heyday as a major port was brief, from the 1850s to the 1880s, many historical buildings from the period still stand in town. A major preservation effort has made Jefferson one of the most visited towns in Texas. East Texas produce from a 200-mile radius was shipped down Big Cypress Bayou on side-wheelers to New Orleans and Saint Louis via the Red River and the Mississippi.

The dining room and ballroom in Excelsior House, a hotel that has been operating in Jefferson for well over a century.

By 1870 the town was second only to Galveston in trade volume. Building materials and furniture were shipped up from New Orleans for many of the fine houses built during Jefferson's era of prosperity. The shipping era came to an end rather abruptly in 1874 when the Red River "raft," a huge, mucky clog of fallen trees, silt, and debris that extended seventy miles upriver from Shreveport, was removed by the U.S. Army Corps of Engineers, causing the water level of Big Cypress to drop precipitously.

Jefferson Historical Society Museum

The Jefferson Historical Society offices and museum are housed in the 1888 Romanesque Revival old post office and federal building designed by William A. Ferret. The museum is a repository of art as well as historical artifacts. The Moseley Art Gallery has European and American paintings, a Flemish tapestry, nineteenth-century French furniture, wood carvings, cloisonné, Capo-di-Monte porcelain, Belleek china, and art glass. The Hobart Key Indian Collection has Caddo artifacts. In the basement of the museum is the Texas collection, including an outfitted country store and a steam engine. Other exhibits cover the life of Sam Houston, the Civil War, steamship commerce, and antebellum society.

LOCATION: 223 Austin Street. HOURS: 9:30–5 Daily. FEE: Yes. TELEPHONE: 214–665–2775.

Excelsior House

This hotel has been in continuous operation since its opening, in the 1850s, and was restored and furnished in 1961 to reflect the days when accommodations in Jefferson were elegant. There are fourteen rooms in the original frame wing (ca. 1858) and in a brick addition of 1872. The Jessie Allen Wise Garden Club, which owns and operates the hotel, restored all the original furniture and installed wallpaper and fabrics in keeping with the originals. Formal drawing and dining rooms were the scene of many Queen Mab balls and part of Jefferson's Mardi Gras celebrations in the 1870s. Some guests whose names can be seen on old registers have included Presidents Ulysses S. Grant and Rutherford B. Hayes, John Jacob Astor, William Henry Vanderbilt, Oscar Wilde, and Jay Gould. Across the street is the **Jay Gould Private Railroad Car (Atalanta),**

also administered by the garden club. This luxuriously appointed car, which Gould used for traveling on his Texas & Pacific Railroad, was apparently abandoned after the "robber baron's" death, in 1892. In the 1930s, during the oil boom in Kilgore and attendant housing shortage, oil companies started bringing in railroad cars for families to live in. Recognized in Kilgore years later by someone from Jefferson, the car is much as it was, built of fine woods including curly maple and walnut and appointed with brass fixtures, a German silver sink, and stained-glass windows.

LOCATION: 211 West Austin Street. HOURS: 9–4 Daily. FEE: Yes. TELEPHONE: 214–665–2513.

The Greek Revival **Captain William Perry House** (Walnut and Clarksville streets, private), built in 1858, belonged to the owner of Excelsior House. Built in 1872 for Benjamin H. Epperson, a prominent attorney, legislator, railroad promoter, and confidant of Sam Houston, the steamboat-era **House of the Seasons** (409 South Alley Street, 214–665–8880), an Italianate two-story frame house (a rare style in northeast Texas) has a square central cupola with interpretations of the seasons rendered in its four stained-glass windows. The cupola tops a dome that retains its original frescoes. Many of the furnishings are original to the house.

Freeman Plantation

This Greek Revival raised cottage, very much in the bayou style, was built in 1850 for Williamson M. Freeman and has interesting outsized columns. Freeman, a native of Georgia, grew cotton and sugarcane on an estate of 1,000 acres and owned a mercantile business in Jefferson. Slaves built this house meticulously, with handmade materials including clay bricks for the fourteen-inch-thick lower-floor walls and columns, and custom-cut notched and pegged framing timbers. The exterior walls above the brick are made of cypress. The columns were fashioned from pie-shaped bricks that were stuccoed and painted. The house is fully furnished with antebellum antiques.

LOCATION: Route 49, 1 mile west of Jefferson. HOURS: Tours at 2:30 and 3:30 Thursday–Tuesday. FEE: Yes. TELEPHONE: 214–665–2320.

OPPOSITE: *The posh private car of railroad magnate Jay Gould is preserved in Jefferson, whose citizens refused to allow Gould's railroad to run through the town.*

Thomas J. Rogers acquired the **Captain's Castle** or **Rogers-McCasland Home** (403 East Walker Street, 214–665–2330), a one-story Greek Revival cottage, in the 1850s. In 1878 he bought a two-story house of the same period, had it moved on cypress logs pulled by teams of mules and oxen, and placed it in front of the original house so that the roof of the second house sloped down to join that of the first. The present owners have furnished the house with period antiques. Other houses of interest include the **French Townhouse** (502 East Walker Street, 214–665–2760), a French Gothic cottage; the **Alley-Carlson House** (501 East Walker Street, private), which was built in 1865 by the son of one of the founders of Jefferson; the **Beard House** (212 North Vale at Henderson Street, 214–665–2606), a one-story frame residence with Victorian elements, furnished with period antiques of Federal, Empire, and Victorian periods; and the **Brownhouse** (112 Vale Street, 214–665–2310), the **Atkins-Lemmon House** (407 East Walker Street, 214–665–3679), and **Blue Bonnet Farm** (Route 59, about a mile south of Jefferson, 214–665–3635), all Greek Revival buildings dating from 1842 to 1866. The Jessie Allen Wise Garden Club is headquartered in the oldest house in town, called the **Presbyterian Manse** (Alley and Delta streets), a Greek Revival cottage built in 1830, with additions dating to 1850, that was used at the turn of the century as the Presbyterian manse.

The commercial district of Jefferson includes the **Jefferson Playhouse** (Market and Henderson streets), a Greek Revival residence built in 1860, acquired for a Catholic school nine years later, and then bought by a Jewish congregation. In 1870 they built a Classically inspired synagogue and attached it to the original residence. The Jessie Allen Wise Garden Club acquired the building in 1954, and it is now a theater. The **Planters Bank** (Austin Street at the bayou), built in 1852, is typical of the commercial architecture on the waterfront, with French doors and ornamental ironwork.

MARSHALL

Founded in 1841, Marshall—named for Chief Justice John Marshall—was by 1861 one of the wealthiest and largest cities in Texas, and it became an important manufacturing and military center during the Civil War. After the fall of Vicksburg, Marshall was made Trans–Mississippi Division headquarters. Confederate history is explored at the **Harrison County Historical Museum** (Peter Whetstone Square, 214–938–2680), which occupies twenty-three rooms of the Classic Revival courthouse of 1901, designed by James Riely Gordon. Marshall got the railroad that Jefferson did not, and around it grew what is today called the **Ginocchio National Historic District,** centered on the **Ginocchio Hotel** (707 North Washington), a Mission-style edifice built by C. G. Lancaster in 1896. The nearby **Allen House Museum** (610 North Washington) is a ca. 1877 frame house with a double verandah and period furnishings. Marshall's **First Methodist Church** (300 East Houston) is a stately Greek Revival edifice of 1861 whose massive squared-off columns were mocked by an early critic for looking like "large chimneys."

Starr Family State Historic Site

This beautifully preserved Italianate house was built in 1870, reputedly by New Orleans shipwrights, for James Franklin Starr, son of the illustrious Dr. James Harper Starr, who served as both surgeon general and secretary of the treasury of the Republic of Texas as well as agent of the postal service of the Confederacy west of the Mississippi. Some materials, such as cypress window sashes and doors, window glass, stair railings, hardware, and carpets, came up from New Orleans, along with carpenters—or (if true) shipwrights. An addition to the house was built in 1875 to house Mrs. Starr's mother, but more significant alterations came in the 1930s at the hands of the Starrs' daughter, who was enamored of the then-popular Colonial Revival style. Today the house has a mixture of nineteenth- and twentieth-century furnishings.

LOCATION: 407 West Travis Street. HOURS: 9–11, 1–4 Wednesday–Sunday. FEE: Yes. TELEPHONE: 214–935–4087.

Outside of Marshall, on F.M. 1997, are the ruins of the **Marshall Arsenal,** about forty brick and stone buildings making up an arsenal that was particularly important for the Confederacy after the Union took control of the Mississippi River.

LONGVIEW

Rich natural resources drew settlers to Longview, established in 1870 as the railroads advanced through Texas. The town was named by the Southern Pacific Railroad surveyors who were impressed by the long view from a hillside overlooking a piney woods. The discovery of the East Texas Oilfield in the 1930s tripled Longview's population and transformed this agricultural community into a business and industrial center.

The history of the area is explored at the **Gregg County Historical Museum** (214 North Fredonia Street, 214–753–5840), housed in a bank building of 1910. Exhibits include reproductions of early rooms—a banker's office, a parlor, a general mercantile store, and the inside of a log cabin—as well as displays of local farming artifacts and weapons. At the **Caddo Indian Museum** (701 Hardy Street, 214–759–5739) are prehistoric and historic Caddo artifacts as well as Spanish trade items from the early 1800s and Anglo-American documents.

TYLER

Established in 1846, Tyler is a major shipping center for East Texas truck farms and orchards. For years it was a petroleum center; the seemingly bottomless East Texas Oilfield, discovered in 1930 and one of the greatest fields in the world, is just twenty-five miles east of Tyler. The **Carnegie History Center** (125 South College, 214–593–7989) is housed in one of the many Carnegie libraries built around the country in the early twentieth century, this one a Renaissance Revival brick structure with limestone detailing. Collections include displays on Smith County and Civil War history and Indian artifacts, and a 1930s kitchen.

The **Goodman Museum** (624 North Broadway, 214–597–5304) is the former Goodman-LeGrand House, built as a dogtrot in 1859 by a bachelor named Samuel Gallatin Smith, who called the house "Bonnie Castle." Dr. Samuel A. Goodman and his son, Dr. William H. Goodman, owned the house after Smith and made Greek Revival additions. The collections include medical instruments, among them those of the younger Dr. Goodman, Indian artifacts, antique furniture, and photographs of early life in Smith County. The recently restored **Bonner-Whitaker-McClendon House** (806 West Houston Street, 214–592–3533) was built in 1880 with an addition in 1910 and is a mix of themes: Italianate, Eastlake, and Classic Revival. Approximately two-thirds of the furniture is original to the house.

HENDERSON

The seat of Rusk County, Henderson was founded in 1844 and named for James Pinckney Henderson, a lawyer and military man who raised a good number of men to fight in the Texas Revolution and went on to serve the government of the republic, and as the first governor of the state of Texas. The town of Henderson thrived on lumbering in the early days, then on agriculture and oil. In the waiting room and office of the 1901 Missouri-Pacific Railroad Depot, the **Depot Museum** (514 North High Street, 214–657–4303) tells the story of Rusk County through displays of artifacts and documents. On the grounds is the Arnold Outhouse, a Victorian privy with facilities for three, built in 1908 for a prominent local attorney. A log cabin built in 1841, a Missouri-Pacific caboose, a country doctor's office, an agricultural barn, a broom factory, and a syrup mill are also on the grounds.

The **Howard-Dickinson House** (501 South Main Street, 214–657–6925) has the distinction of being the first brick house in Rusk County, built in 1855, and was known to have been visited often by Sam Houston, a relative of the builder. It has been made a house museum and is furnished with antebellum antiques.

The **Texas State Railroad Historical Park** (Route 84, between Palestine and Rusk, 214–683–2561) is dedicated to railroading's age of steam. Restored turn-of-the-century trains leaving from reconstructed depots of the same period make fifty-mile round-trip runs from the towns of Palestine and Rusk, crossing the Neches River over a 1,100-foot bridge and passing each other at the Mewshaw Siding. The Texas State Railroad was constructed in 1896 to serve industries related to the state penitentiary at Rusk, which was turned into a mental hospital in 1913. The track was conveyed to the Texas Parks and Wildlife Department in 1972.

JIM HOGG STATE HISTORICAL PARK

This 177-acre park was part of the original "Mountain Home" plantation of Joseph Lewis Hogg, a Cherokee County pioneer and the father of James Stephen (Jim) Hogg, the "people's governor" from 1891–1895. The elder Hogg, a brigadier general in the Civil War, died at Corinth, near the Shiloh battlefield, in 1862. The Hogg family cemetery is within the boundaries of the park. The museum house is an approximate one-third-scale replica of the Hogg plantation frame house built by the family in 1846. In addition to memorabilia of and historical displays about the Hogg family, the house has one room devoted to printing (Governor Hogg, as a 16-year-old, worked at the local paper after the Civil War) and a collection of pioneer furniture including cowhide-covered chairs and a hand-carved table.

LOCATION: Route 84, 2 miles east of Rusk off Park Road 50. HOURS: *Park:* September through May: 8–5 Thursday–Monday; June through August: 8–8 Thursday–Monday. *Museum:* 10–4 Thursday–Monday. FEE: None. TELEPHONE: 214–683–4850.

CROCKETT

The frontiersman, Whig politician, and Alamo hero Davy Crockett of Tennessee gave his name to this Texas town, founded in the 1830s alongside the Old San Antonio Road, because he had camped near here on his way to the Alamo. (His camp was at Davy Crockett Spring, still flowing, on West Goliad at Route 7/21.) The **A. T. M. Monroe House** (South 7th and Clark streets, private) is believed to have been built in 1847 by Armistead Thompson Monroe, great-nephew of President James Monroe. The spacious two-story residence has wide porches and a deck with entrances from the upper floor. A decorative railing on the roof suggests a frontier lookout. The Monroes' second Crockett home, the **Monroe-Crook House** (707 East Houston Avenue, 409–544–5820), was built in 1854 in the Greek Revival style. It is furnished to the period. The **Downes-Aldrich House** (206 North 7th Street, 409–544–4804) is one of the best examples of Queen Anne–Eastlake Victorian architecture in the state. Built in 1893 from plans of the Knoxville, Tennessee, architectural firm of George F. Barber and Co., the house possesses elaborate millwork, decoratively patterned shingles, and generous porches and galleries. Inside, pattern competes with pattern in the wallpaper, mantels, woodwork, and paths of light traced by the windows.

The **Mary Allen Seminary for Colored Girls** (803 North 4th Street), later Mary Allen College, was established in Crockett by the Board of Missions for Freedmen of the Presbyterian Church in the United States from a local black parochial school operated by the Reverend Samuel Fisher Tenney. In **David Crockett Memorial Park** stands the one-room **Strode-Pritchett Log Cabin** (Beasley Drive, 409–544–3255), built around 1843 some twelve miles east of

The Queen Anne and Eastlake Downes-Aldrick House, built in 1893 using mail-order plans which were adapted to the owners' wishes.

Crockett. The cabin was relocated in Crockett Park and restored with a wooden shingled roof, split log sidings, and mud cat chimney. The **Houston County Visitors Center Museum** (303 South 1st Street, 409–544–3255) is housed in the waiting rooms, ticket office, baggage room, and freight room of a depot built of brick, concrete, and glass—the third constructed by the Great Northern Railroad, in 1909. The former freight room features a floor made of wooden railroad-track cross ties. Exhibits detail the history of the county's fifty-three communities and five incorporated towns.

MISSION TEJAS STATE HISTORICAL PARK

The reconstructed log building in this park commemorates the first Spanish mission in Texas, Mission San Francisco de los Tejas, founded in 1690 by Fray Damian Massanet and Franciscan priests to bring Christianity to the Indians and to secure Spain's dominion over Texas. Built to serve the Hasinai (the Spanish mistakenly called them "Tejas," the tribe's word for "friends"), the original mission was located on San Pedro Creek. The site of the reconstruction was determined by the discovery of an old cannon thought to have been buried by the Spanish in 1693 when they abandoned the mission—most of the once-friendly Indians had been killed by disease brought to their communities by the Spanish soldiery. Those few who survived kept their distance from the mission, except to steal horses and cattle. The Spanish burned the mission on their departure. An attempt to reestablish the Tejas mission came in 1716 in response to French activity in Texas; it was again abandoned in 1719, reestablished in 1721, and finally in 1731 moved to San Antonio—along with the other east Texas missions that had been feebly operating in the interim. Mission San Francisco de los Tejas was reestablished in San Antonio as Mission San Francisco de la Espada. In 1935 the Civilian Conservation Corps built the present building. In 1974 the Texas Parks and Wildlife Department moved an authen-

This mound is one of three at Caddoan Mounds State Historic Site that have yielded important information about the Indian confederacy that once occupied much of northeastern Texas. The Spanish explorer Coronado was impressed by the ingenious construction of the grass houses built by the Caddo.

tic Anglo-American log house to the park, the home of Joseph Redmund Rice, Sr., built between 1828 and 1838, one of the oldest log houses in Texas and one of the longest occupied—until 1919.

LOCATION: Route 21 and Park Road 44, Weches. HOURS: 8 AM–10 PM Daily. FEE: Yes. TELEPHONE: 409–687–2394.

CADDOAN MOUNDS STATE HISTORIC SITE

This important archaeological site is responsible for much of what scholars know about the Caddo culture. The early Caddo established themselves in this area about A.D. 800; the village was the southwesternmost Caddoan ceremonial center. The Caddo of this period seem to have been led by a ruling class that lived on or around the ceremonial temple mounds built by the commoners of the tribe, who also tilled the fields. Theirs was a sophisticated prehistoric culture. But, in the thirteenth century, this site was abandoned. The Caddo continued to live in east Texas and were present when the Spanish arrived. They lived in east Texas until forced west in 1840 by troops of the Republic of Texas. The first systematic excavations at the Caddoan Mounds were performed from 1939 to 1941 under a WPA grant, and careful excavation and study of the site continue. Two temple mounds and a burial mound are preserved here. There is also a reconstruction of an early Caddo dwelling, built using the materials and techniques of the Caddo.

LOCATION: Route 21, 6 miles southwest of Alto. HOURS: 8–5 Wednesday–Sunday. FEE: Yes. TELEPHONE: 409–858–3218.

NACOGDOCHES

Nacogdoches, one of Texas's oldest towns, is steeped in history and legend. The Caddo Indians left traces of pyramidal mounds here; **Indian Mound,** in the 500 block of Mound Street, is the only one remaining. The town itself has its roots in the settlement of the Nacogdoche and Nacao Indians of the Caddo confederacies; legend has it that an old Caddo chief of a community on the Sabine had two sons, Nacogdoche and Natchitoche; when they came of age he sent the first to the setting sun, the second to the rising sun, and thus the present-day communities of Nacogdoches and Natchitoches, Louisiana, were founded. The road marked between the two towns became El Camino Real (Old San Antonio Road) and was the major route into Texas for more than a century.

In response to the threat of French expansion in east Texas, the Spanish built the Mission Nuestra Señora de Guadalupe de los Nacogdoches among the Nacogdoche and Nacao in 1716. In 1773, when Spain was forced to realize that the mission efforts in east Texas were flagging and increasingly expensive, the crown removed the missions and their settlers to San Antonio, where settlement leader Gil Y'Barbo and his neighbors were not happy to live. They were granted permission to head east again, but only as far as the Trinity River. But Comanche attacks and river floods prompted Y'Barbo to return to Nacogdoches in 1779, which is the year from which the present-day settlement dates.

Adolphus Sterne House (Hoya Library and Museum)

This early pioneer Texas house was built in 1830 by Adolphus Sterne, a German-Jewish immigrant who settled in Nacogdoches in 1826. A prominent merchant and Texas revolutionary leader, Sterne aided Hayden Edwards in the Fredonian rebellion: He procured munitions in New Orleans and hid them in bales of dry goods and barrels of coffee, but he was found out by the Mexican authorities, imprisoned in the Old Stone Fort, and ordered to be shot—a fate from which he was saved by Masons intervening on his behalf. Sterne is sometimes called the "Financier of the Texas Revolution"; at the outbreak of the conflict, he recruited and equipped a company of the New Orleans Grays (U.S. volunteers for the Texas independence effort) and paid for their passage to Natchitoches. They traveled overland to Nacogdoches, where Sterne entertained them in this house before they headed west to their deaths with Fannin at Goliad and Travis at the Alamo.

The widowed Mrs. Sterne sold the house in 1869 to a fellow German immigrant, farmer, and landowner, Joseph von Hoya. The restoration and furnishing of the house created rooms that reflect both the Sternes' and the Hoyas' lives here; one parlor has early Texas furniture, another Victorian pieces. The Texana Room has books about Texas and genealogical materials, and there is also a children's library.

LOCATION: 211 South Lanana Street. HOURS: 9–12, 2–5 Monday–Saturday. FEE: None. TELEPHONE: 409–560–5426.

Stone Fort Museum

This museum is housed in a replica of the structure Don Antonio Gil Y'Barbo, the founder of the present-day city of Nacogdoches, built in about 1780 as his home and as the formal *portales* to the Spanish District of Texas. During its history, the original building served various purposes. From 1806 until the Magee-Gutiérrez Expedition of 1813, William Barr and Samuel Davenport operated a trade business exporting deer hides and horses provided by the Indians. Three filibustering expeditions by expansionist adventurers of the nineteenth century used the stone house as their headquarters: the Magee-Gutiérrez expedition, Dr. James Long's filibuster of 1819, and the Fredonia Rebellion in 1826. The stone house served as offices in 1829, and in 1832 Mexican soldiers barricaded themselves in the house when their attempt to seize weaponry here was resisted. During the Texas Revolution, the building functioned as a meeting place for recruits. After a heated town debate the building

The Stone Fort Museum, a replica of an eighteenth-century house built by the founder of Nacogdoches, was constructed using some of the original stones.

was torn down in 1902 to make way for a modern commercial building. In 1936 some of the original stones were used to build the present replica structure authorized by the Texas Centennial Commission and the State Board of Control. The museum collection focuses on the prehistory and history of east Texas prior to 1900, with emphasis on nineteenth-century technology. Exhibits include textile and agricultural tools, furniture, and local history exhibits.

LOCATION: On the campus of Stephen F. Austin State University. HOURS: 9–5 Tuesday–Saturday, 1–5 Sunday. FEE: None. TELEPHONE: 409–568–2408.

The Greek Revival brick edifice at Mound and Hughes streets was the main building of **Old Nacogdoches University** (713–564–0084) from 1858, when it was built, until 1895, although during the Civil War it served as a hospital and quarters for Confederate troops and for a short while afterward housed federal troops. Now on the campus of Nacogdoches High School, the building has a museum filled with early Texas domestic and church furniture, antique clothing, historic documents, farm implements, a schoolroom display, and various local memorabilia. Several early east Texas houses furnished with a wide variety of antiques have been moved to **Millard's Crossing** (5020 North Street, 409–564–6969), a museum complex. The two-story frame **Millard-Lee House,** built in 1837 as an inn, is now decorated in Victorian wicker and houses one of the best private collections of early Texas maps and papers. Also on the site are the **Millard-Burrows House** (1840); a white wooden **chapel** built in 1843; and the **Watkins Homestead** of 1895, a simple frame cottage.

SAN AUGUSTINE

East of Nacogdoches on the heavily traveled El Camino Real, San Augustine was first an Ais Indian village, in which the Spanish established Mission Nuestra Señora de los Dolores de los Ais in 1716. Anglo-Americans began coming into the area in the 1820s and made of it one of Texas's finest Greek Revival villages. The **Ezekial Cullen House** (205 South Congress, 409–275–5110) was built in 1839 for a significant figure in the days of the revolution and the republic. Cullen fought at the Siege of Bexar and served at the third congress of the Texas Republic (1838–1839), where he wrote the bill that set aside public lands for the endowment of two universities.

Cullen, it was said, had come to Texas with a law degree, a manservant, and $10,000. A descendant, oil millionaire Hugh Roy Cullen of Houston, bought the house in 1952 and financed the restoration. The furnishing of the house is to the early Texas period. The attic floor of this one-and-a-half-story cottage was used by Cullen as a ballroom. Another fine cottage by the builder of the Cullen House, Augustus Phelps, is the **Matthew Cartwright House** (912 East Main Street, private), built in 1839 for a Republic legislator. The **Horn-Polk House** (717 West Columbia, private) is a later Greek Revival residence (1858) built for a cabinetmaker and gunsmith.

The **Heritage Village Museum** (Route 190, just west of Woodville, 409-283-2272) is a reconstructed historical village with approximately thirty restored buildings, including the **Collier Store,** with its original wares on display; a railroad station reconstructed from the materials of a former stop on the Texas & New Orleans line (one of the few railroads in the state to begin operating before the Civil War); and the **Tolar Log Cabin,** built in 1866.

ALABAMA-COUSHATTA INDIAN RESERVATION

One of only two Indian reservations in Texas, this is the home of the Southern forest tribes Alabama and Coushatta, set aside in 1854 under the auspices of Sam Houston, who was able to reward the two tribes for their neutrality during the Texas Revolution. The reservation's 4,600 acres include the only remaining virgin forest of the great Big Thicket. The Alabama and Coushatta, who had lived in the area since 1800, would not sell their trees even during the desperate days of the Great Depression. Tours through the woods show now-rare species of native hardwoods as well as other plants and wildlife. A living Indian village features tribal members in traditional dress making jewelry and baskets. Tribal dances are a regular event during the summer. At the Historical Museum are displays relating the history of the two tribes, who were pushed to Texas from the Mississippi and Tennessee River areas.

LOCATION: Route 3, off Route 190 between Livingston and Woodville. HOURS: June through August: 10–6 Daily; September through May: 10–5 Friday–Saturday, 12:30–5 Sunday. FEE: Yes. TELE-PHONE: 409–563–4391.

HUNTSVILLE

This town, founded in 1835, is sometimes called "the Mount Vernon of Texas" because Sam Houston, first president of the republic, called Huntsville home. The **Huntsville Chamber of Commerce** (Route 30 at Avenue N, 409–295–8113) provides information about the town's sites. Sam Houston is buried at **Oakwood Cemetery** (Avenue I and 9th Street), on land deeded in 1847 for community burial by Huntsville's founder, Pleasant Gray. Houston's grave is marked with a 1911 monument inscribed with Andrew Jackson's words "The World Will Take Care of Houston's Fame." Commercial buildings of interest in Huntsville include the **Gibbs Brothers Building** (Sam Houston and 11th Street), housing the firm founded by Thomas Gibbs, one of the earliest Huntsville settlers; and the 1883 **Henry Opera House** (12th and University). The **Gibbs-Powell Home** (1228 11th Street, 409–295–8113) was built in 1862 by Thomas Gibbs, a close friend of Sam Houston. The Queen Anne **Thomason-Cole Home** (1207 Avenue J), built in 1891, with Shingle-style additions in 1905, was built by local physician and philanthropist John William Thomason. The two-story Greek Revival **Rogers House** (1418 University Avenue, private) was built in 1844 by George Washington Rogers, a pioneer developer who was largely responsible for Huntsville's prominence as one of Texas's most important cultural, political, and educational centers in the mid-1800s.

Sam Houston Memorial Museum

This complex of seven buildings is on 15 acres of Sam Houston's original 174-acre estate. Sam and Margaret Houston moved to Huntsville in 1847, and built a dogtrot house now known as the **Woodland Home.** As governor, Houston had led the Texas Unionists in a vain fight to prevent the state from joining the Confederacy. He had addressed a crowd from the balcony of a Galveston hotel, predicting the bloody consequences of secession: "Let me tell you what is coming . . . . Your fathers and husbands, your sons and brothers, will be herded at the point of the bayonet . . . . The North is determined to preserve this Union . . . they will overwhelm the South." Houston was removed from office by the Secessionists. Upon his return to Huntsville in 1862, Houston tried to repurchase or rent the Woodland Home, but, viewed as a traitor, he was turned away. Finally he was able to rent **Steamboat House,** where he died in 1863 (his last

Steamboat House, where Sam Houston died in 1863 in disfavor, a Unionist in a staunchly Confederate state.

words were "Texas . . Texas . . . Margaret . . ."). The house was moved to this site from its original location near Oakwood Cemetery.

The museum displays many personal items, including Houston's dueling pistols and sword, samples of the woodcarving he did to relax, and correspondence to his wife. General Santa Anna's polychrome leather, gold, and brass saddle is on display, along with Houston's law office, outfitted with his desk and bookcase, a reconstructed kitchen, smokehouse, and a blacksmith shop.

LOCATION: 1826 Sam Houston Avenue. HOURS: 9–5 Tuesday–Sunday. FEE: None. TELEPHONE: 409–294–1832.

The Walls enclose the original site of the first permanent penitentiary in Texas, now the main unit of the Texas Department of Criminal Justice, Institutional Division. The Huntsville State Prison is a legendary place, sung about in blues songs and once home of the annual Texas Prison Rodeo held until 1986 in the arena next door.

Back downtown, on the south side of the courthouse square, is the
Texas Prison Museum (1113 12th Street, 409–295–2155), a fascinating repository of prison artifacts, including contraband weapons
taken from prisoners and the famous "Old Sparky," the electric chair
whose function was replaced in the last few years by lethal injections.

BIG THICKET NATIONAL PRESERVE

South of the Piney Woods is the biologically diverse Big Thicket
region of east Texas. Originally covering over 3,000,000 acres, Big
Thicket is often described as a biological crossroads. Here elements
of the southwestern deserts, central plains, eastern forests,
Appalachian Mountains, and southeastern swamps bump up against
each other. As a result, an extraordinary variety of plants and animals live in the Big Thicket, including some species found in other
states but nowhere else in Texas. Human development has eliminated the black bears, red wolves, and cougars that once roamed the
area, but deer, alligator, beaver, otter, squirrel, armadillo, and pos-
sum still thrive. Approximately three hundred species of birds are
resident in the area or migrate through. The importance of water
can be seen in the numerous streams and bayous that crisscross the
area. The area is as rich in cultural history as in natural history. The
Indians of east Texas hunted in the Big Thicket, but never lived in
it; early Spanish settlers avoided the "impenetrable woods" and early
Anglo-Americans made their way around rather than through the
Big Thicket, settling on the fringes. In the early nineteenth century,
Big Thicket became a refuge for outlaws, runaway slaves, gamblers,
horse thieves, and hermits. Farmers, who also hunted and trapped,
eventually moved into the area. Extensive lumbering ultimately
reduced the original forest to mere fragments. Today, Big Thicket
National Preserve, encompassing 84,550 acres, protects the giant
magnolias and beech trees, spreading dogwood and hawthorns, towering cypress and tupelo trees, orchids and wildflowers, and the
streams and pools. The richness and diversity of Big Thicket are
such that there may still be species of plants and animals that man
has yet to discover. Big Thicket National Preserve is managed by the
National Park Service. The **Visitor Information Station**
(409–246–2337) is located on F.M. 420 approximately seven miles
north of Kountze.

OPPOSITE: *The office where Sam Houston practiced law before he was elected governor of Texas.*

WEST
TEXAS

OPPOSITE: Hornos, *communal beehive ovens, near the Ysleta Mission in El Paso.*

The settlement of west Texas is a story of adaptation to land that is harsh, beautiful, and secretive—and goes on for miles and miles and miles, the source of all the clichés about how *big* Texas is. No written record of much that happened in the way of human history remains. Most of the early architecture has crumbled, although some is preserved on the grounds of small museums. Here the open landscape is the attraction, but the weather is the burden—rainfall is described as "deficient" or, in good seasons, as merely "critical." Inhabitants have never been numerous. The rugged part of Texas west of the Pecos River is desert and dry mountains, with a few mountain havens of pine forests and cool air. The journalist Griffin Smith, Jr., wrote that "men have never managed to 'develop' the trans-Pecos: They simply *cling* to it, wresting what they can from the obstinate land." To the east of the Pecos, the scrub-covered limestone slab called the Edwards Plateau is only slightly more hospitable to human pursuits; the rolling plains and finally the high plains, the lands where the buffalo roamed, were the domain only of the Native Americans until their underground secrets of water and oil were discovered and exploited by whites.

The earliest settlements in west Texas were established about 12,000 years ago in the Panhandle. The dry climate has preserved their records in the bones of mammoths and bison and the early peoples' weapons and tools. Before the Spanish explorers arrived in the sixteenth century, the only known pueblos in Texas were along the Canadian River in the Panhandle. There Indians built multi-roomed stone dwellings and traded with similar peoples in what is modern-day New Mexico and Arizona. The Apache and Comanche came to Texas in the 1500s; the mobility of these two roving tribes was greatly enhanced when they acquired horses from the Spaniards in the mid-1600s. The Apache and Comanche traveled light and lived in buffalo-hide tepees that could be dismantled in minutes.

Along the Rio Grande in the late sixteenth century, the Spaniards encountered the Jumano and their adobe structures and moved on to what is now New Mexico. Spanish settlements in the seventeenth century along the upper stretches of the river in Texas were successful only in the present-day El Paso area. In their search for gold and treasure, the Spanish virtually ignored the harsh mountains of the trans-Pecos, which became the range of the Lipan Apache. In the mountainous deserts of the trans-Pecos, the Apache and later the Comanche used watering holes and springs and creeks

Catching Wild Horses *by George Catlin, a painter who spent eight years documenting the "native looks and history" of Indians on the American frontier (detail).*

unknown to the Spaniards. The Spaniards established a few presidios (forts) and missions just above the canyons of the Big Bend in the 1700s, but Apache raids, which included the capture of some Spanish and the making of slaves out of captives, discouraged long-term commitment. Some Indians and settlers who had joined the mission communities stayed behind after the presidios were abandoned in the early 1800s. Their descendants still live in tiny villages on the river, where adobe, stone, and cane remain the building materials of choice and the Rio Grande floodplain nurtures agriculture in the midst of the Chihuahuan desert.

To the north, the Llano Estacado, or Staked Plains, cover the Panhandle and extends south of the cities of Midland and Odessa. The name of the region was probably derived from the stakes that were used as landmarks on this barren plain. "Not a stone, not a bit of rising ground, not a tree, not a shrub, nor anything to go by," observed Coronado as he passed through the area on his quest for the golden cities. Early American explorers of what was to become

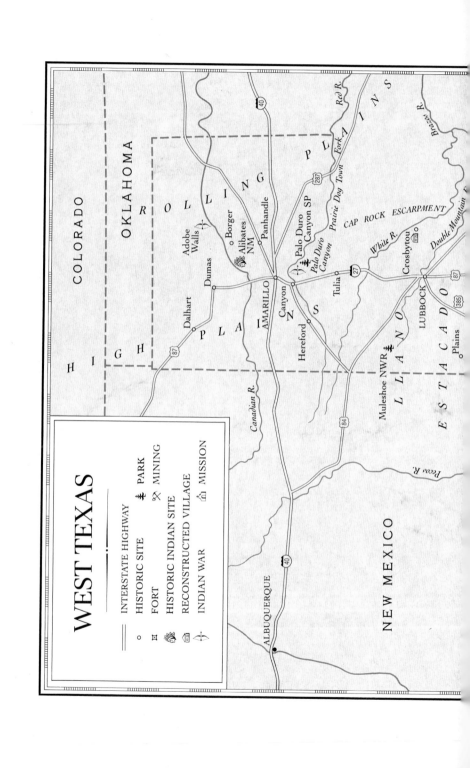

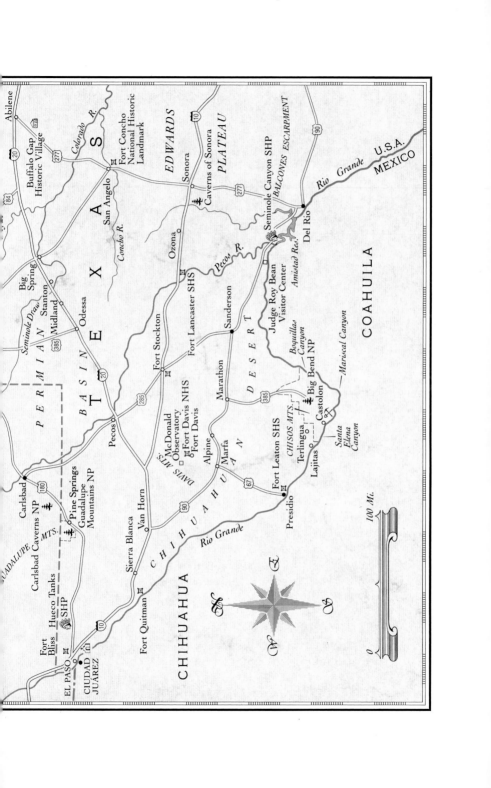

The men and horses of Troop D, Third Cavalry, in a photograph taken while they were stationed at Fort Davis in the 1880s. A museum devoted to the Third Cavalry is located at Fort Bliss in El Paso.

west Texas shared the Spanish impression that the region was simply a vast, arid wasteland. One *empresario* grant from the Spanish king stretched as far as the Pecos River, but the land was never settled; the lack of aboveground water and the threat of Apache and Comanche raids proved too formidable. When Texas joined the Union in 1845, it was in part to get federal assistance with the "Indian problem" in the west: Texas might have owned title to the land, but the Comanche owned it by possession. Only the Comancheros—Mexicans who traded with the Comanche from the late eighteenth century until the Indians were forced onto a reservation—could travel there freely. However, in the late 1840s and 1850s, pioneers and forty-niners started to move in. During the years between statehood and the beginning of the Civil War, the U.S. Army garrisoned nine forts in Texas west of the Pecos River to protect mail and emigration routes from Indian reprisals against the white men's trespass and to secure the border. Secretary of War Jefferson Davis advocated a war to quell the Apache in the 1850s, but then the Civil War broke out and delayed the confrontation. When the Civil War ended in 1865, settlers again followed the route of the forts as they set up trading posts and cattle ranges (the beginnings of many of the present-day towns). After 1872 the Texas Rangers, a paramilitary force armed with repeating weapons, went after the Indians rather than waiting for them to attack.

The Comanche on the high plains had fled from a reservation in Oklahoma Indian Territory where they had been placed in 1859. Like the Apache in the trans-Pecos, the Comanche held out against the white man. They were eventually starved out with the help of buffalo hunters. A single hunter might kill 1,000 to 2,000 buffalo in a three-month hunting season. In spite of belated protests by Texans, the Indians' food supply—herds that numbered millions of buffalo and stretched to the horizon—was eliminated with the approval of the U.S. Army.

It took more than the removal of the Comanche to make the Plains profitable for whites. In both the trans-Pecos and the Plains, there sprang up vast ranches, a few of which covered nearly ten entire counties. Railroads made it easier to ship buffalo hides to markets in the north and east and to import the comforts of home, such as lumber, furniture, and windmills. (Some people still alive today grew up on the Plains in dugouts built of sod blocks—warm in winter, cool in summer, like their adobe counterparts to the southwest.)

Better well-digging technology and the use of windmills to power pumps helped convert the Plains to irrigated farmland after the discovery in the late 1870s of the vast Ogallala Aquifer, which lies under most of the Plains. Barbed wire was introduced in the Plains in the 1870s by the cattle kingdoms, owned for the most part by outsiders who had no love or need for the customs of the shared range; the fencing put an end to the open range and to many smaller ranchers. In the twentieth century oil changed the landscape. Almost every county in the Plains and part of the trans-Pecos has or has had oil underneath it. Where there was oil, there was drilling; boomtowns sprang up and died, and some of them turned into manufacturing centers. Oil rigs are ubiquitous across the Plains, though a few silos compete for supremacy. After the oil runs out, it is likely that agriculture will reign on the Plains—until the water runs out.

This tour starts at El Paso, proceeds through the trans-Pecos and eastward into the Edwards Plateau, then heads north through the Permian Basin and up into the rolling plains and finally the high plains of the Panhandle.

EL PASO

In the farthest western corner of Texas, the city of El Paso spreads along the mountain pass created by the Rio Grande as it cuts through the Franklin Mountains. Human habitation in the area goes back thousands of years; the Tanpachoa were the first people known to have lived on the Rio Grande in these parts. Alvar Nuñez Cabeza de Vaca may have been the first Spaniard to see the pass, in the 1530s, on his journey west from the Gulf Coast at present-day Galveston to the Pacific coast of Mexico near Culiacán. El Paso del Norte, "the pass of the north," was actually discovered in 1598 when it was reached by the New Mexico–bound expedition of Juan de Oñate. Oñate, very rich and married to the granddaughter of Cortés, had contracted with the crown to settle New Mexico and was named its governor. "Therefore," he declared to his party of priests, settlers, and soldiers upon their arrival, ". . . I take possession, once, twice, and thrice, and all the times I can and must, of the . . . lands of the said Rio del Norte, without exception whatsoever," and nailed a cross to a nearby tree, finishing off with a prayer for peaceful possession.

For almost two centuries El Paso del Norte was virtually the only protected route north from Mexico; even to get to the San Antonio missions and those as far as east Texas the Spaniards would make the extremely out-of-the-way loop up through El Paso and then east. The present-day Ciudad Juárez began as a way station on the Camino Real, the route between Mexico City and Santa Fe. It grew into a town after 1659, when a little church to serve the Manso Indians was built of branches and mud (rebuilt in 1668, Our Lady of the Guadalupe of El Paso, or Guadalupe Mission, still stands in Juárez, Mexico—and is the oldest mission in the area).

The first permanent settlement in what would become El Paso began during the great Pueblo Revolt against the Spanish in New Mexico in 1680, which forced the colonizers and some of the Christianized Tigua to flee south along the Rio Grande. The missionaries established the Ysleta Mission in 1680, and a village grew around it. Ysleta, now part of the city of El Paso, is the oldest continuously occupied settlement in Texas. The towns that became El Paso and Juárez grew together until the Mexican War divided them. Today the two cities constitute the largest international metropolitan border area in North America. Paso del Norte was renamed Juárez in 1888 for the Mexican hero and president Benito Juárez.

Downtown El Paso and Ciudad Juárez in the Mexican state of Chihuahua, from the Franklin Mountains.

The next settlement north of the river was on land granted in 1827 to Juan María Ponce de León, who established a ranch, planted cotton and wheat, and started a small vineyard watered by the Rio Grande. In 1849, after the Mexican War, the colorful Irish-Kentuckian trader and one-time U.S. consul to Chihuahua James Wiley Magoffin settled in the area with his wife and built a compound that came to be called Magoffinsville. In the 1850s a federal commissioner observed that the town belonged "wholly to James W. Magoffin, Esq., an American, long resident in Mexico, whose energy and public spirit will undoubtedly make it the principal place on the frontier." The third small settlement was made after Ponce de León's death in 1852, when his ranch was sold to Franklin Coons. Coons became the area's first postmaster and called his community Franklin. But Coons could not finish paying for his real estate, so the land was resold in 1854 to William T. Smith. The name Franklin was changed to El Paso after the town was surveyed by the state in 1858. Meanwhile, downriver, Concordia El Alto Ranch was established by

Hugh Stephenson on land his father-in-law, Juan Ascarate, had been granted by the Mexican government in 1836 (Concordia Cemetery, El Paso's Boot Hill, is on the site today). Upriver from Franklin, Simeon Hart and his wife, Jesusita, built a mill in 1850, around which grew the small village of Hart's Mill. During most of this early settlement, the rest of Texas—on the other side of the wide deserts and Comanche-ruled plains—hardly knew El Paso existed.

A U.S. Army post (later named Fort Bliss) was established in El Paso in 1849 to enforce the Treaty of Guadalupe Hidalgo between Mexico and the United States, which included terms requiring the United States to protect citizens of both countries from hostile Indian raids. The city of El Paso was incorporated in 1873, and a census recorded 23 Anglos and 150 Mexicans at the time. Railroads came in the 1870s and 1880s. El Paso epitomized the Wild West—it was a regular stopping place not only for traders and gold seekers

A stained glass dome, made in 1912 by the Tiffany Studios, in El Paso's Paso del Norte Hotel, where, in 1968, presidents Lyndon Johnson of the United States and Gustavo Diaz-Ordaz of Mexico celebrated the final resolution of the Chamizal border disputes, which were based on the changing Rio Grande riverbed.

but also for outlaws, cattle rustlers, and men of ill repute. Much killing occurred during the 1870s in the Salt War, a dispute about private ownership and the imposition of fees to remove salt from previously public salt lakes in the area. (The Texas Rangers finally put an end to the violence.) The notorious gentleman-outlaw John Wesley Hardin was shot in the back of the head in El Paso in 1896.

In 1909 Presidents William H. Taft and Porfirio Díaz met in El Paso to discuss the political and economic crisis in Mexico. Meanwhile Francisco Madero and his supporters plotted against Díaz in the same city. In May 1911 one of the first major battles of the Mexican Revolution erupted on the streets of Juárez. On the other side of the Rio Grande, the citizens of El Paso—many of whom sided with the revolutionaries—stood on their balconies to watch with cameras and binoculars. Mexicans seeking safety poured into El Paso during the revolution. Francisco "Pancho" Villa plotted against the Mexican government and recruited followers in El Paso (and at one point brought his wife and son to the city for safekeeping). Villa turned against the United States when it backed the government of Venustiano Carranza. When Villa's men raided a town in New Mexico in 1916, Woodrow Wilson ordered General John J. "Black Jack" Pershing and a large force to set out from El Paso on a punitive expedition. (One local paper likened the action to sending the El Paso police to hunt for a jackrabbit turned loose in Oklahoma.) After eleven months of searching for Villa, Pershing gave up.

The main branch of **El Paso Tourist Information** (Santa Fe and San Francisco, 915–534–0686), located in the Civic Center Plaza, provides information about historic sites in the city. Also in the Civic Center is the **Americana Museum** (915–542–0394), devoted to local history and the fine arts. Among the architectural landmarks downtown is the triangular Beaux-Arts **Toltec Building** (747 East San Antonio Avenue) built in 1910 by the English architect John J. Huddart. The **Paso del Norte Hotel** (115 South El Paso Street) was built between 1910 and 1912 by Trost & Trost in a Sullivanesque style with an interior art-glass dome purportedly designed by Tiffany Studios. It accommodated such guests as Pancho Villa, President Taft, and General Pershing. Trost & Trost was headed by Henry Charles Trost, who was born in Ohio, graduated from art school at the age of 17, and worked as a young man in Pueblo, Colorado, and possibly for a year or so in Galveston in the 1880s with the architect Nicholas J. Clayton. A master at Spanish Colonial Revival design,

Trost also embraced the Prairie style and fashioned his own house built in 1908 in El Paso (1013 West Yandell Drive, private) after the Susan Lawrence Dana house in Springfield, Illinois, by Frank Lloyd Wright. Most of the significant buildings in El Paso were designed by Trost & Trost, including the Art Deco/Neo-Gothic **Bassett Tower** (301 Texas Avenue).

San Jacinto Plaza was El Paso's first city square and is said to be where Juan de Oñate discovered a Pueblo garden on his way to New Mexico in 1598. The two-story redbrick Classic Revival **Union Depot** (Coldwell and San Francisco) dates from 1906 and was the first in the United States built expressly for international railroad traffic, which peaked during the Second World War at thirty trains daily. The station, whose architect, Daniel H. Burnham, also designed Union Station in Washington, DC, has been painstakingly restored—stained-glass windows were found beneath layers of paint and new Italian marble replaced the original stone. The Spanish Colonial Revival **Plaza Theater** (125 West Mills Avenue, 915–542–3922) of 1930 was one of the last "atmospheric theaters" built in the United States and features twinkling stars in the ceiling and a cloud machine. The adobe ruins of **Old Fort Bliss** at Hart's Mill can be explored near the river (1800 block of Doniphan Drive). The **Sunset Heights Historic District** (roughly bounded by Route I-10, North Oregon, Hesig, and River Avenue) comprises some of the best early-modern residential architecture in the state—Prairie style, "American four-square," and bungalow.

El Paso Centennial Museum/University Museum

Founded during the Texas centennial celebrations in 1936, this museum is devoted to "the preservation, documentation, and exhibition of human and natural history." It features some 148,600 artifacts, including a collection of rock crystals and minerals from the area; pottery, stone tools, and shell jewelry from the prehistoric ruins of Casas Grandes; dinosaur bones from the Big Bend of Texas; and fossil remains from local Ice Age deposits. Over the entrance a limestone bas-relief by the El Paso artist Tom Lea depicts the arrival of Cabeza de Vaca at El Paso del Norte.

LOCATION: The University of Texas at El Paso, University Avenue and Wiggins Road. HOURS: 10–4 Tuesday–Saturday. FEE: None. TELEPHONE: 915–747–5565.

Chamizal National Memorial

This national memorial park, which has a twin park across the Rio Grande, commemorates the conclusion of a century-long land dispute between the United States and Mexico over an approximately 600-acre tract called the Chamizal. The Rio Grande was notorious for changing its course until large-scale irrigation and damming sapped its force. After the Mexican War a change in the course of the river could, and did, precipitously change the boundary between the two countries, which had been established by the Treaty of Guadalupe Hidalgo as being at the center of the Rio Grande. Most such problems were amicably resolved following accepted international principles regarding rogue-river boundaries: It was agreed that alluvium (gradual erosion or creation of new land) changed the boundary; but in a case of avulsion (sudden desertion of the riverbed to cut a new course), the boundary remained where the river had run before. In the latter part of the nineteenth century, the Chamizal was cut off from Mexico, and in accordance with the rogue-river principles, Mexico laid formal claim to the tract in 1895. But whether the course changed because of alluvium or avulsion was never quite clear; the resulting impasse was made more complicated by the issue of Cordova Island, a piece of Mexico on the west side of the Chamizal, which jutted into El Paso as a result of earlier attempts at flood control. Over the years the Chamizal dispute became much more than a boundary problem; it became a symbol for Mexican nationalism and Yankee imperialism. The case was arbitrated in 1911, but the United States refused to abide by the decision to split the tract between the two countries because, it claimed, the arbitration commission's mandate was to decide which country owned the whole, not pieces of it. In 1962 U.S. president John F. Kennedy and Mexican president Adolfo López Mateos instructed engineers to come up with a practical solution; the two leaders agreed on a compromise boundary along a concrete channel cut through Cordova Island and the Chamizal, which would ensure that the river stayed put. In 1964 Presidents López Mateos and Lyndon Johnson met at the river to declare the dispute officially resolved. The visitor center houses a screening room, a museum, and a graphic arts gallery.

LOCATION: 800 South San Marcial Street. HOURS: 8–5 Daily. FEE: None. TELEPHONE: 915–534–6277.

Magoffin Home State Historic Site

The Magoffin House is a study in felicitous cultural amalgamation. One of the few remaining examples of the Territorial style, it is a large one-story house with two-and-a-half-foot-thick adobe walls. Rough-hewn wooden *vigas* (projecting roof rafters) support the fourteen-foot ceilings; simple classical pediments and pilasters adorn windows and doors; and ornate Victorian furnishings, some of them made in Mexico, fill the rooms. A massive central hall, or *zaguán,* leads from the front of the house to a courtyard, and the rest of the house forms a U around it. Built in 1875 by Joseph Magoffin, the son of James Wiley Magoffin, one of the founders of El Paso, this house is a near-replica of the father's original 1849 house, which was destroyed by a flood in 1868. James Wiley Magoffin, who married Maria Gertrudis Valdez de Veramendi of San Antonio (the same family into which Alamo hero James Bowie married), was El Paso's first

The Territorial-style Magoffin House combines southwestern materials and construction techniques with architectural details imported from the East. Its adobe walls are covered with plaster that has been scored to resemble blocks of stone.

civic leader and grand host. He was a former trader, U.S. consul, and peacemaker, visited by all persons of consequence who made it as far as El Paso in the days when few but Santa Fe Trail riders knew or cared how to get there. Magoffinsville, which Magoffin built in the Mexican style around a plaza, was where the U.S. boundary commissioner John Russell Bartlett had his headquarters during the first official boundary survey. Fort Bliss was located at the settlement in 1854. Magoffin was known for entertaining his visitors and neighbors lavishly. Bartlett wrote of a dinner and ball for the Mexican Boundary Commission at which a "new-fashioned chandelier"—a pork-barrel hoop wrapped in elegant scarlet material and fitted with sardine-tin candleholders—"shed such a ray of light upon the festal hall, as rendered the charms of the fair señoritas doubly captivating . . . and all danger of crossing the river [to return home] was obviated by the company remaining 'til eight o'clock the following morning." When the Rio Grande flooded in 1868, both the civil and military buildings

The Knabe square piano in the Magoffin house, made in Baltimore, was probably shipped to a Texas port and then carried overland to El Paso. Above it hangs a portrait of James Wiley Magoffin, painted in 1852 by Henry Cheever Pratt.

at Magoffinsville were destroyed. James Wiley Magoffin died that same year. When El Paso sided with the Confederates, Magoffin lands were confiscated. It was not until 1873 that Joseph Magoffin regained his family's property and thus became one of the city's leading landholders. He went on to become active in the civic and political affairs in the city, serving four terms as mayor; once again the Magoffin home was the center of social life in El Paso. Most of the furniture in the museum is original to the house, brought over-land by wagon from Saint Louis or shipped to ports in Texas and then hauled to El Paso (when the railroads came in the early 1880s a hefty, elaborately carved Knabe piano arrived from Baltimore). Some pieces were crafted locally, in curious combinations of Victorian and Mexican motifs.

LOCATION: 1120 Magoffin Avenue. HOURS: 9–4 Wednesday–Sunday. FEE: Yes. TELEPHONE: 915–533–5147.

A detachment of the U.S. Border patrol displays an unmistakable message, as pho-

The Border Patrol Training School was based in El Paso until 1961; an alien detention center still exists in the city, which sees enormous traffic, legal and illegal, between Mexico and the United States. The **Border Patrol Museum** (915–533–1816) is located in the **Cortez Building,** originally a Spanish Colonial Revival hotel built by Trost & Trost in 1926. Exhibits in the museum trace the history of the border patrol from its founding in 1924 to the present. Housed in a 1910 Trost & Trost Classic Revival mansion built for W. N. Turney, a state senator, the **El Paso Museum of Art** (1211 Montana Avenue, 915–541–4040) has permanent holdings in nineteenth-century Mexican and Southwestern art, pre-Columbian artifacts, and modern regional painting and sculpture.

Prior to the founding of **Saint Clement's Episcopal Church** (810 North Campbell at Montana) in 1870, there was no Protestant church between Brownsville and Santa Fe. Sited near the river, the church was known as "the watchtower of the Rio Grande," yet the

tographed by Eugene Omar Goldbeck in 1926, two years after the service was founded.

pockmarked bell suggests that the church served as target practice for some of El Paso's gunfighters. The present church, built in 1907 by S. E. Patton, a local architect, has beautiful stained-glass windows and a magnificent five-by-eight-foot mosaic, designed by Tiffany Studios, which depicts the transfiguration of Christ with the desert mountains of the Southwest in the background.

The **El Paso Museum of History** (12901 Gateway West, at Route I-10 and Americas Avenue, 915–858–1928) uses dioramas depicting the travels of the conquistadors and the founding of the El Paso missions to re-create the history of the city. Displays include a blacksmith shop, a Victorian parlor, and frontier furnishings and dress.

Fort Bliss (U.S. Army Air Defense Center)

Fort Bliss was a fort with no name—or rather only the name "the post opposite Paso del Norte"—when it was established in 1849 as a stronghold for enforcing the river boundary between Mexico and the United States as declared in the Treaty of Guadalupe Hidalgo. The post was moved from Smith's Ranch to Hart's Mill to Magoffinsville and renamed in 1854 for Colonel William Wallace S. Bliss, an adjutant general during the Mexican War. When the Civil War broke out, Fort Bliss became the Confederate army's Southwest headquarters until the troops deliberately burned the fort and moved east; subsequently Union forces raised the U.S. flag over the ruins and rebuilt the fort. Destroyed again in the flood of 1868, the fort was rebuilt on higher ground. The garrison at Fort Bliss kept order in El Paso after the Civil War, but by 1877 the troops were deemed unnecessary and were removed to Fort Davis in the Davis Mountains. The fort was recommissioned in 1878 for the Salt War and later, in 1885 and 1886, served as a refitting post during the campaigns against the Apache chief Geronimo and during General Pershing's futile search for Pancho Villa just prior to World War I. When war broke out the fort became a major troop-training center. Today Fort Bliss, situated in the central part of town, is the U.S. Army Air Defense Center for guided missile research and combat training.

There are four museums associated with the fort. **Fort Bliss Museum** (Pleasonton and Pershing roads, 915–568–4518) is located in four reconstructed adobe buildings from the original

OPPOSITE: *One of four adobe structures reconstructed at Fort Bliss, originally established in 1849 to assert U.S. authority over lands acquired after the Mexican War.*

Magoffinsville post. Period rooms include a blacksmith shop, a harness shop, military barracks, a kitchen, and spinning and weaving rooms; costumed guides re-enact daily life on the frontier. The **U.S. Army Third Cavalry Museum** (near the intersection of Forrest and Chaffee roads, Building 2407, 915–568–1922) presents the history of the Regiment of Mounted Riflemen, the second-oldest continuously serving regiment in the United States. The regiment was founded in 1846 and fought in the Mexican War, the Civil War, against the Indians, and in all other U.S. wars to the present. The **U.S. Army Air Defense Artillery Museum** (Pleasonton Road, Building 5000, 915–568–5412) features dioramas and exhibits on the history of air-defense artillery as well as an outdoor weapons park with weapons and equipment from World War II to the present. The **U.S. Army Museum of the Noncommissioned Officer** (Biggs Army Airfield, Staff Sargeant Sims Street and Barksdale Avenue, Building 11331, 915–568–8646) depicts the history of the U.S. Army and the noncommissioned officer from the Revolutionary War to the present; uniforms, photographs, and archival material are on display.

Mission Trail

In Texas, only San Antonio rivals the El Paso area's wealth of Spanish Colonial architecture, which is concentrated in the Lower Valley south of town along the river. The three missions here were originally on the south side of the river, once on an island that became part of the mainland when the fickle Rio Grande changed its course. These missions are the oldest continuously occupied communities in the state. From El Paso the first stop on the Mission Trail (a twelve-mile route with roadside markers) is **Ysleta Mission** (131 South Zaragoza Street), which was originally Mission de Corpus Christi de la Isleta del Sur. Ysleta, the first mission and pueblo in Texas, was founded in 1680 by Franciscans and the Christianized Tigua expelled from New Mexico in the Pueblo Revolt. A small part of the mission church, now called Church of Our Lady of Mount Carmel, dates from the 1600s, but much of the stuccoed adobe structure with a shiny silver beehive-domed tower was rebuilt after floods and fires and thus dates variously from 1744, 1849, and 1907. Adjoining Ysleta is the **Tigua Indian Reservation.** The Tigua have lost virtually all the land they once held by treaty. In 1751 Spain granted the Tigua about 20,000 acres; in 1871 the Texas

El Paso's Ysleta Mission, founded in 1680, was built on land that for many years belonged to Mexico. A change in the Rio Grande's course has placed it in U.S. territory.

legislature incorporated the settlement (without the Tigua's consent), and the tribal lands were sold, reducing Tigua possessions to about 300 acres. In spite of efforts at restitution on the part of the U.S. government, the Tigua tribe today owns only about 66 acres, some of which has been in cultivation since 1682. The **Tigua Indian Museum** (122 South Old Pueblo Road, 915–859–7913) has exhibits on the tribe's long history in the area.

Socorro Mission (Nuestra Señora del Socorro) was established on October 13, 1680, which makes it one day younger than Ysleta. The earliest buildings were washed away by the Rio Grande. The present church dates from 1840, although its thick stuccoed-adobe walls and distinctive stepped parapet with *campanario* (bell tower) are more authentically Spanish Colonial in style than some of the older buildings in the area. Because the mission has not been greatly altered over the years, it is considered to be the most representative of the early El Paso valley missions. Floods have situated the mission church alternately in Mexico and the United States; the last

one placed it in Texas, where it remains. Also of historic interest in the town of Socorro are **Casa Ortíz,** an adobe house built in 1840 with cottonwood *vigas* supporting a roof of branches, cattails, and mud (now a small center for antique shops and art galleries), and **Tienda de Carbajál,** a large adobe hacienda built before 1850, transformed in the 1870s into Juan Carbajál's store. Local legend says the building's only present occupant is a ghost.

San Eliceario Presidio Chapel served the presidio established in 1774 to protect the Lower Valley missions, whose soldiers had until then been nearer to the Guadalupe Mission in Paso del Norte. The church was built in 1789, and restored after fires in 1935 and 1944. The presidio moved again before 1814, but the town of San Elizario remained. It became the El Paso County seat in 1850 and continued as such for the next twenty-six years. The Salt War broke out on the plaza in 1877 as a result of political and ethnic tensions.

WILDERNESS PARK MUSEUM

This museum traces the evolution of weather from the rainy period, which began 15,000 years ago, to the desert conditions, which began about 7,000 years ago. Exhibits demonstrate the adaptation of people to the desert environment. A time tunnel re-creates the era of the Hunter-Gatherers, the introduction about 4000 B.C. of the gods of wind and rain to western Texas, the Mimbres art tradition from A.D. 900 to 1140, the Apache raid in Janos, Mexico, against the Chihuahua in 1880, and the lives of the Tarahumara Indians who have lived relatively untouched by modern civilization in the copper canyons of Chihuahua, Mexico. The museum presents dioramas and murals of archaeological sites in the area, displays of primitive tools, weapons, and jewelry, and an exhibit on the pictographs at the Hueco Tanks. A nature trail passes replicas of a Pueblo ruin, a kiva, and a pithouse. The route to the museum along Transmountain Road cuts through the Franklin Mountains at the old Smugglers' Gap and was used by cattle rustlers in the nineteenth century.

LOCATION: 2000 Transmountain Road, north of El Paso. HOURS: 9–5 Tuesday–Sunday. FEE: None. TELEPHONE: 915-755-4332.

OPPOSITE: *This modest frame church, constructed in 1910 in Mentone, is the oldest building in Loving County.*

HUECO TANKS STATE HISTORICAL PARK

The lack of water is the most pressing problem in the trans-Pecos, and for many years the Hueco Tanks in the Hueco Mountains east of El Paso held one of the few sources of water between the city and the Pecos River, about a hundred miles to the east as the bird flies. The so-called tanks ("hueco" means hollow in Spanish) are depressions of various size in syenite porphyry rock, surrounded by huge piles of the rock. Rainwater collects in these nonporous tanks and is protected from wind and sun by the towering rock piles; in an otherwise parched landscape, the rocks can hold a year's supply of water. These cisterns were formed naturally, and for more than 10,000 years, the oasis they created has been used by people and animals alike. Some of the most impressive rock art in Texas is found at Hueco Tanks. The pictographs date from the Desert Archaic culture (about 8000 B.C.), the earliest human habitation, to the Jornada Branch of the Mogollon (about A.D. 1000) to the Mescalero Apache, whose nineteenth-century rock pictures depict horsemen, myths, and snakes. Once whites found the water, travelers made the tanks a stop on their itineraries (some of the forty-niners carved their names in the rocks), and the Butterfield Overland Mail Route (1858–1861) from Saint Louis to San Francisco made a rest stop here.

> LOCATION: Route 62/180 East to Ranch Road 2775 (Hueco Tanks Road). HOURS: 8 AM–10 PM Daily. FEE: Yes. TELEPHONE: 915–857–1135.

Within the **Guadalupe Mountains National Park,** the tiny village of **Pine Springs** contains the tumbledown stone ruins of an early Butterfield Overland Mail Route station established in 1858. A few red-bark madrone trees grow near the campground, but most seedlings die in the wild. After a summer rain the color of the bark deepens to a brilliant, glittering crimson in the sunlight. The early Indians called the madrone tree the naked Indian.

The mining town of **Van Horn** lies in a basin formed by the Sierra Diablo and the Van Horn and Apache mountains. Pioneers and forty-niners traveling from San Antonio to California stopped at this way station on the Old Spanish Trail. The **Culberson County Historical Museum** (Route I-10 at Route 90, 915–283–2043) is housed in the 1906 Clark Hotel and features exhibits on talc and silver mining as well as a frontier barroom.

PECOS

Home of the Pecos cantaloupe, this town was founded in 1881 as a stop on the Texas & Pacific Railroad. Pecos, a center for ranching, oil production, and irrigated farming, is situated near the muddy Pecos River, which separates the rest of Texas from the trans-Pecos. "Pecos" is an Indian word meaning crooked. The town went on to become one of the wildest cowboy and outlaw towns in the region. On July 4, 1883, the foremen of several area ranches sponsored a steer-roping and bronc-riding contest for local ranch hands, and thus occurred the world's first rodeo (although towns in Arizona and Wyoming make the same claim), which is commemorated in Pecos with an annual national-circuit rodeo. The **West of the Pecos Museum** (120 East 1st Street, 915-445-5076) is housed in two attached buildings: a red-sandstone saloon, built in 1896 by former Texas Ranger R. S. Johnson, and the Orient Hotel, which operated until the 1950s. The museum is devoted to Western heritage and features an assortment of pioneer equipment, dress, and memorabilia. Markers in the saloon indicate where two gunfighters landed dead on the floor. There are also exhibits on Mexican-American and black history.

FORT DAVIS

Fort Davis is in the once volcanic Davis Mountain range, both of which were named in the 1850s for Jefferson Davis, then the U.S. secretary of war. The town grew up around one of the forts on the west Texas frontier established to protect trade and travel routes from the Apache and Comanche. Neither soldier nor civilian could have asked for a more beautiful wilderness setting—because they interrupt moisture-bearing winds, the Davis Mountains are greener than most of the other starkly gorgeous ranges in the trans-Pecos. Today Fort Davis is the county seat of Jeff Davis County, a ranching-supply center and a major base for touring the scenic trans-Pecos. On the town square is the restored Colonial Revival **Limpia Hotel,** built in 1913 by the Union Trading Company. **Indian Lodge** in **Davis Mountains State Park** (four miles northwest of Fort Davis via Route 118) is a "pueblo motel" on a mountainside, built by the Civilian Conservation Corps in the 1930s. The walls are adobe, up to eigh-

OVERLEAF: *Ridged gypsum dunes, west of the Guadalupe Mountains on the Texas-New Mexico border.*

teen inches thick, and some of the rooms have furniture crafted by the workers. The park's **interpretive center** (915–426–3337) covers the natural history of the area. A four-mile hiking trail in the park connects it to Fort Davis National Historic Site.

Fort Davis National Historic Site

Limpia Creek in Limpia Canyon was one of the few good watering places in the arid trans-Pecos for the growing hordes of travelers to the West, and thus it was logical to build a military outpost nearby. To protect travelers from the Mescalero-Apache and Comanche whose range Fort Davis occupied, soldiers spent much of their time escorting mail and freight trains through the mountains and pursuing various raiding bands when they attacked civilians. This went on more or less continuously, and with limited success, until the outbreak of the Civil War, during which the fort was taken by Confederates and then abandoned. When U.S. troops returned in June 1867 to reestablish the fort, they found that the cottonwood and pine buildings had been virtually destroyed by the Apache. The new post was constructed of stone and adobe. After the war it was garrisoned by blacks, and the first black graduate of West Point, Henry Ossian Flipper, served as its acting commissary of subsistence. One of the largest forts in the West, it was active until 1891. The compound, against the dramatic mountain backdrop, includes numerous adobe, stone, and wood structures, some completely restored, some left in ruins. A museum in the enlisted men's barracks contains archival collections and historic photographs. There are also living-history demonstrations.

LOCATION: Routes 17 and 118 on the north side of town. HOURS: June through August: 8–6 Daily; September through May: 8–5 Daily. FEE: Yes. TELEPHONE: 915–426–3224.

MCDONALD OBSERVATORY

Just seventeen miles north of Fort Davis, the University of Texas McDonald Observatory at Mount Locke was built in 1938 from the bequest of William J. McDonald, a wealthy east Texas lawyer, banker, and amateur astronomer who hoped finer astronomical observation

OPPOSITE: *A line of adobe and stone houses, known as Officer's Row, faces larger barracks for enlisted men across the Parade Ground at Fort Davis. The Overland Trail passes just behind the barracks.*

The north squad room of the enlisted mens' barracks at Fort Davis has been restored to its appearance in the summer of 1884, when it was occupied by twenty-six members

would help farmers by allowing more sophisticated weather and seasonal forecasts. Mount Locke was chosen as the site because it is 6,791 feet high and far from city lights and hazy, dusty, or polluted air. Although the dome that houses the observatory's world-class 107-inch reflecting telescope is open daily for tours, the public is allowed (by reservation) to look through the telescope on only one night each month (these evenings are often reserved a full six months in advance). Solar-viewing sessions are held daily when weather permits.

LOCATION: Spur 78, off Route 118 North. HOURS: 9–5 Daily. FEE: None. TELEPHONE: 915–426–3640.

MARFA

Founded in 1881 as a water stop on the Texas & New Orleans Railroad, Marfa was named by the railroad president's wife for a heroine in a Russian novel and was where the prized Highland Hereford cattle—heartier than Longhorns—were introduced to the region. Hollywood took over the town for various Westerns in the twenties and thirties. The Second Empire **Presidio County**

of Troop H of the Tenth U. S. Cavalry, a black regiment stationed at the fort between 1875 and 1885. The south squad room housed an additional thirty-six soldiers.

Courthouse (1886) was designed by the noted San Antonio court-house architect Alfred Giles and topped by a Liberty statue. Exhibits at the **Presidio County Museum** (221 North Mesa, 915–729–8178) cover the history and development of the county from prehistoric times to the present. Just on the edge of town, **Fort D. A. Russell,** originally Camp Marfa, was the headquarters of the Big Bend Military District and supplied the cavalry during the Mexican Revolution border troubles. Activity at the fort was officially discontinued in 1932, and to mark the departure of the oldest cavalry regiment in the United States (First Cavalry), the regiment's oldest horse, "Louie," was given his own military review. Reactivated during World War II, the fort trained chemical warfare battalions and was the site of a German prisoner-of-war camp. Privately owned since 1949, the fort is now the headquarters of the Chinati Foundation, established by the Minimalist sculptor Donald Judd, who has erected on the grounds a line of giant concrete sculptures, filled buildings that used to hold ammunition with smaller boxlike steel sculptures, and installed works of art in the fort's gymnasium as well. Judd lives in the former quartermaster's house in town. The mysterious Marfa

Lights are an unexplained phenomenon occasionally seen in these parts at night.

ALPINE

The largest town in the mountain region of Texas (population 5,500), Alpine is also the seat of the largest county in the state—larger, it is often pointed out, than the state of Connecticut. Alpine developed in the 1880s as a ranching and mining center, which it remains today, and was also on the Southern Pacific Railroad line. The dignified brick Second Empire **Brewster County Courthouse** was built in 1887 by Tom Lovell. The exhibits at the **Museum of the Big Bend** (915–837–8143) depict Indian life, European exploration, settlement, and town building. The displays include a general store, blacksmith shop, and a bullet-ridden stagecoach. The archaeological collection traces life in the Big Bend back 12,000 years. The museum is on the campus of Sul Ross State University, named for Lawrence Sullivan Ross, a famous Indian fighter and governor of Texas.

BIG BEND NATIONAL PARK

The Rio Grande, cutting deep canyons through desert mountains, formed the Big Bend of Texas. Here the land and the river are so wild and rugged that these waters were not successfully navigated until 1899 (the Boundary Commission appointed nearly fifty years earlier to survey the border charted this area only from afar). This vast part of the Chihuahuan desert and the pine-forested Chisos Mountains was a stronghold of the Mescalero Apache, the supreme trial of the U.S. Cavalry, and after the Apache's defeat, the last Texas frontier of true-grit American frontier settlers—railroads never ventured farther south than Alpine, leaving the Big Bend cut off from "civilization" far longer than any other part of Texas. Established as a national park in 1944, the Big Bend is still one of the most rugged and isolated areas in the park system. What hikers and backpackers do today for fun—very carefully—prospectors, ranchers, miners, smugglers, and soldiers used to do knowing that their lives depended on how they did it.

The Apache held that the Great Spirit, having completed making the Earth, used the Big Bend as a dumping ground for leftover

OPPOSITE: *The steep-walled Mariscal Canyon, one of three large canyons that run through Big Bend National Park.*

rocks. The huge variety of plant and animal life in the Big Bend—in five separate life zones from the floodplain to the Chisos Mountains—has adapted to survive on a minimum amount of water; nineteenth-century map makers marked the Big Bend "The Bad Lands." The Spanish were not interested in the Big Bend, certain from the looks of it that it held no riches. The Apache and Comanche knew the whereabouts of springs and *tinajas* (water pooled in rocks) that the luckless Spanish missed at the cost of death by thirst. The Indians easily crossed the river at secret fords to snatch Spanish cattle and horses, sometimes taking Spanish men as slaves. This they did in response to slave taking by the conquerors. The few presidios on the river were all abandoned by 1810, leaving the little villages to fend for themselves. The Mexicans fared hardly better; a legend has it that at the height of Apache depredations into Mexico in the 1820s and 1830s the governor of Chihuahua, which then encompassed the Big Bend, hired an Irishman to kill all the Apache. The Irishman eventually returned to the governor with a scalp claim of nearly $30,000, but the governor refused to pay because there were so many Mexican scalps among the booty. The violence continued from the 1850s to the 1870s with fighting between the U.S. Cavalry and the Apache. After the Apache were eradicated from the Big Bend, American farmers and ranchers moved in and were followed by mercury-mining outfits. The Mexican Revolution brought numerous border skirmishes between the Villistas and the Texas Rangers and the U.S. Army. During Prohibition Mexican adventurers turned from banditry to the more lucrative occupation of smuggling liquor. After Prohibition farming and ranching held sway until overgrazing destroyed the grassland in this part of the Big Bend. The mines were abandoned by the 1950s. The national park, which encompasses more than 700,000 acres, was established in 1944, and some of the plant life depleted by overgrazing is reappearing.

Ruins of early Mexican and white settlements dot the park. **Luna's Jacal** on the Maverick Road is the stabilized ruin of a house built about 1800 by Gilberto Luna, a Mexican farmer. His house was near the Comanche War Trail, the route the Indians took to northern Mexico for seasonal rustling from Mexican herds; but Luna and his family lived peaceably with both the Comanche and the Apache. Luna grew cotton and corn in the desert by irrigating with water he hauled by hand from a distant spring. His house, or *jacal*, is typical of the earliest primitive structures in the area; one wall is a large, flat boulder, against which the rest of the house was constructed of lime-stone and sandstone blocks. The roof, now cemented over, was fash-ioned of cane, ocotillo, and mud spread over pole roof beams sup-ported by forked poles. The interior is barely five-and-a-half feet high. Luna was said to be 109 years old when he died in 1951.

The **Castolon Historic District** consists of the **Alvino House,** pos-sibly the oldest adobe structure in Big Bend National Park, and the remains of a cavalry encampment—barracks, latrine, canteen, stable, and officers' quarters—called Camp Santa Elena, which was built in 1916 to guard the border after Pancho Villa's raids on Glenn Springs and Boquillas created fear that the mining operations at Terlingua would also be vulnerable to attack. When the border troubles ended, the army sold the station in 1925 to W. R. Cartledge, who operated it as a trading post. Castolon is now a ranger station, with a store occupying the barracks.

The ruins of the Mariscal Mine, where cinnabar—red mercuric sulfide—was mined from 1884 until World War II, in Big Bend National Park.

The presence of cinnabar, or mercury ore, in the Big Bend, although indicated by red pictographs all through the mountains and canyons, was unknown until the 1880s, when someone set a hot branding iron on a rock and mercury droplets appeared. The mining life was not easy. Precious water for both mining operations and the workers (Mexicans who earned on the average $1 per twelve-hour day) had to be packed in by burro from five miles away; the wood for the smelting furnace came from twenty miles away. The **Mariscal Mine,** active from 1900 to 1923, reopened briefly during World War II, by which time it still had "one post office and a population of fifty and could only be reached by pack train." Ruins at Mariscal include the mine shafts and buildings made of stone, adobe, concrete, and brush.

On the floodplain between Castolon and Santa Elena Canyon, five structures make up the ruins of **Rancho Estelle,** named by the Mexicans for the land's first owner, L. V. Steele, an itinerant mining prospector who had inherited it through marriage from a wealthy Mexican rancher named Miguel de la O. In 1918 Rancho Estelle was bought by James Sublett of Sweetwater and his partner Elbert W. Dorgan, an eccentric German city planner and architect from the Midwest. Sublett's small adobe-and-rock house overlooks the valley. Dorgan's, larger at 1,200 square feet, is divided by a two-way fireplace of petrified wood, which once supported the roof as well. Both houses are now roofless. A cane structure on an adjacent mountain terrace was built by a Mexican laborer on the ranch and is typical of early valley architecture. The old settlement of **Hot Springs,** homesteaded in 1909 by J. O. Langford, was developed as a resort in the twenties. The foundation of the old bathhouse still fills with water from the springs at a constant 105 degrees. The limestone motel, post office, and trading post still stand.

Just outside the park's western boundary are three communities of historic significance in the Big Bend. The ghost town of **Terlingua** was the region's most prosperous mercury-mining town during the early part of the century. It was home to the Chisos Mining Company and its highly successful boss, Howard E. Perry. Perry's hilltop mansion awaits restoration. The old store and mining offices now house shops, and some of the town's rock and adobe houses

OPPOSITE: *Jumping cholla cactus near Mule Ears Peak in Big Bend National Park.*

have been restored and reoccupied. The town of **Lajitas** is at the San Carlos Ford of the Rio Grande and was on a branch of the Comanche Trail. It centers on a much altered but still atmospheric trading post where fur trappers once traded their skins for goods. On Route 118, **Study Butte** is another ghost town with a few inhabitants, former home to the Study Butte Mine.

FORT LEATON STATE HISTORICAL PARK

On the gorgeous River Road from the Big Bend to Presidio, this "fort" was actually a civilian settlement started in 1848 by Benjamin Leaton, an American scalp hunter formerly in the hire of the Mexican governments of Chihuahua and Sonora. The site was at La Junta de los Rios, downstream from the confluence of the Rio Grande and the Rio Conchos flowing north from Mexico. Cabeza de Vaca had encountered an Indian village at Ojinaga in 1535. The Franciscans established a mission on the north side of the Rio Grande in the 1680s. The Presidio de la Junta de los Rios, also known as Presidio del Norte and El Fortín de San José, was established nearby in 1759, moved south of the river in 1767, and was abandoned by 1810.

By the time Leaton started his farm, the presidio had been abandoned for nearly forty years, but a small civilian settlement of farmers and goat herders remained across the river. By the spring of 1849, a visitor to Fort Leaton wrote, "Leaton has in a few months accomplished a great amount of severe labor, fortified himself in a good position, secured his stock, and carried to considerable extent his farming operations. . . . His fort is a collection of adobes . . . with a lookout and wall which encloses also his corral . . . the place would make a strong defense against Indians." This last was true, but in a turnaround from his former scalp-hunting days, Leaton began trading with bands of Apache and Comanche, and soon was being charged by both the Mexicans and the Americans with encouraging the Indians to raid Mexican settlements so they could use stolen livestock to buy arms and ammunition from Fort Leaton. To this day locals call Fort Leaton "el fortín" rather than dignify the place with the name of Leaton, *un mal hombre.*

Fort Leaton was on the San Antonio–Chihuahua Trail and saw a lot of traffic in goods and silver between the United States and Mexico. Chihuahua was an important mining town and the nearby town of Presidio supplied goods for Mexican citizens. The trail linked Chihuahua to San Antonio and the port of Indianola. Exhibits in twenty-five rooms of Fort Leaton cover the story of the violent Americans who settled here, the development of farming culture in the valleys of La Junta de los Rios from the time of the Indians, and the Spanish, Mexican, and American settlements. Other displays explore native traditions and customs that still exist in this area.

LOCATION: River Road (F.M. 170), 4 miles southeast of Presidio. HOURS: 8–4:30 Daily. FEE: Yes. TELEPHONE: 915–229–3613.

FORT STOCKTON

Built at the site of a now tragically depleted desert oasis that came to be called Comanche Springs—gushing water that flowed at the rate of 80 million gallons a day was used by people for thousands of years before the Comanche came from the north—Fort Stockton was established in 1859 at the crossroads of the Old San Antonio Road and the Comanche War Trail, abandoned during the Civil War, and regarrisoned with black soldiers until the fort closed in 1886. Fort Stockton was one base for U.S. secretary of war Jefferson Davis's camel experiment, which brought those animals to west Texas to be tested in the desert against the army's less-adaptable mules. The camels delivered a superior performance once the soldiers got used to their peculiarities—males were prone to taking chunks out of each other's legs if left unguarded for a moment—and might have changed the military landscape if the Civil War had not intervened. (The camels scattered—some fell prey to humans, some ended up hauling salt in Nevada.)

The adobe and stone buildings of **Old Fort Stockton** (Williams Street between 4th and 5th streets) include the 1868 officers' quarters, 1867 guardhouse, and a cemetery whose headstones indicate that few men lived past the age of 40. Also in the historic district is the Gothic Revival **Saint Stephen's Episcopal Church** (East 2d and Spring) of 1896, the first Protestant church in Texas west of the Pecos (a building moved here from the town of Pecos). **Courthouse Square** features the Pecos County Courthouse (1912); the town's first schoolhouse, built in 1883; and the old jail (1884).

The **Annie Riggs Memorial Museum** (301 South Main Street, 915–336–2167) is the epitome of frontier Victorian architecture, built by a group of local businessmen and opened in 1901 as the

A string of camels, incongruously accompanying a covered wagon, cross a West Texas river bound for Jefferson Davis's camel experiment in the Big Bend in this small painting by an unknown artist who may have been a soldier.

Koehler Hotel. In 1904 the small hotel was bought by Annie Riggs, daughter of the first judge of Pecos County. Built of adobe bricks with a wraparound wooden verandah and ornamental shingle patterns on the gables, the hotel was constructed around a courtyard, to which many of the rooms had access. Period rooms in the museum include a typical guest room, the dining room (meals were 35 cents), and the parlor, into which Mrs. Riggs did not allow children. The exhibits feature a turn-of-the-century dress collection; ranching gear; and Ice Age artifacts, including 22,000-year-old mammoth tusks, found eight miles away. Native plants such as yucca, sotol, and creosote can be seen in the terraced garden. The **Fort Stockton Historical Society,** housed in the museum, offers self-guided tours of local historic sites.

FORT LANCASTER STATE HISTORICAL PARK

Established in 1855 on the old military road between San Antonio and El Paso near the junction of Live Oak Creek with the Pecos

River, Fort Lancaster is now a stabilized ruin, rectangles of adobe wall and limestone chimneys on a site that once had twenty-five buildings. The Camel Corps stopped here for a few nights. Fort Lancaster, like most of the frontier forts, was abandoned after the Civil War began—its garrison marched to San Antonio to surrender to or join the Confederates—but unlike the others it was reoccupied only briefly in 1868. The abandoned post was later used as a military bivouac and a campground for travelers. The museum in the visitor center displays pictographs and artifacts from the nearby **Live Oak Creek Archaeological District**. The military history of the fort is documented with photographs and maps.

LOCATION: Off Route 290, just east of Sheffield. HOURS: 8–5 Wednesday–Sunday. FEE: None. TELEPHONE: 915–836–4391.

OZONA

Ozona is both the county seat and the only town in Crockett County. The town is located on the Edwards Plateau, 31,000 square miles of limestone slab from 1,500 to 3,000 feet above sea level, and has become a wool-production center for the area's sheep ranchers. The **Crockett County Courthouse** (907 Avenue D) is a rusticated-limestone structure built in the Second Empire style in 1902 by the architect Oscar Ruffini, who designed several grand courthouses in the region. The **Crockett County Museum** (404 11th Street, 915–392–2837) contains artifacts from the prehistoric Indian occupation of the Ozona area. Furniture, weapons, implements, and memorabilia from early ranchers are also on display, as well as artifacts from nearby Fort Lancaster.

Local speleological authorities speak of the **Caverns of Sonora** (eight miles south of Sonora off Route I-10, 915–387–3105) as among the most beautiful in the world. The caverns are 95 percent "living"— that is, crystal formations continue to grow into fantastic formations along the eight miles of passages.

JUDGE ROY BEAN VISITOR CENTER

The world associates with Texas a few outrageous men, among them, Judge Roy Bean. This Texas Highway Department shrine to that controversial peacemaker goes a long way toward keeping myths about the state alive, attracting over 100,000 visitors a year. In 1881 Bean hastily established a saloon in a tent in a town named after the local scorpions, Vinegaroon; the scorpions sprang up when the Southern Pacific Railroad began construction on its Sunset Route through Dead Man's Gulch. To quell rowdy behavior Pecos County appointed Roy Bean as its first justice of the peace in 1882. Bean moved his establishment to the railroad town of Langtry (some say that it was named for one of the railroad's engineers, others for Bean's idol, the English actress Lillie Langtry), and up went the still-standing **Jersey Lilly Saloon,** definitely named for Miss Langtry. Above the saloon sign went "Justice of the Peace," and next to that Bean's famous motto: "The Law West of the Pecos." Actually there was little *other* law west of the Pecos, at least little stationary law—the Texas Rangers and the U.S. Cavalry did their legal work on the move—and so more than a few criminals and accused innocents ended up at Langtry. Judge Roy Bean's court and saloon were one and the same—his brand of justice was shaped by instinct and an occasional perusal of the 1879 *Revised Statutes of Texas* (on display at the visitor center). Fines often included a round of drinks for the "jury," chosen on the spot when an accused lawbreaker was brought around. The outcome of a case could depend on how things were going in the saloon, what kind of customers were there, what sort of mood they were in, or on Bean's racial sympathies. Bean received national publicity in 1896 when he arranged for a heavyweight prizefight to take place on a sandbar in the Rio Grande just below Langtry—in defiance of federal and state law.

The visitor center uses six dioramas with accompanying audio programs to re-create typical scenes in Roy Bean's Langtry. Outside the desert garden has plants labeled with Indian and pioneer lore.

LOCATION: Loop 25, off Route 90, Langtry. HOURS: 8–5 Daily. FEE: None. TELEPHONE: 915–291–3340.

SEMINOLE CANYON STATE HISTORICAL PARK

Seminole Canyon is thought to be named for a group of black soldiers who were stationed in the 1870s at Fort Clark, to the west of the present-day town of Brackettville. These men were descendants of slaves who fled to live among the Seminole in Florida. The canyon shows evidence of human habitation 12,000 years ago, and some of North America's oldest known pictographs, painted 8,000 years ago, can be seen at **Fate Bell Shelter** and other sites. There are guided tours to the pictograph shelters daily. A museum in the visitor center uses archaeological exhibits to retrace the history of the canyon area from prehistoric habitation to modern-day ranching.

LOCATION: Off Route 90 between Comstock and Langtry. HOURS: *Museum:* 8–5 Daily. *Tours:* 10 and 3 Wednesday–Saturday. FEE: Yes. TELEPHONE: 915–292–4464.

SONORA

During the late nineteenth century, ranchers and their families roamed through western Texas searching out grazing lands for their cattle and sheep. The area where the town of Sonora was built was just a grassy oasis studded with live oak trees. Except for the river, which was miles away, there was no source of water in the area. In November 1888 the Adams family decided to drill for water using a horse-powered rig on the grassy hill with the live oaks. On February 10, 1889, they hit water. Hundreds of people who had been living in tents on the plains converged around the well during the next six weeks. Much of the original town that sprang up around "the water lot"—now the courthouse lawn—is still standing. Oscar Ruffini built the Second Empire **Sutton County Courthouse** between 1891 and 1893. Houses rather than commercial buildings encircle the courthouse and jail, and eight of the original live oaks still grace the square. Two of the six old houses still standing on Prospect Hill were built in 1891; two elaborate Queen Anne–style residences were built around 1915.

Just north of the courthouse, the **Miers Home Museum** (307 Northeast Oak Street, 915–387–5144), re-created as an early frontier dwelling, was the fifth house built in Sonora. It started out as a two-story board-and-batten house for Isaac Miers, his wife, and seven children. The house was enlarged when one of the Miers daughters decided that she could not be courted properly in the midst of the family's goings-on and asked her brothers to add a private parlor. When it was built in 1891, the **Old Jail Museum** (309 Northeast Oak Street, 915–387–2880) was the first limestone building in town; today it presents the regional history of Sutton County.

FORT MCKAVETT STATE HISTORICAL PARK

General William Tecumseh Sherman thought Fort McKavett "the prettiest post in Texas." Established in 1852 as the Camp on the San Saba, the fort was renamed several months later in honor of Captain Henry McKavett, who had been killed in the Mexican War. Unlike many frontier garrisons, Fort McKavett had plentiful water close by, abundant game, and good river-bottom soil for growing vegetables to enliven the troops' usual fare of beans and salt pork. But like most pre-Civil War garrisons, Fort McKavett suffered from a shortage of uniforms and weapons and, perhaps most importantly, horses. The few mounted soldiers were sent on Indian patrols and escorted pioneers and gold seekers heading west on the Upper El Paso Road.

By 1859 most of the Indian activity had moved north, and Fort McKavett was abandoned. During the Civil War the Comanche reasserted themselves in the absence of the army deterrent, and local citizens moved into the fort to defend themselves. The fort was reestablished in 1868 and was soon manned by black cavalry troops. The fort was closed in 1883. The fifteen restored buildings include the officers' quarters, barracks, hospital and morgue, schoolhouse, bakery, and the post headquarters. Ruins of other buildings remain on the site. Interpretive exhibits on the military and civil history and archaeology of the fort are presented in the museum.

LOCATION: Route 190 and F.M. 864, 23 miles southwest of Menard. HOURS: 8–5 Daily. FEE: Yes. TELEPHONE: 915–396–2358.

BUFFALO GAP HISTORIC VILLAGE

For thousands of years the buffalo migrated southward through the mile-wide gap in the rolling hills of the Callahan Divide. The Comanche followed the buffalo and camped under the huge live-oak trees that mark the site of Buffalo Gap. The white buffalo hunters appropriated the Indian campgrounds and made Buffalo Gap an early headquarters for their systematic slaughter. This historic village comprises nine structures from the pre-railroad settlement, including the 1879 stone **Old Taylor County Courthouse-Jail** on William Street, the only nineteenth-century building original to the site. Western artifacts, including buffalo guns, are displayed inside. Other buildings include the **Marshall House** (1881), which has its original pioneer furniture. The **Texas & Pacific Railroad Depot,** built in 1881, was moved to this site from nearby Clyde. In addition, a two-room schoolhouse, a blacksmith shop, a country store, and a doctor's office. Buggies and wagons are on the grounds of the village.

LOCATION: William and Elm streets, off Route 89 south of Abilene. HOURS: Mid-March through mid-November: 10–7 Monday –Saturday, 12–7 Sunday; mid-November through mid-March: 10–6 Friday–Saturday, 12–6 Sunday. FEE: Yes. TELEPHONE: 915–572–3365.

SAN ANGELO

Fort Concho, founded at the confluence of the North and South Concho rivers in 1867, was the center of the line of forts on the western frontier. The small community of *jacales* and adobe houses that was to become San Angelo grew up around it. In its earliest days the town was called Over-the-River by the soldiers at the fort. B. J. Dewitt opened a trading post in town and called it Santa Angela for his sister-in-law, who was a nun at the Ursuline Convent in San Antonio. The San Angelo area (the city's name was later masculinized) was on the Butterfield Stage Line before there was a fort or a community; buffalo hunters ravaged the area between 1874 and 1878; and the Goodnight-Loving Trail passed directly through here. Over time sheep and goats outnumbered the cattle in this rocky country; today San Angelo is the largest primary wool market in the nation. The Ohio-born architect Oscar Ruffini brought a civilizing influence to town after the railroad came through in 1888, building more than three dozen structures in the city, among them the **J. J. Rackley Building** (118 South Chadbourne Street) of 1890, a two-story Italianate commercial structure, and the **Hagelstein Building, Runkles Building,** and **Harris Building** in the same block. Also of interest are the **San Angelo National Bank Building,** the **Schwartz Building,** and the **Raas Building** (20–26 East Concho), three brick-and-stone buildings with fronts of cut stone, cast iron, and wood, built between 1884 and 1886.

Fort Concho National Historic Landmark

One of the best-preserved and beautifully designed frontier forts in Texas, Fort Concho was built of limestone with pecan-wood rafters by German craftsmen from Fredericksburg, a center of fine workmanship in the Hill Country. Two of the most famous military officers in Texas were in command here—Benjamin Grierson, organizer of the black troops, and Ranald Mackenzie, the man ordered by

General William T. Sherman to solve "the Indian problem" on the frontier. Mackenzie's campaign lasted five years and was helped along by the ongoing depletion by civilian hunters of the Indians' food supply, the buffalo. Fort Concho was decommissioned in 1889 and was almost immediately taken over by San Angelo for commercial storage and civilian housing. Sixteen of the original limestone buildings still stand at Fort Concho, five have been reconstructed, and there is one stabilized ruin. Some of the buildings have been restored. Costumed "soldiers" in the enlisted men's Barracks V recreate the routines of military life here at the fort. Barracks VI presents displays on the Indian Wars and military life. The **Ruffini Building,** the former shotgun cottage where the architect lived and worked, was moved to the fort's grounds in 1951.

LOCATION: 213 East Avenue D. HOURS: 10–5 Tuesday–Saturday, 1–5 Sunday. FEE: Yes. TELEPHONE: 915–657–4441.

The Headquarters building at Fort Concho, built in 1876 under the direction of Colonel Benjamin Grierson. The fort was established in 1867 to protect settlers in western Texas after the Civil War.

ODESSA

Meeting the southern end of the Llano Estacado is the area known as the Permian Basin—an ancient seabed buried thousands of feet under the sand and stretching 300 miles across Texas and New Mexico—where the first deposits of the second-largest oil field in the world were discovered in the 1920s. Consequently a boom came to this little railroad town, which is reputed to have been named by Russian-immigrant rail workers because its location resembled the steppes in the Ukraine on which the city of Odessa is situated. When oil was discovered in the Permian Basin, the University of Texas and Texas A & M University owned much of the land, which had been thought to be worthless desert. Odessa's **Presidential Museum** (622 North Lee Street, 915–332–7123) has a large collection of portraits, photographs, cartoons, memorabilia, and campaign materials relating to the highest office in the United States. Exhibits include the

The re-constructed enlisted men's Barracks V at Fort Concho, originally built in the early 1870s, has been furnished as it would have been when the infantry was stationed there in the 1880s.

Dishong Collection of First Lady dolls. The **White-Pool House** (112 East Murphy Street, 915–333–4072) is the oldest remaining structure in Ector County. The two-story redbrick residence was built in 1887 with milled porch details and Italianate elements.

MIDLAND

The site of this city was on the Comanche War Trail and the Emigrant Trail to California. In 1881 the Texas & Pacific Railroad made a water stop in this former buffalo range and called it Midway because it was about equidistant from El Paso and Fort Worth. Within three years several other towns were calling themselves Midway as well, and under pressure from the U.S. Postal Service, Midway became Midland. Midland was just another agricultural town until the overnight oil boom in the twenties when the town developed as the managerial and financial center for the Permian Basin oil fields.

Permian Basin Petroleum Museum

Creative displays illustrate the history and technology of the oil industry with dioramas of oil-field workers, audio-visual shows, and "sensory" programs—at one simulation exhibit, visitors stand inside a rig and feel the heat and noise of a wild well; at another, the force of a nitroglycerin explosion. Antique and modern equipment is on view both inside and outside the building. The geological history of the Permian Basin is explored—visitors walk underneath "the sea" as it might have been 230 million years ago to learn how the vast oil bed formed over time. Rock samples from deep within the earth are on view. Other exhibits include prehistoric artifacts from the area, cowboy gear, and paintings by Western artists.

> LOCATION: 1500 Route I-20 West, exit 136. HOURS: 9–5 Monday–Saturday, 2–5 Sunday. FEE: Yes. TELEPHONE: 915–683–4403.

The **Museum of the Southwest** (1705 West Missouri Avenue, 915–683–2882) is housed in the Turner mansion, built during the 1930s with interior details such as marble fireplaces and hand-painted tile floors, for a prominent local ranching and oil family, . The museum's collection focuses on Southwestern art and Indian artifacts. In addition, there is a planetarium and exhibits designed for children.

STANTON

The Texas & Pacific Railroad established the way station of Grelton here in 1881, then persuaded some German Catholics in Kansas to resettle around it. The settlers changed the name of Grelton to Marienfeld, or Field of Mary, and established a Carmelite monastery, which became a convent and boarding school for the Sisters of Mercy a few years later. The **Old Convent** (201 East Carpenter Street) was the only Catholic school between Fort Worth and El Paso. The newcomers cultivated fields of wheat and rye, surrounded by barbed wire. The fencing led to some archetypical rancher-farmer conflicts—tempers flared and fences were cut by cowhands from the nearby Long S Ranch, established by the famous and wealthy pioneer rancher Christopher Columbus Slaughter. The farmers survived the dispute but were virtually defeated by the Dry Blizzard, which began in 1886. A few held on; most moved along. Protestants moved into the area and recultivated with tougher crops such as cotton. In 1889 they changed the town's name to Stanton, after Abraham Lincoln's secretary of war, Edwin M. Stanton.

A fine small museum, the **Martin County Historical Museum** (207 East Broadway, 915–756–2722) has indoor exhibits on local history and an outdoor exhibit that includes an early Eclipse windmill. Without windmill power for pumping water, the vast prairies of northwest Texas might never have been settled. The **Old Jail Visitors Center** (Courthouse Square, 915–756–3386) is housed in the 1908 red-sandstone Martin County Jail, which was built around the cells of the original jail of 1884.

BIG SPRING

The original big spring, now a trickle in the city park, was a watering hole for animals and humans long before the Comanche came down to the south plains in the eighteenth century and made this point in Sulphur Draw (a draw is a wide gully) a stop on the Comanche War Trail. The first recorded use of the spring by whites occurred in 1849, when a wagon train escorted by U.S. troops under Captain Randolph B. Marcy marked the spring as a campsite on the Overland Trail to California. It also became a stop on the Santa Fe Trail. In the 1870s, after the Comanche were forced out, ranchers such as C. C. Slaughter moved into the area. Big Spring was the scene of occasional gunplay between ranch hands and construction workers on Jay Gould's Texas & Pacific Railroad (finished in 1882). Texas & Pacific built fancy shops to attract new settlers, and the town gained a decidedly glamorous air when Gould convinced the young earl of Aylesford to visit Big Spring in his search for a place to relax and hunt with his impressive gun collection. Other Englishmen followed and became ranchers, but most were forced out by the drought of 1894. Aylesford stayed and established a meat market (now the Finch Building at 121 Main Street) so he could be sure to get the proper cuts of mutton.

The Texas & Pacific master mechanic Joseph Potton hired S. B. Hagart, a Fort Worth architect, to build a house of Pecos sandstone and Queen Anne detailing in 1901. The **Potton-Hayden House** (200 Gregg, 915–263–7641) preserves the family's turn-of-the-century furniture and other household items. The **Heritage Museum** (510 Scurry Street, 915–267–8255) focuses on ranching and pioneer history in Big Spring and Howard County and houses the world's largest collection of longhorns and a large collection of phonographs.

SNYDER

A trading post for buffalo hunters was founded here by Pete Snyder in 1878, and around it grew a "community" called Robbers Roost. This assembly of buffalo-hide tents and dugouts attracted more than its share of undesirables. After the buffalo were gone, Snyder saw some farming and ranching—and fence-cutting episodes that flared some dangerous tempers—but the town was quiet until 1950, when the Canyon Reef Oil Field was discovered. Scurry County, of which Snyder is the seat, is said to produce more oil than any other county in the United States. The **Scurry County Museum** (Route 350 South, 915–573–6107), on the campus of Western Texas College, offers exhibits on the Comanche era, buffalo hunting, ranching, farming, and the oil business.

LUBBOCK

In 1890, just south of the Yellow House Draw and north of where Texas Tech University is today, a developer established a small town called Monterrey. A few months later another developer set up a town on the other side of the canyon, called North Town. Both developers were hoping to attract settlers with cheap lots and com-

At a stag dance at the Lazy S Ranch, the designated female wears a lace-trimmed apron.

peted for a time. In 1891, in a spirit of compromise, they decided to consolidate at a neutral site about a mile downstream—which meant, among other things, that they moved an eighteen-room hotel across the canyon. They called the third site Lubbock, after the Texas Revolutionary hero Thomas S. Lubbock. Today Lubbock is a large commercial center of one of the richest agricultural areas in the state, a high, flat land speckled with grain elevators and plant-ed in cotton. The Panhandle is an archaeological area of tremen-dous importance. The **Lubbock Lake National Historic Landmark** (North Indiana Avenue and Loop 289, 806–742–2442) is a rich repository of tools and artifacts of early Clovis and Folsom man, as well as animal remains, including those of the horse, camel, bison, and giant armadillo up to six feet long. Excavated material dates back as far as 12,000 years.

National Ranching Heritage Center

This impressive outdoor complex is probably the most comprehensive record of ranch architecture and life in Texas. Over thirty structures have been moved to the center's fourteen acres from all over the state, and each is painstakingly restored as an authentic record of settlement from the early days of the Republic of Texas to the turn of the century. A sampling includes buildings moved from some Panhandle-area ranches, including Las Escarbadas, established around 1886 and one of seven division headquarters for the 3,050,000-acre XIT Ranch; the Masterson JY Bunkhouse (ca. 1880), moved from King County; C. C. Slaughter's Long S. Whiteface Camp, established about 1890, first as a headquarters, then a line camp; the JA Milk and Meat Cooler (ca. 1880), where meat was hung in the path of prevailing breezes and perishable goods were cooled in crocks covered with wet rags and set in a trough of running water; John B. Slaughter's carriage house with the rancher's private saddle room; the Blankenship Cowchip House (ca. 1907), for winter-fuel storage; and the three-story Victorian Barton House (ca. 1909), a more sophisticated ranch house than most built at the time. Four kinds of windmills, a Fort Worth & Denver steam locomotive, and cattle-shipping pens from the King Ranch are also on view. The complex is landscaped with berms to keep modern Lubbock out of sight while visitors explore the past with costumed tour guides. The center is operated by the **Museum of Texas Tech** just to the west, whose collections and exhibits cover the arts, natural history, archaeology, and pioneer history of the area.

> LOCATION: 4th Street and Indiana Avenue, Texas Tech University campus. HOURS: *Museum:* 10–5 Tuesday–Wednesday, Friday–Saturday, 10–8:30 Thursday, 1–5 Sunday; *National Ranching Heritage Center:* 10–5 Monday–Saturday, 1–5 Sunday. FEE: None. TELEPHONE: 806–742–2442.

The **Muleshoe National Wildlife Refuge** (twenty miles south of Muleshoe on Route 214, 806–946–3341), the oldest national wildlife refuge in Texas, is one in a chain of refuges for migratory birds in the central flyway. Located on the high plains of west Texas, Muleshoe was established as a wintering area for up to 100,000 huge, gray sandhill cranes, which join flocks of ducks and geese on the alkaline lakes of the refuge (the lakes dry up in summer).

In **Crosbyton,** the **Crosby County Pioneer Memorial Museum** (101 Main Street, 806–675–2331) is a furnished replica of a rock house built in 1876 by the pioneer farmer Henry Clay Smith in an area that was inhabited by buffalo hunters and ranchers. Exhibits and a diorama depict life in Crosby County from early days to the present; there is a reconstructed half-dugout on the grounds.

TULIA

The small Swisher County seat of Tulia, settled by employees of the vast JA Ranch, is named for nearby Tule Creek and Tule Canyon and holds the record for the lowest temperature ever recorded in Texas, twenty-three degrees below zero in 1899. A tragic scene of devastation took place near here on September 28, 1874, in the Battle of Palo Duro Canyon: In the closing days of his ruthless campaign to stamp out the Indians on the Llano Estacado, the Indian fighter Captain Ranald Mackenzie (whom the Comanche called Three Fingers, because he had lost two in the Civil War) surprised an Indian encampment in Palo Duro and led thousands of soldiers in a roundup of 1,500 horses, which he then drove west into Tule Canyon and slaughtered. As the Indians fled on foot, the sound of rifle fire and screaming horses followed them for miles. "For years afterward," wrote historian T. R. Fehrenbach in *Lone Star,* "thousands of horse bones lay whitening here, a stark monument on the Plains." The few hundred Comanche and Kiowa remaining in the Panhandle were hunted down by U.S. troops or suffered through the winter until they were able to make their way to the reservation in Oklahoma. A historical marker seventeen miles east of Tulia on Route 86 notes the site where the horses were massacred.

Charles Goodnight and John Adair's vast JA Ranch was established in the Palo Duro Canyon only a year after the Indians were removed. At one time the ranch extended for more than seventy-five miles through much of four counties; today it is the largest and oldest ranch in the Texas Panhandle. The **Swisher County Archives and Museum Association** (127 Southwest 2d Street, 806–995–2819) has a fine collection of pioneer home furnishings, tools, and equipment. The museum contrasts two styles of frontier life: The Elegant House demonstrates how a well-to-do family might have lived around 1910, and the Jowell House suggests how a poor family might have lived in the 1920s. A log cabin that served as a line camp on the JA Ranch is also located on the museum grounds.

The flat land of the Texas Panhandle near Tulia is well suited for grazing such breeds of cattle as the Hereford, which can flourish on a diet of grass alone.

HEREFORD

This Panhandle city was named after the Hereford cattle, and today is a major feedlot center. Hereford is the seat of Deaf Smith County, named after the Texas Revolution hero Erastus "Deaf" Smith, the "Texas Spy." The **Deaf Smith County Museum** (400 Sampson Street, 806–364–4338), housed in a 1927 Catholic school, has among its more interesting exhibits a half-dugout, a shelter frequently built by early white settlers on the treeless and rockless plains; a country store equipped with merchandise and equipment from early Hereford businesses; a millinery store; a wagon yard; and ancient Indian arrowheads made from Alibates flint. The **National Cowgirl Hall of Fame and Western Heritage Center** (515 Avenue B, 806–364–5252) is dedicated to honoring Western women, including rodeo cowgirls. The center has an extensive collection of photographs of cowgirls, as well as early and contemporary western painting. Memorabilia include hats, boots, spurs, buckles, western costumes, trick ropes, and trick saddles. A one-and-a-half-story white house with Classic Revival elements, the **E. B. Black Historical House** (508 West 3d, 806–364–4338) was built in 1909 for a local businessman and philanthropist.

CANYON

The T-Anchor Ranch was established in the valley of Palo Duro Creek on the edge of the Palo Duro Canyon soon after Charles Goodnight moved his ranching operation into the canyon itself. Canyon, at the northernmost part of the 120-mile canyon, is still a ranching center and stepping-off point for touring this beautiful cut made by the Prairie Dog Fork of the Red River, a surprise in the midst of the high plains.

Panhandle-Plains Historical Museum

This inviting, spacious museum—the oldest state-supported museum in Texas—is housed in an Art Deco building of 1933 whose entrance is surrounded by tiles bearing the brands of the famous ranches of the area. The Hall of Texas History just inside the entrance gives an overview to the rest of the museum's galleries, which feature murals by Ben Carlton Mead and Harold Bugbee, as well as military uniforms. Extensive exhibits on three floors explore paleontology and geology, the Plains Indians, a pioneer town, oil and gas, western art, documentary photography, historic fashions, natural history, and transportation. A research center with archival materials is also open to the public. On the grounds of the museum is the **T-Anchor Ranch Headquarters,** built in 1877, the oldest intact structure in the Panhandle. Ranch outbuildings also still stand.

> LOCATION: 2401 Fourth Avenue. HOURS: September through May: 9–5 Monday–Saturday, 2–6 Sunday; June through August: 9–6 Monday–Saturday, 2–6 Sunday. FEE: Yes. TELEPHONE: 806–656–2244.

PALO DURO CANYON STATE PARK

Nomads hunted mammoths in Palo Duro Canyon 12,000 years ago, according to the dating of projectile points and animal bones. Coronado saw the 120-mile canyon—a haven of grass, trees, and water in the semi-arid plains—on his search for the golden cities, but few other whites saw it before the late nineteenth century. For nearly 200 years the canyon was the domain of the Comanche, who apparently convinced bands of Apache, Cheyenne, and Arapaho to go elsewhere. Comancheros—Mexicans who traded with the Comanche—lived or camped in parts of the canyon, as did the buffalo hunters after them. In 1874 the Battle of the Palo Duro Canyon, farther south in Tule Canyon, ended that, making room for Charles Goodnight, perhaps the most famous cattle rancher in Texas history, who moved his ranching operation from Colorado to the Palo Duro Canyon a year after the Comanche were removed. A mud, stone, and log dugout similar to the one first used by Goodnight has been constructed at the first water crossing on the park road. Also marked is the site where Colonel Ranald Mackenzie came upon the Kiowa and Comanche encampment, where thence began the last major battle involving Indians in Texas.

> LOCATION: Park Road 5, 12 miles east from Canyon via Route 217. HOURS: *Visitor Center:* 8–5 Daily. *Interpretive Center:* June through August: 11–7 Wednesday–Sunday. FEE: Yes. TELEPHONE: 806–488–2227.

In **Umbarger,** a few miles west off Route 60, **Saint Mary's Catholic Church** (218 West 13th Street) was built in 1929. The interior of the church is decorated with freehand figures, inscriptions, and stenciled accents done in 1945 by Italian prisoners of war interned at a camp near Hereford.

AMARILLO

The commercial and cultural capital of the Panhandle, the attractive city of Amarillo is an oasis of dignified houses on tree-lined streets set in rolling, semi-arid ranchland. When the Fort Worth & Denver City Railroad started construction through these parts in 1887, a community of tents called Ragtown sprang up. A promoter named J. T. Berry, thinking to take advantage of the development a railroad always brought to an area, marked off a town site in a low-lying area near the tracks and called it Oneida. A cattleman named Henry B. Sanborn, who owned the Frying Pan Ranch, did the same thing a mile away by Amarillo Creek (named by the local *pastores* and *Comancheros* from New Mexico for the yellow soil and hills along its banks). Sanborn owned the ranch with Joseph F. Glidden, who had invented the practical form of barbed wire; Sanborn, as his

The Harrington House in Amarillo, completed in 1914, is operated by the Panhandle Plains Historical Society. It was designed for the Landergin family by Shepard, Farrar & Wiser, an architectural firm in Kansas City.

agent in Texas, was thus partly responsible for changing the face of American ranching. Sanborn built a fancy hotel and painted it bright yellow in honor of the town's name, offered free lots as inducements, and convinced the railroad to stop at Amarillo as well as at Oneida. These tactics won settlers and, eventually, the county seat. Amarillo today is a world-class cattle market and site of the largest helium reserves in the world.

A prosperous cattle rancher named John Landergin and his brother, Pat, built the Neo-classical **Harrington House** (1600 South Polk Street, 806–374–5490) in 1914. It was later acquired by the prominent oil and gas producer Don Harrington and his philanthropist wife, Sybil., who donated the house and its contents to the Panhandle Plains Historical Society in 1983. Harrington House has unusual appointments for this part of the world, including eighteenth-century parquet floors, a carved pine mirror of 1697, George III–style mirrors, a Regency side cabinet of 1810, an Aubusson rug, and a banquette with eighteenth-century needlepoint cushions.

PANHANDLE

Panhandle is the seat of Carson County, through which some of the earliest Spanish explorers passed, the first being Coronado in 1541. The county's economy is based on ranching, agriculture, oil and gas industries, and defense work—Pantex, the assembler of all U.S. nuclear and thermonuclear bombs, is located here.

Carson County Square House Museum

This indoor-outdoor museum is one of the finest small pioneer museums in Texas. The outdoor exhibits, which are always open, depict the branding of cattle, the wildlife of the Panhandle, an old-time bank, a blacksmith shop, and a reconstructed half-dugout with pioneer furniture. Also outside is a Santa Fe Railroad caboose. The main museum building is called the Square House, built of twenty-four-foot lengths of pine hauled by ox cart from Dodge City, Kansas. The oldest aboveground dwelling in town, it was built in 1887 as part of the cattle operation of the Niedringhaus Brothers, who, before they came to the Panhandle from Saint Louis, invented graniteware—the speckled-enamel and tin dishes from which many cowboy outfits ate during cattle drives and roundups. The exhibits chronicle Indian culture, the buffalo hunters, cattle ranching, the discovery of oil, and the area's agricultural development. The museum has one of the finest collections of painting on paper by Native Americans. The Freedom Hall, installed for the Texas sesquicentennial in 1986, includes among its commemorations of American freedoms a display exploring those freedoms lost by American Indians.

LOCATION: 5th and Elsie streets. HOURS: 9–5:30 Monday–Saturday, 1–5:30 Sunday. FEE: None. TELEPHONE: 806–537–3524.

In Bates Canyon is the **Alibates Flint Quarries National Monument** (six miles south of Fritch off Route 136, 806–857–3151), comprised of flint quarries that were mined for ancient tools and weapons as long ago as 10,000 B.C. and for other purposes as recently as the turn of the century. Flint in one house in Amarillo is said to have been carted from the site by "touring car." National Park Service tours are the only way to see the multicolored quarries, and specimen collecting is strictly forbidden. The quarries' name is a smoothing out of its namesake, a cowboy called Allie Bates.

The history of the Battle of Adobe Walls is explored in **Borger** at the **Hutchinson County Museum** (618 North Main Street, 806-273-6121), through an exact-scale replica of Adobe Walls and a life-size painting of Chief Quanah Parker, who led the attack against the buffalo hunters. Museum exhibits also document the 1926 oil boom that created the town—45,000 men and women descended on Borger in eight months.

ADOBE WALLS

On June 27, 1874, Kwahadi Comanche led by Chief Quanah Parker (whose white mother, Cynthia Ann Parker, was captured as a child) and Kiowa warriors led by Lone Wolf attacked a buffalo hunters' fort called Adobe Walls. Cheyenne and Arapaho joined the force—they were all furious over the slaughter of the buffalo. The warriors rode toward the camp under the protection of a Kwahadi prophet named Isatai, who assured them they would win the fight to

In this view of a Comanche village in Texas, painted in 1834 by George Catlin, the women prepare buffalo hides to make tepees. The depletion of the buffalo on the Texas plains was supported by the government as a way of controlling the Comanche.

save the buffalo, that they would be impervious to the bullets of the buffalo hunters; but that was not to be the case. A buffalo hunter named Billy Dixon killed a Cheyenne warrior from a mile away; the Indians were shocked and demoralized, and in further fighting, fewer than thirty buffalo hunters, using their high-powered rifles, cut down many of the several hundred Indian warriors. Adobe Walls was merely the prelude to the final Comanche defeat three months later, at the Battle of Palo Duro Canyon. It was the first battle in a series of fourteen involving 3,000 United States troops. They converged in a circle on the Texas panhandle to break the southern Plains Indians' resistance. There are two monuments to the Indians and the whites who fought at Adobe Walls, and three marked graves. (The site is off a ranch road approximately twelve miles north of Stinnett on Route 207, follow signs.)

In the town of **Dumas**, the **Moore County Historical Museum** (Dumas Avenue and West 8th, 806–935–3113) displays a model of an early Rock Slab Indian dwelling and exhibits related to immigrant settlers on the high plains, such as a church with a working pump organ, a pioneer kitchen, samples of different kinds of barbed wire, and a "branding board" of area brands.

In the town of **Dalhart**, the **XIT Museum** (108 East 5th Street, 806–249–5390) commemorates the biggest ranch in Texas, created by one of the state's most famous real estate deals. In 1882 the state of Texas contracted with a group of Illinois investors, organized as the Capitol Syndicate, to grant them 3,050,000 acres of public land on the high plains in exchange for financing the building of the new state capitol in Austin. (The investors paid $3,224,593.45, somewhat less than half of the actual construction costs.) When the area was apportioned into counties in 1891, the ranch covered parts of ten counties in the western half of the Panhandle. Although it was said that the name stood for "Ten in Texas," it was devised because, as a brand, XIT was virtually unalterable by cattle thieves. The owners began selling off pieces of the ranch in 1901. The museum's exhibits include a turn-of-the-century parlor, bedroom, and kitchen, a pioneer chapel, an antique gun collection, and a collection of Indian arrowheads and grinding stones.

OPPOSITE: *Quanah Parker was the son of a white woman, Cynthia Parker, who as a child was captured by Comanche raiders in Limestone County, Texas, and lived with the tribe for twenty-five years before being recaptured by Texas Rangers. Quanah remained with the tribe, becoming the last Comanche to hold the title of chief.*

EASTERN OKLAHOMA

OPPOSITE: *The polychrome roof of Tulsa's Philtower, headquarters of the Phillips Petroleum Company.*

In the language of the Choctaw, *okla* means "people" and *humma* means "red." This is the land of the red people—Indian territory. Oklahoma is unique among all the states in having once been reserved by the federal government exclusively for Native Americans. White settlers were prohibited, it was said, "as long as grass grows and water runs." For more than half a century, Indians held most of the land in common and governed themselves by tribal law, until in the 1870s they began to be overrun by settlers. Even today, this population includes members of more than sixty tribes. Emblazoned on the state flag is the Osage war shield crossed by a peace pipe, perhaps a somewhat sanitized symbol of the final surrender of Indian territory to the forces of westward expansion.

Indians arrived in Oklahoma more than 20,000 years ago; they were hunters who killed immense Columbian mammoths with nothing but flint-pointed spears. When the climate warmed some 12,000 years later, beasts such as the bison and antelope were hunted by so-called Paleo People. In the period from A.D. 900 to 1450 a group of Mound Builders we call the Spiro People developed a sophisticated network of towns, farmed and traded, and created wonderful works of art—heads carved from rock crystal and ornaments of etched tortoiseshell. Other groups had probably vanquished the Spiro People before 1541, when the Europeans arrived. Spain sent Francisco Vásquez de Coronado and 1,500 of his men to investigate rumors of fabulous towns to the north—places so rich that the residents wore golden hats and sheathed the doors of their houses in pure turquoise. But in the Oklahoma Panhandle, Coronado found only the temporary camps of Plains Apache, who hunted "hump-backed cows," or bison. Coronado's expedition—the first European visit to Oklahoma—produced the first written accounts of the land, but found no golden cities.

Soon the French appeared as well. After Réne-Robert Cavelier Sieur de La Salle explored the Mississippi Valley in the 1680s, French fur trappers came to eastern Oklahoma in search of pelts, marking the land with such place names as the Verdigris River and the Sans Bois Mountains. They established trading posts among the Wichita and Caddo, and intermarried, founding towns on the Arkansas and Red rivers. The first successful American exploring party entered

OPPOSITE: *A repoussé profile of a male found in the Craig Mound, the largest surviving mound from a group built by the Spiro culture on the Arkansas River in eastern Oklahoma.*

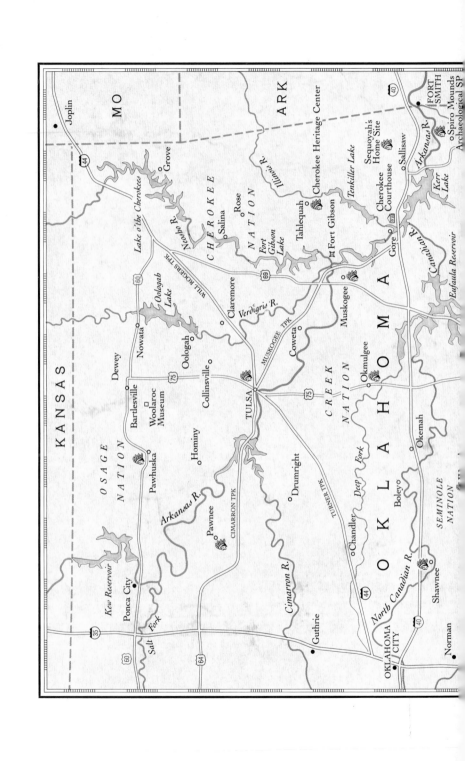

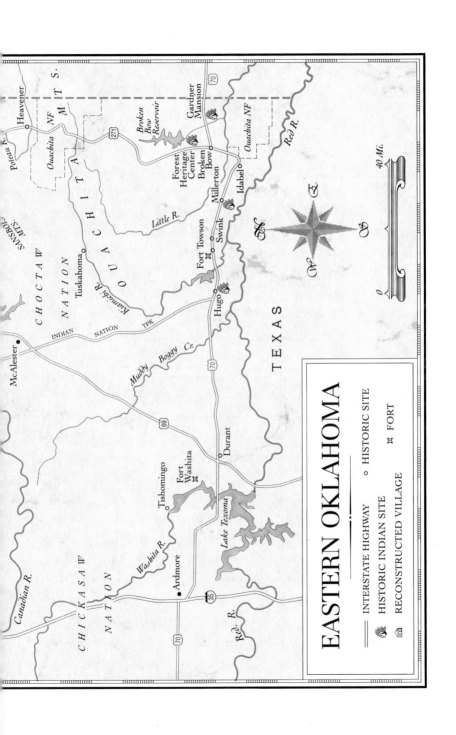

EASTERN OKLAHOMA

— — INTERSTATE HIGHWAY   ○ HISTORIC SITE

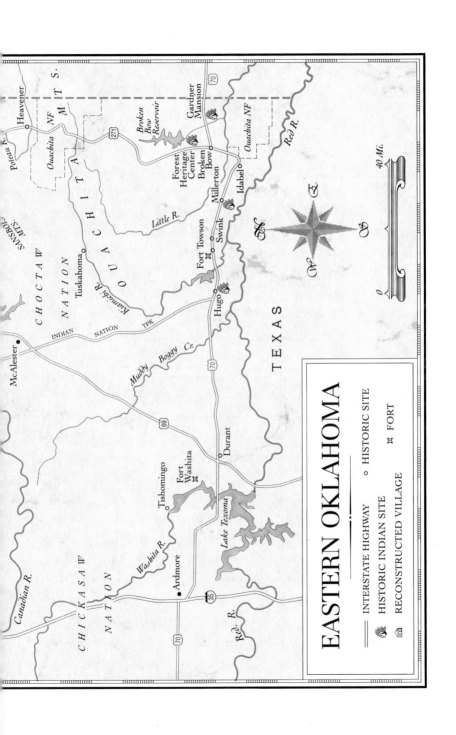 HISTORIC INDIAN SITE   ¤ FORT

 RECONSTRUCTED VILLAGE

40 Mi.

0

Oklahoma in 1806, led by James Wilkinson, a lieutenant serving as a member of the Zebulon Pike expedition. At that time various Indian tribes occupied the territory: Plains Apache, Kiowa, and Comanche in the west, Wichita and Caddo in the southwest, Cheyenne and Arapaho in the northwest, the warlike Osage in the northeast, and Quapaw in the east. In 1819 the United States and Spain divided their possessions at the 100th meridian and the Red River, lines that later became Oklahoma's southern and western borders. During the first two decades of the 1800s, fur traders settled in Oklahoma. Jean Pierre Chouteau and Joseph Bogy both operated posts at the Three Forks, where the Arkansas, Verdigris, and Grand rivers joined. Indians brought bear oil and skins to trade for tobacco, cloth, and weapons. Other traders made their way into west-central Oklahoma.

In a sequence replicated elsewhere on the frontier, traders were followed by settlers who built log cabins, planted crops, and imported livestock. To protect the settlers from Osage raids and to guard U.S. territory, in 1824 the government built Fort Gibson near the Three Forks, and Fort Towson on the Kiamichi River. Oklahoma seemed to be following the path that led many other western territories to statehood. However, in 1825 the federal government prohibited pioneers from settling in Oklahoma and reserved the land as Indian Territory, a place to relocate Indians who blocked the march of American civilization east of the Mississippi. Cherokee, Creek, Choctaw, Chickasaw, and some of the Florida Seminole—known as the Five Civilized Tribes—owned fertile lands for growing crops and cotton, lands that white settlers coveted. So they were the first to be removed to Oklahoma, forcibly escorted by troops. Government forces burned houses and farms, shot resisters, drove away livestock, and even opened Cherokee graves to loot silver jewelry. "I fought in the Civil War," a militiaman recalled years later, "and have seen men shot to pieces and slaughtered by thousands, but the Cherokee removal was the cruelest work I ever knew." Faced with hunger, unsanitary conditions, extreme weather, disease, and heartbreak, about 4,000 of the 16,000 who started the journey perished and were buried along the way. The Indians called the route to Oklahoma the Trail of Tears. Cholera ravaged the Choctaw, and some Creek walked to Oklahoma in shackles.

OPPOSITE: *Cypress trees in Beavers Bend State Park, near Broken Bow.*

Once settled, the deportees started over bravely. Each nation established a new capital—Tahlequah for the Cherokee, Okmulgee for the Creek, Wewoka for the Seminole, Tishomingo for the Chickasaw, and Tuskahoma for the Choctaw—and constructed a stone or brick capitol building. All but the Seminole capitol have survived. The five tribes feared the fierce western Indians and disliked the plains, so they remained in the forested eastern portion of their new territory. The Creek and Seminole, especially, clung to the traditional ways of hunting and fishing and tilling small farms; but many Indians started large-scale plantations, with black slaves, and became wealthy enough to send their sons to New England universities. "On the whole," note the historians Wayne and Anne Morgan, "the children of the Five Civilized Tribes were better educated and more concerned about learning than were their white counterparts on the frontier."

The Five Civilized Tribes were divided by the Civil War—some leaders sided with the Confederacy in 1861. The Confederates raised four Indian regiments, numbering about 5,000 men. These Confederate Indians first battled 7,000 Creek and Seminole men, women, and children who were Union sympathizers or neutralists. The war ravaged Oklahoma. After the hostilities had ended, returning Indians found their houses burned, their cattle driven off, their fields wasted. Furthermore, the federal government declared that the tribes would have to allow railroads to build tracks across Oklahoma, and cede the entire western half of Indian Territory to the government so that tribes from other parts of the United States could be resettled there. After the Civil War, the Five Civilized Tribes recovered from their economic losses and were soon cultivating farms and running herds of cattle. They laid plans for a territorial government of the united tribes, with statehood as an eventual goal. Indian Territory rebuilt war-ravaged towns and began new ones, established freight lines, attracted steamboat traffic, and marketed its herds in neighboring regions. In the absence of slaves, the tribes hired white tenants and laborers to work the land. The civil rights of the newly freed slaves were limited, however, and the tribes practiced Southern-style segregation. All-black townships such as Boley, Red Bird, and Foreman came into being. "Modernizing" seemed attractive to the tribes, and one observer noted that "instead of ceremonials and peace councils we hear now of railroad deals and contracts with cattle syndicates." Freight and passenger trains were

Cherokee making their way to Oklahoma from Georgia along the Trail of Tears, painted by Robert Lindneux in 1952 (detail).

rolling across eastern Oklahoma by the early 1870s, when the Katy (Missouri, Kansas & Texas Railway Company) arrived, followed by the Frisco, Santa Fe, Rock Island, and other lines. Crisscrossing the territory, the tracks soon created chains of new towns. A lumber industry developed in the southeast and coal mining began on Choctaw lands to furnish roadbeds and fuel steam engines.

Since experienced miners were rare and asked high wages, the railroads brought in European immigrants to work the coal seams. Other whites poured into Indian Territory: intruding farmers who defied the exclusion laws, cattle ranchers who leased grazing land, and workers. Eventually white outsiders outnumbered the Indians. However, since these outsiders had no right to live in Indian Territory, they received no land titles, no political rights, no education for their children in the tribal schools. Soon a rough alliance formed among the white residents, railroad promoters, and aspiring homesteaders who had missed out on good farmland elsewhere in the West. They called for the federal government to open at least part of the Indian Territory and let settlers in.

In 1889 the government designated the unassigned lands in the middle of Indian Territory for a land opening, the first of several runs that saw home seekers swarming into western Oklahoma. This opening was accomplished by the Dawes Allotment Act, which gave each Indian an allotment of 160 acres and left the "surplus" Indian lands available as homesteads. Indian leaders had gathered at Muskogee in 1905 to resist annexation to Oklahoma Territory and to plan the Indian state of Sequoyah, for which they wrote a constitution. Congress ignored the Indians and their superbly drafted document and created a unified state in 1907.

Oil would define eastern Oklahoma in the new age of statehood. As early as 1859, a Cherokee drilling a water well had accidentally struck oil, which flowed for a year until the gas pressure gave out, yet not until 1897 did the first commercial well gush forth in Bartlesville. Since there was no method for getting the oil to market until 1899 when the Santa Fe Railroad arrived, the well was capped. But the "oil rush" could not be similarly contained. A mad wave of speculation and drilling swept the state. Near Tulsa the Red Fork field was hit in 1901. Thomas Gilcrease of Tulsa was a former schoolteacher who craved excitement and found it in gushers; the wildcatter discovered the fabulous Glenn Pool in 1905. Tulsa became known as the "Oil Capital of the World," and by the time of statehood in 1907, about 40 million barrels of oil were being pumped out of Oklahoma each year. Tulsa was awash with oil profits, and petroleum barons endowed a university and fine museums such as the Philbrook in gratitude. The city's Gilcrease Museum, with its collection of more than 10,000 pieces relating to the Old West and the American Indian, brings the story of eastern Oklahoma full circle. The collection was started by a white oilman who found his fortune in what had once been Indian Territory.

This chapter travels through eastern Oklahoma, beginning with Salina and moving south to Tulsa and its surrounding towns. Next the route proceeds through the southeast region, moving from Shawnee to Okmulgee, Tuskahoma, and Tishomingo.

SALINA

Salina, which grew on the site of the old Chouteau trading post, is acknowledged as Oklahoma's first permanent white settlement. The Chouteau family were French fur traders based in Saint Louis who enjoyed a monopoly on the Osage trade at the end of the 1700s. Major Jean Pierre Chouteau established a post on the Grand River and convinced 3,000 Osage to relocate here in 1802. In a region rich with pelts, tallow, honey, and other goods, Chouteau prospered, and by 1809 he had become a partner in the Saint Louis Missouri Fur Company. His son August Pierre attended West Point and built a two-story log house. He had two wives and many children and surrounded himself with a retinue of Indians and slaves. Washington Irving was lavishly entertained by this frontier lord, and he described his 1832 stay in *A Tour on the Prairies*. The **Chouteau Memorial** (Route 20 East, 918–434–2224) displays family artifacts, including clothing, a fiddle, furniture, and photographs.

About four miles west of the town of **Grove** stands **Har-Ber Village** (Har-Ber Road, 918–786–6446), a collection of 100 relocated log buildings, including a saloon, stage depot, jail, and cabins. Displays include glassware, dolls, pipes, minerals, outlaw Belle Starr's piano, a papoose diaper made of sealskin, and a vest belonging to Ulysses S. Grant. Little is left of the neighboring town of **Cayuga** except the **Cayuga Mission** (east of Number 10 Bridge across Elk River), built of stone in 1894 by a visionary Wyandot Indian, Mathias Splitlog. In addition to beginning a ferry on Cowskin Creek, he established a wagon-manufacturing business, mills, and much of the town. The church shows Gothic Revival influence, with two towers and a bell from Belgium. Mathias Splitlog did not live to see its completion; the first service observed there was his funeral.

DEWEY

After establishing Bartlesville, pioneer rancher and entrepreneur Jacob Bartles founded the town of Dewey in 1898 and named it for the hero of Manila Bay. The next year Bartles built the **Dewey Hotel** (801 North Delaware, 918–534–9978), a vernacular frame building with turrets, a corner tower, and other Victorian Gothic elements. The Dewey Hotel is now a museum, and its collection includes period furnishings, such as an oak rolltop desk from Bartles's store and a black walnut bedroom set built for his wife's parents. There are also artifacts of the Delaware Indians. **Prairie Song** (Route 1, 918–534–2662) is a replica of a prairie village of the 1800s with a pioneer house, school, and chapel. There is also an Amish-style barn, wash house, and mule shed.

BARTLESVILLE

Bartlesville took shape on a meander of the Caney River in the Cherokee nation in 1875, when Jacob Bartles bought a gristmill and proceeded to add a trading post, stables, and a water system and then installed the area's first electrical generator. In 1885 two of Bartles's former clerks, William Johnstone and George Keeler, built a rival trading post on the river nearby. The town of Bartlesville was incorporated in 1897. That same year Johnstone and Keeler, together with the Cudahy Oil Company, hauled an abandoned drilling rig seventy miles over mud-bogged roads and drilled Oklahoma's first commercial oil well. The well produced more than 100,000 barrels and launched the state's petroleum industry. An exact reproduction of the **Nellie Johnstone Number 1** stands in Johnstone Park.

With the arrival of the Santa Fe tracks nearby in 1899, Bartlesville grew from a wildcatters' town into a city. In 1917 two brothers, Frank and L. E. Phillips, incorporated their oil and gas properties as the Phillips Petroleum Company; their first three wells

The elaborate Frank Phillips Home in Bartlesville was completed in 1909, only four years after Phillips, who was raised on a farm in Iowa, had arrived in Oklahoma territory to enter the oil business.

had been "dusters" but the next eighty-one hit. The **Frank Phillips Home** (1107 South Cherokee Avenue, 918–336–2491) was erected for the oilman and his wife in Classic Revival style in 1909; it had twenty-six rooms, imported woodwork, and baths featuring gold fixtures and a barber chair. Their Japanese butler amassed his own fortune in the stock market; Phillips might have been the world's only millionaire with a millionaire for a butler.

The H. C. Price Company, makers of oil pipeline equipment, hired Frank Lloyd Wright in 1956 to design **Price Tower** (6th Street and Dewey Avenue, 918–333–2927). The nineteen-story, 221-foot-tall building has floors cantilevered from a central shaft, each "similar to the branch of a tree from its trunk," said the architect. It is based on a diamond modular of thirty- to sixty-degree triangles, sheathed in copper and glass and supported entirely by four interior columns.

WOOLAROC

The remarkable legacy of oilman Frank Phillips, Woolaroc (WOOds-LAkes-ROCks) consists of a wildlife preserve, a lodge, and a museum. A private buffalo herd and other grazing animals roam 3,500 acres of prairie and forest. Phillips's rustic, nine-bedroom lodge of Arkansas pine logs, built in 1926, has been a getaway for presidents, movie stars, artists, and industrialists—Harry Truman, Rudy Vallee, Pawnee Bill, and Edna Ferber were among the guests. The oilman entertained his company with a Steinway grand piano covered with pine bark and with an unusual steer's head—when Phillips pushed a hidden button, the longhorn's eyes lit up, its nose exhaled puffs of smoke, and the voice of Oklahoma's favorite son, Will Rogers, came from its mouth. The front porch of the lodge offers a fine view of Clyde Lake and the surrounding Osage Hills. The museum's displays include the airplane that Phillips sponsored in a California-to-Hawaii race in 1927, a 95-million-year-old dinosaur egg, and artifacts from the Spiro Mound archaeological site. Among the exhibits of Indian culture are a Chippewa birch-bark canoe, nineteenth-century Navajo blankets, a bow and arrow made by Geronimo, and a portion of a scalp taken at the Osage Indian Agency in 1874. The collection also includes a saddle used by Theodore Roosevelt; an 1869 Concord Express stagecoach that traveled 625,000 miles; Buffalo Bill's saddle

OVERLEAF: *Derricks in an early Tulsa oil field. Oil became Oklahoma's premier industry with the opening of the Red Fork-Tulsa field in 1903.*

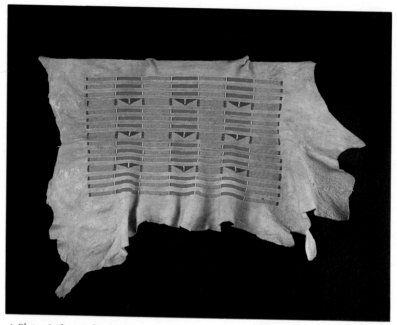

A Plains Indian girls' puberty robe, in the collection of the Woolaroc Museum.

and revolvers; and a full chief's costume given to Phillips when he was adopted into the Osage tribe. Works by Charles M. Russell, Frederic Remington, and Frank Tenney Johnson are on exhibit.

LOCATION: Route 123, 14 miles southwest of Bartlesville. HOURS: 10–5 Tuesday–Sunday. FEE: Yes. TELEPHONE: 918–336–0307.

PAWHUSKA

This rough country made the Osage extremely wealthy when oil was developed beneath it just before World War I. Oil-lease auctions in Pawhuska brought the Osage more than $250 million by the mid-1930s—as much as $15,000 each year for every man, woman, and child—and made them the richest Indians in the United States. They were famous for driving long, shiny cars. Agency Hill rises above town and is where the **Osage Agency** was built in 1872. The complex consists of the original frame office building and a sandstone agency building, as well as facilities for administering today's tribal affairs. In a sandstone building nearby, the **Osage Tribal Museum** (600

Grandview Avenue, 918–287–2495) displays Osage artifacts, such as ribbon work, war items, and dolls; portraits; and historical photographs. The 1894 Osage Council House later became the **City Hall** (Main Street and Grandview Avenue), built of rock-faced stone and topped with a bell tower. The **Osage County Historical Museum** (700 North Lynn Avenue, 918–287–9924) fills the Santa Fe depot of 1923 with displays of Indian, pioneer, western, and oil-industry artifacts.

Founded in 1886 on the site of an earlier Osage village, **Hominy** prospered during the oil boom of the 1920s. The **Drummond Home** (305 North Price, 918–885–2374), a Victorian house erected in 1905, contains clothing, documents, photographs, and 98 percent of the original furnishings from the oil-boom era. Frederick Drummond, a Scotsman, was an Indian trader and rancher.

PAWNEE

The **Pawnee Indian Agency** (Agency Road, 918–762–3621) was established after the tribe was relocated from Nebraska in 1874. The complex consists of the old sandstone agency building and a two-story superintendent's house. A teacher at the agency school, Major Gordon W. Lillie, was a proponent of opening Indian Territory to white settlers. When this occurred in 1893, the pioneer town of Pawnee took shape. Lillie, a cowboy, Indian interpreter, and frontiersman, was known to the Indians as Pawnee Bill—the name he adopted for his Wild West Show in 1888. From 1908 to 1913, he combined his show with William F. Cody's as "Buffalo Bill's Wild West and Pawnee Bill's Far East" ("East" connoting elephants). The **Pawnee Bill Museum** (west of Pawnee on Route 64, 918–762–2513) occupies the showman's 1910 ranch house, a stone and half-timbered building with the original furnishings. Billboards, costumes, a stagecoach, Indian artifacts, and a diorama of the Wild West Show are on display.

A small town sparked by the railroad in 1887, **Oologah** is the site of the **Will Rogers Birthplace** (off Route 169, three miles northeast of town, 918–341–0719). His large boyhood home is not quite in accord with the legend of Rogers's humble beginnings. His father was a successful rancher and banker, and his was one of the leading families in the region. The house was built of logs with frame additions. "Just before my birth my mother, being in one of these frame

rooms, had them remove her into the log part of the house," Rogers once said. "She wanted me to be born in a log house. She had just read the life of Lincoln. So I got the log-house end of it okay; all I need now is the other qualifications." The house was moved from its original site a mile away and contains period furnishings.

WILL ROGERS MEMORIAL

In one person, Will Rogers embodied both strains of Oklahoma's genetic makeup. Born in 1879 and officially nine-thirty-seconds Cherokee, he used to say, "My ancestors didn't come on the *Mayflower,* but they met the boat." He grew up as a rancher, however, and later signed love letters to his future wife: "Your Injun Cowboy." No fan of school, Rogers said that he "got bogged down in the fourth grade for about six years"; he preferred to practice rope tricks. As the trick-roping "Cherokee Kid," he traveled to South Africa with a Wild West show and appeared at the Saint Louis Exposition of 1904 with Zack Mulhall's rodeo, which he accompanied to New York's Madison Square Garden. Rogers became a popular vaudeville performer—his specialty was lassoing a horse and rider simultaneously with two ropes. His career soared, and by 1906 he was performing in London for Edward VII. Audiences enjoyed not only Rogers' roping, but his humorous comments on events of the day. Spotted by Florenz Ziegfield, he was a great success when he joined the *Follies* in 1915. The first of his seventy films came in 1918. Later he moved his family to Beverly Hills, where he was made an honorary mayor: Rogers was known and loved for his generosity to friends and the needy all over the world. In 1919 he began writing articles; he was eventually syndicated in 350 newspapers, more than any journalist before him. Traveling as America's "Goodwill Ambassador to the World," Rogers played polo with the king of Spain, chatted with George Bernard Shaw, and reported "their angle" in his homespun way. He flew whenever possible and was a tireless booster of government support for aviation. In 1935 he flew to Alaska with his friend Wiley Post, whom he termed the world's greatest pilot. Their plane crashed near Point Barrow; both men were killed. "When I die," Will Rogers said many times, "I want my epitaph to read, 'I never met a man I didn't like.'" These words are

OPPOSITE: *Will Rogers, billed as an "expert lariat thrower" in vaudeville shows, posing with his rope in an early publicity shot.*

carved on the base of a huge statue of the humorist at the Will
Rogers Memorial. Dioramas of his life, excerpts from his films and
newsreels, a Charles Russell bronze of Rogers, and a saddle collection are on display, along with many personal mementoes: the typewriter (battered in the crash) on which he turned out some 2 million words, his "gag book" of jokes, polo gear, and family photos. He
is buried at the memorial.

LOCATION: West Will Rogers Boulevard (Route 88), Claremore.
HOURS: 8–5 Daily. FEE: None. TELEPHONE: 918–341–0719.

TULSA

Tulsa began when the Creek were relocated from Alabama in the
1830s. Heads of families often met under a huge oak tree to purify
themselves, feast, and dance; this **Council Tree** still stands at 18th
Street and Cheyenne Avenue. The first party of whites to travel here
(aside from fur traders) in 1832 included Washington Irving, who
commented on the "rich and varied country . . . alluvial bottoms

The Art Deco style crown of Tulsa's Phythian Building.

Tulsa's Union Depot, built in 1931, in one of many buildings constructed in the Art Deco style during a period of prosperity from oil production.

matted with vegetation . . . [and] broken and rocky hills." By 1848 the first store was started, and by 1879 a post office had been established. During the 1880s Texas cattle ranchers grazed their herds in the area, and both the Creek and whites started farming. But the town itself took root only because of a railroad and a legal technicality. In 1882 the Atlantic & Pacific (Frisco) laid tracks that stopped in Cherokee country, a mile short of the river. But since non-Indians were not allowed to trade on Cherokee land, white settlers asked the railroad to extend the tracks one more mile into Creek territory, where they could obtain a bond for doing business. That done, the Tulsa commercial district grew up around the terminal. Tulsa prospered as a trade center for a wide area, especially after tracks were laid across the river to meet the cattle drives at a new terminal called Red Fork. The discovery of oil in 1901 at Red Fork spread the name of the town around the world. To ensure the link between their city and future oil development in Red Fork, Tulsa citizens financed a toll bridge and enticed oilmen to build homes in their community where, said boosters, "ordinances prevent the desolation of our homes and property by oil wells." To safeguard Tulsa's position, the Commercial Club convinced three more railroads to run tracks through the city by providing helpful land surveys and large cash "bonuses." Tulsa became a shipping hub for the oil industry's products and equipment. In 1905 the nearby Ida Glenn Number 1 discovery well came in, and soon the Glenn Pool was pumping more oil than any field on earth. A "black gold" rush began, and Tulsa began billing itself as the "Oil Capital of the World." But amid the prosperity a race riot erupted. By 1921 blacks made up 10 percent of the population in Tulsa; the local branch of the Ku Klux Klan had also grown. Two days of violence and arson destroyed the black district and left thirty-six people dead, 1,000 injured. Careful rebuilding of neighborhoods and white–black relationships improved matters thereafter. Meanwhile, Tulsa grew as an aviation center; both American Airlines and Braniff began their passenger service here. The city also developed into a cultural capital when oilmen such as Waite Phillips and Thomas Gilcrease donated important art galleries.

Gilcrease Museum

This museum was founded by Thomas Gilcrease, who was part Creek and grew up in Indian Territory. When he was nine years old, Gilcrease received a 160-acre allotment in the center of what became the Territory's first major oil-producing field, near present-day Tulsa. He educated himself with the earnings from his oilfield and went on to build a fortune. Starting in 1910 when almost no one was interested in Americana and continuing for the next forty years, Gilcrease built his collection, focussing on the discovery and development of the New World, in particular the settlement of the West. The collection is rich in American landscapes from 1870-1890, especially those of Thomas Moran. Gilcrease was proud of his Indian heritage; the museum's native American art ranges from eighteenth-century hide paintings to twentieth-century Taos paintings. The contrasting views of Indian life held by Frederic Remington, Charles M. Russell, and George Catlin are apparent in nearly 600 works by those artists. Also represented are James McNeill Whistler, John Singer Sargent, Winslow Homer, and John James Audubon. The museum's holdings include 10,000 works of art, 250,000 artifacts, and 10,000 rare books and documents. Among

OPPOSITE: *A late-nineteenth-century elk hide, probably Sioux, shows chiefs and warriors. It is now in the collection of the Gilcrease Museum.*

the artifacts is a letter, written in 1512 by Diego Columbus (the discoverer's son) to the Archbishop of Toledo, containing the earliest known description of the island of Hispaniola and accounts of the first exploratory expedition to Cuba.

LOCATION: 1400 Gilcrease Museum Road. HOURS: 9–5 Monday–Saturday, 1–5 Sunday. FEE: Yes. TELEPHONE: 918–582–3122.

The **Tulsa County Historical Society Museum** (918–585–5520) is also on the Gilcrease Museum grounds and occupies the **Thomas Gilcrease House,** where the oilman lived after 1914 with his first and second wives. Inside the sandstone building are exhibits on Tulsa history, correspondence, and early furnishings.

In the downtown area several buildings reflect the Art Deco trend. The **Union Depot** (3 South Boston Avenue, 918–583–6900), built in 1931 and now restored as offices, incorporates many Art Deco designs on its exterior walls and retains the original interior colors of gray, coral, green, and crimson, as well as zigzag motifs on glass doors, bas-relief ornaments, and other stylistic touches. Another example of adaptive reuse for offices is the 1917 **Tulsa Municipal Building** (124 East 4th Street), which harks back to an earlier Classic Revival style. The **Philcade** (511 South Boston Avenue, 918–581–3011) is an example of Zigzag Moderne, an early Art Deco style. Built in 1930, it has ornate window grillwork, bronze chandeliers, and stylized foliage above the windows that conceals bird and animal imagery. The facade blends terra-cotta, metalwork, and brick. A tunnel connects the building to the twenty-eight-story **Philtower** (across 5th Street, 918–585–2377); both buildings were put up by oilman Waite Phillips, who feared kidnapping and planned the tunnel as a way to move about safely and secretly. The Philtower is notable for its polychrome roof tiles. The celebrated **Boston Avenue United Methodist Church** (1301 South Boston Avenue) dates to 1929 and has been called "an elegant Art Deco finger pointing toward heaven." Its pleated tower rises 225 feet. The **Fenster Museum of Jewish Art** (1223 East 17th Place, 918–582–3732) displays the Southwest's largest collection of ceremonial and aesthetic Judaica, which spans nearly 4,000 years. Included is a nineteenth-century silver-gilded Polish Torah crown.

OPPOSITE: *The dramatic spiral staircase, based on a French design, of Tulsa's Mid-Continent Building, an Art Deco skyscraper designed by John Coultis. A drawing of the building hangs on the wall.*

In the Riverview district, the **McBirney Estate** (1414 South Galveston, private) was erected in 1927 by a one-time Irish janitor, James H. McBirney, who became an important banker. This brick Jacobean Revival-style mansion is located in a neighborhood that McBirney developed along the Arkansas River; it features half-timbering, a Tudor arched entry portal, and leaded-glass windows. The grounds once included a small golf course and trout pools fed by natural springs. The **Harwelden Mansion** (2210 South Main Street, 918–584–3333) is a Tudor Gothic Revival-style landmark, built by the oilman Earl Palmer Harwell in 1923 with four levels and thirty rooms. **Westhope** (3704 South Birmingham Avenue, private) was designed in 1929 by Frank Lloyd Wright for his cousin, newspaper publisher Richard Lloyd Jones. Concrete blocks were cast on the premises and assembled into sprawling sections with vertical bands of windows.

Philbrook Museum of Art

Waite Phillips, an Iowa farmboy who made a fortune in oil, began work on Villa Philbrook in 1926, inspired by the country villas of Renaissance Italy. Along with serpentine columns, Venetian lanterns, and coffered ceilings, this Jazz Age house also has a lighted-glass dance floor inspired by a Paris nightclub. An open loggia leads to twenty-three acres of gardens: an informal English garden, a rock garden, and a formal Italian garden with a "water staircase." It is said that Phillips and his wife built the mansion to give their children a place to entertain their friends; in 1938, after the children were grown, he donated the house to Tulsa as an art museum. The collections include Indian artifacts, Italian Renaissance art, African and Oriental art, and American and European paintings.

LOCATION: 2727 South Rockford Road. HOURS: 10–5 Tuesday–Saturday, 1–5 Sunday. FEE: Yes. TELEPHONE: 918–749–7941.

Sapulpa, a town near the bountiful Glenn Pool oil district, takes its name from Chief Sapulpa, a Creek farmer of the 1850s. The **Sapulpa Historical Museum** (100 East Lee, 918–224–4871) displays pioneer clothing, furniture, a kitchen, and Frisco Railroad articles.

OPPOSITE: *The Philbrook Museum of Art is housed in a villa designed as a residence for Waite Phillips, a brother of Frank Phillips of Bartlesville.*

Six years after its founding in 1891, **Chandler** was virtually destroyed by a cyclone. The story of the town is told at the **Museum of Pioneer History** (717 Manvel Avenue, 405–258–2425), which re-creates daily life in the early years of Lincoln County. The exhibits include a pioneer kitchen and doctor's office, a printing press, farm tools, and clothing. There are also displays of Sac and Fox relics, such as moccasins and beadwork, and the memorabilia of Marshal Bill Tilghman, a former buffalo hunter who helped settle Dodge City, Kansas, before he became Chandler's marshal. The **William M. Tilghman Homestead** (off Route 18, two miles northwest of town, private), a log cabin later enclosed by frame construction, was built by Tilghman in 1891. After he was elected sheriff of Lincoln County in 1901, Tilghman purchased the **Tilghman Home** (209 West 8th Street, private) and moved to Chandler so he could be near the courthouse and jail. The brick house, built in 1898 by O. B. Kee, has five patterns of fish-scale shingles and a mansard-style frame roof.

The Shawnee Friends Mission, established in 1871, provided schooling and some social services to the Shawnee until 1924. This frame building, constructed in 1885 and now undergoing restoration, replaced the mission's first log structure.

SHAWNEE

After the Civil War, President Ulysses S. Grant tried to pacify the Plains tribes by sending Quakers to Oklahoma as "peace policy agents" for the Shawnee Indians. The area around what is now the town of Shawnee was a trading hub for the Shawnee Indians and a logical place to establish the **Shawnee Friends Mission** (two miles south of Shawnee on Gordon Cooper Road). The frame meeting-house of 1885 still stands, with its original bronze bell in the belfry. A log home built in 1882 by the Bourbonnais family is located close by. The nearby **Potawatomi Indian Museum** (1901 South Gordon Cooper Drive, 405–275–3121) displays the headdresses, beadwork, and feather flag of the tribe. The Indian lands in this area were first opened to white settlers on September 22, 1891. At the start of the land run, a young woman named Etta Ray simply stepped over the line and staked a 160-acre claim; the town of Shawnee was estab-

The Bourbonnais log house, built in 1882, was moved to a site near the Shawnee Mission from Shawneetown, a neighboring village that was abandoned when its inhabitants joined the land run of 1891.

Shawnee's Richardsonian Romanesque Santa Fe Depot, completed in 1903, is now a museum specializing in local history.

lished on her farm and several other parcels. With the arrival of three railroad lines between 1895 and 1904, Shawnee became a cotton and agricultural shipping center. When the Seminole and nearby oil fields boomed in the 1920s, Shawnee became an oil town. Local history is recounted at the **Santa Fe Depot Museum** (614 East Main Street, 405–275–8412); the exhibits include an organ that landed in a farmer's field after a 1924 tornado, a 1917 pickup truck, and the buckskin dress of a Potawatomi woman who married into the Bourbonnais family. The red limestone building of 1903 is one of the few large Richardsonian Romanesque depots surviving in the Southwest; its tower is patterned after a Scottish lighthouse.

WEWOKA

The Seminole moved to the Wewoka area in 1866. The influx of white settlers in Florida had forced the Seminole to abandon their earthen homes; in Florida, a treaty signed in 1832 called for their removal to Indian Territory. But the warrior Osceola and his followers waged a prolonged fight against surrendering their Florida homeland. By 1842 about 3,000 of the tribe had moved to Oklahoma, many under military guard, and the government finally stopped pursuing the rest, who had taken refuge in the Florida Everglades. White settlers moved to Wewoka after the railroad arrived at the turn of the century; the oil boom started in the 1920s. The **Seminole Nation Museum** (524 South Wewoka Avenue, 405–257–5580) displays canes and teakettles used by the Indians during their march west, household furnishings used by the white settlers, and a replica of an early drilling rig.

BOLEY

After the Civil War, the Indians of the Five Civilized Tribes were required to treat their former slaves as citizens and provide them with land. The Indians passed laws to segregate their former slaves in schools and public accommodations. From 1865 to 1910, twenty-six all-black towns were founded in Oklahoma. In 1903 the Fort Smith & Western Railway suggested that blacks be given an opportunity to govern themselves, and the town of Boley was started around the railroad tracks. When Booker T. Washington visited in 1905, he applauded Boley as an attempt "to do something to make the race respected; something which shall demonstrate the right of the Negro . . . to have a worthy and permanent place in the civilization that the American people are creating."

Okemah, which comes from the Creek word for "big chief," was founded in 1902. At one time the entire town was surrounded by a barbed-wire fence to keep out the longhorns, which grazed by the thousands on the nearby plains. The Dust Bowl balladeer Woody Guthrie was born here in 1912. The **Territory Town Museum** (Route I-40, five miles west of town, 918–623–2604) features artifacts from the Civil War and the Indian and Oklahoma territories, including a strongbox and shotgun owned by the Wells Fargo Company.

The Creek (an English name, not an Indian one) suffered more than any other tribe on their Trail of Tears. Virtually all the infants, small children, and old people—more than 40 percent of the tribe—died during the removal from Alabama and Georgia to Indian Territory. The Creek comprised two factions: The Upper Creek tended to adhere to traditional values and withdrew from white culture by moving west in the early 1830s; the Lower Creek embraced more of the values of the white settlers, including their religion, and they were relocated in the late 1830s. In 1868 **Okmulgee** became the capital of the Creek. In 1878 the tribe built the **Creek Council House Museum** (Town Square, 918–756–2324) as its capitol building. The council house is made of sandstone and topped with a louvered cupola; the museum displays plumed turbans, clothing, jewelry, and baskets made by the tribe. The Creek were served by the **Nuyaka Mission** (off Route 56, twelve miles west of Okmulgee, private), built in 1882 by Presbyterians and the tribal council as a joint project. Funds were also raised by Alice Robertson, who was later elected Oklahoma's first congresswoman. The frame superintendent's house (which was also the boys' dorm for the mission school) still stands. Nuyaka is a corruption of "New Yorker," the name of a Creek town in Alabama.

TAHLEQUAH

When the western Cherokee and the newly arrived eastern contingent met in 1839 at Tahlequah to reunite the tribe, they wrote a constitution. The tribe chose Tahlequah as a permanent capital, but the site was nothing more than a campsite and council ground until 1843. The next year the *Cherokee Advocate,* Oklahoma's first newspaper, was published in both Cherokee and English in Tahlequah. Princeton-educated William Ross, the nephew of principal chief John Ross, served as editor. In 1845 the Cherokee government decreed that the public square be cleared of houses to make way for important tribal buildings. The **Cherokee National Capitol** (101 South Muskogee, 918–456–0671), built of brick to replace a log structure burned during the Civil War, now stands on the square. Occupied in 1870, the Italianate building housed the tribal legislature and new chambers for the supreme court, then served as Cherokee County Courthouse from 1907 to 1979; it now contains a small display of Cherokee material. Originally, the tribal court met in the brick **Cherokee Supreme Court Building** (Water Avenue and Keetoowah Street), built in 1845 as the first permanent structure in Cherokee country. The **Cherokee National Prison** (Water Avenue and Choctaw Street, 918–458–0577), built of sandstone in 1874, once contained a gallows. Today the jail serves as the tribal library.

Cherokee public high schools were established in 1846 with the authorization of seminaries for males and females. Built with turrets and a tower in 1887, the brick **Cherokee Female Seminary** (918–456–5511) has become Seminary Hall on the campus of Northeastern State University, which, according to the National Historic Register, is the alma mater of more Indian students than any other accredited institution. A simple frame building once functioned as the **Indian University of Tahlequah** (320 Academy, private), a school for Cherokee youth founded by Baptists in 1867.

Park Hill, located about three miles south of Tahlequah, was the premier center of learning in Indian Territory. It was the site of the 1836 Park Hill Mission, established by a Presbyterian, Samuel Austin Worcester. The steamboat on which he had shipped his printing press sank in the Arkansas River, and only by heroic effort did Worcester salvage it. "This single piece of equipment," notes the historian Arrell Gibson, "became one of the most important devices ever brought to Oklahoma" and helped create the "Athens of the

A reconstructed Cherokee dwelling, at left, alongside a rounded osi, *a winter dwelling in which the inhabitants would light a fire during the day so the retained heat would warm them at night, at the Cherokee Heritage Center.*

American Southwest." The Park Hill Press published the annual *Cherokee Almanac*, textbooks, and much of the Bible in Cherokee; it also did printing for other tribes (11 million pages for the Choctaw alone). Park Hill was the original site of the Cherokee Female Seminary, a three-story brick structure built in 1851 and destroyed by fire in 1887. Three surviving brick columns from the seminary have been incorporated in a tribal museum.

CHEROKEE HERITAGE CENTER (TSA-LA-GI)

The **Cherokee National Museum,** located on forty-four acres, offers exhibits on tribal life before and after relocation and a display on the Cherokee syllabary devised by Sequoyah. Artifacts include a knife made by Jim Bowie for a Cherokee brigadier general of the Confederacy and wooden "booger masks" used in dances that parodied problems in tribal life, including the improper behavior of non-Cherokee. The Ancient Village imaginatively re-creates a sixteenth-century Cherokee settlement. Indian craftspeople demonstrate pottery, basket making, beadwork, canoe making, and other skills of daily life. Adams Corner Rural Village presents a typical Cherokee community during the period from 1875 to 1890, with a general store, hunter's cabin, parsonage, and school. An outdoor amphitheater is the site of the Trail of Tears Drama, which depicts the Cherokee story from relocation to statehood.

> LOCATION: Willis Road off Route 62, 3 miles south of Tahlequah.
> HOURS: June through August: 10–8 Monday–Saturday, 12–6
> Sunday; September through May: 10–5 Monday–Saturday, 1–5
> Sunday. Trail of Tears Drama performed early June through Labor
> Day. FEE: Yes. TELEPHONE: 918–456–6007.

The 1843 **Murrell Home** (Murrell Road, three miles south of Tahlequah off Route 82, 918–456–2751) served as a social and political gathering place in the Cherokee nation. John Murrell was a white merchant who married a niece of the principal chief of the Cherokee. His large frame house with Greek Revival elements illustrates the gracious way of life achieved in remote Indian Territory—a wine cellar, servants' quarters, fine cabinetwork, and tree-shaded grounds. One of Oklahoma's few surviving antebellum mansions, it displays Indian artifacts, costumes, and early furnishings.

FORT GIBSON MILITARY PARK

Designed to stem Osage hostilities and defend the nation's south-west boundary against invasion by Spanish forces, Fort Gibson was erected in 1824 near the strategic junction of the Grand, Verdigris, and Arkansas rivers—the Three Forks. Oklahoma's first military post, Fort Gibson was connected to Fort Smith in Arkansas via Oklahoma's first road, and its officers included the future president Zachary Taylor, Confederate commander Robert E. Lee, and Confederate president Jefferson Davis. The fort was an important hub of frontier life; a nearby neighbor was Sam Houston, who had abandoned the governorship of Tennessee to live among the Cherokee with whom he had spent part of his youth. Washington Irving set out from Fort Gibson on his 1832 tour. The Stokes Commission set up headquarters at the fort in 1832 to expedite the relocation of the Five Civilized Tribes. To squelch the threat of aggression by the resident Osage, in 1833 the army established its first permanent cavalry unit, the First Regiment of U.S. Dragoons.

A replica of a cannon of 1841, facing the reconstructed officers' quarters at Fort Gibson Military Park.

The mounted corps wore elaborate and hot uniforms that featured orange sashes, gold braid, and hats topped with white horsehair pom-poms. In 1834 these troops were sent to make a show of power to the western Indians. Unfortunately, virtually every soldier fell ill with fever—150 men died, including the commander, General Henry Leavenworth. Nonetheless, the western Indians did sign treaties. The artist George Catlin made drawings and notes as a member of this expedition. The fort, deserted in 1857, became active again during the Civil War, when it was held by Confederate forces and then captured by Union troops as a base for further military operations. A trade center and supply depot, Fort Gibson was served by steamboats on the Arkansas River. It was abandoned in 1890. The seventy-acre military park includes a reconstructed stockade, the original stone barracks, a powder magazine, a commissary, blacksmith shop, adjutant's office, bakery, and hospital.

LOCATION: Route 80, Fort Gibson. HOURS: 9–5 Monday–Saturday, 1–5 Sunday. FEE: None. TELEPHONE: 918–478–2669.

MUSKOGEE

Muskogee is another name for the Creek Indians, who were relocated to the area beginning in 1829. The town took shape in the early 1870s with the arrival of the Missouri, Kansas & Texas (Katy) Railway. Hopeful settlers and glint-eyed promoters had waited patiently while a railroad bridge was built across the Arkansas River, then they boarded the first train and alighted in a fever to erect houses and shops. Although Muskogee was in Indian Territory, settlers ignored laws prohibiting trespassing because the Indian courts could not enforce them. The pioneer outpost had a corn crib as its first school and an empty boxcar for its first church. Muskogee lay on the busy Texas Road, which ran north as a thoroughfare for cattle herds along what is now Cherokee Street. Dust poured into houses, and children were warned not to play in the area lest the animals trample them.

In 1874 the Union Agency for the Five Civilized Tribes was installed in Muskogee and ensured the town's future importance. Originally the agency was to be near Checotah, but legend says that Muskogee boosters poured salt in the well of the rival settlement,

OPPOSITE: *The officers's quarters at Fort Gibson, which housed officers, enlisted men, and offices, were among the earliest structures in the fort. Originally constructed beginning in 1824, they were reconstructed in the 1930s.*

A gorget, or collar, made of shell, found in the Spiro mounds. OPPOSITE: *A bauxite effigy pipe from the Spiro culture, ca. 1200-1350.*

making the water unfit to drink, and thus secured the facility. The city became a meeting place for leaders of the Five Civilized Tribes; noncitizens of Indian Territory also poured in. When the Dawes Commission set up here in 1897 to allot land to individual tribal members and enroll every Indian, there was an influx of lawyers and real estate agents. Muskogee was also the site of the fruitless Sequoyah Convention of 1905, during which Indian leaders drafted a constitution for a separate Indian state. As Oklahoma approached statehood, Muskogee gained six railroad lines and an oil industry, which began in 1903 with a gusher that actually splattered houses at the edge of town; the next year the city's first refinery was built.

The **Five Civilized Tribes Museum** (Agency Hill, Honor Heights Drive, 918–683–1701) occupies the former Indian agency building, a two-story, Italianate structure erected in 1875 when the Five Civilized Tribes consolidated their governments. It has since served as everything from a tearoom to Boy Scout headquarters. Now a museum and art gallery, it presents the history and artifacts of the Cherokee, Choctaw, Creek, Chickasaw, and Seminole.

Oklahoma history was the specialty of Grant and Carolyn Foreman. They wrote nearly twenty books in the **Thomas-Foreman Home** (1419 West Okmulgee Street, 918–682–6938), a plain frame cottage built in 1898 by Carolyn's father, Judge John Thomas. The original furnishings and Indian artifacts are on display. The **Ataloa Lodge Museum** (Bacone College campus, 918–683–4581, ext. 283) displays Indian arts and crafts, such as rugs, baskets, and pottery by Maria Martinez, on the campus of Bacone College, established in the early 1880s for Indians but later opened to whites. Adjacent to the campus is the site of Fort Davis, a Confederate post established in 1861 to command and supply Indian troops; it was burned by Union soldiers in 1862. Only an earth mound topped with a flagpole remains. The **USS *Batfish* Submarine** (Port of Muskogee, off Muskogee Turnpike, 918–682–6294) was commissioned in 1943, sank three enemy subs in as many days, and is now in permanent dry dock near the city port. The control room, passageways, and torpedo tubes are on view.

Gore was the original capital of the Cherokee nation in Oklahoma; in 1843, with the arrival of 12,000 Cherokee from the Trail of Tears, the capital was moved to Tahlequah. The complex at the **Cherokee Courthouse** (two-and-a-half miles southeast of Gore on Route 64, 918–489–5663) features a nineteenth-century log cabin and reproductions of the original Cherokee courthouse and council house.

Sequoyah's Home Site (Route 101, 918–775–2413) is located eleven miles northeast of the town of **Sallisaw.** Sequoyah (George Guess; ca. 1770–1843) was the only person in history, so far as is known, to create a full alphabet—or, more properly, a syllabary; his system of eighty-six characters used one symbol for each sound in his native Cherokee language. Sequoyah undertook the task in about 1809 in Arkansas after observing "talking leaves," the white people's written pages. After years of ridicule by his tribe, who thought he was practicing black magic, and the intolerance of his wife, who once burned all the bark and material on which he had written, Sequoyah perfected his system in 1821. Almost anyone could learn it in a matter of weeks, and a contemporary noted that "the whole [Cherokee] nation became an academy for the study of the system." Virtually overnight, the Cherokee became literate. In 1828 the tribe launched its own newspaper, the *Cherokee Phoenix.* The next year Sequoyah was "relocated" from Arkansas to near Sallisaw, where this practical genius served as a tribal leader. The hewn-log cabin on his farmstead was built in 1829; Sequoyah's hand-forged farming utensils are on display inside.

Seven miles northeast of **Spiro**, the **Spiro Mounds Archaeological State Park** (Spiro Mounds Road, off Route 9/271, 918–962–2062) reflects an age of high achievement in Oklahoma prehistory from A.D. 850 to 1450. A group of Mound Builders called the Spiro People lived in a network of towns and built earthen mounds up to thirty-six feet high. They planted corn, melons, and tobacco. The Spiro People traded for pearls, which came from the Gulf of Mexico, and crafted copper axes and ornaments made of conch and tortoiseshell. They left twelve mounds; a home, a mortuary, and a temple have been reconstructed. The visitor center displays artifacts and murals of these early people.

In the town of **Heavener** is the **Heavener Runestone State Park** (Route 1, Morris Creek Road, 918–653–2241). Discovered by Choctaw in the 1830s, the Runestone—twelve feet high, ten feet wide, and sixteen inches thick—has eight symbols etched into its west face that are believed to be letters from two runic alphabets (one A.D. 300 and the other A.D. 800) once used by pre-Columbian Norsemen. Seven miles southwest of town is the **Peter Conser House** (off Route 59, 918–653–2493). Built in 1894 by the district chief of the Choctaw Lighthorsemen, a corps of Indian police, the frame building has been restored with its original contents.

The Choctaw were the first of the Five Civilized Tribes to agree to removal; they left their homes in Mississippi starting in 1820. They farmed the new territory, sometimes with slave help. In 1834 the Choctaw wrote the first constitution drafted in Oklahoma. In 1884 they moved their capital from Chahta Tamaha (Choctaw City) to **Tuskahoma**. The **Choctaw Council House Historical Museum** (off Route 271, three miles north of Tuskahoma, 918–569–4465) is a square brick building with Second Empire elements that served as the center of tribal government from 1884 until statehood in 1907. The museum displays a small number of Choctaw artifacts.

In the 1830s the area around **Broken Bow** became Choctaw territory; previously it had been the home of the Caddo Indians, who raised corn and lived in dome-shaped houses. Caddoan pottery is displayed in town at the **Memorial Indian Museum** (2nd and Allen streets, 405–584–6531). The **Forest Heritage Center** (Route 259, 405–494–6497), ten miles north of Broken Bow in **Beavers Bend**

State Park, focuses on Indian and pioneer cultures in the forests of the South as well as exhibits of artifacts of the early logging and lumber industries. The largest cypress tree in Oklahoma, more than 2,000 years old, stands near the **Gardner Mansion** (Route 70, six miles east of Broken Bow, 405–584–6588). This frame house, built in the 1880s, was the home of the Choctaw principal chief Jefferson Gardner. Historic and prehistoric Indian artifacts are on view.

Named for Ida and Belle, daughters of a railroad official, **Idabel** is the site of the **Magnolia Mansion** (601 Southeast Adams, 405–286–3200). Also called the Spaulding-Olive House, the mansion was designed in Classic Revival style for George Spaulding, an Oklahoma lawyer and judge, in 1910. Antiques, glassware, and Victorian furniture are on display; magnolia blossoms appear as a decorative motif in the house. Just south of town, the **Museum of the Red River** (812 East Lincoln Road, 405–286–3616) focuses on Indian art and life in North and South America. Exhibits tell the story of the Caddoan confederacy and the Choctaw. Caddoan pottery, pre-Columbian art, and a variety of Native American tools are displayed.

Millerton was one of the first towns in Choctaw country and is the site of Oklahoma's oldest surviving house of worship. The **Wheelock Church** (off Route 70, two miles north of town, 405–286–3448) is built of limestone, and its walls are nearly two feet thick. It was erected in 1846 by a congregation of Choctaw under the Reverend Alfred Wright. Dr. Wright named the church and mission after Dr. Eleazar Wheelock, the founder of Dartmouth College. An Indian parishioner, who took the name Allen Wright to honor the missionary, proposed a name for Indian Territory in 1866 that was later used for the state: Oklahoma, or Land of the Red People. Two miles northeast of **Swink** stands the **Chief's House** (off Route 70, 405–873–2492), built about 1832 and said to be Oklahoma's oldest residence. The two-story log structure was occupied by Choctaw district chief Thomas LeFlore, who operated a 1,000-acre farm here. The rooms contain period furnishings.

Fort Towson (off Route 70, 405–873–2634) was established in 1824 to pacify the frontier. In contrast to other military posts, it was a model of proper behavior, with an active temperance society and numerous religious services. The fort was abandoned and reactivated several times; it served as a Confederate post during the Civil

War. Stand Watie, a Cherokee brigadier general, surrendered the Cherokee, Creek, Seminole, and Osage Battalion near Fort Towson on June 23, 1865, to Lieutenant Colonel Asa Mathews. This was the last formal surrender of any significant body of Confederate troops. Only the foundations of the fort remain. A replica of the sutler's store is outfitted as it was in 1832. Glassware, flint, and parts of guns are among relics displayed in a museum.

Established by future president Zachary Taylor, **Fort Washita** (off Route 199, sixteen miles northwest of Durant, 405–924–6502) was built on the nation's southwestern frontier in 1842 to protect the relocated Chickasaw and Choctaw from raids by Plains Indians. Fort Washita served as the Chickasaw Agency and offered a good market for the tribe's farmers, who sold their meat, eggs, and vegetables, including 7,000 bushels of corn every year, to the garrison. During the California gold rush, emigrants gathered into groups at Durant to make a safer crossing of hostile territory. Union soldiers abandoned the fort in 1861, and Confederate troops moved in. The fort was burned in 1865. The U.S. government returned the site to the Chickasaw in 1870. Today the south barracks and the original cabin of Confederate general Douglas Cooper have been reconstructed.

TISHOMINGO

A treaty in 1855 allowed the Chickasaw to purchase a portion of the Choctaw domain for $150,000. The Chickasaw wrote a constitution and established their national capital at Tishomingo the following year. The **First Chickasaw Capitol** (1856) was a log building that is now enclosed within the **Chickasaw Council House Museum** (Court House Square, 405–371–3351); the museum displays demonstrate the advanced culture and education of the tribe. A second capitol burned, but a **Third Chickasaw Capitol** (Court House Square) was built of granite blocks in 1898; from 1907 to 1988 it served as the county courthouse. The Chickasaw nation has recently repurchased this land. The **Bank of the Chickasaw Nation Museum** (West Main Street, 405–371–2175) occupies the Richardsonian Romanesque building, erected of rock-faced granite in 1901, that served as the official Chickasaw bank depository from 1901 to 1907. The ground-floor offices were used as the city hall between 1916 and 1976, and one of Oklahoma's oldest Masonic lodges occupied space on the second floor from 1915 to 1985.

WESTERN OKLAHOMA

OPPOSITE: *Elaborately carved and overscaled corbels brace an exterior staircase at the Marland Mansion in Ponca City.*

It was called "the world's greatest horse race." On the morning of April 22, 1889, about 50,000 landless and hopeful people jammed the four borders of the unassigned lands, a swath of 2 million acres in central Oklahoma. To the swift would go the 160-acre homesteads and town lots that had been surveyed on the empty, wildflower-strewn prairies. At high noon the starting guns boomed, and seekers sprang into the promised land on horseback, in buggies, trains, ox carts, and even on high-wheeled bicycles. By sundown the luckier families were cooking dinner under the stars and bedding down their children on their own parcels of land. Entire cities—Guthrie and Oklahoma City among them—popped into existence. As an eyewitness reporter for *Cosmopolitan* wrote: "Ten thousand people had 'squatted' upon a square mile of virgin prairie that first afternoon, and as the myriad of white tents suddenly appeared upon the face of the country, it was as though a flock of white-winged birds had just settled down upon the hillsides and in the valley."

Oklahoma's first land run completed a long process; the barriers protecting the Indian lands of Oklahoma had begun to crumble years earlier. In 1866 the Five Civilized Tribes—the Cherokee, Choctaw, Chickasaw, Creek, and Seminole—signed treaties ceding to the federal government the western portion of their Oklahoma holdings, and the government of the United States started relocating tribes there from the East. Agricultural bands such as the Delaware, Potawatomi, Shawnee, Sac and Fox, Kaw, and Kickapoo began to till farms and tend livestock on a checkerboard of reservations. But the 1867 Medicine Lodge Council, held just north of Indian Territory, revealed different dynamics when a U.S. delegation met with the chiefs and 7,000 members of the Plains tribes. Tepees of buffalo hide spread along the riverbanks for miles, and the event was covered by newspaper reporters, including Henry M. Stanley (later of "Dr. Livingstone" fame in Africa). At the council, Indians who had lived for centuries as roving hunters—Comanche and Kiowa, Cheyenne and Arapaho—were urged to become sedentary dwellers on reservations. They loathed the idea. Among the great Indian orators present, Comanche chief Ten Bears said: "I was born upon the prairies, where the wind blew free, and there was nothing to break the light of the sun. I was born where there were no enclosures, and where everything drew a free breath. I want to die there, and not within walls." And Kiowa chief Satanta said of his people: "When we settle down, we grow pale and die."

On September 16, 1893, more than 100,000 settlers poured into a section of north-western Oklahoma known as the Cherokee Outlet during the largest land rush in the state's history. A photographer, who knew what to expect from accounts of earlier rushes, constructed a special platform from which to record the sight.

Not surprisingly, the federal commissioners had their way; treaties assigned the Plains Indians to reservations. But when the government's promised gifts and rations failed to arrive, the four tribes promptly rode on the warpath against settlements in neighboring states. To suppress the fierce Plains raiders, the army built military posts. Fort Supply in the Cherokee Outlet (a strip of land just south of the Kansas border) became the western vanguard in 1868. The escort for the fort's supply train of 450 wagonloads of equipment, weapons, and building materials was General George Armstrong Custer and the Seventh Cavalry. Custer struck south in heavy snow and attacked the camp of Cheyenne chief Black Kettle in the Battle of the Washita, which has been called "the classic example of . . . Custer's stupidity, sadism, and greed." Taking the Indians by surprise, the troops killed warriors, women, and children, torched the lodges, and shot a herd of 875 ponies—while the regimental band played. In 1869 General Philip H. Sheridan established Fort Sill on the rim of the Wichita Mountains; Fort Reno followed in 1874. That year General Nelson Miles made a sweep for "hostiles"

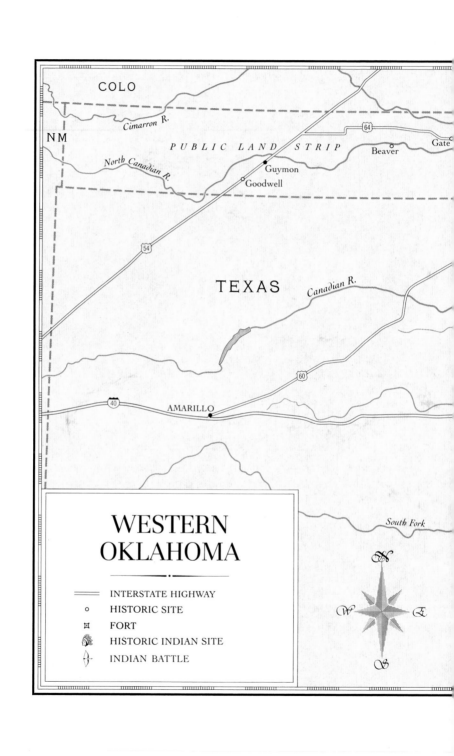

COLO

Cimarron R.

NM

PUBLIC LAND STRIP

North Canadian R.

64

Beaver

Gate

● Guymon

○ Goodwell

54

TEXAS

Canadian R.

60

40

AMARILLO ●

South Fork

WESTERN OKLAHOMA

════════ INTERSTATE HIGHWAY

○ HISTORIC SITE

⌑ FORT

HISTORIC INDIAN SITE

INDIAN BATTLE

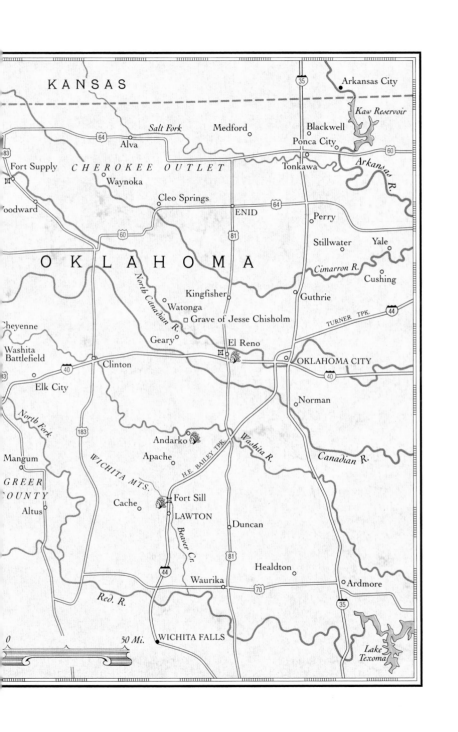

KANSAS

Arkansas City

Kaw Reservoir

Salt Fork   Medford   Blackwell
64   Alva   Ponca City   60

Fort Supply   CHEROKEE OUTLET   Tonkawa   Arkansas R.
83
Woodward   Waynoka

Cleo Springs   ENID   64

60   Perry

OKLAHOMA   Stillwater   Yale

81   Cimarron R.   Cushing

North Canadian R.   Kingfisher
Watonga   □ Grave of Jesse Chisholm   Guthrie

Cheyenne   Geary   El Reno   TURNER TPK.   44

Washita
Battlefield   40   Clinton   OKLAHOMA CITY

83   Elk City   40

North Fork   Norman

183   Andarko   Washita R.

Mangum   Apache   H.E. BAILEY TPK.   Canadian R.

GREER
COUNTY   WICHITA MTS.   Cache   Fort Sill
Altus   LAWTON

Beaver Cr.   Duncan

81   Healdton

44   Waurika   70   Ardmore

Red R.   35

0   50 Mi.   WICHITA FALLS   Lake
Texoma

THE SIGNAL

People having Certificates to enter the Strip will please line up by 11 o'clock tomorrow morning, Saturday, September 16th., 1893, in a space Two Miles East of the City Limits, and One Mile West of same. The Signal to enter Strip will be Fired Precisely at 12 M., tomorrow ☞Santa Fe Time, by Capt. Hardie 3rd Cavalry, from a point opposite the Registration Booths. This Signal will be repeated along the line by soldiers. Those desiring to go by the Railroad will please have their Certificates in their hands.

F. H. HARDIE,
Captain 3d Cavalry Commanding

JOURNAL PRINT.

A broadside announcing the start of the 1893 Cherokee Strip land run gives explicit instructions to the hopeful settlers.

and forced many bands to lay down arms at Fort Sill. The last to surrender were Comanche under Quanah Parker in 1875. The Indian era in Oklahoma was drawing to a close.

On the plains the buffalo, upon which hunting tribes depended, were being killed off by commercial hide hunters, including Wild Bill Hickok, Pat Garrett, and Buffalo Bill Cody. The slaughter left Indians hungry and angry, and the grasslands open for a new venture—range cattle. By the late 1860s, Texas cattle ranchers were driving their herds north to railheads in Kansas cow towns. Four main trails crossed Indian Territory. In western Oklahoma, cattle caravans plied the Great Western and the Chisholm trails, the latter being the most famous cow highway on the entire frontier. Ranchers also eyed the vast grasslands in sections of Indian Territory not being farmed by Indians, such as 6 million acres in the Cherokee Outlet. Ranchers developed huge herds there, sometimes paying grazing fees to the tribe, sometimes not. Eventually the more permanent ranchers formed the Cherokee Strip Livestock Association and established exclusive grazing rights to the entire area for an annual lease of $100,000. Farmers, meanwhile, had noticed ranchers were making handsome profits in Indian Territory, where they were shut out: Naturally, they wanted in. Railroads also began pressuring the government to admit settlers to Indian Territory, where they would stimulate the growth of towns, farms, and industries and thereby generate higher revenues for the railroads. Merchants in Kansas border towns took up the cry because nearby settlers would boost retail sales.

About 1879 there arose a group of professional promoters known as Boomers. Among them was a railroad attorney, Elias C. Boudinot, who trumpeted a claim that 14 million acres of Indian Territory were actually in the public domain and therefore legitimately open to homesteaders. (Remarkably, Boudinot himself was part Cherokee.) Boomers made speeches, published pamphlets,

Oklahoma Boomers await the signal that marked the start of the Cherokee Outlet land run of 1889.

called public meetings, all presenting Oklahoma as a promised land of golden opportunity. During the early 1880s, pioneer families inspired by Boomer propaganda came streaming into the towns of southern Kansas, where with religious fervor David L. Payne organized them into camps. Payne's favorite quotation was: "And the Lord commanded unto Moses, 'Go forth and possess the Promised Land.'" In violation of U.S. law, Payne's hopeful colonists repeatedly followed him into Oklahoma, and although they were turned back by the cavalry, the publicity began to sway public sympathy and prevent punishment. (The savvy Payne always invited newspaper reporters and photographers to come along and document his Boomer "raids.") After Payne's death in 1884, his lieutenants took over the campaign, which was developing into a cause for the poor and landless—as long as they were not Indians.

Finally Congress bought unused tracts of land from various Oklahoma tribes. In 1889 President Benjamin Harrison announced that the unassigned lands, located in west-central Indian Territory, would be opened to white settlers. Foreseeing that more than 50,000 home seekers would be vying for the 12,000 available claims, planners set up a land run to ensure everyone an equal chance.

Many of the hopeful settlers massed along the Kansas border, especially in Arkansas City and Caldwell. A corps of pickpockets worked the crowds in the Kansas railroad stations, while con men sold newcomers "prime lots" in nonexistent towns. Land seekers in covered wagons formed enormous camps on the Kansas line, while others grouped on the eastern and western edges of the unassigned lands or on the south side where they could board Santa Fe trains heading through the center of the tract. To be fair, on the day of the race these trains moved at walking speed; homesteaders simply jumped off when they saw land they liked. The race went not only to the swift, however, but to the sneaky. Sooners—men who crept into the territory "sooner" than everyone else and hid there in ravines and brush—managed to stake claims to homesteads and town lots minutes after trumpets and pistol shots started the legitimate home-seekers racing from the borders. Among the Sooners were corrupt deputy marshals and government and railroad officials. To make it appear that they had been among the high-noon throng, Sooners used to lather their horses with soap to make them look hard-ridden. Many among this group—nicknamed the "8 o'clock crowd"—were evicted later or had their claims invalidated in court.

Many rushees put down roots on quarter sections (160 acres) of farm land, but most settled in new towns such as Norman, Guthrie, and Oklahoma City, along the Santa Fe tracks. The settling was finished by sundown. "Creation! Hell! That took six days," declared a character in Edna Ferber's *Cimarron*. "This was done in one." Next came the necessity of building communities and establishing a government. In 1890 Congress created the Oklahoma Territory and provided a capital at Guthrie, a governor, a legislature, and courts. The territory officially annexed "No Man's Land," the Oklahoma Panhandle, which had been separated from Texas by the Compromise of 1850 and remained unattached to any territory or state. This strip was also called Robber's Roost, because of the jailbirds who flocked there. It was a retreat for outlaw bands, such as the Doolin and Dalton gangs, who roamed the frontier robbing banks, trains, and stagecoaches. The act also provided that any additional land openings would become part of Oklahoma Territory. "Indian Territory" now referred only to the eastern section of the old domain. To accommodate the increasing demand for homesteads, the government appointed the Jerome Commission to negotiate agreements with most of the tribes on western reservations. Communal titles to their lands were eliminated, and in exchange each Indian man, woman, and child was given a 160-acre allotment. The U.S. government bought the "extra" tribal land—millions of acres—for homesteaders. In 1891 Oklahoma's second land run threw open the Sac and Fox, Iowa, and Shawnee-Potawatomi reservations; then, in 1892, the Cheyenne and Arapaho territory. In the land run of 1893, 100,000 people exploded into the Cherokee Outlet. "One pioneer woman was so eager for a claim," reports the official state biography, "that she wrapped herself in a feather mattress so her son could push her out of the wagon without having to stop and jeopardize his own chances for a good claim. The plan worked, but the son was never seen again." Homesteaders were so frantic to claim good farmland after the recent drought years on the prairies that violence marred the opening. "It is an astonishing thing," the *New York Herald* observed, "that men will fight harder for $500 worth of land than they will for $10,000 in money."

Settlers homesteaded Greer County, a section along the Red River claimed by Texas but declared part of the Oklahoma Territory by the Supreme Court in 1896. During the run into the Kickapoo reservation in 1895, about half the claims had been grabbed by

Sooners; so to open the domain of the Kiowa, Comanche, Apache, Caddo, and Wichita tribes in 1901 the government decided to hold a lottery instead of a run. Tales of gold and silver in the Wichita Mountains lured about 165,000 persons to take part in a drawing for just 15,000 parcels. During the next few years, surplus land on various small reservations was sold to settlers, and in 1906 the Osage domain, the last reservation west of the Five Civilized Tribes, was divided among tribe members with no surplus and became part of Oklahoma Territory.

Life was not easy for the new settlers on the western plains. They often lived in sod houses or dugouts that leaked rain and harbored vermin. Women cooked over fires of buffalo chips, suffered loneliness, and lost their children to disease. The land also suffered; poor farming methods caused such serious soil erosion that homesteads sometimes had to be abandoned.

After Indian Territory was allotted to individual members of the Five Civilized Tribes and their governments were "abolished," it was possible to contemplate statehood for the unified Indian and Oklahoma territories. A state constitution was written at a convention in Guthrie, and in 1907 President Theodore Roosevelt accepted Oklahoma into the Union. With prices for farm products rising, railroads laying tracks, towns bustling with new industries, and a building boom in progress, Oklahoma's future looked bright. Political life, however, had its ups and downs. After a storm of debate, voters moved the capital to Oklahoma City in 1910. During the volatile 1920s, two governors were thrown out of office for maladroit administration and abuse of power. After trying to start a utopian agricultural colony in Bolivia, "Alfalfa Bill" Murray was elected governor of Oklahoma in 1931. During his four-year term, Murray, an underdog with a reputation for fighting wealth and smugness, used state troopers to enforce his orders, and he declared martial law thirty-four times. He used to discourage visitors from approaching him too closely by chaining their chairs to the wall of his office. Alfalfa Bill kept the nation amused, as did a spate of Oklahoma elections during the 1930s in which candidates with the same names as famous people ran for office: Daniel Boone, Oliver Cromwell, and Patrick Henry. An Oklahoma City switchboard operator named Mae West received 65,000 votes, while public school teacher Will Rogers won a seat in Congress. The state needed such diversions during the Great

Depression, when drought parched the farmlands and ferocious windstorms eroded the soil and darkened the sky with dust. Images of Oklahoma's abandoned, rutted farms and its bony, underfed families fleeing the Dust Bowl in jalopies were immortalized in John Steinbeck's *The Grapes of Wrath*.

This chapter begins in Oklahoma City and loops westward to El Reno and Cheyenne; returning eastward through Mangum, Fort Sill, Lawton, Ardmore, Anadarko, and Norman. Next it proceeds northward to Guthrie, Stillwater, Yale, Perry, and Ponca City; and loops westward through Enid, Kingfisher, Fort Supply, and Beaver.

A mesa in the Glass Mountains, part of the Blaine Escarpment—a large formation of gypsum—that extends across western Oklahoma. OVERLEAF: *Cowboys at a water hole in the Oklahoma Panhandle, recorded by an itinerant photographer.*

OKLAHOMA CITY

The unassigned lands, where Oklahoma City lies, had been reserved
for the Creek and Seminole but never occupied. When the area was
thrown open for Oklahoma's first land run on April 22, 1889, the
"city" consisted of only a Santa Fe depot, a stagecoach yard, a "shack
to serve as a post office," and a few other frame buildings. At high
noon settlers stampeded in from the borders by horse, buggy, and
train. By that afternoon a man on the train observed: "All I could
see was a lot of tents arranged in a haphazard way, much like someone had thrown a handful of white dice out on the open prairie." To
heighten the confusion, promoters sold lots they did not own to the
desperate and gullible. Two separate land companies surveyed and
developed the infant city. The Seminole Land and Improvement
Company worked north of Grand (today's Sheridan) Avenue, and

*The Vermont marble staircase in the State Capitol in Oklahoma City, above which
are murals memorializing the citizens of the state who lost their lives in World War I.
Painted in the late 1920s, the murals were commissioned by Frank Phillips.*

the Oklahoma Colony Company worked south. Their respective streets did not align where they met the avenue. In addition, "the government had not made any provisions for city lots," according to historian Pendleton Woods. "This resulted in a great amount of turbulence with fights, lot jumping, illegal sales, and hasty confusion."

Despite the turmoil a community of perhaps 10,000 people had come into existence before sunset: Oklahoma City residents say their town was "born grown." A public assembly chose a temporary municipal committee solely on the basis of looks—each nominee was paraded across the platform to garner cheers or jeers—a reasonable method in a community where few people knew anyone. Later the settlers elected a council and a "Boomer," William Couch, as provisional mayor. A little over a month later, the new town had no paved streets or sidewalks, but boasted numerous shops, restaurants, hotels, and banks.

Settlement, one of four historical murals in the capitol painted by Charles Banks Wilson, includes a banner proclaiming "Go Forth to Possess the Promised Land," the Biblical exhortation to Moses that was the motto of David L. Payne's "Boomers."

In 1900 Theodore Roosevelt was the guest of honor at the Roughriders' Ball, which, because of the heat, was held in a partially built furniture store whose open sides offered natural air conditioning. By 1910 six railroad lines crossed the settlement and assured its position as a supply center. That year Governor Charles Haskell, a Democrat, arranged a referendum to try to wrestle the capital away from Guthrie, a Republican stronghold. When voters chose Oklahoma City, Haskell immediately nabbed the state seal and set up a new capitol in the Lee-Huckins Hotel. The move brought an influx of government workers to Oklahoma City and stimulated a building boom, which included the city's first skyscraper, the twelve-story Colcord Building. Textile mills and meat-packing plants were erected, and around the time of World War I the city became a major distribution center for Oklahoma cotton. Then, in 1928, oil was discovered in the city. The first well, drilled near today's Southeast 59th Street and Bryant Avenue, transformed Oklahoma City into a boom town, dizzy with wildcatters, hustlers, and lease promoters. In 1936 derricks were even planted on the statehouse lawn, making it the world's only capitol whose grounds include operating oil wells. Among other firsts associated with Oklahoma City were the invention of the parking meter in the mid-1930s and the shopping cart in 1937.

The **Oklahoma State Capitol** (Northeast 23d Street and Lincoln Boulevard, 405–521–3356) is one of the nation's few capitols without a dome. That traditional feature was eliminated because of a lack of funds and a wartime steel shortage when the building was erected between 1914 and 1917. Built of granite and limestone, the capitol's architecture includes Greek and Roman elements. Portraits of illustrious Oklahomans such as Jim Thorpe and Will Rogers hang in the rotunda; historical murals decorate the ceiling. For years oil was pumped from beneath the building.

Two blocks east is the **Governor's Mansion** (820 Northeast 23d Street, 405–521–2491), a Dutch Colonial residence completed in 1928 and faced with limestone to match the capitol. Furnishings include the original dining-room suite. The grounds feature an Oklahoma-shaped swimming pool.

State Museum of History

As a repository of the Oklahoma Historical Society, this museum traces the state's past, beginning with the Spiro Mound culture of

A.D. 900. The extensive Indian collection includes artifacts from the Five Civilized Tribes and other groups relocated to Indian Territory during the nineteenth century, such as a bison-hide tepee from the 1860s and fans used in peyote ceremonies. Among the pioneer relics is a wagon used in two Oklahoma land runs and the eagle-quill pen used by President Theodore Roosevelt to sign the statehood bill. Other items range from Civil War battle flags to a Skylab spacesuit worn by Oklahoma astronaut Owen Garriott.

LOCATION: 2100 North Lincoln Boulevard. HOURS: 8–5 Monday–Saturday. FEE: None. TELEPHONE: 405–521–2491, ext. 64.

The **Capitol-Lincoln Terrace Historic District** (roughly between 13th Street, 23d Street, Lincoln Boulevard, and Kelley Avenue) includes more than 150 residences from the 1920s. During the oil boom, this enclave of the wealthy was popular as it was close to both downtown and the offices of state government. However, "whipstock" drills, angled right under some of the houses to drill oil, led to a number of lawsuits.

The **Oklahoma Heritage Center** (201 Northwest 14th Street, 405–235–4458) fills a 1917 brick Greco-Georgian mansion with collections of American and European paintings and furniture, Meissen china, and unusual antique canes. Many furnishings belonged to the family of one-time owner Robert Hefner, a judge, oil man, and Oklahoma City mayor. The third-floor ballroom displays sculptures and portraits of inductees into the Oklahoma Hall of Fame. The **Overholser Mansion** (405 Northwest 15th Street, 405–528–8485) was erected by Henry Overholser, the "Father of Oklahoma City," in 1903. He was an entrepreneur whose vision helped develop the pioneer community. Even before the land run, he shipped eight prefabricated two-story buildings to the site; later he erected an opera house that had leather seats, held an audience of 2,500, and contained the largest stage in the West. Overholser also helped bring railroads and waterworks to Oklahoma City. His chateauesque-style brick mansion contains the original furnishings, including furniture in French and Oriental motifs; period costumes are exhibited in the third-floor ballroom.

Downtown is the twelve-story **Colcord Building** (Robinson and Sheridan avenues), Oklahoma's first reinforced-concrete skyscraper. It was erected in 1910 and is referred to as a "significant example of

At Oklahoma City's Harn Homestead, a recently constructed exhibit barn includes an indoor windmill like one used by Harn.

a Sullivanesque skyscraper outside of Chicago" by the National Register of Historic Places. Faced with terra-cotta and detailed in copper and marble, the building contains the city's first high-speed elevators. The stone **Federal Building** (Robinson Avenue and 3rd Street) was built in the Second Renaissance Revival style in 1912; an Art Deco tower was added in 1937. **Central High School** (700 block of Robinson Avenue) blends Gothic Revival style with Jacobethan Revival; the stone building of 1910 has an arched Tudor entry and a crenelated tower. The **Museum of the Unassigned Lands** (4300 North Sewall, 405–521–1889), in the northeast section of the city, displays artifacts from the state's first land run. The exhibit includes land-office items, a territorial parlor and kitchen, a model of Oklahoma City in early 1889, and a display of brick making.

The **Harn Homestead and 1889er Museum** (312 Northeast 18th Street, 405–235–4058) occupies ten acres homesteaded during the land run of 1889. On the site is the two-story frame house erected in

The Harn Homestead parlor is furnished with pieces from the 1889er Society, descendants of participants in the land rush.

1904 by William Harn, who prosecuted Sooners that committed perjury to protect their illegal claims. A civic leader, Harn donated forty acres for the capitol and other state buildings. A stone-and-cedar barn contains farm equipment and a working windmill; on the grounds are a restored one-room schoolhouse of 1897 and a four-acre working farm that uses the kind of seeds planted at the turn of the century. The **Forty-fifth Infantry Division Museum** (2145 Northeast 36th Street, 405–424–5313) traces Oklahoma's military heritage from the Coronado expedition of 1541 to the present. Memorabilia include items the division seized in Hitler's apartment: a black cape, monogrammed silver picture frames, and copies of *Mein Kampf*. Also on exhibit are World War II cartoons by Bill Mauldin; an outdoor display of military aircraft, artillery, and vehicles; and a military firearms collection from the Revolutionary War to the present, which includes one of three surviving Confederate sniper rifles made by Whitworth.

The collections of the **Oklahoma Firefighters Museum** (2716 Northeast 50th Street, 405–424–3440) include the state's first fire station (1869), hand- and horse-pulled equipment dating back as far as 1736, fire engines, and an array of shoulder patches. Also, a fifty-eight-foot-long mural of firefighting equipment, *The Last Alarm*, by Lynn Campbell, is painted on the museum's south wall.

Kirkpatrick Center

The center features a planetarium with a forty-foot dome; a tropical conservatory and a Japanese garden; and the Omniplex Science Museum, with 250 hands-on science exhibits such as a walk-in set of teeth. The International Photography Hall of Fame and Museum features works by Mathew Brady, Edward Steichen, and others. In addition, seventeen galleries display Native American, African, and Oriental art. The center's museum of air and space has exhibits on the history of flight and replicas of the Wright Brothers' plane and a lunar lander. Antique clocks, Boehm porcelain birds, and a railroad parlor car of 1929 are also on display.

> LOCATION: 2100 Northeast 52d Street. HOURS: June through August: 9–6 Monday–Saturday, 12–6 Sunday; September through May: 9:30–5 Monday–Friday, 9–6 Saturday, 12–6 Sunday. FEE: Yes. TELE-PHONE: 405–427–5461.

The **National Cowboy Hall of Fame and Western Heritage Center** (1700 Northeast 63d Street, 405–478–2250) honors America's western legacy and the frontier spirit through three halls of fame—great westerners, rodeo, and great western performers—as well as an extensive collection of western art from such artists as Russell, Remington, and Schreyvogel. A "west of yesterday" street includes a sod house, gold mine, jail, Overland stage depot, and saloon, furnished with authentic artifacts.

The **Fairchild Winery** (1600 Northeast 81st Street, private), built of sandstone in 1893, was Oklahoma's first winery and may be the oldest structure within the city limits.

EL RENO

A few months after the land run of April 1889, the town of El Reno took shape where two Rock Island Railroad routes crossed. The town developed into a transport hub and distribution center, serving the region and nearby Indian lands. When the Cheyenne-Arapaho reservation was opened to whites in 1892, El Reno was a staging area for the settlers preparing to sweep in. In 1901 the town's population briefly ballooned to nearly 150,000 during the lottery to distribute homesteads on the Kiowa-Comanche reservation. The 1906 Rock Island depot now contains the **Canadian County Historical Museum** (300 South Grand Street, 405–262–5121); a caboose, Indian artifacts, pioneer furniture, and photographs from Fort Reno are on exhibit. Also on the site are the wooden El Reno Hotel of 1892; a barn containing farm machinery and a fire truck; and a 1918 Red Cross canteen built of telegraph pole "logs," which served traveling soldiers during World War I.

Fort Reno (three miles west of El Reno and two miles north, off Route 66, 405–262–5291) was established in 1874 to control the marauding Kiowa, Comanche, Cheyenne, and Arapaho. The pres-

Students and teachers at the Indian school at the Darlington Agency, photographed around 1890.

ence of cavalrymen helped pacify the area for white settlers, although the soldiers were later called upon to eject the would-be settlers called Boomers and, just before the land rush of 1889, to secure the borders of the unassigned lands against Sooners rushing in early. By 1890 the Rock Island line arrived. (Western Oklahoma's first telegraph line was strung from the post to Wichita, Kansas, in 1876, and eight years later the state's first working telephone lines linked the nearby Darlington Agency with the fort.) After 1908 Fort Reno operated as a remount station, breaking and training horses for other army posts. During World War II the facility served briefly as a POW camp for captive German and Italian soldiers, and in 1949 it became an agricultural research facility. Grouped around the former parade ground are a number of old brick buildings including a barracks, a chapel, and a guardhouse. The grave of Ben Clark, Custer's head scout, lies in the rock-walled cemetery.

The **Darlington Agency** (six miles northwest of El Reno, off Route 81) was founded in 1870 for the Cheyenne and Arapaho by an Indian agent, Brinton Darlington, one of the Quakers sent by President Ulysses S. Grant in an effort to employ honest Indian agents. The agency became a stop on the Chisholm Trail, on which western artist Frederic Remington journeyed in 1882, when he painted a number of works here and at Fort Reno. In 1909 Indian administration was moved to nearby Concho, and nothing survives of the original agency but two homes of the 1870s.

Indian scout Ed Guerrier would not recognize the spelling of **Geary,** a town established in 1898 and named for him—the West has its own way with the French language. Eight miles northeast of town at Left Hand Spring is the **grave of Jesse Chisholm.** Son of a Scottish father and Cherokee mother, Jesse Chisholm (1805-1868) was an Indian trader who knew the tribes well and supposedly spoke fourteen Indian dialects. This skill aided the government when he served as an Indian-country guide and acted as an interpreter negotiating the release of white captives. From one of his trading posts, near Wichita, Kansas, he blazed a wagon trail south to the Red River. This route became famous as the Chisholm Trail, one of the great western cattle highways—although Jesse Chisholm apparently never owned a cow. He was liked and trusted, and his simple stone grave marker reads: "No one ever left his home cold or hungry." Chisholm died here on the land of his friend Left Hand, a chief of the southern Arapaho.

Elk City, a trading and farming hub, is the home of the **Old Town Museum** (Route 66 and Pioneer Road, 405–225–2207), a gingerbread-bedecked house displaying late-Victorian furnishings and rodeo artifacts from the nearby Beutler Brothers ranch. Across the street the **Whited Grist Mill,** a frame building of vernacular construction, was the town's first mill. It served Elk City from 1904 to 1944.

The town of **Cheyenne** began with the Cheyenne Indian Agency in 1891 and became the county seat after the 3 million acres of the Cheyenne-Arapaho reservation were opened to settlers the next year. The **Black Kettle Museum** (Routes 283 and 47, 405–497–3929) contains Indian, pioneer, and cavalry artifacts, and a diorama of the Battle of the Washita. The **Washita Battleground** (two miles northwest of Cheyenne on Route 47A) was the site of General George A. Custer's attack on the village of Chief Black Kettle's sleeping Cheyenne in November 1868. After a forced march with the Seventh Cavalry through a blizzard, Custer had the regimental band play during the charge. Although his troops were victorious—killing 150 men, women, and children, destroying the village, slaughtering the Indians' pony herd, and collecting hundreds of saddles and buffalo robes as booty—the battle has nonetheless been called Custer's "dress rehearsal for disaster." As in the Battle of Little Bighorn eight years later, he disregarded the warnings of his scouts and risked attacking superior forces. Monuments and a map document the battle's progress.

MANGUM

Greer County was originally claimed by Texas, which had granted land here to veterans of the Civil War. Texas cattle ranchers also had entered the area. But in 1884 the federal government ordered the ranchers and settlers to stay out, pending the resolution of a surveying error which indicated that the county should actually be part of Oklahoma. The proper borderline, said the government, was the Red River, not the north fork of the Red River. Texans ignored the decree until 1896, when the U.S. Supreme Court decided in favor of Oklahoma. Congress did allow prior settlers to file claims on their land, and the town of Mangum was a center of die-hard Texans. The **Old Greer County Museum and Hall of Fame** (222 West Jefferson Street, 405–782–2851) traces the history of the county through Indian artifacts, cowboy gear, home furnishings, horse-drawn farming equipment, and a replica of an early dugout home. More than a hundred granite monuments etched with the portraits and biographies of area pioneers stand on the museum's eastern grounds.

After a flood on Bitter Creek drove settlers from low-lying land nearby, **Altus** ("higher ground") took shape in 1891. It became a hub for the area's cotton, wheat, and alfalfa farms. The **Museum of the Western Prairie** (1100 North Hightower, 405–482–1044) depicts life on the plains, with exhibits of fossils, Indian relics, and pioneer artifacts, including a reassembled half-dugout house. The Great Western cattle trail, which ran nearby, is evoked by a drover's journal of 1876.

CACHE

Located in the foothills of the Wichita Mountains, Cache derives its name from tales of Spanish gold supposedly lost among the peaks; but no one has found a glimmer. Ten miles west of Lawton in **Eagle Park** (Route 115, off Route 62, 405–429–3238) are several relocated buildings: the 1865 "picket house," built with vertical logs, that served as officers' quarters at Fort Sill; the 1896 Saddle Mountain Indian Mission; the 1902 Cache railroad depot; and the house of outlaw Frank James. The **Quanah Parker Star House** (1890), residence of the great Comanche chief (ca. 1845-1911), is also in the park. Parker's father was Chief Peta Nocone, and his mother, Cynthia Ann Parker, was a white Texan taken captive as a child and raised by the tribe. (She died in 1864, shortly after Texas Rangers forced her to return to white civilization.) At first Parker fiercely resisted the U.S. Army. But in 1875 he bowed to the inevitable and led his warriors into Fort Sill—they were western Oklahoma's last band to capitulate. Parker proceeded to help his people adapt to the "white man's road." On his allotted land, Parker erected a twelve-room house with a verandah around both stories. When a brigadier general visited one day, Parker noticed the stars on the leader's uniform and painted huge white stars on the red roof of his house to show that he was leader of the Indians. Over the years Parker served as an Indian policeman, judge, and envoy to Washington. A shrewd businessman, he negotiated grazing leases that brought great prosperity to the tribe. At one time Quanah

Parker had five wives; when Theodore Roosevelt advised him to give up all but one wife, the chief responded: "You tell them which one I keep!"

U.S. ARMY FIELD ARTILLERY AND FORT SILL MUSEUM

On his exploration in 1852 of the country north of the Red River, Captain R. B. Marcy camped on the future site of Fort Sill and recommended it as the site for an army post "to command the respect of the Indians." Camp Wichita was established by General Philip Sheridan in 1869 on the edge of the Wichita Mountains. Soon renamed Fort Sill, its job was to pacify the raiding tribes of the southern plains. One by one, the bands surrendered at the fort, and Fort Sill served as the Kiowa-Comanche Agency until 1878. During the Boomer era, its soldiers helped eject early-bird settlers from the Indian lands, and when the Kiowa-Comanche-Apache reservation was opened for white settlement in 1901, the government withheld the vast military facility. From 1894 to 1913 the Chiracahua Apache were lodged at the fort as prisoners of war; Geronimo was here until his death in 1909. Although the government considered abandoning the fort, new construction was undertaken in 1910 to accommodate the U.S. Army Field Artillery. In 1915 the army's First Aero Squadron was stationed here. The facility now sprawls over nearly 100,000 acres. The museum includes twenty-three buildings of the "Old Post," eight of which are open to visitors, including the guardhouse and the commissary storehouse. These are occupied by exhibits on Fort Sill and on field artillery since the American Revolution; flags, uniforms, weapons, and Indian artifacts. The 1870 stone corral, built to keep Indians from capturing the fort's livestock, now houses a carriage museum; the stone chapel is still in use. The porch of the commanding officer's quarters was the scene of an attack upon General William Tecumseh Sherman by the Kiowa leaders Satanta, Setank, and Big Tree during a council in 1871. The Comanche chief Quanah Parker and other Indian leaders are buried in the post cemetery, while Geronimo lies in the Apache prisoner of war cemetery. Buildings of the "New Post" include the 1911 general officers' quarters, made of stuccoed concrete with Spanish Colonial Revival elements. One outdoor exhibit is "Atomic Annie," a large cannon that

The Murray-Lindsay Mansion in Lindsay, built in 1879 by Frank Murray.

in 1954 became the first artillery piece to fire an atomic projectile. Also at Fort Sill are the **Medicine Bluffs,** a crescent of four porphyry and granite bluffs, rising 320 feet high, where Indian ceremonial and religious activities were held.

> LOCATION: 4 miles north of Lawton on Route I-44. HOURS: 9–4:30 Daily. FEE: None. TELEPHONE: 405–351–5123.

LAWTON

Lawton was Oklahoma's last town to rise from the prairie in a single day. On August 6, 1901, the lots were auctioned off, and by nightfall there was a tent city with 25,000 pioneers and 400 businesses. In what the *Saturday Evening Post* called the "Mecca of the land-hungry pilgrims," bidders had to pay cash in full within thirty minutes or else lose their $25 deposits. In the lottery for land alongside the town site, the first-place winner, Mr. Wood, chose an unusually shaped parcel a mile long and a quarter-mile wide, so as to gain as much valuable property as close to Lawton as possible. However, his strategy totally blocked the second-place winner, Miss Mattie Beal, from holding any town frontage. Citizens nicknamed him "Hog" Wood, while the publicity surrounding Miss Beal's drawing almost immediately brought her more than 500 marriage proposals.

The **Museum of the Great Plains** (601 Ferris Avenue, 405–353–5675) exhibits a railroad depot and engine, a replica of a trading post of the 1840s, a living prairie dog village, and the skull and tusks of a mammoth. Displays trace the human presence on the plains from prehistory to white settlement. At B Avenue and 5th Street stands the **Carnegie Library,** a 1922 brick building of modified Federal style. The **Mattie Beal House** (5th Street and Summit Avenue, private) was built in 1909 by the woman who drew the runner-up claim in the land lottery. Of eclectic style, the stuccoed house contains fourteen rooms on two stories. The **Fort Sill Indian School** (one mile north of Lawton on Route 277, private) was established for Comanche children in 1892; the earliest stone buildings of the boarding school date to 1894.

When the Rock Island Railroad announced plans to come through the area in 1889, the clever Chickasaw wife of William Duncan chose as her tribal allotment a 500-acre parcel that was in the direct path of the tracks. When she sold her lots, this became the town site of **Duncan.** By the 1920s agriculture and oil became the mainstays of the town. The **Stephens County Historical Museum** (Route 81 and Beech Street, 405–252–0717) has Indian arrowheads and other artifacts; pioneer items, such as carriages, dolls, and lacework; and a velocipede, the forerunner of the tricycle.

Laid out in 1902 as a Rock Island watering station, the town of **Waurika** lies near hills where nourishing buffalo grass provided good grazing for Texas herds on the Chisholm Trail to Kansas railheads. The **Chisholm Trail Historical Museum** (Routes 70 and 81, southeast of Waurika, 405–228–2166) recounts the story of this famous cow highway over which millions of beef were driven from 1867 to 1889. On display are exhibits on local pioneer times, including a wagon, brands, guns, saddles, and other cowboy gear.

A town that took thirty years to develop, **Healdton** finally boomed in 1913 when a nearby field began gushing oil. The story of the billion-dollar Healdton Field is told at the **Healdton Oil Museum** (East Main, on Route 76, 405–229–0317), which displays oil-field rigs and equipment.

ARDMORE

When the Santa Fe laid tracks across Chickasaw country in 1887, Ardmore became a shipping center for cotton and farm products. A settler recalled the public watering trough in the center of Main Street and "the cowboys standing at the well with their ten-gallon white hats, black-and-white checked shirts, and slant-heeled boots. The spot seemed to be attractive to the town's hogs, also, as they had made a wallowing ground." After a widespread fire in 1895, the town rebuilt more solidly in stone and brick. With the discovery of the Healdton Field in 1913, Ardmore became an oil town served by a pipeline and a refinery. Two years later the bonanza backfired when the explosion of a railroad tank car full of casing-head gas killed forty-three people, flattened Main Street, and—so they say—knocked horses to their knees eight miles away. The town rebuilt itself from the rubble.

The **Carter County Historic Museum and Genealogy Library** (35 Sunset Drive, 405–226–3857) houses a furnished 1800s log cabin, pioneer tools, an 1895 firehouse with a horse-drawn pumper truck, a cash register and typewriter collection, a courthouse of 1911, and a genealogy library.

ANADARKO

Although Anadarko was founded by white settlers in 1901 during the land run onto surrounding reservations, its character and attractions are Indian. It has been a center of Indian administration since 1878, when the Kiowa, Comanche, Apache, and Wichita agencies were combined here. The town's name is a mutation of Na-Da-Ka, the name of a Caddoan tribe. The **National Hall of Fame for Famous American Indians** (115 Route 62 East, 405–247–5555) is an outdoor exhibit of bronze busts of notable Native Americans, including Sacajawea, Quanah Parker, Pocahontas, Sequoyah, Chief Joseph, Geronimo, and Jim Thorpe. Just west on Route 62 is the **Southern Plains Indian Museum and Crafts Center** (405–247–6221), which displays the arts of tribal peoples of southwestern Oklahoma: beadwork; music and dance materials, such as a hoof rattle and wooden flutes; a Ghost Dance shirt; a peyote box and drums from a Native American church; and articles of warfare—tomahawks, eagle-

OPPOSITE: *A blockhouse at the reconstructed mid-nineteenth-century fur trading post at the Museum of the Great Plains in Lawton. Gun ports were placed so that men stationed inside could cover all approaches to the post.*

ABOVE *and* OPPOSITE: *A Wichita lodge at Indian City U.S.A., constructed of cedar poles thatched with swamp grass with a smoke hole at the top. It contains tools and foodstuffs used by this Caddoan tribe.*

feather bonnets, and buffalo-hide shields, which were hung outside to acquire some of the sun's power. Occupying the old Rock Island depot, the **Anadarko Philomathic Museum** (311 East Main Street, 405–247–3240) recaptures the pioneer days with railroad memorabilia, military uniforms and equipment, a doctor's office, country store, and Indian artifacts.

Indian City U.S.A. (two-and-a-half miles south of Anadarko on Route 8, 405–247–5661) offers visitors a sampling of Indian life with seven authentic Indian villages. On view are Navajo hogans, Apache brush wickiups, a forty-foot-high Wichita council house, a Kiowa winter tepee camp, Caddo wattle-and-daub houses, Pawnee earth lodges, and a Pueblo stone-and-adobe dwelling. Inside are cooking utensils, cradles, weapons, and musical instruments. Tours are conducted and dances performed by members of each tribe. The museum building exhibits costumes, beadwork, basketry, arrowheads, Hopi kachinas, silverwork, and other Indian arts.

The country store at the Anadarko Philomathic Museum contains farmyard and kitchen tools like those used in frontier Oklahoma

NORMAN

After being settled in the 1889 land run, Norman grew steadily with the University of Oklahoma, founded in 1890. "It is not claimed for this city that she will ever be a great metropolis," noted the *Norman Transcript* in 1893, "but it is a city of homes, and one of the most desirable places of residence of which the mind can conceive." The **Norman and Cleveland County Historical Museum** (508 North Peters Avenue, 405–321–0156) is located in a house built in 1899, with gables, stained-glass windows, and one turret, by William S. Moore, who gave his job description as "capitalist." Eight furnished period rooms illustrate the life of an upper-middle-class family in territorial Oklahoma. This is one of many vintage homes in the silk-stocking neighborhood. The partially restored 1929 **Center Theater** (101 East Main Street, 405–321–9600) was built in the Spanish Gothic style with brick and wood, stained-glass windows and chandeliers, heraldic crests, and a cantilevered balcony. The theater was one of the first in the United States to present "talkies."

There are about 5 million items in the collection of the **Oklahoma Museum of Natural History** (1335 Asp Avenue, 405–325–4711), including dinosaur bones and Spiro Mound artifacts. Greek and Roman relics, such as mosaics and coins, are on display, along with Plains Indians material, such as pottery, blankets, and costumes, and pioneer items. The **Boyd House** (407 West Boyd, 405–325–2151), which once housed University of Oklahoma presidents, was built in 1906 by the university's first president, David Ross Boyd. A frame clapboard residence with Georgian Revival elements, it now serves as the university visitor center.

GUTHRIE

On the morning of the land run in April 1889, Guthrie was an unprepossessing sight: a depot, two section houses, and a water tank. But to developers and hustlers it looked quite alluring, for Guthrie had one of the two land offices in the new territory and

Sign painters such as Walker & McCoy of Guthrie, photographed in 1889, did a brisk business in land-rush boom towns, providing signs for the various businesses essential to the burgeoning settlement.

The business office of the Guthrie State Capital, the frontier newspaper published by Frank Greer, was a mail-order bank teller's cage, ordered from a supplier in Quincy, Illinois, with custom-designed signs over the various windows.

was to be a rail hub. In the minds of settlers, Guthrie was the place to be. Sooners felt the same way, and even before the starting guns popped along the borders of the unassigned lands, unprincipled men had sneaked in and staked out the best lots. Legitimate settlers, who arrived soon after noon, had to claim land on the outskirts or buy lots from real estate agents. When the last of fifteen trains full of settlers pulled in near midnight, the new arrivals had to step gingerly over sleeping pioneers and roped-off claims. A prairie of grass and cottonwoods had been transformed into a tent city of perhaps 15,000 people. William Sydney Porter, the author who went by the name O. Henry, visited the nascent city and wrote about it in "Cupid á la Carte": "Guthrie was rising . . . like a lump of self-raising dough. It was a boom town of the regular kind—you stood in line to get a chance to wash your face; if you ate over ten minutes you had a lodging bill added on; if you slept on a plank at night they charged it to you as board the next morning."

Because more settlers had arrived than could be accommodated on the town's 320-acre plot, citizens held a meeting and created three more town sites: East Guthrie, West Guthrie, and Capitol Hill. According to historian Don Odom, town ordinances varied: "In West Guthrie a man could call his dog in a loud and profane manner, but if he did so in East Guthrie, he could be fined $20. The Capitol Hill City Council deemed it a misdemeanor for a woman to appear on the streets dressed in a man's clothing or other sensational attire." All the townships raised operating revenue by taxing anything that moved or sold something, from peddlers' wagons to lawyers and lumberyards. Even gamblers who set up games on the street became a revenue source via $5 fines for operating stud-poker or chuck-a-luck tables.

When Congress created the Oklahoma Territory in 1890, Guthrie was declared the capital. The four cities were consolidated

A row of Chandler & Price electric presses and composing tables holding forms, furniture, and type cases, used for job printing, in Guthrie's State Capital Publishing Museum.

as a single entity, thereby lessening confusion and stimulating an immediate expansion in the business district. A number of tuberculosis patients came to town around 1900, and bricks on city streets were incised with the admonition "Don't Spit on Sidewalk." Guthrie set up Oklahoma's first free school district, and by 1900 a number of civic amenities—from running water and electricity to streetcars—were available. Meanwhile, mills and shops hummed, and four newspapers churned out copy. By 1906 Guthrie was visited by forty-two passenger trains daily, operated by nine different railroads.

The national government had declared Guthrie the capital until 1913, but the state's first governor was a Democrat, Charles Haskell; he held a referendum in 1910 and had the capital moved from the "Republican nest" of Guthrie to Oklahoma City. Guthrie never quite recovered. It grew slowly, changed little. But few of its historic buildings fell to the wrecker's ball, and today the downtown area is a virtual museum of nineteenth-century buildings. The **Guthrie Historic District** (bounded by 14th Street, College Avenue, Pine Street, and University Avenue) encompasses thousands of commercial structures, public buildings, and houses dating from 1889 to 1907. A number of the eclectically styled commercial buildings were designed by the French architect Joseph Foucart.

The **State Capital Publishing Museum** (2d Street and West Harrison Avenue, 405–282–4123) is a stone-and-brick structure designed by Foucart and built in 1902; its four-story open tower is topped with a modified onion dome. It was built to house the plant of the *State Capital,* Oklahoma's first newspaper, whose first edition was out by 4 P.M. on the day of the land opening and "went like hotcakes," according to publisher Frank Greer. The issue was printed in Kansas and the copies brought in by wagon. Ironically, the venomous attacks on Governor Haskell in the *State Capital* helped provoke Haskell to move the capital to Oklahoma City in 1910. In a political vacuum, Greer's newspaper went bankrupt, and he moved away. The publishing museum displays cases of hand-set type, Mergenthaler Linotype machines, and Miehle cylinder presses. There is an exhibit of antique typewriters on the first floor, and a restored Victorian salesroom.

The **Victor Building** (1st Street and West Harrison Avenue) was designed by Joseph Foucart in 1893 and uses a medley of window styles. The building has housed a drugstore, territorial offices, a third-floor ballroom, and saloons. Tunnels once linked the basement to other downtown buildings. Across the street is the **Harrison House** (124 West Harrison Avenue, 405–282–1000), a bed-and-breakfast inn that encompasses a 1902 bank and three other buildings, including the **Pollard Theatre** (405–282–2800), whose auditorium has been restored to its appearance in 1929, with eight murals.

The **Guthrie Scottish Rite Masonic Temple** (Oklahoma Avenue and Capital Boulevard, 405–282–1281) claims to be the largest structure in the world reserved for Masonic activities. It cost $3 million to erect from 1920 to 1929 and has hundreds of stained-glass windows, gold doorknobs, carpets custom-woven to match the painted ceilings, an Egyptian auditorium, Victorian reading salons, a billiard room, a marble atrium, and a Classic Revival exterior.

The steps leading to the Guthrie Scottish Rite Temple, located on a piece of land originally reserved for the Oklahoma State Capitol, are organized in sets of three, five, seven, and nine, numbers with symbolic importance to the Masonic order.

Period furnishings and artifacts from ancient civilizations decorate the rooms. The brick Convention Hall, where the state legislature held two sessions prior to the relocation of the state capital to Oklahoma City in 1910, is part of the temple. The **Carnegie Library and Oklahoma Territorial Museum** (402 East Oklahoma Avenue, 405–282–1889) was the state's first library; the domed brick-and-stone library was built in 1902 with funds provided by Andrew Carnegie. Charles Haskell took the oath of office on the front steps. The connecting museum displays a hearse and a springboard wagon, a homestead house, toys, documents from the 1906 constitutional convention, and an exhibit on the movers and shakers of government in early Oklahoma.

STILLWATER

Five years before the land run of 1889, a caravan of 200 Boomers led by William Couch had illegally entered Indian Territory and built dugouts on Stillwater Creek. Despite the Boomers' assertion that the Indian Territory was legally available for homesteading, the cavalry escorted them back to Kansas. But during the land rush of April 22, 1889, Stillwater became a town at last. After convincing the territorial legislature to pick it as the site for the Agricultural and Mechanical College (today known as Oklahoma State University), the town was able to end its isolation when it lured the Santa Fe Railroad to build a spur in 1900. Stillwater quickly developed into a trade center. The **Sheerar Cultural and Heritage Center** (7th and Duncan streets, 405–377–0359) features antique American glass and china, 4,000 buttons, and early parking meters, an Oklahoma invention.

The **Old Central Museum of Higher Education,** at Oklahoma State University (University Avenue, 405–624–3220), was the only permanent college building constructed between 1894 and 1900. Its exhibits depict the history of higher education in Oklahoma. The **Oklahoma State University Museum of Natural and Cultural History** (103 USDA Building, 405–744–6531) houses photographic displays and collections of historic clothing, farm implements, pioneer furniture, African artifacts, and gems and minerals. The **Pfeiffer Farm Collection** (three miles east of Stillwater on Route 51, at Payne County Fairgrounds, 405–377–1275) has tractors and trucks dating from the 1920s to the 1950s, threshing machines, plows, a manure spreader, and other agricultural machinery. Farm tools such as hay hooks, potato diggers, and milk cans are also on display.

Cushing, an agricultural town founded on the Turkey Track Ranch in 1892, boomed after 1912, when the huge Cushing oil field came in. Within three years it was producing nearly 200,000 barrels of oil a day. Refineries and tank farms popped up, and a network of pipelines radiated from the town. At the **Cimarron Valley Railroad Museum** (Kings Highway, south of Route 33, 918–225–1657) the Santa Fe depot (1916) (relocated from the nearby town of Yale) bulges with uniforms, caps, badges, lanterns, dining-car china, and other train memorabilia. A Frisco wooden caboose and an oil-tank car of 1917 can be seen on tracks outside.

YALE

A small town based on farming and oil, Yale is the site of the **Jim Thorpe House** (706 East Boston, 918–387–2815), a five-room clapboard bungalow where the Olympic champion lived from 1917 to 1923. Thorpe was born in Indian Territory in 1887 and was five-eighths Indian, mostly Sac and Fox. In the 1912 Olympics in Stockholm, he won both the decathlon and the pentathlon—the first and only athlete to take gold medals in these two grueling events in the same Olympic year. Dubbed the "World's Greatest Athlete" by King Gustav of Sweden, Thorpe was stripped of his medals in 1913 because he had unknowingly broken the Olympic amateur rules by playing semiprofessional baseball two years before the 1912 games. Thorpe died in 1953; however, his medals were restored to his family and his feats to the record book in 1982. Today his house is decorated with family furnishings and awards from his days as an All-American halfback at the Carlisle Indian School.

PERRY

During the land run of 1893, about 100,000 eager home seekers stampeded into the Cherokee Outlet, a strip of land stretching for 200 miles along the Kansas border. A Santa Fe train full of settlers stopped about a mile from the town site of Perry, which was surveyed but empty; the passengers ran for it and staked their claims. The new city had so many saloons and gambling halls that three federal marshals were dispatched to keep order until a municipal government could be formed.

The collection of the **Cherokee Strip Museum** (West Fir Avenue, 405–336–2405) re-creates the old days with artifacts of the Otoe Indians, a small local tribe. The museum also houses pioneer and ranching antiques: tools, household belongings, brands, and saddles. Various structures on site include the remains of an outdoor jail, an 1895 frame schoolhouse with original furnishings, and a northern Cheyenne tepee. Unpublished manuscripts detailing homesteaders' memories of the land run are also on display.

TONKAWA

The Nez Percé Indians were driven from their homeland in Oregon and Idaho and forced onto a reservation in north-central Oklahoma in 1879; the city of Tonkawa is named for their successors. The Tonkawa were excellent scouts and were employed by

Three small boys pose for a camera recording the publicity for the Miller Brothers 101 Ranch Wild West Show in Ponca City.

frontier military units to search out the camps of hostile Indians. The Kiowa, Comanche, and Kickapoo retaliated by accusing the Tonkawa of cannibalism as an excuse to persecute them. The Tonkawa were nearly exterminated before they received their land allotments in 1885; the rest of the old Nez Percé reservation was opened to settlers in 1893. The next year Tonkawa town was laid out.

The **Tonkawa Tribal Museum** (at Fort Oakland, on the east edge of town, 405–628–2561) contains moccasins, pottery, beadwork, and other Tonkawa artifacts. The **A. D. Buck Museum of Science and History** (1300 East North Avenue, at Northern Oklahoma College, 405–628–2581, ext. 477) displays a pioneer icebox and milk cans, beaded picture frames, and artifacts from World Wars I and II. The science collection includes mounted birds and mammals representative of Oklahoma wildlife.

PONCA CITY

Ponca City took shape shortly after the 1893 land run, when some businessmen decided to leave the Santa Fe's designated station, Cross, and move a few miles south, to be near a good spring. Cross and Ponca City were rivals until the citizens of Ponca offered the railroad agent free property in town and moved his house from Cross. In exchange, the agent asked the Santa Fe to move the depot to Ponca. Happy Poncans rode the first train and handed out cigars, flowers, and cards proclaiming: "The train stops in Ponca City the same as in Chicago." The city soon eclipsed Cross and became an agricultural center with stockyards alongside the railroad tracks.

After 1907 the town became the base of operations for oilman Ernest Whitworth Marland, who drilled a successful discovery well on the Miller brothers' 101 Ranch and started a spate of oil-field development on the plains around Ponca City. Marland improved the town by helping to develop a depot, hotels, a golf course, polo fields, and his own houses, whose gardens he opened to the public. He became governor of Oklahoma in 1934, but his oil empire was taken over by the Continental Oil Company, and Marland ended up living in the gatehouse of his own estate. The **Marland Mansion and Estate** (901 Monument Road, 405–767–0420), built

The Ponca City oil baron E. W. Marland, who dreamed of living in a palace, commissioned architect John Duncan Forsythe to build him one in the Italian Renaissance style. A Latin inscription on the balcony says "A man's home is his castle."

in 1928, contains fifty-five rooms—including a ballroom with a gold-leaf ceiling and two Waterford crystal chandeliers—and a leather-lined elevator. The rooms are decorated with murals, mosaics, and elaborate grillwork. Modeled on the Davanzati Palace in Florence, Italy, the stone house was originally surrounded by 2,500 acres of land.

The nearby **Pioneer Woman Statue and Museum** (Route 77 and Lake Road, 405–765–6108) centers on a seventeen-foot bronze statue financed by E. W. Marland in 1930 and designed by Bryant Baker as a symbol of the pioneer spirit in American women. The museum exhibits the household goods, furniture, and clothing of women who made the Cherokee Strip land run in 1893.

Marland's first home, a Spanish Colonial Revival mansion of 1916, contains Oklahoma's first indoor swimming pool and is now the **Ponca City Cultural Center and Museums** (1000 East Grand

Many of the ceilings in the Marland Mansion were painted by Vincent Margliotti, a Florentine mural painter.

Avenue, 405–767–0427). Inside are Indian relics of Oklahoma, the Southwest, Pacific Northwest, and Central and South America; and artifacts dating to the Revolutionary War period. Also on display are memorabilia of the 101 Ranch and the Wild West Show, and the relocated studio of Bryant Baker.

Blackwell was established during the 1893 land run into the Cherokee Outlet and was developed by A. J. Blackwell, a real estate promoter, self-styled Baptist "prophet," and two-time alleged murderer. Originally known for its oil and zinc industries, the town is now a farming and ranching center. The **Top of Oklahoma Historical Society Cherokee Outlet Museum** (300 South Main Street, 405–363–0209) occupies the Blackwell Electric Park Pavilion, a 1912 Mission-style building that was erected "as a salute to electricity when the majority of Americans and most

Oklahomans did not have domestic electric power," according to the National Historic Register. The museum contains artifacts and exhibits on settling the Cherokee Outlet, including furniture, clothing, and farm implements.

A farm town settled during the Cherokee Outlet land run of 1893, **Medford** is the site of the **Grant County Museum** (Cherokee and Main streets, 405–395–2888), which features antique furniture, clothing, and farm equipment.

ENID

The Chisholm Trail ran through the future site of Enid, where there were good springs, and so the area was well known before the 1893 Cherokee Outlet land run. Advance surveys laid out town lots in preparation for the galloping hordes—15,000 men and women in the first six hours of the run. Although the Rock Island line crammed settlers into cattle cars to haul them to the site, the railroad refused to stop in the new town after settlement. A freight train was wrecked after persons unknown sawed through a trestle. A federal act was quickly passed, requiring trains to make certain stops: Enid was one of them. As a wheat center and oil refinery, Enid was able to attract the Santa Fe and Frisco lines.

The Geronimo, an early automobile, was manufactured in Enid. The **Museum of the Cherokee Strip** (507 South 4th Street, 405–237–1907) exhibits materials from settlement days, including Cheyenne beadwork and a furnished tepee. Also on the site is a barn displaying horse-drawn farm equipment and a Model T Ford.

KINGFISHER

Near what is now the town of Kingfisher, ruts made by cattle herds moving north on the Chisholm Trail remained hidden by grass, wrecking some settlers' wagons during the land run of 1889. The town was once a contender to be the territorial capital. When local judge Abraham Seay became governor in 1892, he built the brick **Seay Mansion** (11th Street and Zellers Avenue, 405–375–5176), in a modified Queen Anne style with a domed tower, in the hope that Kingfisher would become the capital and his house the executive mansion. (His strategy failed.) The house is furnished in period style. Across the street the **Chisholm Trail Museum** (605 Zellers Avenue, 405–375–5176) contains a Sioux ceremonial dress, Sitting

A modest chapel and cemetery in the countryside west of Watonga. OVERLEAF: *In 1936, during the worst of the Oklahoma dust bowls, Arthur Rothstein photographed Arthur Coble, a Cimarron County farmer, fleeing a dust storm with his sons.*

Bull's game bag, and other Indian artifacts as well as items that came up the Chisholm Trail—a rocking chair from Texas, a whiskey jug, and a dutch oven. The log cabin home of Adeline Dalton, mother of the notorious Dalton Gang, is here, along with an early bank, a country school, a church, a chuck wagon, a horse-drawn hearse, and a fire engine.

Watonga takes its name from Black Coyote, an Arapaho chief. It is the site of the **T. B. Ferguson Museum** (519 North Weigel, 405–623–5069), occupying a frame house built for Thompson Benton Ferguson, pioneer publisher of the *Watonga Republican* newspaper, who was named governor of Oklahoma Territory by President Theodore Roosevelt in 1901. Ferguson and his wife were both well-known writers, and while visiting this literary household, novelist Edna Ferber worked on *Cimarron.* The house is furnished with original and period articles. A cavalry remount station and an 1890s jail are located behind it.

During pioneer days there were thousands of sod houses across the American prairies, and one of the few survivors stands some five miles north of **Cleo Springs.** Homesteader Marshall McCully, who lived first in a dugout hollowed into the bank of a ravine, then built this more "luxurious" **Sod House** (Route 8, 405–463–2441) in 1894 using buffalo-grass sod that grew a mile north of the site.

In the college town of **Alva,** site of a land office during the Cherokee Outlet opening of 1893 and of a camp for German prisoners of war during the Second World War, is the **Cherokee Strip Museum** (901 14th Street, 405–327–2030). Thirty-eight rooms contain various historical exhibits, including firearms, clothing, dolls, and artifacts from the German prisoner of war camp. The **Northwestern Oklahoma State University Museum** (Jesse Dunn Hall, 405–327–1700) features fossils, Native American artifacts, and local geological specimens. During the land run of 1893, **Waynoka** took shape around a railroad siding. The Santa Fe depot, an ornate brick building of 1910 with scrolled Flemish gables, is now the **Waynoka Historical Museum** (Waynoka and Cleveland streets, 405–824–4741). Exhibits focus on the Transcontinental Air Transport, the nation's first coast-to-coast air-rail link, which crossed the country in 1929 in forty-eight hours. Passengers switched from plane to train in Waynoka. The museum has an excellent collection of memorabilia celebrating the Transcontinental Air Transport, including old photographs and a landing light from the runway.

The town of **Woodward** was a railroad settlement six years before the 1893 land run into the Cherokee Outlet, and the Western Trail, a route for northbound cattle herds, passed through it. The surrounding land was home to the Cheyenne and Arapaho for many years prior to the railroad. Local history is portrayed at the **Plains Indians and Pioneers Museum** (2009 Williams Avenue, 405–256–6136) through murals, Indian relics, and interpretive exhibits; relocated buildings include a Fort Supply trader's store and the Bank of Fargo.

FORT SUPPLY

Non-Indian settlement of northwestern Oklahoma began in 1868 with **Fort Supply** (Western State Hospital grounds, 405–766–2224). Built as an advance post for General Philip Sheridan's operations against the Arapaho and Cheyenne, the so-called Camp Supply was outfitted with 450 wagonloads of goods and building materials. (General George A. Custer accompanied the supply train, then set off to attack the sleeping Indians of Black Kettle's camp in the Battle of the Washita.) As Indian hostilities decreased, the post became a center for supplies and communications, with trails leading to Fort Reno, Fort Sill, Fort Dodge (in Kansas), and the Texas Panhandle. It was not a luxurious post. The local historian Kent Ruth recounts that in 1872 an officer's wife complained that her dining-room floor was sand, "and almost every night little white toadstools grow up all along the base of the log walls." The post was abandoned in 1893 and taken over ten years later by a state mental hospital. Two sixteen-room frame houses, the brick guardhouse, and a cabin from the early 1870s are all that remain of the original fort.

THE PANHANDLE

The Oklahoma Panhandle was a political anomaly, an overlooked rectangle of land within a cartographic "box" formed by two old borders set in treaties with Spain (in 1821) and Mexico (1848) and the boundary lines of Texas and Kansas Territory. Called No Man's Land, it was not part of any state or territory. Beginning in 1886 squatters flocked to this neutral Strip, only to find that there was no government, no title to the land, and no law. Ruffians and claim jumpers, locally referred to as rail trotters, threatened life and property with impunity. Two factions of settlers each elected local officials and a delegate to Washington in hopes of becoming a new territory called Cimarron, with Beaver as its capital. Congress, confused by the two delegates as well as the cross purposes of politicians from Kansas and Missouri, failed to recognize this territory. Discouraged by the climate, outlaws, and the unresponsiveness of Congress, more than 12,000 settlers left during the Oklahoma land run. When this neglected strip was tacked on to the Oklahoma Territory with the Organic Act of 1890, barely 3,000 citizens were still living in what became the panhandle of Oklahoma. In the small town of **Gate,** the 1912 train depot now houses the **Gateway to the Panhandle Museum** (Route 64, 405–934–2004) which exhibits of frontier household items, farm equipment, and Civil War and railroad artifacts. In **Beaver,** an 1880 sod house is now the **Beaver City Museum** (15 East Main Street, 405–625–4726). Built by pioneer James Lane as a store and home along the Jones and Plummer Trail—an important cattle and stagecoach highway from Texas to Dodge City, Kansas—the house has been integrated into a larger stucco building and displays arrowheads, 6,000 strands of beads, old money, a vintage dental chair, and other eclectic items.

ARKANSAS

OPPOSITE: *The Jefferson County Courthouse in Pine Bluff, originally constructed in 1856 and largely reconstructed after a fire in 1976, contains records from court proceedings in the cabin of Joseph Bonne, who founded the town in 1819.*

One look at a relief map shows that Arkansas is divided into two clearly defined physiographic regions. A line running from the northeast to the southwest corners separates the highlands of the northwest, encompassing the Ozark and Ouachita mountains, from the flatlands of the southeast, dominated by the Mississippi River delta. Arkansas's development, both economic and political, has been shaped by the distinctions between these two areas. Little Rock, capital and largest city, sits in the very center of the state where the hills begin to rise out of the lowlands, at the crossroads of the two main thoroughfares for early settlers, the Arkansas River and the Southwest Trail.

Somewhere along the state's eastern boundary, on the west bank of the Mississippi, the first European explorer set foot in what is now Arkansas in 1541. The exact spot where the Spanish adventurer Hernando de Soto crossed the river has long been debated by historians, but it probably was just south of the present-day city of Helena. De Soto found a highly developed Indian civilization in east Arkansas, with large cities containing ceremonial mounds laid out in patterns based on astronomical observations. By the time French explorers came to the area, well over a century later, the Indian villages they found were only a shadow of those that de Soto had reported—very likely the result of epidemics of diseases, brought by the Spaniards, to which the Indians lacked resistance.

The three main Indian cultures in Arkansas during the period of European exploration were the Quapaw in the southeast, the Caddo in the southwest, and the fierce Osage, who roamed widely throughout their hunting grounds in the mountains of the northwest. During the succeeding eras of French, Spanish, and finally U.S. rule, these, and other tribes resettled here from the east, were gradually pushed farther west until, by 1835, no Indian homelands were left in Arkansas.

The first permanent European settlement in Arkansas was founded in June 1686 by Henry de Tonti, who four years earlier had accompanied René-Robert Cavelier, Sieur de La Salle, on his expedition claiming the Mississippi Valley for France. De Tonti set up a trading post in Quapaw territory on the north bank of the Arkansas River, just above its confluence with the Mississippi. For many years Arkansas Post was the only white settlement in the area, and in 1819

OPPOSITE: *An Osage warrior, a member of a delegation that went to Washington to discuss tribal lands in Arkansas, drawn in 1804 by Charles B.J Fevret de Saint-Memin.*

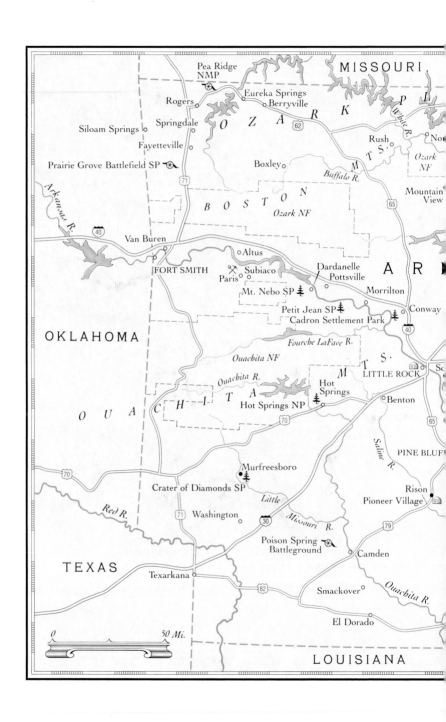

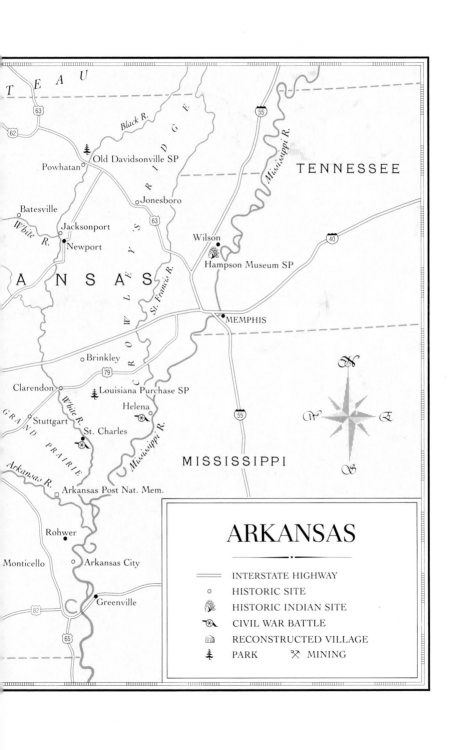

T E A U

63
62

Black R.

R I D G E

55

Mississippi R.

TENNESSEE

Old Davidsonville SP
Powhatan

Jonesboro

Batesville

63

Jacksonport
Newport

White R.

Wilson

Hampson Museum SP

40

A N S A S

C R O W L E Y ' S

St. Francis R.

MEMPHIS

Brinkley

79

Clarendon

Louisiana Purchase SP

White R.

Helena

GRAND

Stuttgart

St. Charles

P R A I R I E

Mississippi R.

55

MISSISSIPPI

Arkansas R.

Arkansas Post Nat. Mem.

Rohwer

Monticello

Arkansas City

82

Greenville

65

ARKANSAS

	INTERSTATE HIGHWAY
o	HISTORIC SITE
	HISTORIC INDIAN SITE
	CIVIL WAR BATTLE
	RECONSTRUCTED VILLAGE
	PARK ⚒ MINING

it became the first capital of Arkansas Territory. Two years later the territorial capital was moved upriver to Little Rock, which soon became, and has remained, the state's largest city, dominant both politically and economically.

Arkansas Territory, sparsely settled at first, grew quickly as the American frontier moved west across the continent. The territory's population—14,200 in 1820—had reached 50,000 by the time Arkansas became a state in 1836. In the 1830s the Southwest Trail between Saint Louis and Texas brought thousands of migrants through Arkansas, and beginning in 1849 Fort Smith became an important supply depot for adventurers headed for the California gold fields; some of these travelers stopped and put down roots in the state. A special convention called in March 1861 to consider Arkansas's secession from the Union first voted against it; two months later (after Fort Sumter in South Carolina was fired upon) a majority voted that the state join the Confederacy, though a substantial minority, especially in the northwest, remained Unionist and sent troops to the Union army. Arkansas was not a major battleground in

Picking cotton, a strain that was introduced to Arkansas soon after the Louisiana Purchase and became its most important crop in the early part of the twentieth century, in 1908.

the Civil War, although the northwest part of the state suffered greatly as Union and Confederate forces fought for control of the region
in the war's early stages. (The Battle of Pea Ridge, in which an
attempted Confederate excursion into Missouri was turned back,
may have been the most important battle fought west of the
Mississippi.) Little Rock fell to Federal troops in 1863, and the
Confederate state capital was moved to Washington, in southwest
Arkansas. By the end of the war, Arkansas, like the rest of the South,
had lost a significant part of its male population, its resources, and its
economic vitality.

The postwar era in Arkansas was a period of political experiment and bitter confrontation. It ended in 1874 after a confusing
month-long armed struggle between factions of Reconstruction
Republicans. The Brooks–Baxter War, as it came to be known,
involved two men who both claimed to be rightful occupants of the
governor's office. Although hundreds of troops massed in Little
Rock, few skirmishes were actually fought, most outside the city, and
the number of deaths that resulted has been reported at between 20
and 200. Eventually President Ulysses S. Grant ruled that Elisha
Baxter was governor; a new election installed Augustus H. Garland,
a Democrat, in the state house, beginning an era of Democratic
dominance in state politics that lasted until the 1960s.

Railroads began to crisscross much of Arkansas in the 1880s,
and they stayed busy hauling out huge old trees from the virgin
forests that covered the eastern part of the state. After the trees were
gone, cotton moved in and dominated agriculture in the state for
decades. The forests of west and northwest Arkansas were protected
for a time by the rugged terrain, but they too eventually fell. Timber
remains an important part of the economy of the state today, especially in the southern half, where extensive pine forests provide trees
for lumber and paper mills.

The mountains of northwest Arkansas were a barrier to travel
during the late nineteenth and early twentieth centuries, just as the
swamps of east Arkansas had been. The swamps were eventually
drained; the mountains were a more formidable obstruction. The
people who settled in the "hollers" of the Ozarks remained relatively
isolated for generations, retaining pioneer speech patterns and passing on folk songs and tales. These determined, sometimes aloof people were the "hillbillies" of stories and jokes. Although their mountain culture is fast disappearing, some of it still survives in small

Ozarks towns and, in an institutionalized form, at the Ozark Folk Center near Mountain View. (Arkansas's modern image was no doubt shaped to a great extent by "Lum and Abner," one of the most popular radio programs of the 1930s and 1940s; its stars were two rustic Arkansas storekeepers in the fictional town of Pine Ridge.)

Cotton and timber were dominant in Arkansas's economy as the twentieth century began, but soon other products took their places. Rice growing began soon after the turn of the century in east Arkansas's Grand Prairie region, where the soil was found to be ideal for retaining the surface water needed for the crop. Northwest Arkansas was a national leader in fruit (especially apple) production in the years between 1890 and 1920. Oil was discovered in south Arkansas in the 1920s, bringing a boom that, while nothing like the one in Texas, nevertheless created an important new refining and marketing industry.

Arkansas's population actually dropped between 1940 and 1955, as more people moved out of than into the state. Arkansas had just begun to try to attract industry in the 1950s when something happened that was to make the name of its capital city known not only

Boxley Valley, part of the protected area known as Buffalo National River.

across the United States, but around the world. Everyone in Arkansas old enough to remember it knows it as "the Fifty-seven Crisis." It was one of the most important incidents in the long struggle for civil rights in America, and undoubtedly the most famous event in Arkansas history. When the Little Rock School Board made plans to integrate Central High School in the fall of 1957, Governor Orval E. Faubus mobilized the Arkansas National Guard to prevent nine black students from attending classes. After a series of court hearings and confrontations, President Dwight Eisenhower federalized the National Guard and sent part of an army infantry division to Little Rock to enforce desegregation rulings. Although Little Rock never again was the scene of such a racially divisive series of events, the stigma left by this early incident in the civil rights movement clouded Arkansas's image for many years. A generation later, the echoes of "Fifty-seven" are just beginning to fade.

This chapter begins with the state capital, Little Rock. It then travels through Eastern Arkansas, from Arkansas City through Jacksonport. The third segment of the chapter traverses Western Arkansas, from Camden to Batesville.

L   I   T   T   L   E   R   O   C   K

There really is—or at least was—a little rock in Little Rock. It served as an Arkansas River landmark beginning in 1722, when the French explorer Bénard de la Harpe searched the area for a fabled giant green rock, which he hoped might turn out to be a huge emerald. La Harpe found no emerald, but he did find a large rock outcropping on the north side of the river and a smaller one just downstream on the south bank. This was called "little rock" by later explorers; it marked the first upland site on the riverbank for travelers who had ascended past the bayous, sandbars, and mud of the lower Arkansas River. Because it was also a convenient fording place, the little rock became an important crossroads in the settlement of the West. The Southwest Trail, the busiest route between Saint Louis and Texas, crossed the Arkansas River here, and a rude settlement grew up at the beginning of the nineteenth century. By the time Arkansas Territory was created in 1819, the village still had only a

handful of residents. The following year, a coalition of land speculators who owned property at Little Rock persuaded the general assembly to move the capital from the soggy, malaria-ridden bottomlands
of Arkansas Post to the nearest elevated location upriver: Little Rock.

What is left of the **little rock** (it was partially destroyed in the
construction of a railroad bridge over the Arkansas River) can be
seen in **Riverfront Park** (Markham Street and La Harpe Boulevard),
a riverside promenade downtown.

OLD STATE HOUSE MUSEUM

At the west end of Riverfront Park is one of Arkansas's most beautiful and historically significant buildings, the Old State House.
Designed by Gideon Shryock and opened in 1836, the year Arkansas
was admitted to the Union, it is an excellent example of the Greek
Revival architecture popular at the time. The building's exterior and
interior walls, as well as its four imposing Doric columns, were built
of handmade brick; the outside was stuccoed and painted, "rusticat-

*Arkansas's Territorial Governor John Pope, originally from Kentucky, hired Gideon
Shryock, a noted Kentucky architect, to design a state house that would "command
the admiration and respect of the passing stranger and have a moral and political
influence on the whole community."* OPPOSITE: *Its walnut staircase was added during
renovations in 1885.*

The restored House of Representatives Chamber in the 1885 additions to the Old State House. Each desk is equipped with a brass spittoon. When the House was in session, the floor would be covered with wood shavings to provide further protection.

ed" in the fashion of the time to imitate granite, which was then unavailable in the area. The state's first governor was inaugurated here in 1836, and the Arkansas general assembly met here from that year until it moved to the present capitol in 1911. The first legislative session in the Old State House was enlivened by the only recorded murder of one Arkansas state legislator by another. (During a discussion of taxes and wolf bounties, one lawmaker made a remark that another took to imply that he had certain canine affinities, at which point a bowie knife was drawn.)

Today the Old State House is an elegant museum, with six rooms furnished to illustrate evolving decorative tastes in the state. The room representing the period 1890–1905, for instance, has a hanging "gasolier," or gas-burning chandelier. One room displays hands-on exhibits: old clothes that children can try on, early kitchen utensils, and a crank phonograph with records. There is a display of Arkansas First Ladies' gowns, and five galleries host changing art and history exhibits. The legislative meeting rooms are upstairs, and on the lawn is "Lady Baxter," a cannon that dates from the Civil War.

"Lady Baxter" was fired only once: to celebrate the end of Arkansas's own mini-Civil War, the strange, month-long 1874 conflict called the Brooks–Baxter War.

LOCATION: 300 West Markham Street. HOURS: 9–5 Friday–Saturday, 1–5 Sunday. FEE: None. TELEPHONE: 501–371–1749.

Across the street from the Old State House is the **Capital Hotel** (Markham and Louisiana streets), an 1877 structure restored in 1983. The Capital has a cast-iron facade, and its lobby features massive marbled columns and a mezzanine skylight. Ulysses S. Grant and Sarah Bernhardt were among the hotel's guests in its early years. The **Pulaski County Courthouse** (Markham and Spring streets) is actually two connected buildings. The original courthouse is a Romanesque Revival structure constructed in 1889 of granite from a site west of the city. The adjoining 1914 addition has an impressive rotunda with marble columns and a stained-glass dome. Across the street is the **Old Post Office Building and Customhouse** (2d and Spring streets), a massive stone Second Renaissance Revival building of 1881, now used by the University of Arkansas at Little Rock School of Law.

Many of Little Rock's most historic structures are located in the **Quapaw Quarter,** just southeast of downtown. American Queen Anne-, Second Empire-, and Colonial Revival-style architecture can be seen in this mix of business and residential buildings. The area takes its name from the Quapaw Line, which once marked the western boundary of treaty lands belonging to the Quapaw Indians. Among the most interesting structures in this area (all private residences) are the **Dibrell House** (14th and Spring streets), built in 1892; the **Augustus Garland House** (1404 Scott Street), dating to 1873; the ca. 1889 **Hanger House** (1010 Scott Street); the 1888 **Hornibrook House** (2120 Louisiana Street); the 1900 **Hotze House** (1619 Louisiana Street); and the **Fordyce House** (2115 Broadway), the **Gibb House** (1801 Arch Street), and the **Foster-Robinson House** (2122 Broadway), all dating to 1904.

Also of interest is the **Villa Marre** (1321 Scott Street, 501–374–9979), a brick Second Empire Italianate building with a ten-foot-deep granite foundation. It was built in 1881 and rented to Governor Jeff Davis around the turn of the century. It is open for tours. Furnishings date from 1858 to 1920, and the ornate carved wood fireplace is original.

The parlor of the Villa Marre, built by a prosperous Little Rock saloon keeper in 1881.
It later was rented by Governor Jeff Davis, some of whose furniture is on display.

The Arkansas Arts Center's **Decorative Arts Museum** (7th and
Rock streets, 501–372–4000) is also known as the **Pike-Fletcher-Terry
House.** The Greek Revival house was built in 1840 by Albert Pike, a
flamboyant, eccentric figure who at various times was a lawyer, soldier, poet, mystic, and Masonic leader. The Pulitzer Prize–winning
poet John Gould Fletcher spent his boyhood here and was deeply
influenced by the experience. "It was from this house," he once
wrote, "that I learned what it was like to have been a Southerner of
the aristocratic sort in the days before the Civil War." The rooms
have been converted into galleries displaying glassware, furniture,
pottery, textiles, and similar objects.

The **Arkansas Museum of Science and History** (9th and
Commerce streets, 501–371–3521), located in **MacArthur Park,** has
exhibits on Arkansas's Native American cultures, pioneer days, prehistory, and geology, including dinosaur bones and other fossils
found in the area. One wing is devoted to an audio-visual display on

the life of Friedrich Gerstäcker, a German traveler who visited Arkansas in the years 1838–1842 and later wrote extensively about his adventures. The museum building was originally constructed as an arsenal in 1842, when it was part of a federal military post. General Douglas MacArthur was born at the post, and it was for him that the present-day city park was named. Just outside the arsenal grounds is the site of the hanging of David O. Dodd, a 17-year-old boy, who during the Civil War was caught trying to smuggle information about Federal troops occupying Little Rock to the Confederates. Dodd went to the gallows on January 8, 1864, after refusing to reveal the source of his information.

Mount Holly Cemetery (Broadway and 12th Street) has been called "the Westminster Abbey of Arkansas" because of the number of historic figures buried there, including ten governors, three U.S. senators, five Confederate generals, David O. Dodd, and twenty Little Rock mayors. Founded in 1843, Mount Holly has tree-shaded paths that meander among its many statues, elaborate mausoleums, and other monuments.

ARKANSAS TERRITORIAL RESTORATION

Taking up an entire block northeast of 3d and Scott streets, the Territorial Restoration comprises a modern reception center and four restored nineteenth-century buildings. The 1830s-era **Hinderliter House,** a log structure covered with cypress planks, is the oldest building in Little Rock. The modest **Brownlee-Noland House** and the **McVicar-Conway House** both date from the 1840s; the former has English boxwood plantings from George Washington's Mount Vernon estate, as well as hand-carved doors and mantels. The **Woodruff House** was built by William E. Woodruff, who founded the *Arkansas Gazette* in 1819. It is the oldest newspaper west of the Mississippi River. Part of the interior of the house has been made into a time line of Arkansas history, displaying newspaper pages from territorial days through the beginning of the Civil War.

LOCATION: 3d and Scott streets. HOURS: 9–5 Monday–Saturday, 1–5 Sunday. FEE: Yes. TELEPHONE: 501-371-2348.

ARKANSAS STATE CAPITOL

Arkansas's capitol, built on a hill that once was the site of the state penitentiary, had a controversial beginning. Construction based on

A desk in an upstairs room of the Jesse Hinderliter House, the oldest house in Little Rock, which is preserved in the Arkansas Territorial Restoration. Hinderliter had sleeping quarters and an office upstairs, and operated a grog shop on the ground floor.

plans by George C. Mann was begun in 1899, but inefficiency and a bribery scandal delayed completion for sixteen years. In 1909 architects changed, and Cass Gilbert finished the project, only slightly changing Mann's plans. The legislature first met in the partially completed building in 1911. The capitol was designed along the lines of the national Capitol in Washington, DC (it has been used as a stand-in for that building in several films). The exterior is of gray limestone; the interior features a handsome marble rotunda and staircases. The two-ton central chandelier and brass front doors were built by Tiffany and Company, of New York. The fourth floor houses exhibits on Arkansas geology and history.

LOCATION: Capitol Avenue and Woodlane Street. HOURS: 9–4 Monday–Friday, 10–4 Saturday, 1–5 Sunday. FEE: None. TELEPHONE: 501–682–5080.

EASTERN ARKANSAS

ARKANSAS CITY

Little evidence remains today that this delta town was an important Mississippi River port for more than fifty years. Arkansas City was a landmark as early as 1834, when it was sometimes called Kate Adams Port, for a well-known Mississippi steamboat that stopped here. The town grew quickly when nearby Napoleon, once a thriving city, was washed away by the Mississippi in the 1870s. However, the Great Flood of 1927 changed the course of the Mississippi, and Arkansas City, no longer on the main channel, began to wither. A marker on the huge Mississippi River levee locates the site of the former port. The **Desha County Courthouse** (Robert S. Moore Avenue) was built in 1900 when Arkansas City was still a regionally important commercial and political center. It has a four-story clock tower, and its eclectic style shows Romanesque Revival elements.

ARKANSAS POST NATIONAL MEMORIAL

Arkansas Post can lay legitimate claim to being the birthplace of Arkansas. Founded in 1686 by Henry de Tonti, La Salle's lieutenant, this settlement on the lower Arkansas River was a center of trade with the Quapaw Indians and a vital part of France's plan to assert its influence in the Mississippi River valley. Arkansas Post remained a French military and commercial outpost almost continuously for nearly a century. It may have been abandoned around 1700, but renewed French interest in trade with the Indians soon brought it back to life. In 1712 King Louis XIV granted a monopoly on colonization rights in the Louisiana territory to a private company. Later, the monopoly was acquired by the Scottish financier John Law, who organized the Mississippi Company in 1718 to develop the region. One of the company's projects was the settling of 1,700 Alsatian homesteaders in Arkansas Post. Meanwhile, French investors, encouraged by Law's vigorous promotional campaign, speculated heavily in the company's stock. In 1720 the stock crashed—the bursting of the so-called "Mississippi Bubble"—wiping out the fortunes of the investors caught holding the stock and erasing the financial backing for colonists. The Alsatians quit Arkansas Post and moved to a site near New Orleans.

*A playhouse built in the 1930s for an only child near De Witt is now part of the
Arkansas Post County Museum.*

Following its defeat by the British in the French and Indian War,
France ceded Louisiana (including Arkansas Post) to Spain, which
controlled the region until ceding it back to France in 1800. In the
meantime, Arkansas Post, then called Fort Carlos III, was the site of
a skirmish between the British and Spanish—like the British assault
upon Saint Louis, a minor episode in the world war of which our
Revolutionary War was one part. After the Louisiana Purchase
(1803), Arkansas Post remained a center of trade. By then, it had
been relocated several times because of flooding on the Arkansas
River. It was named territorial capital when Arkansas Territory was
created in 1819, but two years later lost that position to Little Rock,
which was more centrally located—and on less swampy ground.
Arkansas Post quickly went into decline; a visitor in 1832 reported
that chimneys had fallen down and trees were growing through the
roofs of buildings. A Civil War battle at the site in 1863, and the
resultant naval bombardment, sealed the old post's fate.

Today's 389-acre Arkansas Post National Memorial includes the
locations of several of the Post's former forts and settlements.
Almost nothing remains of the buildings that once were here, but its

location conveys the strategic importance of the site. Exhibits at the visitor center include displays on the fur trade, riverboats and steamships, the Civil War battle for Fort Hindman, and the plants and animals of the region. Pathways lead past sites where a state bank, a tavern, and gin, and other buildings once stood, including the first home of the *Arkansas Gazette,* established here in 1819.

LOCATION: Route 169, 20 miles north of Dumas. HOURS: *Visitor Center:* 8–5 Daily. FEE: None. TELEPHONE: 501–548–2432.

Only two miles from the memorial site is **Arkansas Post County Museum** (Routes 165 and 169, 501–548–2634). Exhibits here include a log "breezeway" house from about 1877, which still has some of its original mud chinking, and an impressively detailed miniature house built in the 1930s as a child's playhouse. (Displayed right next to the latter is, rather disconcertingly, a gallows.) Exhibits in the main building include an original first edition of the *Arkansas Gazette,* dated November 20, 1819, a French crucifix from the early 1700s, and one of a set of spurs from the period of Spanish occupation.

The kitchen of a log dogtrot house, built in Gilette in the 1870s and moved to the Post County Museum, has been furnished as it would have been in the late nineteenth century.

MONTICELLO

Evidence that this was once one of the state's wealthiest towns can be seen in the **North Main Street Historic District,** just north of the downtown square. Many of the imposing houses along this street date from the turn of the century and earlier; there are good examples of Victorian and Queen Anne styles. The **Hotchkiss House** (577 North Boyd Street, private) was built about 1902 by a local architect as his own residence; the two-and-a-half-story structure is an interesting mixture of styles and forms.

The **Drew County Historical Museum** (404 South Main Street, 501–367–7446) is housed in the Cavaness House, a monumental two-story building constructed in 1906 of cement blocks individually molded to mimic stone. Among the items displayed are Civil War weapons and uniforms, a nineteenth-century F. A. O. Schwartz rocking horse (covered with a real horse's pelt), and Indian artifacts.

RISON

The aim of **Pioneer Village** (Cleveland County fairgrounds off Route 35) is to re-create a small Arkansas town of the late nineteenth century. Several buildings have been moved here from their original locations in the area and put on display. The **Mount Olivet Methodist Church** of 1867 is a simple white clapboard structure typical of rural Arkansas churches of its time; the pews were handmade from local timber. The 1902 **Cleveland County Clerk's Office** was moved from the Rison courthouse square; it has been refurbished as a country mercantile. Pioneer Village also includes a Victorian house dated ca. 1892, a two-room "shotgun" cabin, a one-room log cabin, a blacksmith's shop, and a barn. All the buildings have furnishings, tools, and other items relating to their original uses.

PINE BLUFF

Early travelers on the lower Arkansas River noted a place of pine-covered bluffs on the south bank about sixty miles northwest of its confluence with the Mississippi. It was to this site that Joseph Bonne moved his family around 1819 to set up a trading post with the Quapaw Indians. The town that grew up here, first called Mount Marie, was renamed Pine Bluff in 1832, eight years after the Quapaw ceded their lands in the area to the United States. Pine Bluff grew quickly after the 1850s and became an important port for the shipment of cotton. Later it developed into a major rail center, with railroad shops the dominant economic force in the city. Several impressive homes near the downtown area are reminders of Pine Bluff's nineteenth-century affluence. Built in 1850, the **Dexter Harding House** (Route 65 and Pine Street, 501–536–7606) was moved to this site from its original location across town, where Harding operated a sawmill before the Civil War. It is now a visitor center offering information about Pine Bluff's historic homes. The **Jefferson County Courthouse** (Main and Barraque streets) is a reconstruction of the original 1856 building, partially destroyed by fire in 1976. Its tower, topped with a golden dome, is a copy of one that was a longtime landmark in southeast Arkansas. One section of the courthouse serves as the **Jefferson County Historical Museum** (501–541–5402), with displays on the Quapaw, railroads, and riverboats, including a miniature replica.

Private residences of historical interest include the **Hudson-Grace-Borreson House** (716 West Barraque Street), originally built around 1860 as a two-room cabin and expanded and remodeled later in the Second Empire style. The **Trulock-Gould House** (704 West Barraque Street), built in 1876, retains its original exterior appearance. The **Roth-Rosenzweig House** (717 West Second Avenue) is a Queen Anne building of 1894 with decorative cypress shingles. The **Trulock-Cook House** (703 West Second Avenue), built ca. 1903, is Pine Bluff's only remaining example of Shingle-style architecture. **DuBocage** (1115 West Fourth Avenue) was built in 1866 by Judge Joseph Bocage, a prominent businessman, in the Greek Revival style with some Victorian elements. **Trinity Episcopal Church** (703 West Third Avenue) is the oldest Episcopal building still in use in Arkansas. The cornerstone was laid in 1866.

Locomotive 819 was the last 4-8-4 "Northern"-type locomotive to be built by the Saint Louis Southwestern Railway Company at its Pine Bluff shops. Just four inches short of 100 feet in length with its tender, 819 was commissioned in 1943 and retired in 1955. Now fully restored, it is on display at the **Arkansas Railroad Museum** (1400 East Second Avenue, 501–541–1819) at the Cotton Belt railroad shops.

SCOTT

This small community, located among several Arkansas River oxbow lakes, has traditionally been an important center of cotton farming. The **Plantation Agriculture Museum** (Routes 161 and 165,

501–961–1409) has exhibits on cotton cultivation from 1836 to World War II. It is housed in a building dating to about 1912 that once was a country store serving farmers in the area. Nearby is **Marlsgate Plantation** (Bearskin Lake Road, 501–961–1307), an impressive Classic Revival mansion that was built in 1904 for William P. Dortch, a member of a prominent local family of plantation owners. It has been restored and furnished with antebellum antiques.

Toltec Mounds Archaeological State Park

This park preserves an important religious and ceremonial center of the Plum Bayou Culture, Indians who lived from about A.D. 700 to 950. (The misnomer "Toltec" came from an early owner of the site, who believed the mounds here had been built by the people of that name who lived in ancient Mexico.) Toltec Mounds is one of the largest and most complex archaeological sites in the lower Mississippi Valley. Although many of the original mounds were plowed over before the site was protected, scientists know the locations of at least eighteen existing or former mounds. Two of them, rising more than forty feet high, are the largest Indian mounds in Arkansas. The Toltec center is bordered on one side by an oxbow lake and was once surrounded on the other sides by an earthwork six feet high and more than a mile long; only small remnants of the earthwork remain.

The visitor center has exhibits on the Plum Bayou Indians, with examples of artifacts that have been found here. Both self-guided and interpreter-led tours of the site are available.

LOCATION: Route 165, 4 miles south of Scott. HOURS: 8–5 Tuesday–Saturday, 12–5 Sunday. FEE: None. TELEPHONE: 501–961–9442.

STUTTGART

This part of Arkansas's Grand Prairie region was settled by German Lutherans, who arrived here in 1878 and named their new town after a city in their home country. Agriculture in the Grand Prairie

OPPOSITE: *The church and schoolhouse on the re-created small-town street at the Stuttgart Agricultural Museum.*

changed drastically with the introduction of rice at the turn of the century. It soon became the dominant crop, and its success made Arkansas one of the world's leading rice-growing areas—with Stuttgart at the center. (Arkansas's first rice mill was built in Stuttgart in 1906.) The **Stuttgart Agricultural Museum** (921 East 4th Street, 501–673–7001) has an excellent collection of items related to rice farming in the region. One large wing contains several antique tractors, including a 1920 Fordson and an enormous (over twelve-ton) Nichols and Shepard "steam traction engine." The museum also has re-created a small-town street of earlier times, with a mercantile, a doctor's office, a post office, and a grocery store. Part of the museum's main room is devoted to household items from pioneer times, including clothing, furniture, kitchen utensils, and restored musical instruments. The museum's Waterfowlers' Wing celebrates Stuttgart's other passion: duck hunting. (The city calls itself the "Rice and Duck Capital of the World.") There are mounted ducks of several species, along with guns, decoys, and other items related to hunting. Outside are a two-thirds scale model of an early Lutheran church and a prairie house of the type once common in the region.

HELENA

One of the earliest settlers near the southern end of Crowley's Ridge was an immigrant from North Carolina named Sylvanus Phillips, who lived in the area as early as 1797. His last name was eventually given to a county in east Arkansas, and the county's major city was named for his daughter. Helena was an important port on the Mississippi from its beginning, and the nearby high ground offered an escape from the river's frequent flooding. Mark Twain wrote in *Life on the Mississippi* that "Helena occupies one of the prettiest situations on the river." Helena had great strategic importance during the Civil War, and the town was the site of a bloody Confederate defeat. On July 4, 1863, Confederate troops tried to capture the town from well-fortified Union forces, but poor planning and miscommunications led to terrible losses for the Rebels. More than a fifth of the 7,600 Confederate troops involved in the battle were killed, wounded, or captured. The Confederates attacked Helena partly because it was the most important supply depot for Union forces besieging Vicksburg, Mississippi, and on the day of the defeat at Helena, Vicksburg fell to the Federals. (This was also one day after the Union victory at Gettysburg, Pennsylvania.) Some traces of the battle can still be seen on Hindman Hill at the site of **Battery D** (off Military Road), where there are trenches and fortifications used by Union troops. (A sign here reads "No Trespassing," but history-minded persons who do not disturb the site are welcome.)

Some of the southern dead from the Battle of Helena are buried in the **Confederate Cemetery** (within Maple Hill Cemetery, 1801 North Holly Street). Here, on a tree-shaded hilltop, is the **Confederate Monument**, erected in 1892 out of "devotion to the memory of the lost cause," the inscription reads. Memorabilia from the Civil War and exhibits on the county's seven generals can be found in the **Phillips County Museum** (623 Pecan Street, 501–338–3537). The collection includes the bullet that killed Thomas Hindman, fired through a window of his home by an unknown assassin in 1868. The museum also displays Indian artifacts and military items.

Estevan Hall

Helena's historic homes reflect a time when the city was one of wealth. The raised Creole cottage called Estevan Hall is one of the most interesting among the state's oldest and most important residences. The house, begun in 1826 by plantation owner Fleetwood Hanks, was built of locally fired bricks and hand-hewn cypress boards. Estevan Hall has remained in the same family ever since, except for a period during the Civil War when it was occupied by Union army physicians. The house has a long, pillared porch overlooking the Mississippi; from this spot, a family diary records, James Millinder Hanks watched a famous 1870 steamboat race between the *Natchez* and the *Robert E. Lee*. Civil War artifacts displayed in Estevan Hall include a Union cannonball, recently found when a huge magnolia tree in the front yard died a few years ago.

LOCATION: 653 Biscoe Street. HOURS: By appointment. FEE: Yes. TELE-PHONE: 501–338–8247.

The **Edwardian Inn** (317 Biscoe Street, 501–338–9155) was built in 1904 by a local cotton broker. Now restored as a bed-and-breakfast inn, it displays the magnificently detailed woodwork of the original house. Tours of several of the city's historic homes can be arranged through the Phillips County Chamber of Commerce

(501–338–8327), including the **Hornor-Gladin House** (626 Porter Street), built in 1881 in the Italianate style. The **Tappan-Pillow House** (717 Poplar Street) is an 1858 Greek Revival home that was once owned by Confederate general James Tappan. The **Pillow-Thompson House** (718 Perry Street) was built in the late 1890s and is a superb example of a Queen Anne Victorian structure, with the intricate detailing, filigrees, domes, and turrets of that unrestrained style.

In 1921 surveyors discovered two trees that had been blazed as "witness trees" in 1815 by an exploring party setting out into the territory of the Louisiana Purchase. The site is marked by a monument in **Louisiana Purchase State Park** (Route 362, two miles south of Blackton), which also preserves an unusual upland swamp of the type that once covered much of east Arkansas.

HAMPSON MUSEUM STATE PARK

This small museum in the northeast Arkansas town of Wilson houses part of one of the most important collections of Indian artifacts in the South. The items were assembled by Dr. James K. Hampson from his family's Nodena Plantation, a site that has given archaeologists valuable clues about a group of Indians who lived here between about A.D. 900 and 1540. Indians of the Nodena culture grew corn, squash, and beans, supplementing their diet by hunting and fishing. The Nodena site included ceremonial mounds, a central plaza, and a playing field, surrounded by houses and family burial plots. Only a small fraction of the artifacts found by Hampson and others is on display at the museum; Hampson himself excavated more than 1,000 burial sites at Nodena. The museum collection contains jewelry, tools, and pottery, including some beautiful and archaeologically significant pots and other vessels that may have been used in religious ceremonies. The rare painted pottery found here has been given its own archaeological designation: Nodena Red and White.

LOCATION: Lake Drive at Route 61, Wilson. HOURS: 9–5 Tuesday–Saturday. FEE: Yes. TELEPHONE: 501–655–8622.

JONESBORO

The largest city in northeast Arkansas, Jonesboro is located on Crowley's Ridge, a 150-mile-long strip of elevated land composed of the fine wind-blown soil called loess. Founded in 1859, the town grew quickly in the 1880s when railroads arrived, enabling the region's hardwood forests to be exploited. Jonesboro was selected as the site of a new agricultural school in 1909; Arkansas State University is now the state's second-largest college. Two residences of architectural interest are the 1884 **Frierson House** (1112 South Main Street, private) and the 1895 Queen Anne–Eastlake **Bell House** (303 West Cherry, private).

Arkansas State University Museum

One of the state's most important museums, the ASU Museum focuses on the natural and cultural history of northeast Arkansas. The collection of Indian artifacts includes effigy pots, spear points, and arrowheads dating from 10,000 years ago to the sixteenth century. Fossils such as camels' teeth, mastodon bones, and a llama skeleton indicate how the climate of the region has changed over time. "Old Town Arkansas" is entered through a replica of the 1886 Craighead County Courthouse. Exhibits on pioneer life include quilts and coverlets, clothing, farm tools, and a re-creation of a typical nineteenth-century living room, kitchen, and workshed. Special emphasis is given to the decorative arts and military history. The Lutterloh glass collection has representative pieces from many eras, including an H. P. Sinclaire candelabrum. Guns, uniforms, and other items from every major war fought by the United States are also on display.

LOCATION: Arkansas State University campus, Aggie and Caraway roads. HOURS: 9–4 Monday–Friday, 1–4 Saturday–Sunday. FEE: None. TELEPHONE: 501–972–2074.

Old Davidsonville State Park (Route 166, 501–892–4708) preserves a site along the Black River thought to have been a French settlement before the Louisiana Purchase as well as the scant remains of the small town of Davidsonville.

POWHATAN

Powhatan is yet another river town, once prosperous, that fell into decline when railroads supplanted steamboats as the major mode of transportation in the late nineteenth century. The **Powhatan**

Courthouse (Route 25, 501–878–6794), built in 1888, served as the center of justice in Lawrence County until the county seat was moved to Walnut Ridge in 1963. It has been restored and is now a state park, with displays on regional history and pioneer life along the Black River. A stone jailhouse built in 1873 stands nearby.

JACKSONPORT

Situated near the confluence of the White and Black rivers, Jacksonport began as a trading post in the late eighteenth century. The town was laid out in 1833. It became an important shipping port for cotton and timber, enjoying its greatest vigor during the steamboat era. In 1865 it was the scene of the surrender of 6,000 Confederate troops by General M. Jeff Thompson.

Jacksonport State Park (Route 69, three miles north of Newport, 501–523–2143) preserves some of the town's varied history. Its centerpiece is the **Jacksonport Courthouse Museum,** a two-story structure built in 1869 of local bricks set on a foundation of north Arkansas limestone. Inside are uniforms and weapons from the Civil War through World War I; arrowheads, pottery, and other Indian artifacts; and pioneer clothing and household items, including an 1854 melodeon. One exhibit focuses on the button industry, which once employed hundreds of workers along the White River. Mussel shells provided round blanks that were made into shiny buttons, until low-cost plastic killed the industry. Docked nearby is the *Mary Woods II,* a restored 1931 stern-wheeler that was one of the last of its kind to work the White River.

W E S T E R N   A R K A N S A S

CAMDEN

French trappers and traders named this spot on the Ouachita River in the 1780s, calling it Ecore á Fabré, or Fabré's Bluff. In 1844, after a substantial settlement had grown up at the steamboat landing here, residents dropped the difficult foreign name and chose Camden as the new one. At one time before the Civil War, Camden was Arkansas's second-largest city. The town went into decline during Reconstruction, but the arrival of the railroad in 1881 brought a revitalization caused by the growth of the timber industry. Camden still has many of its mid-nineteenth-century homes. The **Graham–Gaughan–Betts Home** (710 Washington Street, 501–836–3125), built in 1858, has a Chinese Gothic exterior and elaborate hand-made interior woodwork. General Steele used it as his headquarters during the siege of Camden. **Tate's Barn** (902 Tate Street, private) is a five-level structure that is an excellent example of a late-nineteenth-century barn.

Camden was occupied by a Federal army for two weeks in April 1864. In March and April, Major General Frederick Steele's army marched south from its base at Little Rock in an attempt to link up with General Nathaniel Banks's army, which was moving up the Red River to seize Shreveport, Louisiana. The combined armies were to expand federal control in Louisiana and then turn east to attack Mobile, Alabama. Steele never had much confidence in the plan, and both armies ran into trouble. Steele's advance was slowed by Rebel skirmishers and blocked, south of the Little Missouri River, in three days of fighting at Prairie d'Ane. Now desperately short of supplies, Steele withdrew east to Camden on April 15 and was encircled

The 1856 Graham-Gaughan-Betts Home in Camden was built in 1856 as a town residence for Major Joseph M. Graham, who had a plantation in Calhoun County. It was designed and constructed by E. Sifford, a local builder and woodworker.

A decanter and glasses that belonged to the Chidester family in the dining room of the McCollum-Chidester House Museum. Reflected in the mirror is a portrait of a young boy by Henry Byrd, an itinerant artist who visited Camden in the nineteenth century.

by Confederates. On April 18, in a bloody ambush at **Poison Spring Battleground** (Route 76, twelve miles northwest of Camden), Confederates captured a Federal wagon train bringing provisions to Camden; one week later, another supply train was captured at **Mark's Mill Battleground** (Route 8, ten miles east of Fordyce). By night Steele's army slipped out of Camden to escape to Little Rock but was forced to halt at the Saline River at Jenkins Ferry until engineers could bridge the river. On April 30 a pursuing Confederate force caught up with the Federals; 1,000 Southerners and 700 Federals were killed at the **Jenkins Ferry Battleground** (Route 46, four miles north of Leola) before Steele's men managed to cross. Thus ended Steele's inglorious campaign.

McCollum-Chidester House Museum

Built in 1847 by Peter McCollum, this house was bought sixteen years later by Colonel John T. Chidester, who operated stage lines and a mail service in the South and Southwest. It was used at various times as the headquarters of both Confederate and Union officers during General Steele's campaign. Upstairs walls still show evidence of bullets that struck them during the war. This was the first house in the city built with finished lumber rather than log planks; bricks used in construction were made on site by slaves. Nearly all the furnishings are original, brought up from New Orleans by Chidester. The handmade cradle, walker, and high chair were used by several generations of Chidester children. Also on display is a reconstruction of one of John Chidester's stagecoaches. On the grounds is the **Leake-Ingham Building,** a small Greek Revival structure of 1850 that was a law office and later Camden's first community library.

LOCATION: 926 Washington Street NW. HOURS: April through October: 9–4 Wednesday–Saturday. FEE: Yes. TELEPHONE: 501–836–9243.

TEXARKANA

The Texas & Pacific Railroad originally intended to build a city some five miles west of the Arkansas-Texas line. But in 1873 the railroad began selling town lots on the state line instead, where it could link up with the Cairo & Fulton Railroad without the latter needing a Texas charter. The junction boomed, attracting three more separate railroads by the turn of the century; separate cities with identical names were established on either side of the state line. The **U.S. Post Office** (5th Street and State Line Avenue), built of half Texas granite and half Arkansas limestone, sits on the state line. The **Texarkana Historical Museum** (219 State Line Avenue, 214–793–4831) is housed in one of the town's oldest buildings, a turreted 1879 brick structure originally occupied by a bank. It displays Caddo Indian tools and pottery, a turn-of-the-century business office, and a Scott Joplin exhibit featuring an extensive collection of the works of the great ragtime composer, who was born in Texarkana.

Ace of Clubs House

The best surviving mansion constructed during the early boom days is the Draughon-Moore "Ace of Clubs" House. It is said that James Draughon, the lumberman and dry-goods dealer who built it, got his inspiration for the architecture from the card that won him a huge poker pot in 1884—the Italianate house does resemble an ace of clubs when viewed from above. Three octagons and a partial octagon are clustered around an octagonal rotunda, with two stories topped by a fifteen-foot cupola, resting on a basement surrounded by a dry moat. Moorish–Spanish Revival porches replaced the original iron galleries in the 1920s. A restoration by the Texarkana Historical Museums highlights a variety of decors from the Draughon-Moore's century as a residence, including a Victorian library, several Edwardian rooms, a kitchen of the 1920s, bedrooms of the 1930s, and an Art Deco Streamlined Modern bath.

LOCATION: 420 Pine Street. HOURS: 10–3 Wednesday–Friday, 1–3 Saturday–Sunday. FEE: Yes. TELEPHONE: 214–793–7108.

WASHINGTON

Washington was once the preeminent city of southwest Arkansas. The town began in 1820 as a way station on the Southwest Trail—just a tavern, a general store, and a blacksmith shop—but its position as the last stop before Texas helped it grow quickly. It was named county seat of Hempstead County in 1824. In the mid-nineteenth century, the town had sixteen doctors, nine blacksmiths, a vaudeville theater, male and female academies, and a brass band. Washington began a slow decline in Reconstruction days when the Cairo & Fulton Railroad bypassed the town, laying its tracks eight miles to the east. Devastating fires in 1875 and 1883 hastened its population loss, and in 1939 the nearby town of Hope became the county seat.

Old Washington Historic State Park

Washington's decline in prosperity led to its present distinction. Because so many residents moved away and few new ones arrived, many buildings were left standing rather than remodeled, torn down, or replaced. Washington has Arkansas's best collection of early- and mid-nineteenth-century houses, churches, and public buildings and is one of the best-preserved villages of its period in the nation. Preservation efforts were begun in 1958 by the Pioneer Washington Restoration Foundation and accelerated in 1973 when parts of the town were designated as Old Washington Historic State Park. Park personnel offer tours of several buildings and sponsor history-oriented events throughout the year.

The **1836 Courthouse** served as the Confederate state capitol after Union forces captured Little Rock in 1863; it houses items from the Civil War. The **1874 Courthouse** serves as the park visitor

OPPOSITE: *Bowie knives at various stages in their manufacture, displayed in a re-created blacksmith shop from the 1820s in Old Washington State Historic Park. The knife was patented by Rezin Bowie, Jim's brother.*

The Music Room in the Grandison Royston House contains the family's Steinway square piano. Some of the furnishings displayed in the house came from Bullock Hall in Georgia.

center. The **Royston House** was built in 1845 for Grandison Royston, one of Arkansas's most influential early politicians; it has Empire-style furnishings along with items from the 1840s and 1850s. The **Purdom House** (ca. 1850), once owned by a local physician, contains exhibits on the history of medicine in early Arkansas. The **Sanders House** of about 1845 was the site of the wedding in 1853 of Sarah Virginia Sanders to Augustus H. Garland, later governor of Arkansas, U.S. senator, and attorney general of the United States under President Grover Cleveland. A reconstructed **blacksmith shop** represents the one in which James Black made one of the first bowie knives for Jim Bowie, the adventurer who died at the Alamo in 1836. The **Goodlett Cotton Gin** (1883) and the **Williams Tavern** (1832) were both moved to Washington from sites a few miles away to enhance the park's re-creation of nineteenth-century Arkansas.

LOCATION: Route 4, 9 miles north of Hope. HOURS: 9–5 Daily. FEE: Yes. TELEPHONE: 501–983–2684.

HOT SPRINGS

Hot Springs, Arkansas's most cosmopolitan city, also possesses its most colorful history, built around an accident of geology: the hot springs themselves. Rainwater that seeps into the ground northeast of the city flows deep into the earth, where it contacts heated rock and slowly makes its way back to the surface through faults in the underlying sandstone. This process takes about 4,000 years and produces an average flow in Hot Springs valley's springs of 850,000 gallons a day. The water from these springs comes out of the ground at 143 degrees Fahrenheit. It is so naturally sterile that the National Aeronautics and Space Administration used it to hold moon rocks while scientists looked for signs of life. Legend—with some historical backing—says that Hernando de Soto was the first European to visit the springs. (One chronicler of his journey wrote about discovering a place with hot, brackish water—very likely this site.) Thousands of years earlier, Indians had been using the hot springs for bathing. So important were the springs that this region was con-

The Hotel Eastman, which opened in 1890, was one of many luxurious hotels that sprang up in the resort town of Hot Springs after the railroad reached it in 1875.

sidered neutral ground, where different tribes came to bathe and hold religious ceremonies in peace.

In 1804 President Thomas Jefferson sent William Dunbar, a planter and naturalist from Natchez, and Dr. George Hunter, a chemist from Philadelphia, to explore the valley of the hot springs. Their report created a new interest in the area. Increasing numbers of people traveled over the rugged mountains to partake of the spring water's allegedly therapeutic qualities, and in 1832 President Andrew Jackson signed a bill setting aside four parcels of land as a federal reservation—an act that can be considered the beginning of the national park system. His action was timely; the springs were attracting so many settlers that a rowdy little town was growing up. In 1851 the city of Hot Springs was incorporated by those who had come to the valley to stay.

A railroad to Hot Springs, completed in 1874, spared visitors a stagecoach trip over the rough local roads, as well as the indignity of holdups by the James and Younger gangs. This new access made possible Hot Springs's development as a world-class resort in the early twentieth century. The city's slogan was "We Bathe the World," with good reason. Theodore and Franklin Roosevelt came to Hot Springs, as did Harry Truman. Babe Ruth bathed here, and tycoons such as Jay Gould and Andrew Carnegie helped make it fashionable.

Hot Springs National Park

The hot springs are the centerpiece of one of America's most unusual national parks. Created from the original federal reservation in 1921, the 5,839-acre park wraps around the business district of the city of Hot Springs and includes extensive mountainous areas nearby. Most of the springs were eventually capped and channeled into a common, federally regulated source of hot water for the city's bathhouses, which were built side by side along Central Avenue downtown in what came to be known as **Bathhouse Row.** These elaborate, beautifully appointed buildings are full of marble, tile, brass, fountains, and stained glass. The **Fordyce Bathhouse** (401 Central Avenue, 501–624–3383), built in 1915, is the grandest and most elaborately furnished of all the bathhouses. A statue of an Indian maiden offering a bowl of flowing spring water to de Soto is its centerpiece; an 8,000-piece stained-glass skylight depicts marine scenes. The bathhouse once offered bathers a library, music room, a bowling alley, and a gymnasium. It serves as the park's visitor center.

The **Buckstaff Bathhouse** (501–623–2308) is the only one that still offers baths to the public. It was built in 1913 in the Classic Revival style, with large Doric columns lining its facade. Behind the **Maurice Bathhouse** are two uncapped, free-flowing hot springs.

The **Medical Arts Building** (236 Central Avenue) is the state's most impressive Art Deco structure. The sixteen-story building, erected in 1929, was for many years the tallest in Arkansas. The **Stitt House** (824 Central Avenue) was built in 1877 in an eclectic style with Italianate touches by one of the city's most prominent early businessmen. It is now a restaurant. The **Williams House** (420 Quapaw Avenue), a fine Victorian brownstone built in 1891 and remodeled around 1914, has been restored as a bed-and-breakfast inn.

West of the city, the **Mid-America Museum** (400 Mid-America Boulevard, 501–767–3461) focuses on science and technology, with participatory exhibits on dinosaurs, weather, aviation, and Arkansas history. Among the displays is a fanciful flying machine designed by the English artist Rowland Emett.

Laid out around a new railroad depot in 1871, **Conway** was designated county seat of Faulkner County two years later. On the grounds of the county courthouse sits the **Greathouse Home** (Faulkner Street just south of Caldwell Street, 501–329–6446). Built between 1825 and 1830, it was the family home of Daniel Greathouse, and later served as an inn on the Butterfield Overland Mail route. The two main rooms of the house, separated by a dogtrot hallway, contain a variety of nineteenth-century furnishings and household items. At **Cadron Settlement Park** (Route 319, five miles west of Conway, 501–329–2986) is a reconstruction of a late-eighteenth-century blockhouse, a two-story structure made from rough-sawed cypress logs.

James Miles Moose, one of the founders of **Morrilton,** built the frame clapboard **Moose House** (711 Green Street, private) there in the late 1860s. Also in town, the **Depot Museum** (101 East Railroad Street, 501–354–8578), located in the Saint Louis, Iron Mountain & Southern Railroad depot of 1915, displays local historical items and Indian artifacts. Twelve miles south of Morrilton, **Petit Jean State Park** (Route 154, 501–727–5441) takes its name from a romantic local legend. Petit Jean ("little John") was a French girl who is said

OVERLEAF: *The gymnasium at the Fordyce Bathhouse in Hot Springs National Park, the largest in the state when it was constructed in 1915, contains rings, punching bags, vaulting horses, and doctor's scales.*

to have disguised herself as a boy to accompany her lover to America. She died while on the journey, and her supposed grave site is located just off Route 154 at the top of Petit Jean Mountain. Also at the park is the **Museum of Automobiles** (501–727–5427), with approximately fifty vintage cars on display. Of special interest are two 1920s-era Climber automobiles, the only surviving examples from Arkansas's only car manufacturer, the Climber Motor Corporation. The company turned out 200 cars and 75 trucks in its Little Rock factory in its three years in business.

POTTSVILLE

Kirkbride Potts moved to the Arkansas River valley from Pennsylvania in the late 1820s. In about 1858 he completed **Potts Tavern** (Main and Center streets, 501–968–1147) to house his wife and eleven children. The tavern was built with slave labor, using wood cut on Potts's land and bricks made on site. It also served as the post office and as a stop on the Butterfield stage line. Owned by the family until 1970, it is now operated as a museum and is one of Arkansas's best-preserved antebellum structures. Upstairs are four bedrooms, each twenty feet on a side, and a twelve-foot-wide central hall. The downstairs area includes displays of stagecoach memorabilia and Kirkbride Potts's original postmaster's desk.

PARIS

Paris was a coal-mining town from the late nineteenth century until recent times, and memorabilia of that industry makes up part of the collection in the **Logan County Museum** (204 North Vine Street, 501–963–3936). The museum is housed in the former Logan County Jail, an 1886 building that held its last prisoner in 1971. The jailer and his family lived downstairs; the cells upstairs now hold displays on railroading, farming, military artifacts, and on Arthur Tillman, who in 1914 became the last man hanged for murder in Arkansas.

VAN BUREN

The first settler arrived at this site on the Arkansas River, just downstream from the first Fort Smith, in 1818. The town that grew up here was once called Phillips Landing; in 1836 it was bought for $11,000 by two local entrepreneurs who believed it was in a good location for growth. Van Buren was an important jumping-off place for people heading west during the gold rush and later became a stop on the Butterfield stage line. The extensively restored **Van Buren Historic District** (Main Street) encompasses a number of significant buildings dating from the late nineteenth century. Information about the area is available at the Chamber of Commerce in the Stick-style 1901 **Van Buren Frisco Depot** (Route 59 and Main Street, 501–474–2761).

The **Crawford County Courthouse** (Main and 3d streets) is called the oldest active courthouse west of the Mississippi, though several in Texas, New Mexico, and Arizona may be older. Built in 1841, it burned in 1877 and was rebuilt in the Italian Villa style. On the courthouse lawn is the **Albert Pike Schoolhouse,** where the famed poet, Civil War general, and author taught for three months in 1833 (the log cabin was moved here from its original location about a mile from Van Buren). **Fairview Cemetery** (Fayetteville Road and Poplar Street) contains the graves of Confederate soldiers killed here on December 28, 1862, when Federal cavalry swept into town and drove out General Thomas Hindman's Confederates. The **Mount Olive Methodist Church** (Lafayette and Knox streets) was built in 1889 for one of the oldest black United Methodist congregations west of the Mississippi. The **King Opera House** (Main and 5th streets), of 1891, which once hosted Jenny Lind and William Jennings Bryan, has been restored and is again the scene of musical and dramatic performances. Nearby is the **Crawford County Bank Building** (633 Main Street), an impressively decorated Queen Anne-style building of 1889. It is now an inn.

The **John Drennen House** (221 North 3d Street, private), built in 1836 by one of the founders of Van Buren, looks much as it did just after the Civil War. The **Wilhauf House** (109 North 3d Street, private), built in the late 1830s, is one of the state's few existing examples of an early workingman's house.

FORT SMITH

The original military post of Fort Smith was founded in 1817 by the War Department in an attempt to interpose federal forces between the Osage Indians, who had been there all along, and the Cherokee, forced to emigrate to the area from their eastern homelands. The site chosen for the post was Belle Point, at the confluence of the Arkansas and Poteau rivers. The first fort was occupied for only seven years before the army moved west with the expanding frontier.

But in 1838, in response to settlers' fears about continuing violence, the army began a second fort near the ruins of the first. Never used for its intended purpose, the new fort was converted into a supply depot in 1845. It was occupied by Confederate and, later, Union troops during the Civil War. By 1871 it was no longer needed by the military and so was handed over to the Federal Court for the Western District of Arkansas. In addition to jurisdiction over western Arkansas, this court was also charged with overseeing the adjacent Indian Territory, an area notorious for its lawlessness and violence. The judge who presided over the court from 1875 to 1896 was Isaac C. Parker, an incorruptible man who dedicated himself to restoring order to the territory. Parker believed strongly in Indian rights, and he was tireless in upholding the law. Seventy-nine executions during his term brought him the inevitable nickname of "Hanging Judge" Parker, but his reputation should be considered in light of the fact that, during the same time period, sixty-five of his deputy marshals were murdered. Parker once said, "People have said that I am a cruel, heartless, and bloodthirsty man, but . . . I have ever had the single aim of justice in view. . . . Do equal and exact justice has been my motto." Parker even had some surprisingly modern ideas about criminal justice. "The whole system of punishment is based on the idea of reform or it is worse than nothing," he wrote. "Moreover, if there is no reform in it, it becomes criminal."

The town that grew up around the second fort once was well known as a tough and dangerous frontier outpost. Civilizing forces were given a boost by the discovery of natural gas and coal deposits in the area. The city of Fort Smith became a major manufacturing center, and its population grew from 11,000 in 1900 to 30,000 just a decade later.

Fort Smith National Historic Site

The foundation of the original Fort Smith and the storehouse and barracks of the second are part of the Fort Smith National Historic Site, administered by the National Park Service. The two forts are located on the bank of the Arkansas River just west of the downtown area of present-day Fort Smith, Arkansas's second-largest city. One room of the barracks that was converted to Judge Parker's courtroom has been authentically restored. Underneath the courtroom is a basement that served as a jail known as "Hell on the Border" for its primitive conditions. South of the barracks is a reconstruction of the 1886 gallows on which the court's sentences were carried out; as many as six condemned criminals could be hanged at one time—and were. The nearby commissary-storehouse served as a residence for court officials and as Parker's chambers. An audio-visual program on Fort Smith's early days is shown in the barracks building, and there are displays of historic documents and artifacts.

LOCATION: Rogers Avenue and 3d Street. HOURS: 9–5 Daily. FEE: Yes. TELEPHONE: 501–783–3961.

Just east of the Fort Smith Historic Site is the **Old Fort Museum** (320 Rogers Avenue, 501–783–7841), housed in the four-story Atkinson-Williams Warehouse of 1906. The museum collection encompasses 25,000 items including Indian artifacts, Isaac Parker's cracked leather judge's chair, an American LaFrance steam fire engine, a 1920s pharmacy with operating soda fountain, and memorabilia of the Fort Smith native William O. Darby, the World War II general who founded the unit known as "Darby's Rangers." Also on display is a huge bell of 1888 that had to be removed from the local courthouse because its weight was damaging the building.

Fort Smith's **Belle Grove Historic District,** a residential area northeast of the downtown commercial area, has a large number of historically significant buildings. One of the best of them is the **Bonneville House** (318 North 7th Street), built in 1864 and sold in 1887 to the widow of General Benjamin Bonneville, the great explorer of the Rocky Mountains and the Columbia River basin. The Baroque structure has cast-iron lintels and windowsills and elaborate brackets supporting its wide eaves. The **Rogers-Tilles House and Patent Model Museum** (400 North 8th Street, 501–782–9014), built in the mid-nineteenth century, is believed to have been the home of John Rogers, a Fort Smith pioneer. One of the oldest houses in the Belle Grove, it was constructed in the traditional vernacular style sometimes called—even so late as this—"Federal." The **J. K. Barnes House** (515 North 6th Street, private), of about 1893, is in the Richardsonian Romanesque style, with curved brick detail and "butter-thin" mortar. The **John Vaughn House** (423 North 6th Street), built about 1879 in the Second Empire style, is occupied by the Fort Smith Art Center.

Just east of the Belle Grove district, the **Joseph Knoble Brewery** (North 3d and E streets), dating from around 1850, is a reminder of a time when a substantial number of Germans settled in Fort Smith. Knoble, a native of Wittenberg, built this three-story brick structure around a beer cellar with a six-foot-thick arched stone ceiling. The **Sparks House** (201 North 14th Street, 501–785–2292), of ca. 1887, has been beautifully restored and is used as a restaurant; the interior woodwork, oak fireplaces, and chandeliers are original.

Located in the heart of the Belle Grove Historic District, the fully restored **William H. H. Clayton House** (514 North 6th Street, 501–783–3000) is the headquarters for the Fort Smith Heritage Foundation. The three-story Italianate structure was built in 1882 as the home of William H. H. Clayton, U.S. attorney for Judge Isaac C. Parker in the late nineteenth century. The downstairs sitting room has an antique rectangular piano and a restoration of the original painted ceiling. One upstairs bedroom features a handsome half-canopied walnut tester bed; another has a brass bed with an unusual curved footboard.

FAYETTEVILLE

Fayetteville, settled in 1828, was so named because several of the early settlers were from Fayetteville, Tennessee. Fayetteville suffered greatly in the Civil War—as did much of northwest Arkansas—as battle lines swept back and forth over the region. It was a Federal headquarters and supply depot and was the target of destructive Confederate raids. One of the most important battles in the state took place nearby at Prairie Grove. In 1871 Fayetteville was selected as the site of what eventually became the **University of Arkansas** (501–575–2000). The university's most historic building, **Old Main,** was completed in 1875. Copied from a building at the University of Illinois in Urbana-Champaign, the Second Empire–style structure with two five-story towers was built almost entirely of local materials.

The **Ridge House** (Locust and Center streets, private) is Fayetteville's oldest building. The original dogtrot cabin of the 1840s was remodeled into its current saltbox form in the 1880s; the first cabin's logs are encased within the present clapboard walls. Across the street is the **Walker-Stone House** (207 West Center Street, private), built in the 1840s by David Walker, a state senator and chief justice of the Arkansas Supreme Court. It was sold in the 1850s to

OPPOSITE: *The 1879 John Vaughn House, now the Fort Smith Art Center, in Fort Smith's Belle Grove Historic District.*

Stephen K. Stone, whose grandson, the distinguished architect Edward Durell Stone, once owned the house. The **Gregg House** (Lafayette Street and Gregg Avenue, private) was built in 1871 by Lafayette Gregg, a prominent lawyer who wrote the bill that made Fayetteville the home of the University of Arkansas; its actual construction was by W. Z. Mayes, who also built Old Main. The centerpiece of Fayetteville's downtown square is the **Old Post Office** (Center and Block streets), a two-story Classic Revival building of 1911 that has been impressively restored as a restaurant and club. The **Washington County Courthouse** (1904) and nearby **Old Washington County Jail** (College Avenue and Center Street) of 1897 are among Fayetteville's most interesting buildings. The courthouse has octagonal corner towers and a central clock tower that commands the view east on Center Street. The old jail's crenelated corner towers are of a lighter-colored stone than the rest of the structure, giving it the look of a European castle.

Headquarters House flies both the stars and stripes and the Confederate flag, as it was occupied by both Confederate and Union forces during the Civil War.

Headquarters House

One of Fayetteville's most historic buildings is known as "Headquarters House." It was occupied alternately by both Confederate and Union forces during the Civil War, and during a Confederate raid on April 18, 1863, it was at the center of the fighting. Two doors in the house show bullet holes from this battle. The Greek Revival house was built in 1853 by Jonas Tebbets, an outspoken Unionist, like many in the area. Tebbets was imprisoned at Fort Smith by the Confederates and later fled north with his family, never to return to Arkansas. Now operated by the Washington County Historical Society, Headquarters House contains Civil War relics and items from the early nineteenth century.

LOCATION: 118 East Dickson Street. HOURS: May through September: 1–4 Tuesday–Friday. FEE: None. TELEPHONE: 501–521–2970.

SPRINGDALE

The original settlement at this site was called Shiloh, taking its name from a Baptist church built around 1840. The town was destroyed in the Civil War; rebuilt after fighting ended, it was renamed Springdale in 1872. The **Shiloh Church** (Huntsville and Main streets), an excellent, late example (1870) of Greek Revival architecture, is the city's oldest surviving building.

Shiloh Museum

The Shiloh Museum is in the top rank of Arkansas's museums. Dedicated to preserving the history of northwest Arkansas, its six buildings occupy an entire block near downtown Springdale. The museum was started in 1965 with the acquisition of the Guy Howard Collection of more than 10,000 Indian artifacts from North and Middle America. Much attention is devoted to agriculture; the fruit and poultry industries to a great degree shaped the development of this part of the state. The extensive Vaughn-Applegate Photography Exhibit includes cameras from the mid-nineteenth century. In addition, several buildings have been moved to the site for display, including a general store of the 1870s that is Springdale's oldest commercial building, a contemporary doctor's office, a log cabin of

*Several generations of the Amos Howard family who settled near Springdale in the
1880s, photographed during a summer celebration. The photograph is part of the
Shiloh Museum collection.*

1853 that once served as a stage stop in nearby Elm Springs, and an
outhouse built in 1931, reported to be in "very good condition."

> LOCATION: 118 West Johnson Street. HOURS: 9–5 Monday–Friday.
> FEE: None. TELEPHONE: 501–751–8411.

PRAIRIE GROVE BATTLEFIELD STATE PARK

In early December 1862, Confederate major general Thomas C.
Hindman made plans to try to drive Federal forces out of northwest
Arkansas. Hindman hoped to surprise a Union division led by
Brigadier General James G. Blunt before reinforcements led from
Missouri by Brigadier General Francis J. Herron could come to
Blunt's aid. When Herron's hard-marching troops arrived on the
scene earlier than expected, Hindman changed his plans and turned
to face Herron's troops at Prairie Grove, on the Fayetteville–Cane
Hill road near the Illinois River. The battle began on the morning of
December 7; Blunt's division joined the battle about 3 P.M., bringing
the total number of troops involved to over 20,000. By sunset the
two armies had sustained combined casualties of 2,500, and neither

side had gained a significant advantage. A shortage of ammunition forced Hindman to withdraw to the south, leaving the Federals in command of the region.

Prairie Grove Battlefield State Park encompasses part of the battleground, including **Borden House,** whose grounds and orchard were the scene of the battle's heaviest fighting. Although the original house was burned the day after the battle, the present version is believed to be an accurate replica, built in 1872. **Morrow House,** moved to the park from its original location nearby, served as Hindman's headquarters the night before the battle. The visitor center offers a diorama of the battle and military artifacts, as well as an oral presentation on the fighting man's daily life during the Civil War. A driving tour leads to significant sites outside the park.

LOCATION: Route 62, 10 miles west of Fayetteville. HOURS: *Battlefield:* 8 AM–10 PM Daily. *Visitor Center:* 8–5 Daily. FEE: None. TELEPHONE: 501–846–2990.

The Morrow House, an 1860s dogtrot cabin moved to Prairie Grove Battlefield State Park, contains rustic furnishings of the period.

SILOAM SPRINGS

A settlement was founded here in the mid-1830s by a German immigrant, Simon Sager. In the late 1870s, a new resort town sprang up nearby around several springs said to have medicinal qualities; it took the biblical name of Siloam Springs and was incorporated in 1881. Exhibits at the **Siloam Springs Museum** (112 North Maxwell Street, 501–524–4011) focus on local history in the years 1880–1920 but also include furniture made by Simon Sager and his brother Christian between 1839 and 1863. The **Crown Hotel** (119 West University Street), originally called the Lakeside, was the city's first brick building; it has been in continuous operation since it opened in 1881. The **Sager Cabin** (John Brown University campus, West University Street) was built around 1835 as the Simon Sager family's first home. The hand-hewn log building is Siloam Springs's oldest structure.

ROGERS

Rogers was incorporated in 1881, just a few months after the first train passed through the area on the newly laid tracks of the Saint Louis & San Francisco Railroad. Parts of its downtown area, including some of its brick streets, have been preserved and restored. The **Applegate Drugstore Building** (116 South 1st Street), built in 1905, the **Bank of Rogers Building** (114 South 1st Street), built in 1906, and the **Mutual Aid Union Building** (224 South 2d Street), built in 1914, are among the most significant. All were designed by A. O. Clark, a Saint Louis architect who came to Rogers to work on Monte Ne, a resort that now lies beneath Beaver Lake, a reservoir formed when the White River was dammed in the early 1960s. The **Rogers Historical Museum** (322 South 2d Street, 501–636–0162) is partially housed in the brick Hawkins House of 1895, which is furnished with Victorian-era furniture and household items. The museum's new Key Wing contains exhibits on local history, a re-creation of three turn-of-the-century Rogers businesses, and a discovery room for children.

PEA RIDGE NATIONAL MILITARY PARK

One of the most important Civil War battles west of the Mississippi River was fought on March 7 and 8, 1862, near Elkhorn Tavern. Confederate major general Earl Van Dorn planned to march from

Arkansas into southern Missouri and retake Saint Louis. When his 16,000-man army approached a strongly entrenched Federal force of 10,000 under Brigadier General Samuel Curtis south of Pea Ridge, Van Dorn abandoned his supply train and slipped behind Curtis's position. Federal scouts (among them, "Wild Bill" Hickok) observed the maneuver. Alerted, Curtis turned his back on his fortifications and prepared to meet Van Dorn's two-pronged attack. On the first day of battle, the Federals held their ground on their left flank southeast of Pea Ridge and gave ground slowly in bitter fighting on their right around Elkhorn Tavern. Exhausted, and low on food and ammunition, the Confederates broke and ran the next day under Curtis's determined counterattack, led by German-American units under General Franz Sigel. The battle is commemorated at Pea Ridge by markers indicating significant battle sites. Elkhorn Tavern, which was at the center of the fighting, burned down shortly

Pea Ridge National Military Park preserves the battlefield where, in March 1862, Union forces turned back a Confederate army on its way to invade Missouri.

after the battle, and the present structure was built soon afterward. At the visitor center are exhibits of Civil War weapons and uniforms and displays recounting the events leading up to the battle.

LOCATION: Route 62, 2 miles west of Garfield. HOURS: 8–5 Daily. FEE: Yes. TELEPHONE: 501–451–8122.

EUREKA SPRINGS

Of all Arkansas's cities, Eureka Springs may have grown the fastest in its early days—testimony to the popularity of spa resorts and the belief in the healing powers of spring water in the late nineteenth century. The first to tout the water of this rugged Ozarks region was Alvah Jackson, a doctor who promoted the water from "Indian Healing Spring" as "Dr. Jackson's Magic Eye Water" in the late 1850s. As word of this miracle elixir spread, people began to settle around the site of the original spring and others found nearby. In

Eureka Springs' Rosalie House, named for a house in Natchez, Mississippi, was built for Mr. and Mrs. J. W. Hill in 1883. Hill, who started with a single horse and buggy, prospered in the transportation business in the fast-growing resort town.

1879, 400 people were living in what had by then come to be called Eureka Springs. (According to tradition, someone who drank the water shouted out the Greek word meaning "I have found it.") The town was incorporated in 1880, and by the next year, dozens of boardinghouses dotted the steep hillsides. The original "Indian Healing Spring," now called **Basin Spring,** is located downtown in Basin Park, part of the **Eureka Springs Historic District,** which encompasses the city's downtown area and much of its residential district.

The railroad arrived in 1883—thanks in large part to the influence of ex-governor Powell Clayton, who had moved to the new resort town—and growth began in earnest. This was the beginning of the era of Eureka Springs's great hotels; more than fifty were built in the next thirty years, including the **Crescent Hotel** (75 Prospect Street), commandingly situated at the top of one of the city's hills. This five-story "castle in the wilderness," built of locally

The parlor of the Castle at Inspiration Point, a house that is stone inside and out, contains early twentieth-century furniture. Other collections in the house include 1920s radios, household appliances, farm implements, and early medical implements.

quarried limestone in 1886, was Eureka's first stone structure. The **New Orleans Hotel** (63 Spring Street), originally called the Wadsworth when it was built about 1900, has fanciful iron grillwork on its balconies. The **Basin Park Hotel** (12 Spring Street), of 1905, is a seven-story structure located next to Basin Park. The **Palace Hotel and Bathhouse** (135 Spring Street) was built in 1901 to offer bathers water from two local springs.

The home built in 1881 by the former governor Powell Clayton is now the **Crescent Cottage Inn** (211 Spring Street). The **Bank of Eureka Springs** (70 South Main) has restored its interior to showcase its oak furniture, brass tellers' cages, antique business machines, and a beautiful potbellied stove. The famed temperance crusader Carry Nation lived in Eureka Springs for three years beginning in 1908. Her home, **Hatchet Hall** (35 Steele Street, 501–253–7324) has remembrances of her saloon-destroying battles against alcohol. Nation suffered a stroke while giving a speech at Basin Park in 1911 and died soon afterward.

One of Eureka Springs's most striking buildings is the **Rosalie House** (282 Spring Street, 501–253–7377), a frothy Queen Anne blend built in 1883, with an abundance of spindles, balls, and semicircles. Its interior features plaster frescoes and gold-leaf decorations. The **Eureka Springs Historical Museum** (95 South Main Street, 501–253–9417) is located in the Califf House, originally built in 1889 as a combination residence and general store. The museum concentrates on local history; among its exhibits are a doll collection, period clothing, and historic photographs.

The **Castle and Museum at Inspiration Point** (Route 62, five miles west of Eureka Springs, 501–253–9462) is an unusual rock structure in a spectacular mountaintop setting. Once a residence, it now houses items of everyday life from the early twentieth century, including antique cars, medical equipment, farm vehicles, and furniture. **Quigley's Castle** (Route 23, four miles south of Eureka Springs, 501–253–8311) calls itself "the Ozarks' strangest dwelling." Hand-built in the 1940s by a local family, its walls are covered with rocks, fossils, marbles, and anything else that caught the builders' eyes. Trees, shrubs, and other plants grow inside the house in bare soil around the edge of the ground floor.

BERRYVILLE

This quiet Ozarks town was for more than thirty years the home of Colonel C. Burton Saunders, a wealthy businessman who was an obsessive collector of firearms. Today the **Saunders Memorial Museum** (115 East Madison Street, 501–423–2563) houses what may be the largest private gun collection in the country. There are guns here that belonged to Pancho Villa, Jesse James, Billy the Kid, Wild Bill Hickok, Annie Oakley, Sam Houston, and many others. Some date back to the earliest days of firearms; there are European dueling pistols, modern automatics, and a complete line of Colt pistols. In addition, the eclectic museum exhibits furniture, Oriental rugs, silver and china, Tiffany lamps, Egyptian wall panels, Indian blankets, and clothing. Berryville's **Heritage Center** (Town Square, off Route 62, 501–423–6312) is housed in the former **Carroll County Courthouse,** built in 1880. Exhibits of local history include a pioneer one-room school, a barbershop, an early-day funeral parlor with handmade coffins, and a moonshine still. Nearby **Pioneer Park** displays a 150-year-old log cabin, a cell from the Carroll County Jail (1905), and an early twentieth-century newspaper office.

BUFFALO RIVER VALLEY

This peaceful valley is now part of the **Buffalo National River** (headquarters in Harrison, 501–741–5443), although private citizens continue to live and farm here under a cooperative arrangement with the National Park Service. The **Villines Mill** (off Route 43, Boxley) once ground corn and wheat for local residents; the ca. 1870 structure is being restored. Also in Boxley is the picturesque **Walnut Grove Baptist Church and School** (off Route 21), a two-story structure built about 1900. The **Parker-Hickman Farmstead** (six miles west of Route 7, north of Jasper), one of the oldest farms along the Buffalo River, chronicles 150 years of Ozark pioneer settlement. The farm, a Historic District, has as its focal point a hand-hewn red-cedar log residence. The corner joinings, curved cornice pieces, and tongue-and-groove flooring attest to a builder with skill and pride in his dwelling.

The discovery of zinc in the Rush Creek valley in the 1880s caused the boomtown of **Rush** to spring up near the mouth of this tributary of the Buffalo River. The town reached its zenith during

World War I, when several thousand people lived in the valley, but it was eventually abandoned when the zinc industry declined. Today a ghost town, Rush is preserved by the National Park Service as part of the Buffalo National River. Several buildings, dating from the late nineteenth century to the 1940s, are still standing, including the general store, a few houses, and an early zinc smelter.

The town of **Norfork** was founded by Jacob Wolf, who in the early 1820s established a trading post where the North Fork River flows into the White River. The **Wolf House** (Route 5, 501–499–5632) was built between 1821 and 1825 and is possibly the state's oldest log cabin. Wolf was a member of Arkansas's territorial legislature, and his "saddlebag" dogtrot house (two stories, with a breezeway through the ground floor) served as Izard County's first courthouse in 1825. One room was the office of County Clerk John Houston, brother of the Texas patriot Sam Houston. The house, which has two stone chimneys and four fireplaces, is in excellent condition today. Among its exhibits are a pre–Civil War kitchen, a re-creation of the original courtroom, early medical tools, and a desk made in 1865 by George Wolf, Jacob's son.

MOUNTAIN VIEW

This picturesque and relatively unspoiled Ozark mountain town has several historic buildings in its downtown area. On Washington Street are the **Commercial Hotel** (1925) and the **Inn at Mountain View,** called the Dew Drop Inn when it was founded in the late nineteenth century. The **Old Mill** (Main Street, 501–269–4514), built in 1915, has been restored and operates seasonally as a working gristmill. Yet it is music, most of all, that made Mountain View famous. The original gathering place for folk musicians was the **Courthouse Square** (Main Street), where people met informally to play traditional songs and, as a happy consequence, keep alive Ozark mountain music that might otherwise have been lost. The courthouse concerts continue today, supplemented by activities at the nearby **Ozark Folk Center** (off Route 9, 501–269–3851), a part of the Arkansas state parks system. Here local residents play folk music and demonstrate woodcarving, blacksmithing, weaving, doll making, pottery, and many other crafts. There is a 1,000-seat auditorium for concerts and folk dancing, and twenty-four small buildings house practitioners of mountain crafts and pioneer skills.

BATESVILLE

Although Batesville's claim to being the second-oldest city in Arkansas is open to debate, there is little doubt that, early on, it was one of the state's most important centers of trade. Located at the confluence of the White River and Poke Bayou, the town was a port of call for steamboats beginning in 1831. In the years before the Civil War, Batesville achieved a high degree of sophistication, thanks to immigrants from Virginia and Maryland who had been socially prominent in the East. The **Lower Main Street Historic District,** centered on the intersection of Main and Central streets, includes several attractive buildings, many of them made of local stone. The **Case Building** (101 East Main Street) was built about 1870 with pressed-tin window trim and decorative brickwork. **Adler Hall** (151 West Main Street) was built around 1880 with brick and cast-iron facade; it was once home to a bank and an opera house. Batesville was a center of marble quarrying in the nineteenth century, and both the **Pioneer Cemetery** (3d and Center streets), of the 1830s, and the **Oaklawn Cemetery** (Sidney and Grays street), of the 1880s, exhibit fine examples of stonework. **Morrow Hall** (7th and College streets) was the first home of Batesville's Arkansas College, the oldest private college in Arkansas still operating under its original charter. Built in 1873, the two-story Italianate brick building is now part of the First Presbyterian Church.

Among Batesville's most interesting residential buildings (all private) are the **Wycough House** (683 Water Street), built in 1878 by a longtime county sheriff, with authentic Victorian colors and stained-glass windows, and the **Cook-Morrow House** (875 East Main Street), of 1909, which uses local marble trim for decorative touches in the brickwork. The **Garrott House** (561 East Main Street), built in 1842 and remodeled in 1880, has picturesque Gothic Revival trim. The **Glenn House** (623 Water Street) was originally built in 1859 as part of the Soulesbury Institute, an early Methodist school. When the school fell on hard times during the Reconstruction era, the building was converted into a residence; it is still owned by members of the family that bought it in 1873.

Spring Mill (eight miles northwest of Batesville on Route 69) dates from around 1869, making it one of the oldest original gristmills in the Ozarks. It uses a turbine to drive the grinding stone instead of the typical large waterwheel, and it is still in operating condition.

Notes on Architecture

SPANISH COLONIAL

SAN JOSE MISSION, TX

Spanish mission churches in the southwest were provincial adaptations of Baroque forms transformed further by local materials and labor. The most simple structures feature massive masonry walls, bell towers, tile roofs, and dependent buildings placed around arcaded courtyards. Elaborate mission churches more closely resemble their European and Mexican models, with vaulting, domes, and ornate doorways ornamented in the Churrigueresque style.

GREEK REVIVAL

OLD STATE HOUSE, AR

The Greek Revival manifested itself in severe, stripped, rectilinear proportions, occasionally a set of columns or pilasters, and even in a few instances Greek-temple form. It combined Greek and Roman forms—low pitched pediments, simple moldings, rounded arches, and shallow domes, and was used in public buildings and many private houses.

GOTHIC REVIVAL

The Gothic Revival brought darker colors, asymmetry, broken skylines, verticality, and the pointed arch to American buildings. New machinery produced carved and pierced trim along the eaves. Roofs became steep and gabled; "porches" or "piazzas" became more spacious. Oriel and bay windows became common and there was a greater use of stained glass.

ITALIANATE

The Italianate style began to appear in the 1840s, both in a formal, balanced "palazzo" style and in a picturesque "villa" style. Both versions of the style had round-headed windows and arcaded porches. Commercial structures were frequently made of cast iron, with a ground floor of large arcaded windows and smaller windows on each successive rising story.

SECOND EMPIRE

STEVE'S HOMESTEAD, TX

After 1860, Parisian fashion inspired American builders to use mansard roofs, dark colors, and varied textures, including shingles, tiles, and, increasingly, ironwork, especially on balconies and skylines. With their ornamental quoins, balustrades, pediments, pavilions, columns, and pilasters, Second Empire buildings recalled many historical styles.

QUEEN ANNE

ROSALIE HOUSE, AR

The Queen Anne style emphasized contrasts of form, texture, and color. Large encircling verandahs, tall chimneys, turrets, towers, and a multitude of textures are typical of the style. The ground floor might be of stone or brick, the upper floors of stucco, shingle, or clapboard. Specially shaped bricks and plaques were used for decoration. Panels of stained glass outlined or filled the windows. The steep roofs were gabled or hipped, and other elements, such as pediments, Venetian windows, and front and corner bay windows, were frequently used.

RICHARDSONIAN ROMANESQUE

SHAWNEE DEPOT, OK

Richardsonian Romanesque made use of the massive forms and ornamental details of the Romanesque: rounded arches, towers, stone and brick facing. The solidity and gravity of masses were accentuated by deep recesses for windows and entrances, by rough stone masonry, stubby columns, strong horizontals, rounded towers with conical caps, and repetitive ornament based on botanical models.

RENAISSANCE REVIVAL OR BEAUX ARTS

U.S. POST OFFICE AND CUSTOMS HOUSE, TX

In the 1880s and 1890s, American architects who had studied at the Ecole des Beaux Arts in Paris brought a new Renaissance Revival to the United States. Sometimes used in urban mansions, but generally reserved for public and academic buildings, it borrowed from three centuries of Renaissance detail—much of it French—and put together picturesque combinations from widely differing periods. The Beaux Arts style gave rise to the "City Beautiful" movement, whose most complete expression was found in the late nineteenth- and early-twentieth century world's fairs in Chicago and San Francisco.

ART DECO

DALLAS HALL OF STATE, TX

The late 1920s was the development of a new architectural style, Art Deco, influenced by the Paris Exposition des Arts Decoratifs of 1925. It is marked by linear, hard edged, or angular composition, frequently achieved by the use of set-backs in the building facade. These buildings were ornamented with stylized decoration executed in the same material as the building itself or in various metals, colored glass bricks, or mosaic tiles. A popular style, it was relatively inexpensive to build.

INDEX

Numbers in *italic* indicate illustrations; numbers in **boldface** indicate maps.

Ace of Clubs House, 457-58
Adobe Walls, TX, 329-30
Age of Steam Museum, 221
Alabama-Coushatta Indian Reservation, 265
Alamo, the, *31*, 33, 34-38, *34*, *35*
Alamo Heights, San Antonio, TX, 55-56
Albany, TX, 240
Alibates Flint Quarries National Monument, 328
Allen Chapel African Methodist Episcopal Church, 225
Alley, Abram and Nancy, Log Cabin, 160
Alpine, TX, 302
Altus, OK, 400
Alva, OK, 424
Amarillo, TX, 326-27, *327*
Americana Museum, 281
Ammansville, TX, 164
Anadarko, OK, 405-06, *408*
Anadarko Philomathic Museum, 406, *408*
Anderson, TX, 164-65
Anderson Baptist Church, 164
Anderson Historic District, 164
Annunciation Church, 98
Antioch Missionary Baptist Church, 98
Apache Indians, 21, 30, 40, 50, 51, 128, 180, 272, 273, 276, 277, 288, 295, 308, 326, 386, 401, 405
Aransas National Wildlife Refuge, 73
Arapaho Indians, 326, 329, 339, 378, 379, 385, 397, 398, 424, 425
Ardmore, OK, 405
Arkansas, **8-9**, 426-83, **430-31**
Arkansas City, AR, 443
Arkansas Museum of Science and History, 440-41
Arkansas Post County Museum, *444*, 445, *445*
Arkansas Post National Memorial, 443-45
Arkansas Railroad Museum, 447
Arkansas State University Museum, 453
Arkansas Territorial Restoration, 441, *442*
Armstrong-Browning Library, 181, *182*

Arneson River Theater, *39*
Ashton Villa, 112
Ataloa Lodge Museum, 372
Atkins-Lemmon House, 254
Austin, Stephen F., 12, 24, 25, 53, 106, 107, 111, *129*, 134, 137, 148, 154, 160, 163, 206; State Historical Park, 163; State University, 263-64, *263*
Austin, TX, 136-37, 139-42, *142*, *143*, 144, *145*, 146-49, *148*, *150*, 151-55, *155*, *156*, 157; Governor's mansion, 141, *142*, *143*; Texas State Capitol, *126*, *138*, 139-40
Ayres, Atlee B., 46, 55, 56, 58, 84, 197

Bachman, Jourdan, Pioneer Farm, 157
Bandera, TX, 198
Bank of the Chickasaw Nation Museum, 375
Barker, Eugene C., Texas History Center, 152
Bartlesville, OK, 344-45
Bastrop, TX, 158
Batesville, AR, 483
Batfish, 372
Bayou Bend, 99, *100*
Bean, Judge Roy, Visitor Center, 311-12
Beard House, 254
Beaumont, TX, 119-20, 122, *122*, *123*, 124
Beavers Bend State Park, *338*, 373-74
Bell County Museum, 175
Belle Grove Historic District, 469, *471*
Bellville, TX, 163
Belton, TX, 175
Belvin Street Historic District, 203
Berryville, AR, 481
Bethlehem Lutheran Church, 168
Bexar County Courthouse, 41, *48*
Big Bend National Park, 302, *303*, 304-05, *305*, *306*, 307
Big Spring, TX, 319-20
Big Thicket National Preserve, 268
Big Tree, 73
Bishop's Palace, *18*, 112-13
Black, E. B., Historical House, 325
Black Kettle Museum, 399
Blackwell, OK, 419
Blue Bonnet Farm, 254
Boerr e, TX, 197-98
Boley, OK, 363

Bonham, TX, 246-48
Bonner-Whitaker-McClendon House, 256
Border Patrol Museum, 287
Borger, TX, 328
Bosque County Courthouse, 237
Bosque Memorial Museum, 237
Boston Avenue United Methodist Church, 357
Bourbonnais log house, 361, *361*
Boyd House, 409
Brackenridge Park, 57
Bremond, John, Jr., House, 144, *145*
Brenham, TX, 166
Brewster County Courthouse, 302
Britton-Evans (Centennial) House, 77
Broken Bow, OK, 373
Brownhouse, 254
Brownsville, TX, 82-84, *83*
Brownsville Art League Museum, 82
Buck, A. D., Museum of Science and History, 417
Buffalo Gap Historic Village, 314-15
Buffalo National River, 481
Buffalo River Valley, AR, 481-82
Burlington-Rock Island Railroad Museum, 185
Burnet, TX, 186
Burr, Aaron, 10-11, 14-15, 17, 158

Cabeza de Vaca, Alvar Nuñez, 20, 108, 128, 278, 308
Cache, OK, 400-01
Caddo Indian Museum, 256
Caddo Indians, 183, 206, 261, 334, 339, 373, 374, 386, 428
Caddoan Mounds State Historic Site, *260*, 261
Cadron Settlement Park, 463
Camden, AR, 454-56, *455*
Cameron, TX, 176-77
Cameron County Courthouse, 84
Camp Verde, TX, 197
Canadian County Historical Museum, 397
Canyon, TX, 325
Capitol-Lincoln Terrace Historic District, 393
Captain's Castle, 254
Carnegie Library and Oklahoma Territorial Museum, 414

Carrington-Covert House, 141
Carroll County Courthouse, 481
Carson County Square House Museum, 328
Carter, Amon, Museum, 228
Carter County Historic Museum and Genealogy Library, 405
Carver, George Washington, Museum, 148
Castle and Museum at Inspiration Point, *479*, 480
Castolon Historic District, 305
Castroville, TX, 58-59
Caswell, Daniel, H., House, 141
Caswell, William T., House, 141
Cat Spring, TX, 163
Catedral Santuario de Guadalupe (Cathedral of the Sacred Heart), 217
Cattleman's Museum, 226
Caverns of Sonora, 311
Cayuga, OK, 343
Center for Transportation and Commerce, 118-19
Center Theater, 408-09
Central Texas Area Museum, 174
Cestohowa, TX, 65
Chamizal National Memorial, 283
Chandler, OK, 360
Chapel of Miracles, 58
Chapel of Our Lady of the Visitation, 85
Cherokee Courthouse, 372
Cherokee Female Seminary, 365
Cherokee Heritage Center (Tsa-La-Gi), *365*, 366
Cherokee Indians, 183, 339, 340, *341*, 353, 364, 365, 366, 367, 370, 372, 375, 378, 467
Cherokee National Capitol, 364
Cherokee National Museum, 366
Cherokee National Prison, 364
Cherokee Strip Museum, Alva, OK, 424
Cherokee Strip Museum, Perry, OK, 416
Cheyenne, OK, 399
Cheyenne Indians, 326, 329, 330, 339, 378, 379, 385, 397, 398, 424, 425
Chickasaw Council House Museum, 375

Chickasaw Indians, 183, 339, 340, 370, 375, 378
Chief's House, Swink, OK, 374
Chisholm, Jesse: grave of, 398
Chisholm Trail Historical Museum, Waurika, OK, 403
Chisholm Trail Museum, Kingfisher, OK, 420-21
Choctaw Council House Historical Museum, 373
Choctaw Indians, 334, 339, 340, 341, 370, 373, 374, 375, 378
Chouteau Memorial, 343
Christ Church Cathedral, 98
Church of the Guardian Angel, 164
Cimarron Valley Railroad Museum, 415
Civil War: AR, 432-33, 441, 444, 450-51, 454, 455-56, 458, 467, 468, 470, 473, 474-75, 476-78; OK, 340, 369, 374-75; TX, 29, 72, 77, 82, 84, 86, 109, 125, 137, 153, 212, 288, 297
Claremore, OK, 351-52
Clarksville Historic District, 153-54
Clayton, Nicholas J., 72, 98, 109, 111, 112, 113, 116, 117, 118, 119, 142, 157, 162, 281
Clayton, William H. H., House, 470
Cleburne, TX, 238
Cleo Springs, OK, 424
Clifton, TX, 237
Cloud-Stark House, 244
Colorado County Courthouse, 162
Columbus, TX, 160, *161*, 162
Comal County Courthouse, 202
Comanche Indians, 16, 21, 26, 30, 32, 50, 51, 67, 86, 128, 136, 137, 180, 183, 184, 189, 194, 229, 239-40, 242, 261, 272, 276, 277, 295, 297, 304, 308, 309, 314, 319, 323, 326, 339, 378, 379, 382, 386, 397, 400, 401, 403, 405, 417
Confederate Air Force Museum, 85
Confederate Cemetery, 451
Confederate Memorial Hall Museum, Columbus, TX, 162
Confederate Museum, "Old South Plantation," TX, 107
Conner, John E., Museum, 81
Conser, Peter, House, 373

Conservation Plaza, 201
Conway, AR, 463
Cook, Abner, 139, 141, 144, 149, 153
Coppini, Pompeo, 38, 63, 127, 140, 148, 151
Coronado, Francisco Vásquez de, 273, 325, 328, 334
Corpus Christi, TX, 76-77, *78*, 79, 79
Corpus Christi Museum, 79
Corsicana, TX, 235-36
Cós, Martín Perfecto de, 25, 32, 33, 35, 41, 69, 105
Cost, TX, 63
Council Tree, 352
Cowboy Artists of America Museum, 197
Crawford County Courthouse, 467
Creek Council House Museum, 364
Creek Indians, 339, 340, 352, 353, 363-64, 369, 370, 375, 378, 390
Crockett County Courthouse, 311
Crockett County Museum, 311
Crockett, Davy, *31*, 36, 258; Memorial Park, 258
Crockett, TX, 258-59
Crosby County Pioneer Memorial Museum, 322
Crosbyton, TX, 323
Cuero, TX, 64
Culberson County Historical Museum, 294
Cullen, Ezekial, House, 264-65
Cushing, OK, 415
Custer, George Armstrong, 149, 153, 379, 399, 425

Dalhart, TX, 330
Dallas, TX, 210, 212-13, *214*, 215-21, *217*, *219*
Dallas County Historical Plaza, 216
Dallas Museum of Art, 217-18
Dallas Museum of Natural History, 221
Dallas Theater Center, 217, *217*
Darlington Agency, *397*, 398
Davis, Jefferson, 29, 197, 295, 367
Davis Mountains State Park, 295, 297
De Golyer Estate, 219-20, *219*
De Leon Plaza, 72
Deaf Smith County Museum, 324
Dealey Plaza, 216

Decatur, TX, 243
Decorative Arts Museum, 440
Deep Ellum, 218
Denison, TX, 245
Denton, TX, 244
Denton County Historical
  Museum, 244
Depot Museum, Henderson,
  TX, 257
Depot Museum, Morrilton,
  AR, 463
Depot Square Historic
  District, 242
Desha County Courthouse,
  443
Dewey, OK, 343
Dewey Hotel, 343
DeWitt County Historical
  Museum, 64
Dinosaur Valley State Park,
  238
Downes-Aldrich House, 258
Drew County Historical
  Museum, 446
Driskill Hotel, 146
Drummond Home, 349
Dumas, TX, 330
Duncan, OK, 403

Eagle Park, 400
East End Historic District,
  113, *114, 115,* 116
Eaton Memorial Chapel, 117
Eddleman-McFarland House,
  232
Edwardian Inn, 451
Eisenhower, Dwight D., 245,
  435; Birthplace State
  Historic Site, 245
El Paso, TX, 278-88, *279, 280,
  284, 285, 288,* 290-91, *291,*
  293
El Paso Centennial
  Museum/University
  Museum, 282
El Paso Museum of Art, 287
El Paso Museum of History,
  288
El Reno, OK, 396-97
Elissa, 116-17
Elk City, OK, 399
Ellis County Courthouse, 232,
  233, 234
Ellis County Museum, 234
Enchanted Rock State Park,
  194, *195,* 196
Enid, OK, 420
Erath County Courthouse,
  239
Escandón, Don José de, 21,
  24, 81, 86
Estevan Hall, 451
Eureka Springs, AR, 478-80,
  478, 479
Eureka Springs Historical
  Museum, 480
Excelsior House, *250,* 251,
  253

Fair Park, TX, *204, 211,* 220-
  21
Fairfield, TX, 185
Fairview Cemetery, Van
  Buren, AR, 467
Faison, N. W., Home and
  Museum, 159
Fannin, James Walker, Jr., 36,
  53, 69, 70, 246
Fannin Battleground, 70
Fannin County Museum of
  History, 246
Fanthorp Inn State Historic
  Site, 164-65
Fayette County Courthouse,
  159
Fayette Heritage Museum and
  Archives/Fayette Public
  Library, 159
Fayetteville, AR, 470, 472-73,
  472
Fenster Museum of Jewish
  Art, 357
Ferguson, T. B., Museum, 421
Festival-Institute, 168
First Baptist Church,
  Beaumont, TX, 120
First Christian Church, Fort
  Worth, TX, 224
First Church, Castroville, TX,
  58
First Methodist Church,
  Corsicana, TX, 235
First Methodist Church,
  Fredericksburg, TX, 191
First Methodist Church,
  Marshall, TX, 254-55
First Methodist Church, Paris,
  TX, 248
First Presbyterian Church,
  Galveston, TX, 117
First Protestant Church, New
  Braunfels, TX, 202
First United Methodist
  Church, San Marcos, TX,
  203
Five Civilized Tribes Museum,
  370, *370, 371*
Fordyce Bathhouse, 462, *464-
  65*
Forest Heritage Center, 373-
  74
Fort Bend Museum, 106-07
Fort Bliss, TX, 288, *289,* 290
Fort Bliss Museum, 288, 290
Fort Concho National Historic
  Landmark, 315-16, *316,*
  317
Fort Croghan Museum, 186
Fort D. A. Russell, 301
Fort Davis, TX, 295, 297, *299,*
  300-01
Fort Davis National Historic
  Site, 297, *299, 300-01*
Fort Gibson Military Park,
  367, *367, 368,* 369
Fort Griffin State Historical
  Park, 239-40

Fort Inglish Museum, 247
Fort Lancaster State Historical
  Park, 310-11
Fort Leaton State Historical
  Park, 308-09
Fort McIntosh, TX, 86, 88
Fort McKavett State Historical
  Park, 314
Fort Reno, OK, 397-98
Fort Richardson State
  Historical Park, 242-43
Fort Sam Houston, TX, 56
Fort Smith, AR, 467-70, *471*
Fort Smith National Historic
  Site, 468-69
Fort Stockton, TX, 309-10
Fort Supply, OK, 424-25
Fort Towson, OK, 374-74
Fort Washita, OK, 375
Fort Worth, TX, 221-26, *224,
  226, 227,* 228-29, *230-31,*
  232
Fort Worth Interpretive
  Center, 223
Fort Worth Museum of
  Science and History, 228
Fort Worth Stockyards
  Historical District, 225, *226,*
  227
Forty-fifth Infantry Division
  Museum, 395
Fredericksburg, TX, 188-89,
  190, 191-94, *192*
Freeman Plantation, 253
Freestone County Historical
  Museum, 185
French Legation, 147-48, *148*
French Townhouse, 254
French, John J., Museum, 120
Frontier Times Museum, 198
Fulton, TX, 73, *74,* 75
Fulton Mansion State Historic
  Structure, 73, *74,* 75

Gainesville, TX, 244-45
Galvan House, 79
Galveston, TX, *18,* 108-09,
  110, 111-13, *114, 115,* 116-
  19, *119;* Old Galveston
  Custom House, 117
Galveston Causeway, 109
Galveston County Historical
  Museum, 118
Gardner Mansion, 374
Garner, John Nance,
  Memorial Museum, 59
Gates, John Warne, Memorial
  Library, 125
Geary, OK, 398
George Ranch Headquarters,
  107
Georgetown, TX, 173-74
Gethsemane Church, 141
Gibbs-Powell Home, 266
Giddings, TX, 171-72
Gilcrease, Thomas, 342, 354;
  House, 357

Gilcrease Museum, 354, *355*, 357
Giles, Alfred, 38, 46, 50, 66, 89, 193, 196, 197, 198, 301
Ginocchio National Historic District, 255
Gladys City Boomtown, 120, *122*
Glenwood Cemetery, 98
Goliad, TX, 65-67
Goliad State Historical Park, 66-67
Gonzales, TX, 61, *62*, 63-64
Gonzales County Courthouse, *62*, 63
Gonzales Memorial Museum, 63-64
Gonzales Pioneer Village Living History Center, 60-61, *61*
Goodman Museum, 256
Goose Island State Park, 73
Gordon, James Riely, 41, 47, 63, 72, 144, 159, *172*, 181, 202, 232, 239, 243, 249, 255
Gore, OK, 372
Gould, Jay, Private Railroad Car (Atalanta), 251, *252*, 253
Grace Episcopal Church, 111
Graham-Gaughan-Betts Home, 455, *455*
Granbury, TX, 239
Granbury Opera House, 239
Grand Opera House, 60
Grant County Museum, 420
Grayson County Frontier Museum, 246
Greathouse Home, 463
Gregg County Historical Museum, 256
Grimes County Courthouse, 164
Grove, OK, 343
Grove, The, TX, 176, *176*
Grove Country Life Museum, The, 176, *176*
Gruene, TX, 202
Guadalupe Mountains National Park, 294
Guthrie, OK, 409-14, *409*, *410*, *411*, *413*
Guthrie Historic District, 412
Guthrie Scottish Rite Masonic Temple, 413-14, *413*

Hall of State/Fair Park National Historic Landmark, *204*, *211*, 220
Hampson Museum State Park, 452
Hanging Tree, 66
Har-Ber Village, 343
Harding, Dexter, House, 447
Harlingen, TX, 85
Harn Homestead and 1889er Museum, 394-95, *394*, *395*
Harrington House, 327, *327*

Harrison County Historical Museum, 255
Harrison House, 413
Harwelden Mansion, 358
Hatchet Hall, 480
Hays County Courthouse, 203
Headquarters House, *472*, *473*
Healdton, OK, 403
Healdton Oil Museum, 403
Heard Natural Science Museum and Wildlife Sanctuary, 246
Heavener, OK, 373
Heavener Runestone State Park, 373
Helena, AR, 450-52
Henderson, TX, 257
Henkel Square, 168
Henrietta Memorial Museum, 81
Henry, O., Hall, 144; Home and Museum, 146-47. *See also* Porter, William Sydney
Hereford, TX, 324
Heritage Association of San Marcos, 203
Heritage Center, Berryville, AR, 481
Heritage House Museum, Orange, TX, 124
Heritage Museum, Big Spring, TX, 320
Heritage Park, Corpus Christi, TX, 77
Heritage Village Museum, Woodville, TX, 265
Hermann, George H., 91, 98, 101, 103; Park, 103
Heroes of Texas Independence Monument, 63
Hertzberg Circus Collection, 40
High Hill, TX, 164
Highlands Mansion, 183
Hill Country Museum, 196
Hill County Courthouse, 236
Hill Junior College, 236; Confederate Research Center and Museum, 236; Murphy, Audie, L., Museum and Weaponry Library, 236
Hillsboro, TX, 236
Hinderliter House, 441, *442*
Historic Brownsville Museum, 82-83
Hogg, Ima, 99, 107, 169, 171, 249, 250
Hogg, James Stephen, 107, 177, 249; Governor Hogg Shrine State Historical Park, 249-50; Jim Hogg State Historical Park, 257-58
Hominy, OK, 349
Hood County Courthouse Historic District, 239
Hopkins County Museum and

Heritage Park, 249
Hot Springs, AR, 461-63, *461*, *464-65*
Hot Springs, TX, 307
Hot Springs National Park, 462, *464-65*
House of the Seasons, 253
Houston, Samuel, 10, 16, 17, 25, 33, 36, 64, 70, *90*, 104-05, 111, 135, 136, 137, 159, 163, 165, 166, 174, 181, 183, 207, 253, 257, 265, 266, 367; Historical Park, 92-93, *92*, *94-95*; Memorial Museum, 266-67, *267*, *269*; Oak, 64
Houston, TX, 89, 91-93, *92*, *94-95*, 96-99, *96*, *100*, 101, *102*, 103-04; U.S. Post Office and Customs House, 97
Houston County Visitors Center Museum, 259
Houston Museum of Natural Science, 103-04
Houston Police Department Museum, 104
Howard-Dickinson House, 257
Hueco Tanks State Historical Park, 294
Humphreys, Kalita, Theater, 217
Huntsville, TX, 266-68, *267*, *269*
Hutchinson County Museum, 329
Hyde Park, Austin, TX, 137

Idabel, OK, 374
Immaculate Conception Cathedral, Brownsville, TX, 83
Immaculate Conception Church, Panna Maria, TX, 65
Imperial Sugar Company, 107
Independence, TX, 166
Independence Baptist Church, 166
Indian City U.S.A., 406, *406*, *407*
Indian Mound, 261
Indianola, TX, 72
Industry, TX, 163
Institute of Texas Cultures, 49

Jacksonport, AR, 454
Jacksonport Courthouse Museum, 454
Jacksonport State Park, 454
Jefferson, TX, 250-51, *250*, *252*, 253-54
Jefferson County Courthouse, *426*, 447
Jefferson County Historical Museum, 447

Jefferson Historical Society
  Museum, 251
Jenkins Ferry Battleground,
  456
Johnson, Claudia Taylor,
  Hall, 144
Johnson, Lyndon Baines, 187,
  283; Library and Museum,
  151-52; National Historical
  Site, 132-33, 187-88; Space
  Center, 106
Johnson, Philip, 103, 216, 228
Johnson County Courthouse,
  238
Jonesboro, AR, 452-53

Karankawa Indians, 20, 21,
  66, 67, 77, 85, 160
Kell House, 242
Kendall County Courthouse,
  197
Kennedy, John F., 215;
  Memorial, 216
Kerrville, TX, 196-97
Kimbell Art Museum, 228-29,
  230-31
King Ranch, 80-81, 80
King William, 49-50, 51
Kingfisher, OK, 420-21
Kingsville, TX, 79-81, 80
Kiowa Indians, 16, 184, 239-
  40, 242, 323, 326, 329, 339,
  378, 379, 386, 397, 401,
  405, 417
Kirkpatrick Center, 396
Kuhlmann-King Historical
  House, 197-98

La Grange, TX, 158-59
Lafitte, Jean, 14, 15, 77, 108
Laguna Atascosa National
  Wildlife Refuge, 84
Laguna Gloria Art Museum,
  154
La Harpe, Bénard de,
  Riverfront Park, 436
Lajitas, TX, 308
Lamar, Mirabeau B., 91, 135,
  136, 207
Landmark Inn State Historic
  Site, 59
La Porte, TX, 104-05
Laredo, TX, 86, 87, 88-89, 88
La Salle, René-Robert
  Cavelier de, 20, 72, 334, 428
Laurel Heights, 55-56
La Villita, 39-40
Lawton, OK, 402-03, 404
Layland Museum, 238
Lee County Courthouse, 172
Lee County Museum, 172
Lewis-Wagner House, 4, 169,
  170, 171
Lindheimer Home, 200-01,
  201
Link-Lee Mansion, 103
Little Church, 40
Little Rock, AR, 435-36, 436,

437, 438-42, 438, 440, 442;
  State Capitol, 441-42
Littlefield Home, 152-53
Littlest Skyscraper, 242
Live Oak Creek
  Archaeological District, 311
Livestock Exchange Building,
  225
Log Cabin Historical Village,
  229
Logan County Museum, 466
Longhorn Caverns, 186
Longview, TX, 255-56
Los Nogales Museum, 60
Louisiana Purchase Park, 452
Lower Main Street Historic
  District, 483
Lubbock, TX, 320-22
Lubbock Lake National
  Historic Landmark, 321
Lucas Gusher Monument, 122
Luna's Jacal, 304-05
Lutcher Memorial Church
  Building, 124

MacArthur Park, 440-41
McCollum-Chidester House
  Museum, 456-57, 456
McDonald Observatory, 298,
  300
McFaddin-Ward House, 122,
  122, 123, 124
Mackenzie, Ranald S., 242,
  315-16, 323, 326
McKinney, Liberty S., House,
  115
McKinney, TX, 246
McLennan County
  Courthouse, 181
McNamara House Museum,
  72
McNay Art Museum, 57-58
Magnolia Mansion, 374
Magoffin Home State Historic
  Site, 284-86, 284, 285
Main Plaza de Las Islas, 40-41
Mangum, OK, 399-400
Marfa, TX, 300-02
Marien Kirche, 194
Mariscal Mine, 305, 307
Market Square, 93, 94
Mark's Mill Battleground, 456
Marland Mansion and Estate,
  376, 417-18, 418, 419
Marlin, TX, 183
Marlsgate Plantation, 449
Marshall, TX, 254-55
Martin County Historical
  Museum, 319
Masonic Grand Lodge Library
  and Museum of Texas, 180
Matthews Memorial
  Presbyterian Church, 240
Maxey, Sam Bell, House State
  Historic Site, 248-49
Medford, OK, 420
Medicine Bluffs, Fort Sill, OK,
  402

Memorial Hall, San Antonio,
  TX, 57
Memorial Indian Museum,
  Broken Bow, OK, 373
Memorial Park, Houston, TX,
  101
Memorial Plaza, Dallas, TX,
  216
Memorial Square, Victoria,
  TX, 71
Menger Hotel, 38
Meridian, TX, 237
Merrell, Captain Nelson,
  House, 172
Mexican Cultural Center, 49
Mexican-American War, 26,
  77, 84
Mid-America Museum, 463
Midland, TX, 318
Miers Home Museum, 313
Milam County Courthouse,
  176-77
Milam County Historical
  Museum, 177
Milam Square, 45-46
Military Plaza, 41
Millard's Crossing, 264
Millerton, OK, 374
Mission Concepción (Nuestra
  Señora de la Purísima
  Concepción de Acuña), 52,
  53
Mission Espada (San Francisco
  de la Espada), 53
Mission Espíritu Santo
  (Nuestra Señora del
  Espíritu Santo de Zuñiga),
  66-67
Mission Rosario (Mission
  Nuestra Señora del
  Rosario), 67
Mission San Antonio de
  Valero, 31, 33, 34-38, 34, 35
Mission San José (San José y
  San Miguel de Aguayo), 53,
  54, 55, 55
Mission San Juan Capistrano,
  53
Mission Tejas State Historical
  Park, 259-61
Mission Trail, 290-91, 291,
  293
Monroe-Crook House, 258
Monte Vista, 55-56
Monticello, AR, 446
Montrose, Houston, TX, 103
Monument Hill and Kreische
  Brewery State Historic Site,
  159-60
Mood-Heritage Musuem, 174
Moore County Historical
  Museum, 330
Morrilton, AR, 463
Morrow Home, 475, 475
Morton Museum of Cooke
  County, 244
Mount Gentilz Cemetery, 59
Mount Holly Cemetery, 441

Mount Olive Methodist Church, Van Buren, AR, 467
Mount Olivet Methodist Church, Rison, AR, 446
Mountain View, AR, 482
Muleshoe National Wildlife Refuge, 322
Murrell Home, 366
Museum of Automobiles, 466
Museum of Fine Arts, 101
Museum of Pioneer History, 360
Museum of Texas Handmade Furniture, *199*, 202
Museum of Texas Tech, 322
Museum of the Big Bend, 302
Museum of the Cherokee Strip, Enid, OK, 420
Museum of the Great Plains, 403, *404*
Museum of the Red River, 374
Museum of the Republic of the Rio Grande, 88-89, *88*
Museum of the Southwest, 318
Museum of the Unassigned Lands, 394
Museum of the Western Prairie, 400
Muskogee, OK, 369-70, 372
Muskogee Indians. *See* Creek Indians

Nacogdoches, TX, 261-64, *263*
National Audubon Society Sabal Palm Grove Wildlife Sanctuary, 84
National Cowboy Hall of Fame and Western Heritage Center, 396
National Cowgirl Hall of Fame and Western Heritage Center, 324-25
National Hall of Fame for Famous American Indians, 405
National Ranching Heritage Center, 322
Nativity of Mary, Blessed Virgin Catholic Church, High Hill, TX, 164
Nativity of the Blessed Virgin Mary Church, Cestohowa, TX, 65
Navarro, José, House, 45
Navarro County Courthouse, 235
Neill-Cochran House, 153
New Braunfels, TX, 198-202, *199, 201*
Ney, Elisabet, 140, 148, 154-55, *155;* Museum, 154-55, *156*
Nimitz Hotel/Admiral Nimitz State Historical Park, 191-93, *192*

Norfolk, AR, 482
Norman, OK, 408-09
Norman and Cleveland County Historical Museum, 408
Norse, TX, 237
North Main Street Historic District, 446
Northwestern Oklahoma State University Museum, 424
Nuevo Santander Museum Complex, 86, 88

Oaklawn Cemetery, 483
Oakwood Cemetery, Austin, TX, 148
Oakwood Cemetery, Huntsville, TX, 266
Odessa, TX, 317-18
Okemah, OK, 363
Oklahoma, **8-9;** eastern, 322-75, **336-37;** western, 376-425, **380-81**
Oklahoma City, OK, 390-96, *294, 295;* Governor's mansion, 392; State Capitol, 392, *390, 391*
Oklahoma Firefighters Museum, 396
Oklahoma Heritage Center, 393
Oklahoma Museum of Natural History, 409
Oklahoma State University Museum of Natural and Cultural History, 414
Okmulgee, OK, 364
Old Central Museum of Higher Education, 414
Old City Park Museum, 213, *214,* 215
Old Davidsonville State Park, 453
Old Fort Museum, 469
Old Fort Parker State Historic Site, 184-85
Old Greer County Museum and Hall of Fame, 399-40
Old Jail Art Center, 249
Old Jail Museum, Gonzales, TX, 63
Old Jail Museum, Sonora, TX, 313
Old Jail Visitors Center, 319
Old Lundberg Bakery, 142
Old Market House Museum, 66
Old Mill, 482
Old Nacogdoches University, 264
Old Round Rock and Old Slave Cemetery, 172, 173
Old Saint Luke's Church, 175
Old Saint Olaf's Lutheran Church, 237
Old San Antonio Exhibit, 40
Old State House Museum, 436, *436, 437,* 438-39, *438*

Old Town Museum, Elk City, OK, 399
Old Victoria County Courthouse, 72
Old Washington County Jail, 472
Old Washington Historic State Park, 458, *459,* 460, *461*
Olmos Park, 55-56
Oologah, OK, 349, 351
Orange, TX, 124
Osage Agency, 348
Osage County Historical Museum, 349
Osage Indians, 339, 343, 348-49, 367, 375, 386, 428, 467
Osage Tribal Museum, 349-50
Our Lady of Loreto Chapel, *68,* 70
Our Savior's Lutheran Church, 237
Overholser Mansion, 393
Ozark Folk Center, 482
Ozona, TX, 311

Padre Island National Seashore, *28,* 79
Palestine, TX, 257
Palm House, 173
Palmito Hill Battlefield, 84
Palo Alto Battlefield, 84
Palo Duro Canyon State Park, 325-26
Panhandle, OK, 425
Panhandle, TX, 328
Panhandle-Plains Historical Museum, 325
Panna Maria, TX, 65
Paris, AR, 466
Paris, TX, 248-49
Park Hill, OK, 365-66
Parker, Cynthia Ann, 184, 185, 229, 329, 400
Parker, Quanah, 184, 185, 229, 329, *331,* 382, 400-01; Star House, 400
Paseo del Alamo, 47
Paseo del Rio, 39, *39*
Paso del Norte Hotel, *280,* 281
Pawhuska, OK, 348-49
Pawnee, OK, 349
Pawnee Bill Museum, 349
Pawnee Indian Agency, 349
Pea Ridge National Military Park, 476-78, *477*
Pecos, TX, 295
Pemberton Heights, 137, 139
Permian Basin Petroleum Museum, 318
Perry, OK, 415-16
Petit Jean State Park, 463, 466
Petroleum Park, 235
Pfeiffer Farm Collection, 414-15
Philbrook Museum of Art, 358, *359*
Philcade, 357
Phillips, Frank, Home, *344,* 345

Phillips County Museum, 451
Philtower, *332*, 357
Pine Bluff, AR, *426*, 446-47
Pine Springs, TX, 294
Pioneer Cemetery, Batesville, AR, 483
Pioneer Memorial Library, Fredericksburg, TX, 193
Pioneer Memorial Museum, Fredericksburg, TX, 191
Pioneer Village, Corsicana, TX, 235-36
Pioneer Village, Rison, AR, 446
Pioneer Woman Statue and Museum, Ponca City, OK, 418
Plains Indians and Pioneers Museum, 424
Plantation Agriculture Museum, 447, 449
Plaza de Armas, 41
Plaza Theater, 282
Poison Spring Battleground, 456
Pollard Theatre, 413
Pompeiian Villa, 125
Ponca City, OK, *376, 416,* 417-19, *418, 419*
Ponca City Cultural Center and Museums, 418-19
Port Aransas, TX, 75-76
Port Arthur, TX, 124-25
Port Arthur Historical Museum, 125
Port Isabel Lighthouse, 82
Porter, William Sydney, 38, 141, 144, 146-47, 410
Potawatomi Indian Museum, 361
Potton-Hayden House, 320
Potts Tavern, 466
Pottsville, AR, 466
Powhatan, AR, 453-54
Powhatan Courthouse, 453-54
Praha, TX, 164
Prairie Grove Battlefield State Park, 474-75, *475*
Prairie Song, OK, 343
Presidential Museum, 317-18
Presidio County Courthouse, 300-01
Presidio County Museum, 301
Presidio de la Bahia, 67, *68,* 69-70
Price Tower, 345
Pulaski County Courthouse, 439

Quapaw Indians, 339, 428, 439, 443, 446
Quapaw Quarter, 439
Quigley's Castle, 480
Quitman, TX, 249-50

Railroad and Pioneer Museum, Temple TX, 175
Ranger Oaks, 60

Raumonda, *161*, 162
Rayburn, Sam: House Museum, 247; Library, 247-48
Resaca de la Palma Battlefield, 84
Rice University, 101, *102*, 103
Richardson, Sid, Collection of Western Art, 223
Richmond, TX, 106-07
Riggs, Annie, Memorial Museum, 309-10
Rio Grande Valley Museum, 85
Rison, AR, 446
River Oaks, 99, 101
Rogers, Will, 349, *350,* 351; Birthplace, 349, 351; Memorial, 351-52
Rogers, AR, 476
Rogers Historical Museum, 476
Rogers-McCasland Home, 254
Rogers-Tilles House and Patent Model Museum, 469
Rosalie House, *478*, 480
Rosenberg Library, 118
Rothko Chapel, 103
Round Rock, TX, 172-73
Round Top, TX, 168
Royston House, 460, *460*
Rush, AR, 481-82
Rusk, TX, 257

Sabine Pass Battleground State Historical Park, 125
Sacred Heart Catholic Church, 113
Saint Anthony Cathedral, 120
Saint Barnabas Episcopal Church, 194
Saint Clement's Episcopal Church, 287-88
Saint David's Episcopal Church, 146
Saint James Episcopal Church, 159
Saint John the Baptist Catholic Church, 164
Saint Joseph's Catholic Church, San Antonio, TX, 38
Saint Joseph's Church, Galveston, TX, 117-18
Saint Louis Catholic Church, 58
Saint Martin's Church, 168
Saint Mary's Cathedral, Austin, TX, 142
Saint Mary's Cathedral, Galveston, TX, 117
Saint Mary's Catholic Church, Umbarger, TX, 326
Saint Mary's Catholic Church, Victoria, TX, 72
Saint Mary's Church of the Assumption, Praha, TX,164

Saint Mary's Church, Fredericksburg, TX, 194
Saint Patrick Catholic Church, 225
Saint Stanislaus Catholic Church, 198
Saint Stephen's Episcopal Church, 309
Salado, TX, 174-75
Salado Methodist Church, 175
Salina, OK, 342-43
Sallisaw, OK, 372
San Agustín Church, *87*, 88
San Agustín Plaza, 88
San Angelo, TX, 315-16, *316, 317*
San Antonio, TX, 30, *31,* 32-41, *34, 35, 39, 42-43,* 44-47, *44, 45, 47, 48,* 49-51, *51, 52,* 53, *54,* 55-58, *55;* City Hall, 41; Spanish Governor's Palace, 44, *44, 45*
San Antonio Missions National Historical Park, 50-51, *52,* 53, *54,* 55, *55*
San Antonio Museum of Art, 56
San Augustine, TX, 264-65
San Eliceario Presidio Chapel, 293
San Felipe, TX, 163
San Fernando Cathedral, 41, *42*
San Jacinto, TX, 33
San Jacinto Battleground State Historical Park, 104-05
San Jacinto Plaza, 282
San Marcos, TX, 202-03
San Pedro Springs Park, 56
Sanguinet & Staats, 46, 213, 223, 224, 229
Santa Ana National Wildlife Refuge, 85
Santa Anna, Antonio López de, 25, 33, 35, 36, 37, 41, 45, 64, 70, 86, 104-05, 135, 163
Santa Fe Depot Museum, 362, *362*
Santa Maria, TX, 85
Sapulpa, OK, 358
Sapulpa Historical Museum, 358
Saunders Memorial Museum, 481
Scott, AR, 447, 449
Scurry County Museum, 320
Seay Mansion, 420
Sebastopol House State Historic Site, 60
Seguin, TX, 60
Seminole Canyon State Historical Park, 312-13
Seminole Indians, 339, 340, 362-63, 370, 375, 378, 390
Seminole Nation Museum,363
Senftenberg-Brandon House, 162

Sequoyah, 366, 372-73; Home Site, 372
Shackelford County Courthouse Historic District, 240
Shawnee, OK, *360*, 361-62, *361, 362*
Shawnee Friends Mission, *360*, 361
Shawnee Indians, 183, 361, 378, 385
Sheerar Cultural and Heritage Center, 414
Shiloh Church, 473
Shiloh Museum, 473-74, *474*
Sidbury, Charlotte Scott, House, 77, *78*
Silk Stocking Historic District, 118
Siloam Springs, AR, 476
Siloam Springs Museum, 476
Sims, Nicholas P., Library, 234
Sixth Floor, Dallas, TX, 215-16
Smith, Ashbel, Building, 119, *119*
Snyder, TX, 320
Socorro, TX, 291, 293
Socorro Mission, 291, 293
Sod House, OK, 424
Sonnenthiel, Jacob, House, *115*, 116
Sonora, TX, 313
Sophienburg Museum and Archives, 200
Southern Methodist University, 218
Southern Plains Indian Museum and Crafts Center, 405-06
Southwest Craft Center, 46
Southwestern University, 173-74
Spanish Governor's Palace, 44, *44, 45*
Sparks House, 470
Spindletop, *1*, 119, 120
Spiro, OK, 373
Spiro Mounds Archaeological State Park, 373
SPJST Museum, 175-76
Spring Mill, AR, 483
Springdale, AR, 473-74, *474*
Stafford Opera House, 162
Stanton, TX, 319
Star of the Republic Museum, 165
Stark, W. H., House, 124
Stark Museum of Art, 124
Starr Family State Historic Site, 255
State Capital Publishing Museum, *410, 411*, 412
State Museum of History, 392-93
Steamboat House, 266-67, *267*
Stephens County Historical Museum, 403

Stephenville, TX, 239
Stephenville Historical House Museum, 239
Sterne, Adolphus, House (Hoya Library and Museum), 262
Steves Homestead, 50, *51*
Stillman House Museum, 83
Stillwater, OK, 414
Stone Fort Museum, 263-64, *263*
Strand Historic District, 116
Strode-Pritchett Log Cabin, 258-59
Study Butte, TX, 308
Stuttgart, AR, 449-50
Stuttgart Agricultural Museum, 450
Sulphur Springs, TX, 249
Sundance Square, 223
Sunset Heights Historic District, 282
Sutton County Courthouse, 313
Sweet Home Baptist Church, 154
Swink, OK, 374
Swisher County Archives and Museum Association, 323
Sydnor's 1846-47 Powhatan House, 111

Tahlequah, OK, 364-65
Tarrant County Courthouse, 223, *224*
Taylor, Zachary, 26, 77, 82, 84, 367, 375
Teague, TX, 185
Temple, TX, 175-76
Temple Beth-El, 235
Terlingua, TX, 307
Terrell Hills, 55-56
Territory Town Museum, 363
Texarkana, AR, 457-58
Texarkana Historical Museum, 457
Texas Baptist Historical Center-Museum, 166
Texas First Ladies Historic Costume Collection, 244
Texas Prison Museum, 268
Texas Ranger Hall of Fame and Museum, 179-80
Texas Revolution, 25, 32-33, 40, 66, 104, 159, 160, 165; the Alamo, 33, 35-37; seige of Bexar, 33, 41, 45-46; battle of Concepción, 53; Gonzales, 61, 63; Presidio de la Bahia, 67, 69-70; "Runaway Scrape," 104, 163; battle of San Jacinto, 33, 64, 70, 104-05
Texas State Cemetery, 148
Texas State Library, 140
Texas State Railroad Historical Park, 257
Texas Wendish Heritage Museum, 172

Texas Women's Collection, 244
Texas, **8-9;** central, 126-203, **130-31;** Gulf coast of, 18-29, **22-23,** 72-81, 108-25; north and east, 204-69, **208-09;** south, 18-72, **22-23,** 81-108; west, 270-330, **274-75**
Thistle Hill, 229, 232
Thomas-Foreman Home, 372
Thorpe, Jim, House, 415
Tigua Indian Museum, 291
Tigua Indian Reservation, 290-91
Tishomingo, OK, 375
Toltec Mounds Archaeological State Park, 449
Tonkawa, OK, 416-17
Tonkawa Tribal Museum, 417
Top of Oklahoma Historical Society Cherokee Outlet Museum, 419-20
Travis, William B., 36, 37, 69, 246
Treaty Oak, 154
Trinity Episcopal Church, Galveston, TX, 117
Trinity Episcopal Church, Pine Bluff, AR, 447
Trube, John Clement, House, 113, *114*
Tulia, TX, 323
Tulsa, OK, *332, 346-47*, 352-54, *352, 353, 355, 356*, 357-58, *359*
Tulsa County Historical Society Museum, 357
Tuskahoma, OK, 373
Tyler, TX, 256
Tyrrell Historical Library, 120

Umbarger, TX, 326
Union Depot, Tulsa, OK, *353*, 357
U.S. Army Air Defense Artillery Museum, 290
U.S. Army Field Artillery and Fort Sill Museum, 401-02
U.S. Army Museum of the Noncommissioned Officer, 290
U.S. Army Third Cavalry Museum, 290
University of Arkansas, 470
University of Saint Thomas, 103
University of Texas, Austin, 149, *150*, 151-53; Texas Memorial Museum, 151
University of Texas at El Paso, 282
Uvalde, TX, 59-60

Van Buren, AR, 466-67
Van Buren Frisco Depot, 467
Van Buren Historic District, 467

Van Horn, TX, 294
Varner-Hogg Plantation State
  Historical Park, 107-08
Vaughn, John, House, 469,
  471
Vereins Kirche, 193
Victoria, TX, 71
Villa Marre, 439, *440*

Waco, TX, *134*, 177-81, *178*
Waco Suspension Bridge, 177,
  178
Wallis, TX, 164
Walnut Grove Baptist Church
  and School, 481
Washington, AR, 458, *459*,
  460, *460*
Washington, TX, 165, *167*
Washington Cemetery, 98
Washington County
  Courthouse, 472
Washington-on-the-Brazos
  State Historical Park, 165,
  167
Washita Battleground, 399
Watonga, OK, 421, *421*
Waurika, OK, 403

Waxahachie, TX, 232, *233*,
  234-35
Waynoka, OK, 424
Waynoka Historical Museum,
  424
Webb County Courthouse, 89
Weches, TX, 259-61
Welcome, TX, 163
Wesley Brethren Church, 163
West of the Pecos Museum,
  295
Wewoka, OK, 362-63
Wheelock Church, 374
White-Pool House, 318
Wichita Falls, TX, 242
Wichita Falls Museum and Art
  Center, 242
Wichita Indians, 128, 183,
  334, 339, 386, 405
Wilderness Park Museum, 293
Williams, Samuel May, House,
  111
Williamson County
  Courthouse, 174
Williamson County
  Courthouse Historic
  District, 174

Wilson, AR, 452
Winedale Historical Center, *4*,
  169, *170*, 171
Wise County Courthouse, 243
Wise County Heritage
  Museum, 243
Witte Museum, 57
Wolf House, 482
Woodward, OK, 424
Woolaroc, OK, 345, 348, *348*
Wooten, Goodall, House, 153
Wright, Frank Lloyd, 217,
  345, 358
Wulff House, 50

XIT Museum, 330

Yale, OK, 415
Ye Kendall Inn, 197
Yorktown, TX, 64-65
Yorktown Historical Museum,
  64-65
Ysleta Mission, 290, *291*
Yturri-Edmunds Home and
  Mill, 50

Zaragoza, Ignacio,
  Birthplace, 71

The editors gratefully acknowledge the assistance of Cynthia Beeman, Robert Blackburn, Ann J. Campbell, Rita Campon, John Collins, Fonda Duvanel, Julia Ehrhardt, Ann ffolliott, Lydia Howarth, Brigid A. Mast, Donald Olson, Robin P. Robinson, Martha Schulman, Tonice Sgrignoli, Catherine Shea Tangney, David Turner, Linda Venator, Wendy Wilson, and Patricia Woodruff.

Composed in Basilia Haas and ITC New Baskerville by Graphic Arts Composition, Inc., Philadelphia, Pennsylvania. Printed and bound by Toppan Printing Company, Ltd., Tokyo, Japan.